D0506517

PEARSON   ALWAYS LEARNING

Materials Selected by Chuck O'Connell

Reader for Introduction to Sociology

Fourth Edition

Cover Art: Courtesy of Blend Images, Photodisc/Getty Images, S. Olsen/K. Mizra, Japan, Norway, Moroc.

Copyright © 2012, 2003 by Pearson Learning Solutions
All rights reserved.

This copyright covers material written expressly for this volume by the editor/s as well as the compilation itself. It does not cover the individual selections herein that first appeared elsewhere. Permission to reprint these has been obtained by Pearson Learning Solutions for this edition only. Further reproduction by any means, electronic or mechanical, including photocopying and recording, or by any information storage or retrieval system, must be arranged with the individual copyright holders noted.

All trademarks, service marks, registered trademarks, and registered service marks are the property of their respective owners and are used herein for identification purposes only.

Pearson Learning Solutions, 501 Boylston Street, Suite 900, Boston, MA 02116
A Pearson Education Company
www.pearsoned.com

Printed in the United States of America

1 2 3 4 5 6 7 8 9 10 V0ZN 17 16 15 14 13 12

000200010271265862

RM/KD

ISBN 10: 1-256-80245-X
ISBN 13: 978-1-256-80245-7

COPYRIGHT ACKNOWLEDGMENTS

Grateful acknowledgment is made to the following sources for permission to reprint material copyrighted or controlled by them:

"On Being Sane in Insane Places," by D.L. Rosenhan, reprinted from *Science* 179, no. 4070 (January 19, 1973), by permission of the American Association for the Advancement of Science.

"Imagine a Country," by Holly Sklar, reprinted from *Z Magazine* (2009), by permission of the author.

"Pig Lovers and Pig Haters," by Marvin Harris, reprinted from *Cows, Pigs, Wars, and Witches: The Riddles of Culture* (1989), Random House, Inc.

"'A Life at Hard Labor': Capitalism and Working Hours," by Juliet Schor, reprinted from *The Overworked American: The Unexpected Decline of Leisure* (1991), by permission of Perseus Books Group.

"Coffee and The Protestant Ethic," by Wolfgang Schivelbusch, reprinted from *Tastes of Paradise*, translated by David Jacobson (1992), Random House, Inc.

"Unintended Consequences of Undercover Work," by Gary Marx, reprinted from *Undercover: Police Surveillance in America* (1988), by permission of University of California Press.

"A Crime By Any Other Name...," by Jeffrey Reiman, reprinted from *The Rich Get Richer and the Poor Get Prison* (1990), Pearson Education, Inc.

"Wealth and Want in the United States," by Michael Parenti, reprinted from *Democracy for the Few, Sixth Edition* (1995), by permission of the author.

"The Global Collapse: A Non-orthodox View," by Walden Bello, reprinted by permission from *the Philippine Daily Inquirer*, February 6, 2009.

"How the Power Elite Dominates Government: A Class Dominance View of the Federal Government," by G. William Domhoff, reprinted from *Who Rules America?* (1998), by permission of the McGraw-Hill Companies.

"Barack Obama as a Ruling Class Candidate," by Paul Street, reprinted from *ZNet*, November 4, 2008, by permission of the author.

"A Propaganda Model," by Edward S. Herman and Noam Chomsky, reprinted from *Manufacturing Consent: The Political Economy of the Mass Media* (1998), Random House, Inc.

"'Black Hawk Down'—Hollywood Drags Bloody Corpse of Truth Across Movie Screens," by Larry Chin, reprinted by permission from the *Intrepid Report*, January 3, 2002.

"Imperialism," by Markar Melkonian, reprinted from *The Weapon of Theory: A Post-Cold War Primer for Marxism* (1996), by permission of Perseus Books Group.

"A Warning to Africa: The New U.S. Imperial Grand Strategy," by John Bellamy Foster, reprinted by permission from *Monthly Review* 58, no. 2 (June 2006)

"A New Silk Road: Proposed Petroleum Pipeline in Afghanistan," by John Maresca, reprinted from *Monthly Review* 53, no. 7 (December 2001).

"Blue Gold, Turkmen Bashes, and Asian Grids," by Pepe Escobar, reprinted from *TomDispatch*, 2009, by permission of the author.

"Nondemocratic Regimes of Mideast Supported by the U.S.A.," by Deborah J. Gerner and Jillian Schwedler, reprinted from *Understanding the Contemporary Middle East* (2008), by permission of Lynne Rienner Publishers.

"Straight Talk on Terrorism," by Eqbal Ahmad, reprinted from *Terrorism, Theirs and Ours* (1998), by permission of Seven Stories Press.

"Vietnam: The Antiwar Movement We Are Supposed to Forget," by H. Bruce Franklin, reprinted from *Vietnam and Other American Fantasies* (2002), by permission of University of Massachusetts Press.

"Why Socialism?" by Albert Einstein, reprinted from *Monthly Review* 54, no. 1 (May 2002), by permission of The Hebrew University of Jerusalem.

Excerpt from *Sin Patron: Argentina's Worker-Run Factories* (July 21, 2007), by Naomi Klein and Avi Lewis, by permission of the Roam Agency.

"Chinese Criticisms of the Soviets," by John Gurley, reprinted from *Challengers to Capitalism* (1988).

"Gender, Relationships, and Communications," by Julia Wood, reprinted from *Gendered Relationships* (1996), by permission of the McGraw-Hill Companies.

"Doing It for Ourselves: Can Feminism Survive Class Polarization?" by Barbara Ehrenreich, reprinted from *In These Times*, November 28, 1999, by permission of the publisher.

"Gendered Violence in Intimate Relationships," by Jacquelyn White and Barrie Boundurant, reprinted from *Gendered Relationships* (1996), by permission of the McGraw-Hill Companies.

"Death on the Home Front—Wars Abroad Continue at Home," by Ann Jones, reprinted from *TomDispatch*, March 31, 2009, by permission of The Frances Goldin Literary Agency.

"America and Political Islam," by Mahmood Mamdani, reprinted from *Global Agenda*, January 29, 2005, by permission of Gelfman Schneider Literary Agents, Inc.

"'Free Trade' and Immigration: A Primer," by Raul Fernandez, January 26, 2008, by permission of the author.

"Arizona's New Laws: An Attempt to Secure Cheap Labor?" by Paul Ortiz, reprinted from *TruthOut*, June 2, 2010, by permission of the author.

"The Duncan Doctrine (Militarizing Minority Schools)," by Andy Kroll, reprinted from *TomDispatch*, January 18, 2009, by permission of the author.

"Looking for Spies of a Different Color," by Vernon Loeb, reprinted by permission from *The Washington Post*, January 12, 2000.

"The Limits of Anti-Racism," by Adolph Reed, Jr., reprinted from *Left Business Observer* 121 (September 2009).

"Civil Religion in America," by Robert Bellah, reprinted from *Journal of the American Academy of Arts and Sciences* 96, no. 1 (winter 1967), by permission of MIT Press Journals.

"Vatican Keeps Up Drumbeat Against War in Iraq," by John L. Allen Jr., March 7, 2003, National Catholic Reporter Publishing Company.

"We Don't Have to Be Saints," by Paul Loeb, reprinted from *Soul of a Citizen: Living with Conviction in a Cynical Time* (1999), St. Martin's Press.

CONTENTS

Race, ethnicity, nationality

Religion

Living with Conviction

PREFACE

This book offers supplementary readings to the main textbook. These readings are organized around the lecture topics of the course and have been selected because they offer thought provoking interpretations of social realities.

THE FIRST WEEK-OPENING REMARKS FOR THE COURSE

There are two readings for this week. The first, "On Being Sane in Insane Places", discusses a clever experiment investigating the ways in which we can become trapped by others' definitions of reality. In doing so, this essay raises questions about the social construction of science and medicine and about intellectual passivity among even the highly educated. The second article, "Imagine a Country", is a report about a modern nation. The author, Holly Sklar, refuses to identify the country; instead she tells us which countries she is not discussing. Why would she adopt this style? What does her approach suggest about the relationship between her message and her audience?

CULTURE

Here are three selections that deal with certain cultural practices and their basis in the economic system of society. In the first article, Marvin Harris investigates the ecological and economic reasons for a religious taboo against eating pork. Juliet Schor, in the second excerpt, explains why we work more than medieval peasants in spite of our modern labor-saving technologies. Finally, Wolfgang Schivelbusch discusses how changes in the mode of economic production led to the demise of beer as a breakfast beverage and its replacement with coffee.

What is the general theoretical thread linking each of these selections? What are the causes for the pig taboo, longer work, and the marketing of coffee? What do these interpretations suggest regarding the development of values and norms of behavior in society?

SOCIAL GROUPS/LANGUAGE AND THOUGHT

We are members of social groups throughout our lives. As individual members we each have some influence on the groups to which we belong. The group, however, generally precedes us in existence and has a structure (a linked set of positions each with a role to play) and a function (purpose) created prior to our entrance as members. The group's positions and roles are the determinants of our behavior. The selection by Gary Marx on police undercover work is a dramatic example of this point. Not all groups in society are equal; some are vastly more powerful than others. Very powerful groups often place their ideology or system of interpretation upon us. Consider how this can be so by reading Jeffrey Reiman's essay on the social definition of crime.

STRATIFICATION

The selections in this section focus on the social relations of economic production or, as it's more commonly called, the class structure. There are three readings: one by Michael Parenti, one by Walden Bello and the other by myself. They all take the position that you cannot understand the state of the two major classes of modern society, capitalists and workers, without understanding the relationship between them. Parenti's chapter looks at the creation of wealth in society and asks "who owns America?" Bello's essay discusses the current global economic crisis and introduces the concept of a *crisis of overproduction* as the built-in de-stabilizer of capitalist economies. My selection is restricted to a discussion of a variety of methods currently used by employers to reduce wages in order to increase profits. The point of my essay is to give you an awareness that wages and profits have an *inverse* relationship and that, in an economy resting on the pursuit of profit, there will always be pressure to reduce wages as much as politically possible.

POLITICS: CLASS DOMINANCE, IMPERIALISM AND WAR

The readings in this section challenge a number of prevailing beliefs about politics in the United States:

- the notion that the American polity is a pluralist system in which power is dispersed among a plurality of interest groups is critiqued by G. William Domhoff in the selection from his classic work *Who Rules America?* By analyzing the *social composition* of cabinet level appointments he demonstrates the dominance of the upper class (capitalist class) in the key executive positions of the federal government. What are the implications of his position for the widespread view that there are substantial differences between the two major political parties, the Democrats and the Republicans? If Domhoff is correct (i.e. if the upper class is a ruling class) and if Parenti is correct (i.e. the capitalist class and the working class have conflicting interests), then how likely is it that the capitalist class will craft government policies for the benefit of the workers (who, by the way, constitute the majority of the society's population)?

- the idea that the presidency of Barack Obama would represent the triumph of new political forces serving those who want government to provide greater measures of social benefit (e.g. universal health care) and who want an end to the wars in Afghanistan and Iraq is challenged by Paul Street in his prescient essay of 2008 "Barack Obama as a Ruling Class Candidate".

- the belief that political discourse and debate in America reflects a wide variety of views disseminated by a "free" press and an educational system encouraging critical thinking is questioned by Noam Chomsky and Edward Herman in their explication of a propaganda model. This selection is the opening chapter from their book *Manufacturing Consent*. The book itself is an exercise in the *sociology of knowledge*—an examination of the economic and political interests shaping both the production and propagation of interpretations of society that reinforce the social position of the upper class and the exclusion of those interpretations undermining the status quo. The key point to note is the process whereby members of the lower classes come to believe that the intellectual positions they hold are not only free of pro-ruling class bias but are also freely chosen rather than forced upon them. As a complement (not a compliment) to the piece by Chomsky and Herman is a review by Larry Chin of the politics of a popular Hollywood film from 2002, *Black Hawk Down*.

- the idea that wars are fought over political values and have humanitarian intentions is countered by Markar Melkonian's essay on imperialism as a central and inevitable outcome of the working of modern capitalist economies. The theoretical discussion offered by Melkonian is supplemented by essays from John Bellamy Foster and Pepe Escobar focusing on the Africa and Central Asia as sites of imperialist rivalries. Sandwiched between the Foster and Escobar pieces is the February 1998 Congressional testimony of Unocal vice-president, John J. Maresca, arguing for greater U.S. government involvement in Central Asia to assist oil companies in building a "new Silk Road" of oil pipelines. Maresca pointed out that the most desirable export routes for carrying oil and gas from Central Asia to world markets are those which the Americans can control (i.e. they would not go though Iran or to China) and which are highly profitable (i.e. provide more favorable "netbacks" to oil producers). His conclusion was that Afghanistan is the desired route for a pipeline from Central Asia to the sea but the country will need to be politically stabilized before construction can begin. Because Unocal cannot stabilize Afghanistan, he urged the U.S. to get involved. Escobar's essay is followed by two charts I prepared—one noting the interlocks between the oil industry and federal offices dealing with foreign policy; the other listing dictatorial regimes in the Middle East consistently supported by the United States. The first chart suggests that many of the men and women who are the decision makers regarding U.S. foreign affairs from the oil industry itself and are thus predisposed to formulate policy that favors their class position. The second chart notes the extensive and long standing U.S. commitment to dictatorships in the Middle East and thus implicitly calls into question the oft-repeated claims that the United States is seeking to promote the growth of democracy in other areas of the world.

The thrust of these readings in politics is that the economic interests of any society's ruling class are the basis for international conflicts, that the main prize is control of the world's energy supply, and that the struggle for control of this prize has been going on for many years and pre-dates the terrorist attacks of September11, 2001. In this light, neither terrorist attacks against the U.S. nor the calls for a cabinet level office of "homeland Security" were unexpected developments. Indeed, a full *seven months before 9/11* a bipartisan committee charged with reviewing national security issued its final report claiming that a direct, catastrophic attack against the United States within the U.S. was likely and that, therefore, the U.S. needed a Cabinet-level office of Homeland Security. The press release describing the final work of the Hart-Rudman Committee report is included here to emphasize the point that, while the *particular* attacks of September 11, 2001, may have been surprising to government leaders, the *general* likelihood of an attack was not. Likewise, the post-9/11 demand to create an Office of Homeland Security was unexpected only in its timing. Also, given prior U.S. commercial interest in Afghanistan (see the reading "A New Silk Road"), were the terrorist attacks of September 11 the *cause* of the subsequent U.S. invasion of Afghanistan or the *catalyst* for a previously contemplated projection of power? This section closes out with brief readings on the topic of terrorism. Of special interest is the discussion, "Straight Talk on Terrorism" by the late Pakistani intellectual Eqbal Ahmad discussing the inconsistencies and contradictions in the government's approach to terrorism. What gets labeled "terrorism" appears to depend less on *what* is done than to *whom* it is done: bombing against friends is terrorism, bombing against enemies is policy. With regard to Osama bin Laden, Ahmad points out that bin Laden's pre-1991 armed exploits on behalf of U.S. foreign policy were, at the time, considered neither terrorist nor a threat to civilization.

POLITICS: RESISTANCE, REBELLION, ALTERNATIVES

In this section we begin with an essay discussing the exercise of political power outside of the framework of electoral politics. In his essay, "Vietnam: The Antiwar Movement We're Supposed to Forget", H. Bruce Franklin argues that U.S. policy options (such as the ability to wage war) were limited by a variety of movements led by working class college students and working class active duty soldiers to resist the war itself. The general cumulative effect was to undercut U.S. ability to deploy more troops, withdrawal from Viet Nam and the abolition of military conscription. The point of including this essay is to indicate that the exercise of political power is not limited to voting for candidates for government offices; rather the collective refusal of workers, soldiers, and students to obey orders is a far greater power than marking a ballot.

After completing the series of assigned readings on stratification and politics you may be asking yourself if there is an alternative way to organizing society. The next two selections explore that possibility. In the first, Albert Einstein argues that it is possible and ethically preferable for all members of society to democratically share the ownership of the means of economic production and produce for the needs of all instead of the profits of a few. It may surprise you that Einstein advocated socialism over capitalism but he certainly was not alone in taking this position. Quite a few outstanding intellectuals, artists, scientists and scholars of the past century were advocates of socialist or communist positions: W.E.B. Du Bois, Pablo Picasso, Isadora Duncan, Pablo Neruda, Bertolt Brecht, Charlie Chaplin, Paul Robeson, Woody Guthrie, Dashiell Hammett, Josephine Herbst, Lillian Hellman, Dalton Trumbo, Zero Mostel, Clifford Odets, C.L.R. James, Helen Keller, John Reed, Ring Lardner, Jr., John Howard Lawson, Meridel Le Seur, Jessica Mitford, Dorothy Parker, Diego Rivera, Pete Seeger, Ben Shahn, Upton Sinclair, I.F. Stone, Paul Sweezy, Kurt Weil, Hans Eisler, Sergei Eisenstein, Aime Cesaire, Cesar Vallejo, Nazim Hikmet, Georg Lukacs, Walter Rodney, Faiz Ahmed Faiz, Antonio Gramsci, Walter Benjamin, Louis Althusser, Howard Zinn, E.P. Thompson, Amilcar Cabral, and Rosa Luxemburg to name a few.

The next selection, "Argentina: Where Jobless Run Factories" by Naomi Klein and Avi Lewis is about the revolutionary politics of the recovered factories movement in Argentina in which unemployed workers occupy factories shut down by their former bosses and restart production *sin patron* (without bosses). The workers collectively manage production and often (but not always) decide to have equal pay for all. The movement was begun by women in the garment industry and spread from there. It operates under the slogan: "Occupy—Resist—Produce." The full meaning of this slogan is: occupy the factories, resist eviction by the authorities, and produce under collective worker control. A key feature of this recovered factories movement is that it extends democracy into the workplace. Because the workers themselves are now also their own managers, they must understand various economic, political, and technical issues and make decisions in worker assemblies. Prior to this, they worked under the dictate of the bosses; prior to this, work itself was not democratically governed.

At the same time that they have extended democracy into the workplace, the workers have also called into question the limitations of electoral politics in a society based on private ownership of the means of production. Their criticism of traditional electoral politics is expressed in another of their slogans: "Our dreams don't fit on your ballots." Think about this. For those of you who want more, the story of the recovered factories movement is told in a fascinating film, *The Take*, by the Canadian filmmakers and journalists Naomi Klein and Avi Lewis.

One of the huge questions facing those who consider alternatives to the political economy of capitalism is the question of the failure of the socialist revolutions of the twentieth century. Arguably the most famous of these revolutions, each having profound effects on world history, were the Russian (1917), Chinese (1949), and Vietnamese (1975) revolutions. Yet, within a matter of only a few generations, each of these revolutionary societies has reverted back to some form of capitalism. Whatever criticism you can make about capitalism itself, the failures of its replacement societies suggest to some that there is no history beyond capitalism. Whether or not such is the case is for history to decide. For our purposes as students of society we should note that our *observation* that the revolutionary societies failed is not the same as an *explanation* of why they failed. In other words, it is obvious that the revolutions failed over time; what is not obvious is why. There is, however, an explanation and it was actually offered many years ago by Chinese revolutionaries who criticized the Soviet Union as a "bourgeois" (i.e. capitalist) state.

The Chinese view is discussed by former Stanford economist, John G. Gurley, in his well written book, *Challengers to Capitalism.* Writing before Gorbachev dismantled socialism in the USSR, Gurley presents the Chinese Marxist criticisms which used *class analysis* to evaluate the politics of the Soviet Union. In the early 1960s, the Chinese claimed that the Soviets had abandoned the vision of an egalitarian society and had restored capitalism to the Soviet Union. The thesis of capitalist restoration was that a new ruling class composed of a "red bourgeoisie" had emerged and lived off the exploitation of the Soviet workers. The new bourgeoisie (capitalist class) was called "red" (the symbolic color of communism) because it camouflaged its class position and interests by espousing Marxist-Leninist ideology. How this could have happened in a society of revolutionaries and without a violent seizure of power is the topic of Gurley's excerpt.

In reading the Gurley selection and thinking about the failure of the socialist revolutions it might be helpful to keep in mind the following comments. What is being discussed is the failure of socialist societies, not the collapse of communism. The expression "collapse of communism" is a misnomer because there were no existing communist societies. Because communism did not exist, it could not collapse. What did collapse, however, were socialist societies. In Marxist theory communism was an egalitarian endpoint to be achieved after completing a transition from capitalism. The transitional social formation was referred to as socialist. It can be thought of as a "half-way house" between capitalism and communism. Its function was to protect the revolution and lay the basis for an egalitarian society. Yet, as a transitional form, socialist societies were full of contradictions: on the one hand, they attacked capitalist practices (such as private ownership of the means of production and production for profit) and, on the other hand, kept several features of capitalist societies (such as wage inequality and hierarchical bureaucracies). The argument, in a nutshell, is that the preservation of these capitalist features formed the basis for the reversal of the revolutionary effort to establish equality and to liberate people from economic exploitation. In other words, the communists weren't communist enough. The underlying point is that the thesis of the restoration of capitalsim allows us to explain the failure of the transitional societies without reference to an alleged universal desire of humans to individualistically pursue profit and self-interest.

GENDER

There are four readings on this topic. Julia Wood's article, "Gender, Relationships, and Communication", discusses the social construction of femininity and masculinity. She points out that gender is not limited to the private and personal but is a principle of social life guiding the structures and practices of society's organizations. Because socially constructed conceptions of gender are embedded in our institutions, our gendered interactions appear natural rather than arbitrary. This implies some questions:

How can individuals learn to take a reflective, critically thoughtful perspective on gender if it is so institutionalized? How can we determine what is useful and what is dysfunctional in our conceptions of masculinity and femininity? The second selection is Barbara Ehrenreich's essay, "Doing It for Ourselves: Can Feminism Survive Class Polarization?". In this piece Ehrenreich discusses how class differences among women lead to different political and economic agendas and how the power and privilege of one class of women may exist at the expense of another class. If Ehrenreich is correct, what does feminism mean in a class-conflicted society? The last two essays deal with the topic of gendered violence. The article "Gendered Violence in Intimate Relationships", by Jacquelyn White and Barrie Bondurant examines the pervasiveness of violence in close relationships—relationships that are supposed to be based on love, care and commitment. Why is it that women are more likely to be assaulted by men they know than by strangers? Why are women (and children) the victims of violence by men? Why does society appear to put a premium on physical aggression by boys and men? To what extent is interpersonal violence a result of a militaristic and imperialistic culture that prepares men to be warriors ready to violently subjugate others? This last question brings us to the final reading, "Death on the Home Front—Wars Abroad Continue at Home", by Ann Jones. In this essay Jones looks at the connections between war and violence against women and men.

RACISM

Racism is often thought of as irrational attitudes and beliefs that lead to discrimination and hate crimes. What is ignored by such a psychologizing and individualistic frame of analysis is the functional role of racism in a structure of labor exploitation. Racism has a long history as a method used by society's upper class for controlling the labor force for purposes of exploitation and for dehumanizing people whose lands will be seized in wars of imperialism. In this section we have a number of essays dealing with current topics concerning racism and its political-economic basis. The first, "America and Political Islam" by Mahmood Mamdani, addresses the notion that Islam is inherently a pre-modern, anti-Western ideology and predisposes its followers to use violence. The second piece, "Who Are the Fanatics?" by Paul Craig Roberts, examines the recent attempt to connect Islam to fascism as manifested in the use of the term "Islamofascism". The next two essays shift our focus to the topic of immigration. We begin with "Free Trade and Immigration: A Primer" by UCI professor Raul Fernandez; in his brief essay he looks at the political and economic basis of immigration. The following essay, "Arizona's New Laws: An Attempt to Secure Cheap Labor?" by Paul Ortiz, speculates on the relationship between the Arizona laws of 2010 targeting the Latino population of the state and the desire of the business class to maintain a low wage immigrant workforce. Then we shift our attention to a topic promoted at the university and throughout the general society: diversity. The first essay, "The Duncan Doctrine" by Andy Kroll, examines neglected points about the politically correct popular celebration of diversity: the desire of society's rulers to increase the diversity of the officer corps in the U.S. military and the creation of military high schools in poor minority neighborhoods to capture sufficient numbers of future recruits. Kroll's article is followed by Vernon Loeb's Washington Post article, "Looking for Spies of a Different Color", about the attempts of the Central Intelligence Agency (CIA) to recruit more people of color for use as operatives and spies around the world. Diversity definitely has its uses. Finally, we conclude with a very thoughtful essay, "The Limits of Anti-racism", by political science professor Adolph Reed Jr. in which he discusses the implications of different meanings of racism and anti-racism.

RELIGION

Robert Bellah's essay, "Civil Religion", discusses the linkage between politics and religious faith through the development of a civil religion in which the secular ideology of nationalism becomes sacralized (made holy). Nationalist politics itself becomes a religion with certain propositions simply taken on faith (e.g. "one nation under God") and with group loyalty becoming a holy obligation (treason is probably the greatest political crime and to be called "unAmerican" is the most dangerous insult). An important implication of Bellah's discussion is the transformation of the various religions of society (e.g. Christianity, Judaism, Islam, Hinduism, etc) into reinforcements for civil religion. Put another way, if civil religion is the dominant faith, where is the integrity of religions that simply meld their teachings into conformity with the dictates of State power? What is the point of belief if it uncritically accomodates to the existing power structure? To illustrate this issue I refer you to the second reading of this section – a brief article from the American newspaper, *The National Catholic Reporter*. Entitled "Vatican keeps up drumbeat against war in Iraq", it notes that the head of the Roman Catholic Church took the position that the U.S. war against Iraq would be an unjust war of aggression. If the war is unjust, then Catholics, if they take seriously the teachings of their religion on the issue of war, should not support the U.S. war in Iraq. Yet how many Catholics in the United States are even aware that the Pope took a position against the war? Probably very few. Certainly, after more than eight years of war in Iraq, American Catholics are not known for their taking a religiously based anti-war position. And this is the point: when religious teachings conflict with the important political and economic interests of the society's ruling class, these teachings are reinterpreted in ways that erase the moral conflict.

LIVING WITH CONVICTION

Sometimes students finish a sociology course overwhelmed and daunted by the many issues and problems discussed. There may be a tendency to feel confused or cynical or hopeless in the face of complexity and powerful social forces. The final reading is about living with faith, hope and conviction in a narcissistic and cynical time. "We Don't Have to be Saints" by Paul Rogat Loeb explains that ordinary people can and do bring goodness into the world.

1

ON BEING SANE IN INSANE PLACES

David L. Rosenhan

On the one hand, it is not uncommon for people who violate explicit *rules written into law to find themselves enmeshed in a formal system that involves passing judgment on their fitness to remain in society. . . . On the other hand, people who violate* implicit *rules (the assumptions about what characterizes "normal" people) also can find themselves enmeshed in a formal system that involves passing judgment on their fitness to remain in society. "If found guilty of insanity," they, too, are institutionalized—placed in the care of keepers who oversee almost all aspects of their lives.*

The fundamental taken-for-granted assumption in institutionalizing people who violate implicit rules is that we are able to tell the sane from the insane. If we cannot do so, the practice itself would be insane! In that case, we would have to explicitly question contemporary psychiatry as a mechanism of social control. But what kind of question is this? Even most of us non-psychiatrists can tell the difference between who is sane and who is not. However, in a fascinating experiment, Rosenhan put to the test whether or not even psychiatrists can differentiate between the sane and the insane. As detailed in this account, the results contain a few surprises.

If sanity and insanity exist . . . how shall we know them? The question is neither capricious nor itself insane. However much we may be personally convinced that we can tell the normal from the abnormal, the evidence is simply not compelling. It is commonplace, for example, to read about murder trials wherein eminent psychiatrists for the defense are contradicted by equally eminent psychiatrists for the prosecution on the matter of the defendant's sanity. More generally, there are a great deal of conflicting data on the reliability, utility, and meaning of such terms as "sanity," "insanity," "mental illness," and "schizophrenia." Finally, as early as 1934, Benedict suggested that normality and abnormality are not universal. What is viewed as normal in one culture may be seen as quite aberrant in another. Thus, notions of normality and abnormality may not be quite as accurate as people believe they are.

To raise questions regarding normality and abnormality is in no way to question the fact that some behaviors are deviant or odd. Murder is deviant. So, too, are hallucinations. Nor does raising such questions deny the existence of the personal anguish that is often associated with "mental illness." Anxiety and depression exist. Psychological suffering exists. But normality and abnormality, sanity and insanity, and the diagnoses that flow from them may be less substantive than many believe them to be.

At its heart, the question of whether the sane can be distinguished from the insane (and whether degrees of insanity can be distinguished from each other) is a simple matter: Do the salient characteristics that lead to diagnoses reside in the patients themselves or in the environments and contexts in which observers find them? From Bleuler, through Kretschmer, through the formulators of the recently revised *Diagnostic and Statistical Manual* of the American Psychiatric Association, the belief has been strong that patients present symptoms, that those symptoms can be categorized, and, implicitly, that the sane are distinguishable from the insane. More recently, however, this belief has been questioned. Based in part on theoretical and anthropological considerations, but also on philosophical, legal, and therapeutic ones, the view has grown that psychological categorization of mental illness is useless at best and downright harmful, misleading, and pejorative at worst. Psychiatric diagnoses, in this view, are in the minds of the observers and are not valid summaries of characteristics displayed by the observed.

Gains can be made in deciding which of these is more nearly accurate by getting normal people (that is, people who do not have, and have never suffered, symptoms of serious psychiatric disorders) admitted to psychiatric hospitals and then determining whether they were discovered to be sane and, if so, how. If the sanity of such pseudopatients were always detected, there would be *prima facie* evidence that a sane individual can be distinguished from the insane context in which he is found. Normality (and presumably abnormality) is distinct enough that it can be recognized wherever it occurs, for it is carried within the person. If, on the other hand, the sanity of the pseudopatients were never discovered, serious difficulties would arise for those who support traditional modes of psychiatric diagnosis. Given that the hospital staff was not incompetent, that the pseudopatient had been behaving as sanely as he had been outside of the hospital, and that it had never been previously suggested that he belonged in a psychiatric hospital, such an unlikely outcome would support the view that psychiatric diagnosis betrays little about the patient but much about the environment in which an observer finds him.

This article describes such an experiment. Eight sane people gained secret admission to twelve different hospitals. Their diagnostic experiences constitute the data of the first part of this article; the remainder is devoted to a description of their experiences in psychiatric institutions. Too few psychiatrists and psychologists, even those who have worked in such hospitals, know what the experience is like. They rarely talk about it with former patients, perhaps because they distrust information coming from the previously insane. Those who have worked in psychiatric hospitals are likely to have adapted so thoroughly to the settings that they are insensitive to the impact of that experience. And while there have been occasional reports of researchers who submitted themselves to psychiatric hospitalization, these researchers have commonly remained in the hospitals for short periods of time, often with the knowledge of the hospital staff. It is difficult to know the extent to which they were treated like patients or like research colleagues. Nevertheless, their reports about the inside of the psychiatric hospital have been valuable. This article extends those efforts.

PSEUDOPATIENTS AND THEIR SETTINGS

The eight pseudopatients were a varied group. One was a psychology graduate student in his twenties. The remaining seven were older and "established." Among them were three psychologists, a pediatrician, a psychiatrist, a painter, and a housewife. Three pseudopatients were women, five were men. All of them employed pseudonyms, lest their alleged diagnoses embarrass them later. Those who were in mental health professions alleged another occupation in order to avoid the special attentions that might be accorded by staff, as a matter of courtesy or caution, to ailing colleagues. With the exception of myself (I was the first pseudopatient and my presence was known to the hospital administrator and chief psychologist and, so far as I can tell, to them alone), the presence of pseudopatients and the nature of the research program were not known to the hospital staffs.

The settings were similarly varied. In order to generalize the findings, admission into a variety of hospitals was sought. The twelve hospitals in the sample were located in five different states on the East and West coasts. Some were old and shabby, some were quite new. Some were research-oriented, others not. Some had good staff-patient ratios, others were quite understaffed. Only one was a strictly private hospital. All of the others were supported by state or federal funds, or in one instance, by university funds.

After calling the hospital for an appointment, the pseudopatient arrived at the admissions office complaining that he had been hearing voices. Asked what the voices said, he replied that they were often unclear, but as far as he could tell they said "empty," "hollow," and "thud." The voices were unfamiliar and were of the same sex as the pseudopatient. The choice of these symptoms was occasioned by their apparent similarity to existential symptoms. Such symptoms are alleged to arise from painful concerns about the perceived meaninglessness of one's life. It is as if the hallucinating person were saying, "My life is empty and hollow." The choice of these symptoms was also determined by the *absence* of a single report of existential psychoses in the literature.

Beyond alleging the symptoms and falsifying name, vocation, and employment, no further alterations of person, history, or circumstances were made. The significant events of the pseudopatient's life history were presented as they had actually occurred. Relationships with parents and siblings, with spouse and children, with people at work and in school, consistent with the aforementioned exceptions, were described as they were or had been. Frustrations and upsets were described along with joys and satisfactions. These facts are important to remember. If anything, they strongly biased the subsequent results in favor of detecting sanity, since none of their histories or current behaviors were seriously pathological in any way.

Immediately upon admission to the psychiatric ward, the pseudopatient ceased simulating *any* symptoms of abnormality. In some cases, there was a brief period of mild nervousness and anxiety, since none of the pseudopatients really believed that they would be admitted so easily. Indeed, their shared fear was that they would be immediately exposed as frauds and greatly embarrassed. Moreover, many of them had never visited a psychiatric ward; even those who had, nevertheless had some genuine fears about what might happen to them. Their nervousness, then, was quite appropriate to the novelty of the hospital setting, and it abated rapidly.

Apart from that short-lived nervousness, the pseudopatient behaved on the ward as he "normally" behaved. The pseudopatient spoke to patients and staff as he might ordinarily. Because there is uncommonly little to do on a psychiatric ward, he attempted to engage others in conversation. When asked by staff how he was feeling, he indicated that he was fine, that he no longer experienced symptoms. He responded to instructions from attendants, to calls for medication (which was not swallowed), and to dining-hall instructions. Beyond such activities as were available to him on the admissions ward, he spent his time writing down his observations about the ward, its patients, and the staff. Initially these notes were written "secretly," but as it soon became clear that no one much cared, they were subsequently written on standard tablets of paper in such public places as the dayroom. No secret was made of these activities.

The pseudopatient, very much as a true psychiatric patient, entered a hospital with no foreknowledge of when he would be discharged. Each was told that he would have to get out by his own devices, essentially by convincing the staff that he was sane. The psychological stresses associated with hospitalization were considerable, and all but one of the pseudopatients desired to be discharged almost immediately after being admitted. They were, therefore, motivated not only to behave sanely, but to be paragons of cooperation. That their behavior was in no way disruptive is confirmed by nursing reports, which have been obtained on most of the patients. These reports uniformly indicate that the patients were "friendly," "cooperative," and "exhibited no abnormal indications."

The Normal Are Not Detectably Sane

Despite their public "show" of sanity, the pseudopatients were never detected. Admitted, except in one case, with a diagnosis of schizophrenia, each was discharged with a diagnosis of schizophrenia "in remission." The label "in remission" should in no way be dismissed as a formality, for at no time during any hospitalization had any question been raised about any pseudopatient's simulation. Nor are there any indications in the hospital records that the pseudopatient's status was suspect. Rather, the evidence is strong that, once labeled schizophrenic, the pseudopatient was stuck with that label. If the pseudopatient was to be discharged, he must naturally be "in remission"; but he was not sane, nor, in the institution's view, had he ever been sane.

The uniform failure to recognize sanity cannot be attributed to the quality of the hospitals, for, although there were considerable variations among them, several are considered excellent. Nor can it be alleged that there was simply not enough time to observe the pseudopatients. Length of hospitalization ranged from seven to fifty-two days, with an average of nineteen days. The pseudopatients were not, in fact, carefully observed, but this failure clearly speaks more to traditions within psychiatric hospitals than to lack of opportunity.

Finally, it cannot be said that the failure to recognize the pseudopatients' sanity was due to the fact that they were not behaving sanely. While there was clearly some tension present in all of them, their daily visitors could detect no serious behavioral consequences—nor, indeed, could other patients. It was quite common for the patients to "detect" the pseudopatients' sanity. During the first three hospitalizations, when accurate counts were kept, 35 of a total of 118 patients on the admissions ward voiced their suspicions, some vigorously. "You're not crazy. You're a journalist, or a professor [referring to the continual note-taking]. You're checking up on the hospital." While most of the patients were reassured by the pseudopatient's insistence that he had been sick before he came in but was fine now, some continued to believe that the pseudopatient was sane throughout his hospitalization. The fact that the patients often recognized normality when staff did not raises important questions.

Failure to detect sanity during the course of hospitalization may be due to the fact that physicians operate with a strong bias toward what statisticians call the type 2 error. This is to say that physicians are more inclined to call a healthy person sick (a false positive, type 2) than a sick person healthy (a false negative, type 1). The reasons for this are not hard to find: It is clearly more dangerous to misdiagnose illness than health. Better to err on the side of caution, to suspect illness even among the healthy.

But what holds for medicine does not hold equally well for psychiatry. Medical illnesses, while unfortunate, are not commonly pejorative. Psychiatric diagnoses, on the contrary, carry with them personal, legal, and social stigmas. It was therefore important to see whether the tendency toward diagnosing the sane insane could be reversed. The following experiment was arranged at a research and teaching hospital whose staff had heard these findings but doubted that such an error could occur in their hospital. The staff was informed that at some time during the following three months, one or more pseudopatients would attempt to be admitted into the psychiatric hospital. Each staff member was asked to rate each patient who presented himself at admissions or on the ward according to the likelihood that the patient was a pseudopatient. A 10-point scale was used, with a 1 and 2 reflecting high confidence that the patient was a pseudopatient.

Judgments were obtained on 193 patients who were admitted for psychiatric treatment. All staff who had had sustained contact with or primary responsibility for the patient—attendants, nurses, psychiatrists, physicians, and psychologists—were asked to make judgments. Forty-one patients were alleged, with high confidence, to be pseudopatients by at least one member of the staff. Twenty-three were considered suspect by at least one psychiatrist. Nineteen were suspected by one psychiatrist and one other staff member. Actually, no genuine pseudopatient (at least from my group) presented himself during this period.

The experiment is instructive. It indicates that the tendency to designate sane people as insane can be reversed when the stakes (in this case, prestige and diagnostic acumen) are high. But what can be said of the nineteen people who were suspected of being "sane" by one psychiatrist and another staff member? Were these people truly "sane," or was it rather the case that in the course of avoiding the type 2 error the staff tended to make more errors of the first sort—calling the crazy "sane"? There is no way of knowing. But one thing is certain: Any diagnostic process that lends itself so readily to massive errors of this sort cannot be a very reliable one.

THE STICKINESS OF PSYCHODIAGNOSTIC LABELS

Beyond the tendency to call the healthy sick—a tendency that accounts better for diagnostic behavior on admission than it does for such behavior after a lengthy period of exposure—the data speak to the massive role of labeling in psychiatric assessment. Having once been labeled schizophrenic, there is nothing the pseudopatient can do to overcome the tag. The tag profoundly colors others' perceptions of him and his behavior.

From one viewpoint, these data are hardly surprising, for it has long been known that elements are given meaning by the context in which they occur. Gestalt psychology made this point vigorously, and Asch demonstrated that there are "central" personality traits (such as "warm" versus "cold") which are so powerful that they markedly color the meaning of other information in forming an impression of a given personality. "Insane," "schizophrenic," "manic-depressive," and "crazy" are probably among the most powerful of such central traits. Once a person is designated abnormal, all of his other behaviors and characteristics are colored by that label. Indeed, that label is so powerful that many of the pseudopatients' normal behaviors were overlooked entirely or profoundly misinterpreted. Some examples may clarify this issue.

Earlier I indicated that there were no changes in the pseudopatient's personal history and current status beyond those of name, employment, and, where necessary, vocation. Otherwise, a veridical description of personal history and circumstances was offered. Those circumstances were not psychotic. How were they made consonant with the diagnosis of psychosis? Or were those diagnoses modified in such a way as to bring them into accord with the circumstances of the pseudopatient's life, as described by him?

As far as I can determine, diagnoses were in no way affected by the relative health of the circumstances of a pseudopatient's life. Rather, the reverse occurred: The perception of his circumstances was shaped entirely by the diagnosis. A clear example of such translation is found in the case of a pseudopatient who had had a close relationship with his mother but was rather remote from his father during his early childhood. During adolescence and beyond, however, his father became a close friend, while his relationship with his mother cooled. His present relationship with his wife was characteristically close and warm. Apart from occasional angry exchanges, friction was minimal. The children had rarely been spanked. Surely there is nothing especially pathological about such a history. Indeed, many readers may see a similar pattern in their own experiences, with no markedly deleterious consequences. Observe, however, how such a history was translated in the psychopathological context, this from the case summary prepared after the patient was discharged.

> This white 39-year-old male . . . manifests a long history of considerable ambivalence in close relationships, which begins in early childhood. A warm relationship with his mother cools during adolescence. A distant relationship to his father is described as becoming very intense. Affective stability is absent. His attempts to control emotionality with his wife and children are punctuated by angry outbursts and, in the case of the children, spankings. And while he says that he has several good friends, one senses considerable ambivalence embedded in those relationships also. . . .

The facts of the case were unintentionally distorted by the staff to achieve consistency with a popular theory of the dynamics of schizophrenic reaction. Nothing of an ambivalent nature had been described in relations with parents, spouse, or friends. To the extent that ambivalence could be inferred, it was probably not greater than is found in all human relationships. It is true the pseudopatient's relationships with his parents changed over time, but in the ordinary context that would hardly be remarkable—indeed, it might very well be expected. Clearly, the meaning ascribed to his verbalizations (that is, ambivalence, affective instability) was determined by the diagnosis: schizophrenia. An entirely different meaning would have been ascribed if it were known that the man was "normal."

All pseudopatients took extensive notes publicly. Under ordinary circumstances, such behavior would have raised questions in the minds of observers, as, in fact, it did among patients. Indeed, it seemed so certain that the notes would elicit suspicion that elaborate precautions were taken to remove them from the ward each day. But the precautions proved needless. The closest any staff member came to questioning these notes occurred when one pseudopatient asked his physician what kind of medication he was receiving and began to write down the response. "You needn't write it," he was told gently. "If you have trouble remembering, just ask me again."

If no questions were asked of the pseudopatients, how was their writing interpreted? Nursing records for three patients indicate that the writing was seen as an aspect of their pathological behavior. "Patient engages in writing behavior" was the daily nursing comment on one of the pseudopatients who was never questioned about his writing. Given that the patient is in the hospital, he must be psychologically disturbed. And given that he is disturbed, continuous writing must be a behavioral manifestation of that disturbance, perhaps a subset of the compulsive behaviors that are sometimes correlated with schizophrenia.

One tacit characteristic of psychiatric diagnosis is that it locates the sources of aberration within the individual and only rarely within the complex of stimuli that surrounds him. Consequently, behaviors that are stimulated by the environment are commonly misattributed to the patient's disorder. For example, one kindly nurse found a pseudopatient pacing the long hospital corridors. "Nervous, Mr. X?" she asked. "No, bored," he said.

The notes kept by pseudopatients are full of patient behaviors that were misinterpreted by well-intentioned staff. Often enough, a patient would go "berserk" because he had, wittingly or unwittingly, been mistreated by, say, an attendant. A nurse coming upon the scene would rarely inquire even cursorily into the environmental stimuli of the patient's behavior. Rather, she assumed that his upset derived from his pathology, not from his present interactions with other staff members. Occasionally, the staff might assume that the patient's family (especially when they had recently visited) or other patients had stimulated the outburst. But never were the staff found to assume that one of themselves or the structure of the hospital had anything to do with a patient's behavior. One psychiatrist pointed to a group of patients who were sitting outside the cafeteria entrance half an hour before lunchtime. To a group of young residents he indicated that such behavior was characteristic of the oral-acquisitive nature of the syndrome. It seemed not to occur to him that there were very few things to anticipate in the psychiatric hospital besides eating.

A psychiatric label has a life and an influence of its own. Once the impression has been formed that the patient is schizophrenic, the expectation is that he will continue to be schizophrenic. When a sufficient amount of time has passed, during which the patient has done nothing bizarre, he is considered to be in remission and available for discharge. But the label endures beyond discharge, with the unconfirmed expectation that he will behave as a schizophrenic again. Such labels, conferred by mental health professionals, are as influential on the patient as they are on his relatives and friends, and it should not surprise anyone that the diagnosis acts on all of them as a self-fulfilling prophecy. Eventually, the patient himself accepts the diagnosis, with all of its surplus meanings and expectations, and behaves accordingly.

The inferences to be made from these matters are quite simple. Much as Zigler and Phillips have demonstrated that there is enormous overlap in the symptoms presented by patients who have been variously diagnosed, so there is enormous overlap in the behaviors of the sane and the insane. The sane are not "sane" all of the time. We lose our tempers "for no good reason." We are occasionally depressed or anxious, again for no good reason. And we may find it difficult to get along with one or another person—again for no reason that we can specify. Similarly, the insane are not always insane. Indeed, it was the impression of the pseudopatients while living with them that they were sane for long periods of time—that the bizarre behaviors upon which their diagnoses were allegedly predicated constituted only a small fraction of their total behavior. If it makes no sense to label ourselves permanently depressed on the basis of an occasional depression, then it takes evidence that is presently available to label all patients insane or schizophrenic on the basis of bizarre behaviors or cognitions. It seems more useful, as Mischel has pointed out, to limit our discussions to *behaviors*, the stimuli that provoke them, and their correlates.

It is not known why powerful impressions of personality traits, such as "crazy" or "insane," arise. Conceivably, when the origins of and stimuli that give rise to a behavior are remote or unknown, or when the behavior strikes us as immutable, trait labels regarding the *behavior* arise. When, on the other hand, the origins and stimuli are known and available, discourse is limited to the behavior itself. Thus, I may hallucinate because I am sleeping, or I may hallucinate because I have ingested a peculiar drug. These are termed self-induced hallucinations, or dreams, and drug-induced hallucinations, respectively. But when the stimuli to my hallucinations are unknown, that is called craziness, or schizophrenia—as if that inference were somehow as illuminating as the others. . . .

THE CONSEQUENCES OF LABELING AND DEPERSONALIZATION

Whenever the ratio of what is known to what needs to be known approaches zero, we tend to invent "knowledge" and assume that we understand more than we actually do. We seem unable to acknowledge that we simply don't know. The needs for diagnosis and remediation of behavioral and emotional problems are enormous. But rather than acknowledge that we are just embarking on understanding, we continue to label patients "schizophrenic," "manic-depressive," and "insane," as if in those words we had captured the essence of understanding. The facts of the matter are that we have known for a long time that diagnoses are often not useful or reliable, but we have nevertheless continued to use them. We now know that we cannot distinguish insanity from sanity. It is depressing to consider how that information will be used.

Not merely depressing, but frightening. How many people, one wonders, are sane but not recognized as such in our psychiatric institutions? How many have been needlessly stripped of their privileges of citizenship, from the right to vote and drive to that of handling their own accounts? How many have feigned insanity in order to avoid the criminal consequences of their behavior, and, conversely, how many would rather stand trial than live interminably in a psychiatric hospital—but are wrongly thought to be mentally ill? How many have been stigmatized by well-intentioned, but nevertheless erroneous, diagnoses? On the last point, recall again that a "type 2 error" in psychiatric diagnosis does not have the same consequences it does in medical diagnosis. A diagnosis of cancer that has been found to be in error is cause for celebration. But psychiatric diagnoses are rarely found to be in error. The label sticks, a mark of inadequacy forever.

2

IMAGINE A COUNTRY: LIFE IN THE NEW MILLENIUM

Holly Sklar

Imagine a country where one out of five children is born into poverty and wealth is being redistributed upward. Since the 1970s, the top 1 percent of households has doubled their share of the nation's wealth. The top 1 percent has close to 40 percent of the wealth—nearly the same amount as the bottom 95 percent of households.

Imagine a country where economic inequality is going back to the future circa the 1930s. The combined after-tax income of the top 1 percent of tax filers was about half that of the bottom 50 percent of tax filers in 1986. By the late 1990s, the top 1 percent had a larger share of after-tax income than the bottom 50 percent.

Imagine a country with a greed surplus and justice deficit. Imagine a country where the poor and middle class bear the brunt of severe cutbacks in education, health, environmental programs, and other public services to close state and federal budget deficits fueled by ballooning tax giveaways for wealthy households and corporations.

It's not Argentina.

Imagine a country which demands that people work for a living while denying many a living wage.

Imagine a country where health care aides can't afford health insurance. Where people working in the food industry depend on food banks to help feed their children. Where childcare teachers don't make enough to save for their own children's education.

It's not the Philippines.

Imagine a country where productivity went up, but workers' wages went down. In the words of the national labor department, "As the productivity of workers increases, one would expect worker compensation [wages and benefits] to experience similar gains." That's not what happened.

— Since 1968, worker productivity has risen 81 percent while the average hourly wage barely budged, adjusting for inflation, and the real value of the minimum wage dropped 38 percent.

— Imagine a country where the minimum wage just doesn't add up. Where minimum wage workers earn more than a third less than their counterparts earned a third of a century ago, adjusting for inflation. Where a couple with two children would have to work more than three full-time jobs at the $5.15 minimum wage to make ends meet.

It's not Mexico.

Imagine a country where some of the worst CEOs make millions more in a year than the best CEOs of earlier generations made in their lifetimes. CEOs made 45 times the pay of average production and non-supervisory workers in 1980. They made 96 times as much in 1990, 160 times as much in 1995 and 369 times as much in 2001. Back in 1960, CEOs made an average of 38 times more than schoolteachers. CEOs made 63 times as much in 1990 and 264 times as much as public school teachers in 2001.

Imagine a country that had a record-breaking ten-year economic expansion in 1991–2001, but millions of workers make wages so low they have to choose between eating or heating, health care or childcare.

A leading business magazine observed, "People who worked hard to make their companies competitive are angry at the way the profits are distributed. They think it is unfair, and they are right."

It's not England.

Imagine a country where living standards are falling for younger generations despite increased education. Since 1973, the share of workers without a high school degree has fallen by half. The share of workers with at least a four-year college degree has doubled. But the 2002 average hourly wage for production and non-supervisory workers (the majority of the workforce) is 7.5 percent below 1973, adjusting for inflation. Median net worth (assets minus debt) dropped between 1995 and 2001 for households headed by persons under age 35 and households that don't own their own home.

About one out of four workers makes $8.70 an hour or less. That's not much more than the real value of the minimum wage of 1968 at $8.27 in inflation-adjusted dollars.

It's not Russia.

Imagine a country where for more and more people a job doesn't keep you out of poverty, it keeps you working poor. Imagine a country much richer than it was 25 years ago, but the percentage of full-time workers living in poverty has jumped 50 percent.

Imagine a country that sets the official poverty line well below the actual cost of minimally adequate housing, health care, food, and other necessities. You were not counted as poor in 2001 (latest available final data) unless you had pre-tax incomes below these thresholds: $9,214 for a person under 65, $8,494 for a person 65 and older, $11,569 for a two-person family, $14,128 for a three-person family, and $18,104 for a family of four. On average, households need more than double the official poverty threshold to meet basic needs.

Imagine a country where homelessness is on the rise, but federal funding for low-income housing is about 50 percent lower than it was in 1976, adjusting for inflation. The largest federal housing support program is the mortgage interest deduction, which disproportionately benefits higher-income families.

Imagine a country where more workers are going back to the future of sweatshops and day labor. Corporations are replacing full-time jobs with disposable "contingent workers." They include temporary employees, contract workers, and "leased" employees—some of them fired and then "rented" back at a large discount by the same company—and involuntary part-time workers, who want permanent full-time work.

It's not Spain.

How do workers increasingly forced to migrate from job to job, at low and variable wage rates, without health insurance or paid vacation, much less a pension, care for themselves and their families, pay for college, save for retirement, plan a future, build strong communities?

Imagine a country where after mass layoffs and union busting, just 13.5 percent of workers are unionized. One out of three workers were union members in 1955. Full-time workers who were union members had median 2001 weekly earnings of $718 compared with just $575 for workers not represented by unions.

Imagine a country where the concerns of working people are dismissed as "special interests" and the profit-making interests of globetrotting corporations substitute for the "national interest."

Imagine a country negotiating "free trade" agreements that help corporations trade freely on cheap labor at home and abroad.

One ad financed by the country's agency for international development showed a Salvadoran woman in front of a sewing machine. It told corporations, "You can hire her for 33 cents an hour. Rosa is more than just colorful. She and her co-workers are known for their industriousness, reliability and quick learning. They make El Salvador one of the best buys." The country that financed the ad intervened militarily to make sure El Salvador would stay a "best buy" for corporations.

It's not Canada.

Imagine a country where nearly two-thirds of women with children under age 6 and more than three-fourths of women with children ages 6–17 are in the labor force, but affordable childcare and after-school programs are scarce. Apparently, kids are expected to have three parents: Two parents with jobs to pay the bills, and another parent to be home in mid-afternoon when school lets out—as well as all summer.

Imagine a country where women working full time earn 76 cents for every dollar men earn. Women don't pay 76 cents on a man's dollar for their education, rent, food or childcare. The gender wage gap has closed just 12 cents since 1955, when women earned 64 cents for every dollar earned by men. There's still another 24 cents to go.

The average woman high school graduate who works full time from ages 25 to 65 will earn about $450,000 less than the average male high school graduate. The gap widens to $900,000 for full-time workers with bachelor's degrees. "Men with professional degrees may expect to earn almost $2 million more than their female counterparts over their work-life," says a government report.

Imagine a country where childcare workers, mostly women, generally make about as much as parking lot attendants and much less than animal trainers. Out of 700 occupations surveyed by the labor department, only 15 have lower average wages than childcare workers.

Imagine a country where most minimum wage workers are women, while 95 percent of the top-earning corporate officers at the largest 500 companies are men, as are 90 percent of the most influential positions, from CEOs to executive vice president. Less than 2 percent of corporate officers at the largest companies are women of color.

Imagine a country where discrimination against women is pervasive from the bottom to the top of the pay scale and it's not because women are on the "mommy track." In the words of a leading business magazine, "At the same level of management, the typical woman's pay is lower than her male colleague's—even when she has the exact same qualifications, works just as many years, relocates just as often, provides the main financial support for her family, takes no time off for personal reasons, and wins the same number of promotions to comparable jobs."

Imagine a country where instead of rooting out discrimination, many policy makers are busily blaming women for their disproportionate poverty. If women earned as much as similarly qualified men, poverty in single-mother households would be cut in half.

It's not Japan.

Imagine a country where the awful labeling of children as "illegitimate" has again been legitimized. Besides meaning born out of wedlock, illegitimate also means illegal, contrary to rules and logic, misbegotten, not genuine, wrong—to be a bastard. The word illegitimate has consequences. It helps make people more disposable. Single mothers and their children have become prime scapegoats for illegitimate economics.

Imagine a country where violence against women is so epidemic it is their leading cause of injury. So-called "domestic violence" accounts for more visits to hospital emergency departments than car crashes, muggings, and rapes combined. About a third of all murdered women are killed by husbands, boyfriends, and ex-partners (less than a tenth are killed by strangers). Researchers say, "Men commonly kill their female partners in response to the woman's attempt to leave an abusive relationship."

The country has no equal rights amendment.

It's not Pakistan.

Imagine a country where homicide is the second-largest killer of young people, ages 15–24; "accidents," many of them drunk driving fatalities, are first. It leads major industrialized nations in firearms-related deaths for children under 15. Increasingly lethal weapons designed for hunting people are produced for profit by major manufacturers and proudly defended by a politically powerful national rifle association. Informational material from a national shooting sports foundation asks, "How old is old enough?" to have a gun, and advises parents: "Age is not the major yardstick. Some youngsters are ready to start at 10, others at 14. The only real measures are those of maturity and individual responsibility. Does your youngster follow directions well? Would you leave him alone in the house for two or three hours? Is he conscientious and reliable? Would you send him to the grocery store with a list and a $20 bill? If the answer to these questions or similar ones are 'yes' then the answer can also be 'yes' when your child asks for his first gun."

It's not France.

Imagine a country whose school system is rigged in favor of the already privileged, with lower caste children tracked by race and income into the most deficient and demoralizing schools and classrooms. Public school budgets are heavily determined by private property taxes, allowing higher income districts to spend much more than poor ones. In the state with the largest gap in 1999–2000, state and local spending per pupil in districts with the lowest child poverty rates was more than $2,152 greater than districts with the highest child poverty rates. The difference amounts to about $861,000 for a typical elementary school of 400 students—money that could be used for teachers, books, and other resources. Disparities are even wider among states, with spending in districts with enrollments of 15,000 or more ranging from $3,932 per pupil in one district to $14,244 in another.

In rich districts kids take well-stocked libraries, laboratories, and state-of-the-art computers for granted. In poor schools they are rationing out-of-date textbooks and toilet paper. Rich schools often look like country clubs—with manicured sports fields and swimming pools. Poor schools often look more like jails—with concrete grounds and grated windows. College prep courses, art, music, physical education, field trips, and foreign languages are often considered necessities for the affluent, luxuries for the poor.

Wealthier citizens argue that lack of money isn't the problem in poorer schools—family values are—until proposals are made to make school spending more equitable. Then money matters greatly for those who already have more.

It's not India.

Imagine a country whose constitution once counted black slaves as worth three-fifths of whites. Today, black per capita income is about three-fifths of whites. Imagine a country where racial disparities take their toll from birth to death. The black infant mortality rate is more than double that of whites. Black life expectancy is nearly six years less. Black unemployment is more than twice that of whites and the black poverty rate is almost triple that of whites.

Imagine a country where the government subsidized decades of segregated suburbanization for whites while the inner cities left to people of color were treated as outsider cities—separate, unequal, and disposable. Recent studies have documented continuing discrimination in education, employment, banking, insurance, housing, and health care.

It's not South Africa.

Imagine a country where the typical non-Hispanic white household has seven times as much net worth (including home equity) as the typical household of color. From 1995 to 2001, the typical white household's net worth rose from $88,500 to $120,900 while the net worth of the typical household of color fell from $18,300 to $17,100.

Imagine a country that doesn't count you as unemployed just because you're unemployed. To be counted in the official unemployment rate you must have searched for work in the past four weeks. The government doesn't count people as "unemployed" if they are so discouraged from long and fruitless job searches they have given up looking. It doesn't count as "unemployed" those who couldn't look for work in the past month because they had no childcare, for example. If you need a full-time job, but you're working part-time—whether 1 hour or 34 hours weekly—because that's all you can find, you're counted as employed.

A leading business magazine observed, "Increasingly the labor market is filled with surplus workers who are not being counted as unemployed."

It's not Germany.

Imagine a country where there is a shortage of jobs, not a shortage of work. Millions of people need work and urgent work needs people—from creating affordable housing, to repairing bridges and building mass transit, to cleaning up pollution and converting to renewable energy, to staffing after-school programs and community centers.

Imagine a country with full prisons instead of full employment. The jail and prison population has nearly quadrupled since 1980. The nation is number one in the world when it comes to locking up its own people. In 1985, 1 in every 320 residents were incarcerated. By 2001, the figure had increased to 1 in every 146.

Imagine a country where prison labor is a growth industry and so-called "corrections" spending is the fastest growing part of state budgets. Apparently, the government would rather spend $25,000 a year to keep someone in prison than on cost-effective programs of education, community development, addiction treatment, and employment to keep them out. In the words of a national center on institutions and alternatives, this nation has "replaced the social safety net with a dragnet."

Imagine a country that has been criticized by human rights organizations for expanding, rather than abolishing, use of the death penalty—despite documented racial bias and growing evidence of innocents being sentenced to death.

It's not China.

Imagine a country that imprisons black people at a rate much higher than apartheid South Africa. One out of seven black men ages 25–29 are incarcerated. Many more are on probation or on parole. Looking just at prisons and not local jails, 10 percent of black males ages 25–29 were locked up at the end of 2001, compared with 1 percent of white males. Black non-Hispanic women are five times more likely to be imprisoned than white non-Hispanic women. Meanwhile, nearly one out of three black men and women ages 16–19 are officially unemployed, as are one out of five ages 20–24. Remember, to be counted in the official unemployment rate you must be actively looking for a job and not finding one. "Surplus" workers are increasingly being criminalized.

Imagine a country waging a racially biased War on Drugs. More than three out of four drug users are white, according to government data, but three out of four state prisoners convicted of drug offenses are black and Latino. Racial disparities in drug and other convictions are even wider when non-Hispanic whites are distinguished more accurately from Latinos.

A study in a prominent medical journal found that drug and alcohol rates were slightly higher for pregnant white women than pregnant black women, but black women were about ten times more likely to be reported to authorities by private doctors and public health clinics—under a mandatory reporting law. Poor women were also more likely to be reported.

It is said that truth is the first casualty in war, and the War on Drugs is no exception. Contrary to stereotype, "The typical cocaine user is white, male, a high school graduate employed full time and living in a small metropolitan area or suburb," says the nation's former drug czar. A leading newspaper reports that law officers and judges say, "Although it is clear that whites sell most of the nation's cocaine and account for 80% of its consumers, it is blacks and other minorities who continue to fill up [the] courtrooms and jails, largely because, in a political climate that demands that something be done, they are the easiest people to arrest." They are the easiest to scapegoat.

It's not Australia.

Imagine a country where the cycle of unequal opportunity is intensifying. Its beneficiaries often slander those most systematically undervalued, underpaid, underemployed, underfinanced, underinsured, underrated, and otherwise under-served and undermined—as undeserving, "underclass," impoverished in moral and social values, and lacking the proper "work ethic." The oft-heard stereotype of deadbeat poor people masks the growing reality of dead-end jobs and disposable workers.

Imagine a country that abolished aid to families with dependent children while maintaining aid for dependent corporations.

Imagine a country where state and local governments are rushing to expand lot-teries, video poker, and other government-promoted gambling to raise revenues, dis-proportionately from the poor, which they should be raising from a fair tax system.

Imagine a country whose military budget tops average Cold War levels although the break up of the Soviet Union produced friends, not foes. This nation spends almost as much on the military as the rest of the world combined and leads the world in arms exports.

Imagine a country that ranks first in the world in wealth and military power, and 34th in child mortality (under five), tied with Malaysia and well behind countries such as Singapore and South Korea. If the government were a parent it would be guilty of child abuse. Thousands of children die preventable deaths.

Imagine a country where health care is managed for healthy profit. In many coun-tries health care is a right, but in this nation one out of six people under age 65 has no health insurance, public or private. Healthcare is literally a matter of life and death. Lack of health insurance typically means lack of preventive health care and delayed or second-rate treatment. The uninsured are at much higher risk for chronic disease and disability, and have a 25 percent greater chance of dying (adjusting for physical, economic, and behavioral factors). Uninsured women are 49 percent more likely to die than women with insurance during the four to seven years following an initial diagnosis of breast cancer.

Imagine a country where many descendants of its first inhabitants live on reser-vations strip-mined of natural resources and have a higher proportion of people in poverty than any other ethnic group.

Imagine a country where 500 years of plunder and lies are masked in expressions like "Indian giver." Where the military still dubs enemy territory, "Indian country."

Imagine a country which has less than 5 percent of the world's population, but uses more than 40 percent of the world's oil resources and about 20 percent of the coal and wood. It is the number one contributor to acid rain and global warming. It has obstructed international action on the environment and climate change.

It's not Brazil.

Imagine a country where half the eligible voters don't vote. The nation's senate and house of representatives are not representative of the nation. They are over-whelmingly white, male, and millionaire. At least 170 senators and congresspeople are millionaires. That's nearly one out of three members of the house and senate. Just 1 percent of the population they represent are millionaires.

Imagine a country where white men who are "falling down" the economic ladder are being encouraged to believe they are falling because women and people of color are climbing over them to the top or dragging them down from the bottom. That way, they will blame women and people of color rather than corporate and government policy. They will buy the myth of "reverse discrimination." Never mind that white males hold most senior management positions and continuing unreversed discrimination is well documented.

Imagine a country with a president who, even more than his father before him, "was born on third base and thought he hit a triple." The president wants to undo affirmative action. Never mind that despite all his advantages he was a mediocre student who relied on legacy affirmative action for the children of rich alumni to get into a top prep school and college. Never mind that he rode his family connections in business and politics.

Imagine a country where on top of discrimination comes insult. It's common for people of color to get none of the credit when they succeed—portrayed as undeserving beneficiaries of affirmative action and "reverse discrimination"—and all of the blame when they fail.

Imagine a country where a then presidential press secretary boasted to reporters: "You can say anything you want in a debate, and 80 million people hear it. If reporters then document that a candidate spoke untruthfully, so what? Maybe 200 people read it, or 2,000 or 20,000."

Imagine a country where politicians and judges whose views were formerly considered far right on the political spectrum now rule both houses of congress and the presidency and increasingly dominate the judiciary.

Imagine a country whose leaders misuse a fight against terrorism as camouflage for undermining democracy. Fundamental civil liberties, including the right not to be imprisoned indefinitely on the word of government officials, are being tossed aside. The attorney general attacked critics of administration policy with McCarthyite words: "To those who scare peace-loving people with phantoms of lost liberty, my message is this: Your tactics only aid terrorists for they erode our national unity . . . They give ammunition to [our] enemies and pause to [our] friends." The attorney general would burn democracy in the name of saving it.

It's not Italy.

It's the United States.

Decades ago Martin Luther King Jr. called on us to take the high road in *Where Do We Go From Here: Chaos or Community?* King wrote:

> "A true revolution of values will soon cause us to question the fairness and justice of many of our past and present policies. We are called to play the good Samaritan on life's roadside; but . . . one day the whole Jericho road must be transformed so that men and women will not be beaten and robbed as they make their journey through life. . . .

A true revolution of values will soon look uneasily on the glaring contrast of poverty and wealth. . . . There is nothing but a lack of social vision
to prevent us from paying an adequate wage to every American citizen
whether he be a hospital worker, laundry worker, maid or day laborer.
There is nothing except shortsightedness to prevent us from guaranteeing
an annual minimum—and livable—income for every American family."

3

PIG HATERS
FROM *COWS, PIGS, WARS, AND WITCHES*

Marvin Harris

Everyone knows examples of apparently irrational food habits. Chinese like dog meat but despise cow milk; we like cow milk but we won't eat dogs; some tribes in Brazil relish ants but despise venison. And so it goes around the world.

The riddle of the pig strikes me as a good follow-up to mother cow. It presents the challenge of having to explain why certain people should hate, while others love, the very same animal.

The half of the riddle that pertains to pig haters is well known to Jews, Moslems, and Christians. The god of the ancient Hebrews went out of His way (once in the Book of Genesis and again in Leviticus) to denounce the pig as unclean, a beast that pollutes if it is tasted or touched. About 1,500 years later, Allah told His prophet Mohammed that the status of swine was to be the same for the followers of Islam. Among millions of Jews and hundreds of millions of Moslems, the pig remains an abomination, despite the fact that it can convert grains and tubers into high-grade fats and protein more efficiently than any other animal. . . .

I shall begin with the problem of the Jewish and Islamic pig haters. Why should gods so exalted as Jahweh and Allah have bothered to condemn a harmless and even laughable beast whose flesh is relished by the greater part of mankind? Scholars who accept the biblical and Koranic condemnation of swine have offered a number of explanations. Before the Renaissance, the most popular was that the pig is literally a dirty animal—dirtier than others because it wallows in its own urine and eats excrement. But linking physical uncleanliness to religious abhorrence leads to inconsistencies. Cows that are kept in a confined space also splash about in their own urine and feces. And hungry cows will eat human excrement with gusto. Dogs and chickens do the same thing without getting anyone very upset, and the ancients must have known that pigs raised in clean pens make fastidious house pets. Finally, if we invoke purely aesthetic standards of "cleanliness," there is the formidable inconsistency that the Bible classifies locusts and grasshoppers as "clean." The argument that insects are aesthetically more wholesome than pigs will not advance the cause of the faithful.

These inconsistencies were recognized by the Jewish rabbinate at the beginning of the Renaissance. To Moses Maimonides, court physician to Saladin during the twelfth century in Cairo, Egypt, we owe the first naturalistic explanation of the Jewish and Moslem rejection of pork. Maimonides said that God had intended the ban on pork as a public health measure. Swine's flesh "has a bad and damaging effect upon the body," wrote the rabbi. Maimonides was none too specific about the medical reasons for this opinion, but he was the emperor's physician, and his judgment was widely respected.

In the middle of the nineteenth century the discovery that trichinosis was caused by eating undercooked pork was interpreted as a precise verification of the wisdom of Maimonides. Reform-minded Jews rejoiced in the rational substratum of the biblical codes and promptly renounced the taboo on pork. If properly cooked, pork is not a menace to public health, and so its consumption cannot be offensive to God. This provoked rabbis of more fundamentalist persuasion to launch a counterattack against the entire naturalistic tradition. If Jahweh had merely wanted to protect the health of His people, He would have instructed them to eat only well-cooked pork rather than no pork at all. Clearly, it is argued, Jahweh had something else in mind—something more important than mere physical well-being.

In addition to this theological inconsistency, Maimonides' explanation suffers from medical and epidemiological contradictions. The pig is a vector for human disease, but so are other domestic animals freely consumed by Moslems and Jews. For example, undercooked beef is a source of parasites, notably tapeworms, which can grow to a length of sixteen to twenty feet within a man's intestines, induce severe anemia, and lower resistance to other infectious diseases. Cattle, goats, and sheep are also vectors for brucellosis, a common bacterial infection in underdeveloped countries that is accompanied by fever, chills, sweats, weakness, pain, and aches. The most dangerous form is *Brucellosis melitensis*, transmitted by goats and sheep. Its symptoms are lethargy, fatigue, nervousness, and mental depression often mistaken for psychoneurosis. Finally, there is anthrax, a disease transmitted by cattle, sheep, goats, horses, and mules, but not by pigs. Unlike trichinosis, which seldom has fatal consequences and which does not even produce symptoms in the majority of infected individuals, anthrax often runs a rapid course that begins with body boils and terminates in death through blood poisoning. The great epidemics of anthrax that formerly swept across Europe and Asia were not brought under control until the development of the anthrax vaccine by Louis Pasteur in 1881.

Jahweh's failure to interdict contact with the domesticated vectors of anthrax is especially damaging to Maimonides' explanation, since the relationship between this disease in animals and man was known during biblical times. As described in the

Book of Exodus, one of the plagues sent against the Egyptians clearly relates the symptomology of animal anthrax to a human disease:

> . . . and it became a boil breaking forth with blains upon man and beast. And the magicians could not stand before Moses because of the boils, for the boils were upon the magicians, and upon all the Egyptians.

Faced with these contradictions, most Jewish and Moslem theologians have abandoned the search for a naturalistic basis of pig hatred. A frankly mystical stance has recently gained favor, in which the grace afforded by conformity to dietary taboos is said to depend upon not knowing exactly what Jahweh had in mind and in not trying to find out.

Modern anthropological scholarship has reached a similar impasse. For example, with all his faults, Moses Maimonides was closer to an explanation than Sir James Frazer, renowned author of *The Golden Bough*. Frazer declared that pigs, like "all so-called unclean animals, were originally sacred; the reason for not eating them was that many were originally divine." This is of no help whatsoever, since sheep, goats, and cows were also once worshipped in the Middle East, and yet their meat is much enjoyed by all ethnic and religious groups in the region. In particular, the cow, whose golden calf was worshipped at the foot of Mt. Sinai, would seem by Frazer's logic to make a more logical unclean animal for the Hebrews than the pig.

Other scholars have suggested that pigs, along with the rest of the animals tabooed in the Bible and the Koran, were once the totemic symbols of different tribal clans. This may very well have been the case at some remote point in history, but if we grant that possibility, we must also grant that "clean" animals such as cattle, sheep, and goats might also have served as totems. Contrary to much writing on the subject of totemism, totems are usually not animals valued as a food resource. The most popular totems among primitive clans in Australia and Africa are relatively useless birds like ravens and finches, or insects like gnats, ants, and mosquitoes, or even inanimate objects like clouds and boulders. Moreover, even when a valuable animal is a totem, there is no invariant rule that requires its human associates to refrain from eating it. With so many options available, saying that the pig was a totem doesn't explain anything. One might as well declare: "The pig was tabooed because it was tabooed."

I prefer Maimonides' approach. At least the rabbi tried to understand the taboo by placing it in a natural context of health and disease where definite mundane and practical forces were at work. The only trouble was that his view of the relevant conditions of pig hate was constrained by a physician's typical narrow concern with bodily pathology.

The solution to the riddle of the pig requires us to adopt a much broader definition of public health, one that includes the essential processes by which animals, plants, and people manage to coexist in viable natural and cultural communities. I think that the Bible and the Koran condemned the pig because pig farming was a threat to the integrity of the basic cultural and natural ecosystems of the Middle East.

To begin with, we must take into account the fact that the protohistoric Hebrews—the children of Abraham, at the turn of the second millennium B.C.—were culturally adapted to life in the rugged, sparsely inhabited arid areas between the river valleys of Mesopotamia and Egypt. Until their conquest of the Jordan Valley in Palestine, beginning in the thirteenth century B.C., the Hebrews were nomadic pastoralists, living almost entirely from herds of sheep, goats, and cattle. Like all pastoral peoples they maintained close relationships with the sedentary farmers who held the oases and the great rivers. From time to time these relationships matured into a more sedentary, agriculturally oriented lifestyle. This appears to have been the case with Abraham's descendants in Mesopotamia, Joseph's followers in Egypt, and Isaac's followers in the western Negev. But even during the climax of urban and village life under King David and King Solomon, the herding of sheep, goats, and cattle continued to be a very important economic activity.

Within the overall pattern of this mixed farming and pastoral complex, the divine prohibition against pork constituted a sound ecological strategy. The nomadic Israelites could not raise pigs in their arid habitats, while for the semi-sedentary and village farming populations, pigs were more of a threat than an asset.

The basic reason for this is that the world zones of pastoral nomadism correspond to unforested plains and hills that are too arid for rainfall agriculture and that cannot easily be irrigated. The domestic animals best adapted to these zones are the ruminants—cattle, sheep, and goats. Ruminants have sacks anterior to their stomachs which enable them to digest grass, leaves, and other foods consisting mainly of cellulose more efficiently than any other mammals.

The pig, however, is primarily a creature of forests and shaded riverbanks. Although it is omnivorous, its best weight gain is from food low in cellulose—nuts, fruits, tubers, and especially grains, making it a direct competitor of man. It cannot subsist on grass alone, and nowhere in the world do fully nomadic pastoralists raise significant numbers of pigs. The pig has the further disadvantage of not being a practical source of milk and of being notoriously difficult to herd over long distances.

Above all, the pig is thermodynamically ill-adapted to the hot, dry climate of the Negev, the Jordan Valley, and the other lands of the Bible and the Koran. Compared to cattle, goats, and sheep, the pig has an inefficient system for regulating its body temperature. Despite the expression "To sweat like a pig," it has recently been proved that pigs can't sweat at all. Human beings, the sweatiest of all mammals, cool themselves by evaporating as much as 1,000 grams of body liquid per hour from each square meter of body surface. The best the pig can manage is 30 grams per square meter. Even sheep evaporate twice as much body liquid through their skins as pigs. Sheep also have the advantage of thick white wool that both reflects the sun's rays and provides insulation when the temperature of the air rises above that of the body. According to L. E. Mount of the Agricultural Research Council Institute of Animal Physiology in Cambridge, England, adult pigs will die if exposed to direct sunlight and air temperatures over 98° F. In the Jordan Valley, air temperatures of 110°F. occur almost every summer, and there is intense sunshine throughout the year.

To compensate for its lack of protective hair and its inability to sweat, the pig must dampen its skin with external moisture. It prefers to do this by wallowing in fresh clean mud, but it will cover its skin with its own urine and feces if nothing else is available. Below 84°F., pigs kept in pens deposit their excreta away from their sleeping and feeding areas, while above 84° F., they begin to excrete indiscriminately throughout the pen. The higher the temperature, the "dirtier" they become. So there is some truth to the theory that the religious uncleanliness of the pig rests upon actual physical dirtiness. Only it is not in the nature of the pig to be dirty everywhere; rather it is in the nature of the hot, arid habitat of the Middle East to make the pig maximally dependent upon the cooling effect of its own excrement.

Sheep and goats were the first animals to be domesticated in the Middle East, possibly as early as 9,000 B.C. Pigs were domesticated in the same general region about 2,000 years later. Bone counts conducted by archeologists at early prehistoric village farming sites show that the domesticated pig was almost always a relatively minor part of the village fauna, constituting only about 5 percent of the food animal remains. This is what one would expect of a creature which had to be provided with shade and mudholes, couldn't be milked, and ate the same food as man.

As I pointed out in the case of the Hindu prohibition on beef, under preindustrial conditions, any animal that is raised primarily for its meat is a luxury. This generalization applies as well to preindustrial pastoralists, who seldom exploit their herds primarily for meat.

Among the ancient mixed farming and pastoralist communities of the Middle East, domestic animals were valued primarily as sources of milk, cheese, hides, dung, fiber, and traction for plowing. Goats, sheep, and cattle provided ample amounts of these items plus an occasional supplement of lean meat. From the beginning, therefore, pork must have been a luxury food, esteemed for its succulent, tender, and fatty qualities.

Between 7,000 and 2,000 B.C. pork became still more of a luxury. During this period there was a sixtyfold increase in the human population of the Middle East. Extensive deforestation accompanied the rise in population, especially as a result of permanent damage caused by the large herds of sheep and goats. Shade and water, the natural conditions appropriate for pig raising, became progressively more scarce, and pork became even more of an ecological and economic luxury.

As in the case of the beef-eating taboo, the greater the temptation, the greater the need for divine interdiction. This relationship is generally accepted as suitable for explaining why the gods are always so interested in combating sexual temptations such as incest and adultery. Here I merely apply it to a tempting food. The Middle East is the wrong place to raise pigs, but pork remains a succulent treat. People always find it difficult to resist such temptations on their own. Hence Jahweh was heard to say that swine were unclean, not only as food, but to the touch as well. Allah was heard to repeat the same message for the same reason: It was ecologically maladaptive to try to raise pigs in substantial numbers. Small-scale production would only increase the temptation. Better then, to interdict the consumption of pork entirely, and to concentrate on raising goats, sheep, and cattle. Pigs tasted good but it was too expensive to feed them and keep them cool.

Many questions remain, especially why each of the other creatures interdicted by the Bible—vultures, hawks, snakes, snails, shellfish, fish without scales, and so forth—came under the same divine taboo. And why Jews and Moslems, no longer living in the Middle East, continue—with varying degrees of exactitude and zeal—to observe the ancient dietary laws. In general, it appears to me that most of the interdicted birds and animals fall squarely into one of two categories. Some, like ospreys, vultures, and hawks, are not even potentially significant sources of food. Others, like shellfish, are obviously unavailable to mixed pastoral-farming populations. Neither of these categories of tabooed creatures raises the kind of question I have set out to answer—namely, how to account for an apparently bizarre and wasteful taboo. There is obviously nothing irrational about not spending one's time chasing vultures for dinner, or not hiking fifty miles across the desert for a plate of clams on the half shell.

This is an appropriate moment to deny the claim that all religiously sanctioned food practices have ecological explanations. Taboos also have social functions, such as helping people to think of themselves as a distinctive community. This function is well served by the modern observance of dietary rules among Moslems and Jews outside of their Middle Eastern homelands. The question to be put to these practices is whether they diminish in some significant degree the practical and mundane welfare of Jews and Moslems by depriving them of nutritional factors for which there are no readily available substitutes. I think the answer is almost certainly negative. . . .

4

"A LIFE AT HARD LABOR"
CAPITALISM AND WORKING HOURS

Juliet Schor

> *The labouring man will take his rest long in the morning; a good piece of the day is spent afore he come at his work; then he must have his breakfast, though he have not earned it, at his accustomed hour, or else there is grudging and murmuring: when the clock smiteth, he will cast down his burden in the midway, and whatsoever he is in hand with, he will leave it as it is, though many times it is marred afore he come again; he may not lose his meat, what danger soever the work is in. At noon he must have his sleeping time, then his bever in the afternoon, which spendeth a great part of the day; and when his hour cometh at night, at the first stroke of the clock he casteth down his tools, leaveth his work, in what need or case soever the work standeth.*
> — *the Bishop Pilkington*

One of capitalism's most durable myths is that it has reduced human toil. This myth is typically defended by a comparison of the modern forty-hour week with its seventy- or eighty-hour counterpart in the nineteenth century. The implicit—but rarely articulated—assumption is that the eighty-hour standard has prevailed for centuries. The comparison conjures up the dreary life of medieval peasants, toiling steadily from dawn to dusk. We are asked to imagine the journeyman artisan in a cold, damp garret, rising even before the sun, laboring by candlelight late into the night.

These images are backward projections of modern work patterns. And they are false. Before capitalism, most people did not work very long hours at all. The tempo of life was slow, even leisurely; the pace of work relaxed. Our ancestors may not have been rich, but they had an abundance of leisure. When capitalism raised their incomes, it also took away their time. Indeed, there is good reason to believe that working hours in the mid-nineteenth century constitute the most prodigious work effort in the entire history of humankind.

Therefore, we must take a longer view and look back not just one hundred years, but three or four, even six or seven hundred. Admittedly, there is a certain awkwardness in this exercise. Such calculations are by necessity rough. Since there are no comprehensive, average figures for any time but the recent past, we must use individual estimates for various types of workers, as well as data representing the typical, rather than average, working day and working year. Also, in medieval times the information that does exist is mainly for men. Descriptions of women's household labors are available, but, to my knowledge, there are no estimates of the amount of time women spent doing them. The greater regularity of women's tasks (cooking, animal husbandry, care of children) suggests their workyear was more continuous, and therefore longer in total, than the male workyear; but we have no direct evidence on this. The other caveat is that because no medieval estimates are possible for America, I have oriented this part of my discussion to Western Europe and mainly England. (For a discussion of "why England?" see the notes.) Despite these shortcomings, the available evidence indicates that working hours under capitalism, at their peak, increased by more than 50 percent over what they had been in medieval times (see figure 1).

Figure 1: *Eight Centuries of Annual Hours*

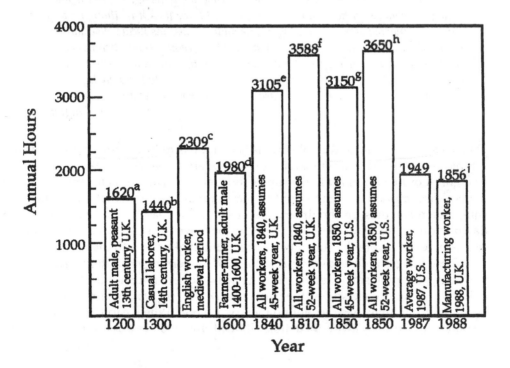

a Calculated from Gregory Clark's estimate of 150 days per family, assumes 12 hours per day, 135 days per year for adult male ("Impatience, Poverty, and Open Field Agriculture," mimeo, 1986).

b Calculated from Nora Ritchie's estimate of 120 days per year. Assumes 12-hour day. ("Labour Conditions in Essex in the Reign of Richard II," in E. M. Carus-Wilson, ed., *Essays in Economic History*, vol. II [London: Edward Arnold], 1962).

c Calculated from Ian Blanchard's estimate of 180 days per year. Assumes 11-hour day. ("Labour Productivity and Work Psychology in the English Mining Industry, 1400–1600," *Economic History Review*, 31 [1 (1978)]: 23.)

d Author's estimate of average medieval laborer working two-thirds of the year at 9.5 hours per day.

e Average worker in the United Kingdom, assumes 45-week year, 69 hours per week (weekly hours from W. S. Woytinsky, "Hours of Labor," in *Encyclopedia of the Social Sciences*, vol. III [New York: Macmillan], 1935).

f Average worker in the United Kingdom, assumes 52-week year, 69 hours per week (weekly hours from ibid.).

g Average worker in the United States, assumes 45-week year, 70 hours per week (weekly hours from Joseph Zeisel, "The Worker in American Industry, 1850-1956," *Monthly Labor Review*, 81 [January 1958]: 23–29).

h Average worker in the United States, assumes 52-week year, 70 hours per week (weekly hours from ibid.).

i Manufacturing worker in the United Kingdom, calculated from Bureau of Labor Statistics data, Office of Productivity and Technology.

Consider a typical working day in the medieval period. It stretched from dawn to dusk (sixteen hours in summer and eight in winter), but, as the Bishop Pilkington has noted, work was intermittent—called to a halt for breakfast, lunch, the customary afternoon nap, and dinner. Depending on time and place, there were also midmorning and midafternoon refreshment breaks. These rest periods were the traditional rights of laborers, which they enjoyed even during peak harvest times. During slack periods, which accounted for a large part of the year, adherence to regular working hours was not usual. According to Oxford Professor James E. Thorold Rogers, the medieval workday was not more than eight hours. The worker participating in the eight-hour movements of the late nineteenth century was "simply striving to recover what his ancestor worked by four or five centuries ago."

The pace of work was also far below modern standards—in part, because the general pace of life in medieval society was leisurely. The French historian Jacques LeGoff has described precapitalist labor time "as still the time of an economy dominated by agrarian rhythms, free of haste, careless of exactitude, unconcerned by productivity—and of a society created in the image of that economy, *sober and modest*, without enormous appetites, undemanding, and incapable of quantitative efforts." Consciousness of time was radically different. Temporal units we take for granted today—such as the hour, or the minute—did not exist. There was little idea of time saving, punctuality, or even a clear perception of past and future. Consciousness of time was much looser—and time had much less economic value.

But the pace of work was slow not only for cultural reasons. On the basis of our knowledge of caloric intake, we can infer that work had to have been a low-energy affair. The food consumption of all but the rich was inadequate to sustain either a rapid pace or continuous toil. (This may be why lords provided substantial meals to laborers during harvests.) A long, hard day of agricultural labor requires well over three thousand calories per day, an amount out of the range of common people. As more food became available over the nineteenth and twentieth centuries, a significant fraction of those additional calories have been burned up by an accelerated pace of work.

The contrast between capitalist and precapitalist work patterns is most striking in respect to the working year. The medieval calendar was filled with holidays. Official—that is, church—holidays included not only long "vacations" at Christmas, Easter, and midsummer but also numerous saints' and rest days. These were spent both in sober churchgoing and in feasting, drinking, and merrymaking. In addition to official celebrations, there were often weeks' worth of ales—to mark important life events (bride ales or wake ales) as well as less momentous occasions (scot ale, lamb ale, and hock ale). All told, holiday leisure time in medieval England took up probably about one-third of the year. And the English were apparently working harder than their neighbors. The *ancien régime* in France is reported to have guaranteed fifty-two Sundays, ninety rest days, and thirty-eight holidays. In Spain, travelers noted that holidays totaled five months per year.

The peasant's free time extended beyond officially sanctioned holidays. There is considerable evidence of what economists call the backward-bending supply curve of labor—the idea that when wages rise, workers supply less labor. During one period of unusually high wages (the late fourteenth century), many laborers refused to work "by the year or the half year or by any of the usual terms but only by the day." And they worked only as many days as were necessary to earn their customary income—which in this case amounted to about 120 a year, for a probable total of only 1,440 hours annually (this estimate assumes a 12-hour day because the days worked were probably during spring, summer, and fall). A thirteenth-century estimate finds that whole peasant families did not put in more than 150 days per year on their land. Manorial records from fourteenth-century England indicate an extremely short working year—175 days—for servile laborers. Later evidence for farmer-miners, a group with control over their worktime, indicates they worked only 180 days a year.

The short workyear reveals an important feature of precapitalist society: the absence of a culture of consumption and accumulation. There was far less interest in and opportunity for earning or saving money. Material success was not yet invested with the overriding significance it would assume. And consumerism was limited—both by the unavailability of goods and by the absence of a middle class with discretionary income. Under these circumstances, the lack of compulsion to work is understandable. Of course, those who object to this characterization argue that free time in the middle ages was not really leisure but underemployment. If work effort was low, they claim it is because the economy provided few opportunities for earning money.

What are we to make of these claims? It is certainly true that holidays were interspersed throughout the agrarian calendar, falling after the peak periods of planting, sowing, and harvesting. And in both agriculture and industry, the possibilities for earning additional income were limited. Yet cause and effect are hard to untangle. If more work had been available, it is not obvious that many people would have taken it. The English case provides considerable evidence that higher incomes led to less not more labor—for example, the casual laborers of the thirteenth century, the farmer-miners of the sixteenth, and even the early industrial workers who resisted work whenever their incomes allowed it. Just after wages were paid, as employers learned, absenteeism, failure to work, and much-decried "laziness" resulted. But wherever one stands on the causes of medieval leisure, one fact remains: steady employment, for fifty-two weeks a year is a modern invention. Before the nineteenth—and, in many cases, the twentieth—century, labor patterns were seasonal, intermittent, and irregular.

The argument I will be making is that capitalism created strong incentives for employers to keep hours long. In the early stages, these incentives took the form of a fixed wage that did not vary with hours. In the twentieth century, this incentive would reappear in the guise of the fixed annual salary, which proved to be a major reason for the white-collar worker's long hours. Other incentives also came into play by the end of the nineteenth century, such as employers' desires to keep machinery operating continuously, and the beneficial effects of long hours on workplace discipline. Later, peculiarities in the payment of fringe benefits would have an impact. Each of these factors has been important in keeping hours long. Of course, there have been countervailing pressures, the most important of which was the trade union movement, which waged a successful hundred-year struggle for shorter hours. But once this quest ended after the Second World War, reductions in hours virtually ceased. Not long after unions gave up the fight, the American worker's hours began to rise.

CAPITALISM AND THE EROSION OF LEISURE

Moments are the elements of profit

—Leonard Homer, English factory inspector

Capitalism steadily eroded the leisure that pervaded medieval society. Telltale signs—in the form of modern conflicts over time—appeared in at least one "capitalist" enclave as early as the fourteenth century, when the textile industry was faced with an economic crisis. The first response of the cloth makers to this crisis was predictable: they announced reductions in wages. But they also tried something new: the imposition of a longer, "harsher" working day. To enforce this new regime, employers introduced what historians believe are the first public clocks, which appeared in textile centers across Europe. These work clocks—or *Werkglocken,* as they came to be called—signaled to workers when they should arrive at work, the timing of meals, and the close of the day. The idea was that the clock would replace the sun as the regulator of working hours. But unlike the sun, the clocks would be under the control of the employer.

As soon as the *Werkglocken* were introduced, they became objects of bitter antagonism. As they were actually not mechanical clocks but bells which were rung manually, workers, employers, and city officials vied for control of them. Workers staged uprisings to silence the clocks, fighting what the historian Jacques LeGoff has termed "the time of the cloth makers." City officials responded by protecting employers' interests. Fines were levied against workers who disobeyed the injunctions of the bells, by coming late to work or leaving early. Harsher penalties—including death—awaited those who used the bell to signal a revolt. Faced with the alliance of employers and state, the workers' resistance failed; and they resigned themselves to the longer hours, the higher pace of work, and the regimentation of the clocks.

The crisis of labor time in the textile industry illustrates two important points about capitalism and work. First, employers used *time* itself to regulate labor. In medieval Europe, consciousness of time was vague. The unit of labor time was the "day." It was tied to the sun and, as I have noted, tended to be approximate. Modern time consciousness, which includes habituation to clocks, economy of time, and the ownership of time, became an important weapon which employers used against their employees. In the words of the English historian E. P. Thompson, time became "currency: it is not passed but spent." As employers consolidated control over their workforces, the day was increasingly split into two kinds of time: "owners' time, the time of *work*"; and "their own time, a time (in theory) for *leisure*." Eventually, workers came to perceive time, not as the milieu in which they lived their life, but "as an objective force within which [they] were imprisoned."

The second point is that working time became a crucial economic variable, profoundly affecting the ability of businesses to survive and prosper. In the textile case, the impetus of the employers to raise hours emanated from an immediate crisis in their geographically widening and fiercely competitive market. In order to earn sufficient profits to survive, employers took advantage of an intensification of labor. They learned that the market system has a structural imperative to exploit labor: those who do not succeed in raising hours of work or accelerating the pace of production may very well be driven out of business by their competitors. The rigors of the market are particularly demanding during the inevitable depressions in trade which lower prices and choke off demand for products.

As capitalism grew, it steadily lengthened worktime. The change was felt in earnest by the eighteenth century. The workday rose in the cottage industries which sprang up throughout the English countryside. Rural people, especially women, took on spinning, weaving, lacemaking, and other handicrafts, in their own cottages, in order to earn a little cash to survive. The time commitment ranged from a few hours a day for the better-off, to eight, ten, or twelve hours a day for those who were poor. And this was in addition to regular domestic responsibilities. Outside the cottage, workdays rose as employers encroached on customary periods for eating and resting. Farm laborers, hired by the day, week, or season, were subjected to tighter discipline and stricter schedules. The invention of factories, in the late eighteenth century, allowed employers to squeeze out the vestiges of precapitalist work habits. Eventually, when artificial lighting came into use, the working "day" stretched far into the night, and scheduled hours climbed.

Some workers—such as the most highly skilled, well-organized male craft workers in England—were able to withstand increases beyond the ten-hour mark. But even in some skilled trades, such as baking and potteries, the men could not hold out. In any case, skilled male workers were a minority of the workforce. The majority of laboring people, in both England and America, would eventually work longer days. Men, women, and children in home-based and factory labor, farm laborers, slaves, domestic servants, and even a large fraction of male craftsmen experienced a progressive lengthening of work hours. Twelve-, fourteen-, even sixteen-hour days were not uncommon.

A second change was the loss of nearly all the regular holidays medieval people had enjoyed. The Puritans launched a holy crusade against holidays, demanding that only one day a week be set aside for rest. Their cause was aided by the changing economic incentives of the market economy, particularly the growing commercialization of agriculture which resulted in more year-round activity. In the sixteenth century, the long rise in holidays was arrested; and during the seventeenth, reversed. The eighteenth saw the demise of the laborer's long-honored Saturday half-holiday. By the nineteenth century, the English agricultural laborer was working six days per week, with only Good Friday and Christmas as official time off. A similar process occurred in the United States, during the nineteenth century, as steady employment grew more common.

Taken together, the longer workday and the expanding workyear increased hours dramatically. Whereas I estimate a range of 1,440 to 2,300 hours per year for English peasants before the seventeenth century, a mid-nineteenth-century worker in either England or the United States might put in an annual level of between 3,150 and 3,650 hours.

Workers' progressive loss of leisure stemmed from structural imperatives within capitalism which had no counterpart in the medieval economy. The European manor survived on its own efforts, mainly consuming what it produced itself. Neither peasants nor their lords were dependent on markets for basic subsistence. They were not exposed to economic competition, nor driven by a profit motive. Their time was their own. Medieval industry was also protected from market pressures. Guilds had strictly defined hours of work, and apparently "few conflicts arose over the time of work." Custom, rather than competition, dictated economic activity. And custom dictated strictly limited work effort.

The growth of markets, both national and international, thrust workers out of their world of custom and into a competitive dynamic. Capitalist businesses, in contrast to medieval manors, strove for maximum profits. They lived or died by the bottom line. Time off was costly, hence bitterly resisted. Whenever one employer managed to squeeze a bit more work out of his workers, others were compelled to follow. As long as a critical mass of employers was able to demand longer hours, they could set the standard. Workers became victims in a larger-than-life struggle for financial dominance. When textile workers in Manchester lost an hour a day, the repercussions would be felt in Lancashire or maybe far across the seas in Lowell. As local outposts were knitted together into a world market, an economic relay system was created—and it operates to this day. American textile workers, who enjoy paid vacations and official five-day weeks, are rapidly losing out to their counterparts in China, where daily, weekly, and hourly schedules are far more arduous.

Given the high value medieval people placed on a leisurely way of life, why did they accede to grueling hours and the loss of their free time? The answer is straight-forward. Capitalists were successful because workers lacked alternatives. In the medieval economy, peasants—whether serfs or freepersons—had secure, time-honored access to land. And land was what nearly everyone depended on for survival. Crop failures might lead to hunger or starvation, but most ordinary people retained *social* rights to some part of their manor's holdings, and hence to food. They were not dependent on the market for their "subsistence." Indeed, a "market" in land did not even exist. Custom dictated its use and disposition.

The growth of a world market led to the uprooting of the peasantry from the land that had sustained them for centuries. Lords enclosed open fields, in order to claim ownership to carry out commercial schemes. Peasants lost control over what had once been a "common treasury" from which they had derived a measure of independence. Now their survival depended on participation in the market in labor. They had become proletarians, reduced to selling time and toil. An analogous fate befell artisans, with the elimination of the more or less assured upward mobility of journeymen into masters promised by the guild system. Increasingly, masters turned themselves into small capitalists and permanently hired apprentices and journey-men. The labor practices enforced by guild traditions were jettisoned in favor of reliance on "what the market would bear."

These changes degraded the status of many common people: "To lose control over one's own (and one's family's) labour was to surrender one's independence, security, liberty, one's birthright." In England, this "commodification" of labor had occurred by the seventeenth century. In the United States, the process took place much later and followed a different path; but by the mid-nineteenth century, similar pressures were operating. In the words of E. P. Thompson, "enclosure and the grow-ing labour-surplus at the end of the eighteenth century tightened the screw for those who were in regular employment; they were faced with the alternatives of partial employment and the Poor Law, or submission to a more exacting labour discipline." As a result, living standards were depressed, and widespread poverty developed. Observers in seventeenth-century England suggest that between a quarter and a half of the rural population lived in poverty. Many commentators maintained that poverty was necessary: "It is only hunger which can spur and goad [the poor] on to labour." The struggle for subsistence had become the paramount fact of life for many people—and in the process, leisure time became an unaffordable luxury.

THE DAILY WAGE AND THE EXPANSION OF WORKTIME

The growth of a world market and the creation of a proletariat were major social developments which formed the backdrop for the rise of working hours. Specific fea-tures of the emerging labor markets also exacerbated pressures toward long hours.

For example, capitalists followed the centuries-old custom of fixing wages by the day, the week, or even the month—in contrast to the modern practice of payment by the hour, which had not been introduced. The daily wage was largely invariant to hours or intensity of labor, a worker earning neither more nor less as the working day expanded or contracted. This flexibility of working hours was a departure from past practice. On medieval manors, serfs' labor obligations to their lords were spelled out in detail, and a certain amount of effort was expected. But with the decline of serfdom, these labor obligations faded away.

The fact that daily wages were fixed gave employers a simple incentive to raise worktime: *each additional hour worked was free.* And because workers were unable to resist the upward pressure on hours, worktime rose dramatically—especially in factories in England and the United States. Marx's famous description of early factories was a harsh reality to the laborers in them: "The 'House of Terror' for paupers, only dreamed of by the capitalist mind in 1770, was brought into being a few years later in the shape of a gigantic 'workhouse' for the industrial worker himself. It was called the factory. And this time the ideal was a pale shadow compared with the reality."

In these "Satanic mills," the custom of a fixed daily wage led the owners to extend hours of toil by whatever means they could manage. They tried "petty pilferings of minutes." They "nibbl[ed] and cribbl[ed] at mealtimes." These methods produced pure profit. One factory operative explained:

> In reality there were no regular hours: masters and managers did with us as they liked. The clocks at the factories were often put forward in the morning and back at night, and instead of being instruments for the measurement of time, they were used as cloaks for cheatery and oppression. Though this was known amongst the hands, all were afraid to speak, and a workman then was afraid to carry a watch, as it was no uncommon event to dismiss any one who presumed to know too much about the science of horology.

Testimony of this sort was not uncommon:

> We worked as long as we could see in summer time, and I could not say at what hour it was that we stopped. There was nobody but the master and the master's son who had a watch, and we did not know the time. There was one man who had a watch. . . . It was taken from him and given into the master's custody because he had told the men the time of day.

Similar strategies were in use in the United States, where factory hours might range from seventy-five to ninety hours a week by the second quarter of the nineteenth century.

Of course, workers did not passively accept the theft of their time. Resistance was widespread and took a variety of forms as workers acquired their own timepieces, failed to show up at work on time, or went on strike to recoup lost leisure. In a New Jersey factory, the young hands went on strike to protest the shifting of the dinner hour. One observer noted: "the children would not stand for it, for fear if they assented to this, the next thing would be to deprive them of eating at all." However, until the second half of the nineteenth century, factory hours in both Britain and the United States rose rather than fell. Workers' position in the market where they sold their labor was not favorable enough to win back their leisure time.

Although the state stepped in, in both countries, government legislation to limit hours was often ineffective. Factory inspectors found themselves unable to enforce the laws: "'The profit to be gained by it' (over-working in violation of the [Factory] Act) 'appears to be, to many, a greater temptation than they can resist . . . In cases where the additional time is gained by a multiplication of small thefts in the course of the day, there are insuperable difficulties to the inspectors making out a case.'"

The incentives to increase hours operated in other parts of the economy as well. Servants were also paid fixed wages. Taken together, farm servants and domestics in middle-class homes made up a significant proportion of workers in both England and the United States in the second half of the nineteenth century. Servants were given room and board, plus some payment, either weekly or perhaps by the season. If their hours of work went up, they received no extra pay. It should come as no surprise, then, that their hours of work were particularly arduous. They would rise in the early hours of the morning and work until evening. The hours of domestic servants frequently expanded to fourteen or fifteen hours a day and were typically above those of factory workers. "I used to get up at four o'clock every morning, and work until ten P.M. every day of the week," recounted one Minneapolis housemaid. "Mondays and Tuesdays, when the washing and ironing was to be done," she began at 2 A.M. Time off was often minimal, as families were reluctant to do without their "help." In the United States, free time was one evening or half-day every week or every other week until the 1880s, after which Sundays were added. But even on a "day off," servants were required to do an average of seven and a half hours.

Similar dynamics operated where labor was formally enslaved. Slaves in the American South received a subsistence living—meager food, clothing, and shelter, which did not vary with their hours of work. Field hands worked "every day from 'fore daylight to almost plumb dark"; and during picking season, lighting kept them going at night, often sixteen hours a day. One slave noted: "Work, work, work. . . . I been so exhausted working, I was like an inchworm crawling along a roof. I worked till I thought another lick would kill me." If the owners were able to squeeze out an extra hour here or there, it was purely to their benefit. Slaves' "wages" did not rise.

Employers (and slaveowners) managed to push working hours to the brink of human endurance because they were far more powerful than the common people they hired (or owned). They had the law on their side, to punish those who went on strike or fled the plantation. They had superior resources, to outlast a work stoppage or buy off opposition. They could also invoke the discipline of the market. When businesses are squeezed from above, workers below may find it impossible to resist. In the end, labor lost the battle over working time because it was just too dependent on capital for its very survival.

5

COFFEE AND THE PROTESTANT ETHIC

Wolfgang Schivelbusch

Toward the end of the sixteenth century, Leonhart Rauwolf, an Augsburg physician, traveled through the Near and Middle East. He noticed that the Turks and Arabs were consuming a hot, blackish beverage much as Europeans drank wine and beer. In his book *Journey to the Lands of the Orient,* published in 1582, Rauwolf wrote: "Among other things they have a good drink which they greatly esteem. They call it 'chaube': it is nearly as black as ink and helpful against stomach complaints. They drink it from earthenware and porcelain cups early in the morning, also in public places without any hesitation. But they take only small sips of it and then pass these cups around, for they are seated next to each other in a circle. To the water they add a berry the natives call 'bunnu' which, but for its size and color, resembles bay tree berries, surrounded by two thin hulls. This drink is very common among them, so that one finds quite a few who serve it in the bazaar, as well as shopkeepers who sell the berries there."

It is difficult to determine precisely when coffee was introduced to Arabic culture. According to legend, Mohammed was cured of narcolepsy with coffee. There are indications in Arabic medical literature that coffee was used medicinally as early as the tenth century. But in the Islamic world, too, it became a popular beverage relatively late, certainly no earlier than the fifteenth century.

Although the dating may be vague, the *logic* of coffee drinking for Arabic-Islamic civilization is incontestable. As a nonalcoholic, nonintoxicating, indeed even sobering and mentally stimulating drink, it seemed to be tailor-made for a culture that forbade alcohol consumption and gave birth to modern mathematics. Arabic culture is dominated by abstraction more than any other culture in human history. Coffee has rightly been called the wine of Islam.

Until the seventeenth century, coffee remained a curiosity for Europeans, mentioned in accounts of journeys to the exotic lands of the Orient. They could not imagine consuming a hot, black, bitter-tasting drink—much less with pleasure. It reminded them too much of hot pitch, which was used in medieval times for battle and torture.

The situation changed around the middle of the seventeenth century. Suddenly a whole set of hitherto unknown exotic substances became fashionable. Together with chocolate, tea, and tobacco, coffee made its entrance upon the stage of European luxury culture. It appeared in several different places at once, then spread in a quasi-strategic pattern of encirclement: in the south it surfaced in the Levantine trade centers, Venice and Marseilles; in the north, in the transshipping ports of the new international trade, London and Amsterdam. From these bridgeheads it quickly conquered the hinterlands. Around 1650 coffee was virtually unknown in Europe, at most used as medication. By about 1700 it was firmly established as a beverage, not, of course, for the entire population but certainly among the trend-setting strata of society.

Court aristocracy added coffee drinking as one more flourish to its cult of luxury. Coffee became as fashionable as the new chinoiserie, or the young blackamoor kept as a sort of mascot in one's retinue. Essentially it was not the drink itself that mattered to court society but how it could be consumed, the opportunities it afforded for display of elegance, grace, and high refinement. The porcelain that was created expressly for coffee drinking at the court was what mattered most—just as all aspects of life in an absolutist regime were determined by the forms of court ceremony. Form replaced content.

Bourgeois society of the same period regarded coffee in a different, quite contrary light. Not form, but substance—the drink—was the focus of interest. The thing itself, in this case, consisted in the actual physiological properties and effects ascribed to coffee. Were one to list all the properties they believed inherent in coffee, the result would be an amazingly motley catalogue of often mutually contradictory virtues. Here is just a small sampling: Coffee is good for colic, it fortifies the liver and the gall bladder, brings relief in cases of dropsy, purifies the blood, soothes the stomach, whets the appetite, but can also decrease it, keeps you awake, but can also induce sleep. It cools "hot" temperaments, but on the other hand it warms up "cold" ones, etc. Coffee, in other words, was viewed as a panacea. There wasn't a positive effect it was not credited with. If we wade through the jumble of properties most commonly imputed to it, however, we come up with two which are actually one and the same: sobriety and the power to sober up a person. In seventeenth- and eighteenth-century medical literature as well as in the general view, coffee was perceived as primarily a sober beverage, in contrast to previously known drinks, all of which were alcoholic. The late seventeenth-century middle classes welcomed coffee as the great soberer. The coffee drinker's good sense and business efficiency were contrasted with the alcohol drinker's inebriation, incompetence, and laziness, most clearly in texts from seventeenth-century Puritan England. "'Tis found already," wrote James Howell in 1660, "that this coffee drink hath caused a greater sobriety among the Nations. Whereas formerly Apprentices and clerks with others used to take their morning's draught of Ale, Beer, or Wine, which, by the dizziness they Cause in the Brain, made many unfit for business, they use now to play the Good-fellows in this wakeful and civil drink."

A BACKWARD GLANCE: THE SIGNIFICANCE OF ALCOHOL BEFORE THE SEVENTEENTH CENTURY

It would be difficult for us nowadays to imagine the crucial role alcoholic drinks played before the hot, nonalcoholic beverages (coffee, tea, and chocolate) assumed their permanent place in the European diet. The former were consumed as both a semiluxury to be enjoyed and a nourishing staple. Medieval people drank copious amounts of wine and beer, especially on holidays—and holidays were quite numerous then (in Paris, for instance, 103 holidays were observed in the year 1660), including church consecrations, weddings, baptisms, burials, and "blue Mondays." On workdays beer and wine were a regular part of the meals.

Prior to the introduction of the potato, beer was second only to bread as the main source of nourishment for most central and north Europeans. "Some subsist more upon this drink than they do on food," wrote Johann Brettschneider, alias Placotomus, in the year 1551, referring not to hard-core drinkers, but to average folk: "People of both sexes and every age, the hale and the infirm alike require it." An English family in the latter half of the seventeenth century—the period when coffee drinking was catching on among the upper classes—consumed about three liters of beer per person daily, children included. Although large breweries already existed by then, beer brewing was still a part of housekeeping, like bread baking and slaughtering—one of the housewife's duties.

The best way to get a sense of how pervasive beer was in the seventeenth century, and often even in the eighteenth, is to remember that breakfast as a rule consisted of beer soup, a now forgotten dish. In rural areas of Germany such soups were still prepared as late as the end of the eighteenth century. The following recipe—which already shows a considerable degree of refinement—comes from that period: "Heat the beer in a saucepan; in a separate small pot beat a couple of eggs. Add a chunk of butter to the hot beer. Stir in some cold beer to cool it, then pour over the eggs. Add a bit of salt, and finally mix all the ingredients together, whisking it well to keep it from curdling. Finally, cut up a roll, white bread, or other good bread, and pour the soup over it. You may also sweeten to taste with sugar."

How unusual the new hot beverages must have tasted to palates accustomed to the ubiquitous beer! The following passage from a letter written by Duchess Elisabeth Charlotte of Orleans illustrates this clearly. Of German origin, and more popularly known as Liselotte von der Pfalz, she complains about the taste of the three new drinks in fashion at the court of Versailles: "Tea makes me think of hay and dung, coffee of soot and lupine-seed, and chocolate is too sweet for me—it gives me a stomachache—I can't stand any of them. How much I would prefer a good *Kalteschale* [a cold soup, often prepared with wine and fruit—Trans.] or a good beer soup, that wouldn't give me a stomachache."

But it was the ritual function of alcohol, above and beyond its nutritional function, that explains what we now regard as the excessive consumption of alcohol in preindustrial societies. Drinking rites are of course still very much with us today. Drinking to someone's health, clinking glasses, the obligation to return another's toast, drinking as a pledge of friendship, drinking contests, etc.—these are rites and obligations one cannot easily evade. To earlier societies they were even more obligatory. Drinkers would work themselves into a state of intoxication that was not merely the result of the alcohol imbibed. It was also psychological in origin, fueled by the frenzy engendered in outdoing yourself offering toasts.

A drinking bout, once under way, usually ended only when its participants lost consciousness. To withdraw earlier was viewed either as an insult to one's drinking companions or as an admission of weakness on the part of the one who "chickened out." Observing a German drinking bout in the sixth century, the Roman author Venantius Fortunatus wrote that the participants "were carrying on like madmen, each competing in drinking to the other's health," and that "a man had to consider himself lucky to come away with his life." This essentially holds true also for the Middle Ages and for Germany up to the sixteenth century. Today competitive drinking to the point where participants lose consciousness is to be found in only a few social settings (rural weddings, Oktoberfest, student fraternities, etc.). It was a normal occurrence in the life of the preindustrial world.

One account of such a drinking contest in 1599 demonstrates how little things have changed in the thousand years between the Old Germanic society and that of the sixteenth century: "These drunkards are not satisfied with the wine they have in front of them, but contend with one another using drinking vessels as they would spears and weaponry. The foremost among them attacks, launching a round of drinks. Soon thereafter he bids those across the room to drink. Others are soon enlisted to join in on all sides with glasses and goblets. These guests and drunkards contend with each other, man to man, in pairs: they must swallow half, then all of a drink in one gulp, and without stopping to take a single breath, or wiping their beards, until they sink into a complete stupor. . . . And just as soon as two heroes emerge victorious, these men guzzle in competition with each other. And whoever is the winner and has best stood his ground carries off the prize. Sometimes the ones who drink the most are awarded honors and presented with trophies as well."

To be sure, there was increasing criticism of these drinking customs in the sixteenth century. The account just quoted, written by a Tubingen professor, Johann Georg Sigwart, is itself an expression of a new view of moderation articulated in a barrage of pamphlets, caricatures, sermons, and books. If the image this propaganda literature created were to be taken as literal truth, one would have to assume that sixteenth-century central Europe saw a sudden explosion of wanton drunkenness and gluttony. "When the city gates are closed, and those who live outside in the surrounding towns leave, they go weaving from side to side, stumbling and staggering, falling into the mud, their legs splayed out wide enough for a coach to pass through." Such descriptions should be taken with a grain of salt. They reflect not so much historical reality as opinion passed off as reality—which is to say that what changed in the sixteenth century was not actual alcohol consumption (which was already so huge that an increase was scarcely possible), but rather the attitude toward drinking.

This new attitude developed during the Reformation. Its chief representatives and advocates were the leading Reformers, above all Martin Luther. The Reformation, redefining the relationship between the individual and God as a *personal* one, at the same time took pains to regulate the relationship of man to alcohol. In so doing the Reformation was laying an essential foundation in both realms for the development of capitalism.

However, the movement to moderation in the Age of Reformation did not have especially lasting results. The numerous prohibitions against toasting rituals, intended to put an end to drinking contests, had to be repeatedly renewed, obviously having failed to achieve the desired effects. Nor were the apostles of moderation themselves the sort of thoroughgoing Puritans the Calvinist churches of seventeenth-century Holland and England were to bring forth. Medieval *joie de vivre* and the Protestant ethic were still inextricably joined in a person like Luther, who preached tirelessly against "Demon Alcohol" (a sixteenth-century descriptive term for alcoholism), yet who also coined the proverb "wine, women, and song"—without which a man would remain a fool his whole life long.

Obviously conditions in the sixteenth century were not yet ripe for any real change in drinking habits. It would take not only Puritan ideology to condemn "Demon Alcohol," but some material basis to make it possible. That came with a more highly developed society and economy, sharper restraints, a higher degree of work discipline—and also a new group of beverages that could replace the old ones. For without substitutes the existing traditions would not disappear. Any substitute for the tried and true would have to have a new kind of appeal—that is, it must satisfy new needs—otherwise it would be unacceptable. These requirements were fulfilled by the new hot beverages that reached Europe in the seventeenth century—above all, coffee.

THE GREAT SOBERER

Coffee awakened a drowsing humanity from its alcoholic stupor to middle-class common sense and industry—so seventeenth-century coffee propaganda would have it. The English Puritan poets seized on this theme, as for example in the following anonymous poem published in 1674:

When the sweet Poison of the Treacherous Grape
Had acted on the world a general rape;
Drowning our Reason and our souls
In such deep seas of large o'erflowing bowls,

. . . .

When foggy Ale, leavying up mighty trains
Of muddy vapours, had besieg'd our Brains,
Then Heaven in Pity . . .
First sent amongst us this All-healing Berry,

. . . .

Coffee arrives, that grave and wholesome Liquor,
That heals the stomach, makes the genius quicker,
Relieves the memory, revives the sad,
And cheers the Spirits, without making mad . . .

Another two hundred years later the nineteenth-century poet-historian Jules Michelet would see coffee fulfill this historic mission as the sobering agent of an entire epoch: "Henceforth is the tavern dethroned, the monstrous tavern is dethroned, which even half a century earlier had sent youths wallowing 'twixt casks and wenches, is dethroned. Fewer liquor-drenched songs on the night air, fewer noblemen sprawled in the gutter . . . Coffee, the sober drink, the mighty nourishment of the brain, which unlike other spirits, heightens purity and lucidity; coffee, which clears the clouds of the imagination and their gloomy weight; which illumines the reality of things suddenly with the flash of truth . . ."

However, in the seventeenth century, coffee was not only considered a sober drink in contrast to alcoholic beverages, but above and beyond that it was credited with the ability to sober up people who were already drunk—a popular belief even today, in spite of all pharmacological evidence to the contrary. Sylvestre Dufour was the author-editor and compiler of a book on the new hot beverages. It had many editions and translations throughout Europe after its publication in 1671 (*Traitez Nouveau et curieux du café, du thé, et du chocolat*). Dufour claimed to have seen the following episode: "Coffee sobers you up instantaneously, or in any event it sobers up those who are not fully intoxicated. One of my friends who had had too much wine sat down at the gambling table one evening after dinner. He was losing considerable sums, because having drunk too much wine, he was confusing hearts with diamonds. I took him aside and had him drink a cup of coffee, whereupon he returned to the game with a completely sober head and clear eye."

There was another series of attributes which the seventeenth century ascribed to coffee, none of them borne out by modern scientific findings. It seems that people of that era perceived coffee to have properties it could not possibly possess, but which they themselves projected onto it. A classic instance of the placebo effect?

If we examine another of these supposed properties, the motivation behind the projections becomes clearer. Michelet speaks in the passage that follows the section quoted above of "antierotic coffee, which at last replaces sexual arousal with stimulation of the intellect." What he had in mind here was the coffeehouse culture of the Enlightenment, the coffeehouse as the gathering place of intellectuals and center for discussion. In seventeenth-century England the idea of coffee as an anti-erotic drink was much more direct and concrete. It was regarded as a substance that reduced sexual energies, even to the point of impotence. It was recommended to clerics who lived in celibacy. In 1764 a broadside caused a great sensation in London. Its title: "The Women's Petition against Coffee, Representing to Publick Consideration the Grand Inconveniencies accruing to their SEX from the Excessive Use of that Drying, Enfeebling LIQUOR. Presented to the Right Honorable the Keepers of the Liberty of VENUS." The text expressed in no uncertain terms the fear that coffee would make "men [as] unfruitful as those deserts whence that unhappy berry is said to be brought." It is easy to identify the sociopolitical impulse behind this complaint: the English coffee houses of this period excluded women, and in their pamphlet the women were rebelling against the increasing patriarchalization of society. That this opposition should use the argument that coffee makes men impotent shows, on the one hand, how powerful this notion was at the time, and on the other, how unpuritanical, indeed how antipuritanical, the women of this time were.

Coffee as the beverage of sobriety and coffee as the means of curbing the sexual urges—it is not hard to recognize the ideological forces behind this reorientation. Sobriety and abstinence have always been the battle cry of puritanical, ascetic movements. English Puritanism, and more generally, the Protestant ethic, defined coffee in this way and then wholeheartedly declared it their favorite drink.

There is no doubt that coffee is to a large degree an ideologically freighted drink. Yet it would be wrong to see only this aspect of it. For coffee undeniably has other properties that made it so well-suited to European civilization as it evolved from the seventeenth century on. Modern pharmacology confirms this. The caffeine in coffee affects the central nervous system. As a standard twentieth-century study states, it enhances "mental activity, speeds perception, and judgment at the same time that it makes them clearer, and it stimulates mental activity without leading to any subsequent depression." It is these properties that make coffee *the* beverage of the modern bourgeois age. The very point at which it was fully inserted into European culture confirms this. The seventeenth century was the century of rationalism, not only in philosophy, but in all the important areas of material life. The absolutist-bureaucratic state was built on the rationalistic viewpoint that originated in this period. Work in the newly burgeoning factories was organized rationalistically. Rationality and accountability characterize the bourgeois spirit that was behind it all.

The seventeenth-century bourgeois was distinguished from people of past centuries by his mental as well as his physical lifestyle. Medieval man did physical work, for the most part under the open sky. The middle-class man worked increasingly with his head, his workplace was the office, his working position was sedentary. The ideal that hovered before him was to function as uniformly and regularly as a clock. (The first example that comes to mind is the famous clocklike regularity of Kant, whose neighbors allegedly set their watches by his precisely timed daily walks.) It is perfectly obvious that this new way of life and work would affect the entire organism. In this connection coffee functioned as a historically significant drug. It spread through the body and achieved chemically and pharmacologically what rationalism and the Protestant ethic sought to fulfill spiritually and ideologically. With coffee, the principle of rationality entered human physiology, transforming it to conform with its own requirements. The result was a body which functioned in accord with the new demands—a rationalistic, middle-class, forward-looking body.

6

UNINTENDED CONSEQUENCES OF UNDERCOVER WORK
FROM *UNDERCOVER: POLICE SURVEILLANCE IN AMERICA*

Gary T. Marx

A seemingly simple sociological principle, but one we could study for years to try to fully comprehend, is that we tend to become the roles we play. In other words, as we play a role over time, the attitudes and expectations attached to that role tend to become internalized into the self—that is, they become a part of who we are, of how we perceive right and wrong, of our understandings of the way things ought to be. This intriguing characteristic of role playing is highly significant for society, for it allows its members to convincingly fulfill their assigned roles.

There are two sides to this picture. The more attractive side is that if we play a positive role, we tend to take on its traits. The less attractive side is that if we play a negative role, we tend to take on its qualities—that is, the negative aspects of roles similarly tend to become part of the self. Marx focuses precisely on this aspect of role playing in discussing police who, after going undercover, no longer are able to distinguish between their roles. The "criminal" role lingers even after the role playing is supposed to be over. In some cases, the criminal role even "engulfs" the person, and the individual never is able to take up where he or she left off.

This article provides observations that you may be able to apply to your own life. Because roles become an essential part of the self—producing either negative or positive traits—to the extent that you have a choice you can play roles that will produce characteristics you admire and avoid roles that might produce a self that you won't like. Remember, what you play is what you become.

The FBI's reputation for integrity and its clean-cut, straight arrow image is attributable in part to J. Edgar Hoover's refusal to allow agents to face the temptations and problems confronting undercover police. Similarly, Los Angeles's Chief William Parker felt that the establishment of personal relations between officers and suspects "would invariably fester into a spot of corruption or prove a source of embarrassment even when capably and honestly conducted." As they recognized, the social and psychological consequences for police who play undercover roles can be severe. He who sups with the devil must indeed have a long spoon. What is there about undercover work that is conducive to negative effects on police, and what are these effects?

Undercover situations tend to be more fluid and unpredictable than routine patrol or investigative work. Agents have greater autonomy, and rules and procedures are less clearly defined. The need for secrecy accentuates problems of coordination, increases the potential for error, and lessens the probability that problems will be discovered.

The major organizational problem of any law enforcement agency—how to supervise a dispersed set of employees—is compounded. Undercover agents are removed from the usual controls and supports of a uniform, a badge, a visible supervisor, a fixed time and place for work, radio or beeper calls, and a clearly bounded assignment. These [controls] have both a literal and symbolic significance. Their formal and visible nature enhances accountability by advertising to police and the public who the individual is and what is expected of him.

SOCIAL AND PSYCHOLOGICAL CONSEQUENCES

Unlike conventional police officers, undercover agents tend to be involved primarily with criminals; the deception is continuous, the criminal environment is pervasive. The agent's ability to blend in, to resemble criminals, and to be accepted are necessary conditions for his effectiveness. As an undercover agent with twenty years of experience put in: "A guy who is two degrees off plumb will survive out there, while a choir boy from MIT will be in a lot of trouble."

To the extent that agents develop personal relationships with potential targets, they may experience pressure, ambivalence, and guilt over the betrayal inherent in the deception. Romantic entanglements are an extreme example; more commonly, agents may come to feel sympathy for their targets and develop an understanding of why they behave as they do. A highly productive officer who, before his undercover assignment, saw the world in black-and-white terms reports he became "a different kind of cop." Going undercover, he learned "what it's like to be on the other side of the fence." He started "seeing the criminal element being just regular people, but caught up in their own thing." Another deep-cover agent says: "Boy, it can get gray out there . . . just because a guy's a criminal doesn't mean you can't like him and that he doesn't have the same interest[s] as you do [e.g., baseball or fishing]." Such attitudes can lead to passivity and even the protection of particular targets. Consider, for example, an agent who came to feel close to a target: "He was a 72-year-old guy. The king pin. There was enough evidence. You go to christenings, weddings, Sunday dinner. It's easy to say hey, it's the other guys. He really isn't so bad. I won't testify against him." The agent may falsely report back that the group cannot be penetrated or that no violations are occurring. The fear of being "made" or "burned" (discovered) may also mean the failure to pursue a case vigorously.

Another agent described the feelings of betrayal he had on concluding an operation when his unknowing target "protected" him. In a sell-bust transaction, the agent arranged for contraband to be sold to a suspect he had befriended. The eventual arrest was arranged in such a way as not to cast suspicion upon the agent. When the arrested suspect was interrogated about his source for the contraband, he refused to "give up" the agent.

In contrast, when the agent plays the role of victim and develops a strong identification in this direction, the result may be an overly aggressive crusade. Joseph Wambaugh describes a member of the San Diego decoy squad who played the role of aliens who had been robbed, stabbed, raped, or terrorized: "He began to feel what *they* felt . . . to *feel* the poverty and fear. It made funny pains in the stomach . . . It made them sigh a lot. Finally it made them mad." In this case, the strong identification meant vigilante actions and personal crusades, as the decoys sought to teach "the crooks that there was a price to pay" for their behavior, regardless of departmental policy and the law.

Covert work is very intense. The agent is always "on." For some agents, the work has an addictive quality as they savor the sense of power, intrigue, excitement, and their protected contact with illegality. They may be both attracted and repelled by the role they play. The strong male bonding and secrecy that are characteristic of police work may take a conspiratorial turn as undercover agents adopt a protective code of silence not unlike that of organized crime.

In his analysis of how patrolmen can avoid becoming corrupted by the use of coercion, William Muir stresses the importance of conversation and interaction with supervisors. The same conditions are likely to reduce the corruption of those licensed to use deception. Yet for the undercover agent these conditions may not be as available. Isolation and secrecy may work against the undercover agent's developing a morality that permits the use of deception in a bounded and principled fashion. Isolation from other contacts and the need to be liked and accepted by members of a criminal subculture can have undesirable consequences. To do well, you must "get your mind inside the bad guy's mind." But "playing the crook" may increase cynicism and ambivalence about the police role and make it easier to rationalize the use of illegal and immoral means, whether for agency or corrupt personal goals. As one agent jokingly put it when asked about his speeding and running stop signs (unrelated to any enforcement effort): "We're here to enforce the law, not to obey it."

When an insensitive supervisor fails to help the agent cope with the moral complexity of the issues or fails to communicate support and questions what the agent does, it may seem to the agent that "everything bad that happens to me comes from the good guys, and everything good comes from the bad guys. You start to wonder." On the other hand, as long as the tactic produces results, some supervisors may not wish to know what agents are doing or what the role is doing to the agent.

The stress the agent experiences can be intense. Some supervisors are more concerned with making cases than with the well-being of their agents. They may not share the priority implicit in the remark of a wise supervisor who said: "Cases will always be there, agents won't." A state police officer who spent two and one-half years undercover reports:

> My nerves are really up. I'm starting to get to where I can't keep a meal down. I would eat with them . . . twenty minutes later, I would be throwing my guts up on the side of the road. I started to feel these chest pains. I really felt like I was having a heart attack. I would have diarrhea on a daily basis.
>
> I go to this doctor . . . I go to my sergeant on the undercover gig the next day and say, "I went to the doc and he wrote this down for you." I figure this is it. I have a note from the doctor saying I'm under stress, too much stress. They'll have to let me out of this job.
>
> He laughs. I say, "What are you laughing about?"
>
> "We got a million dollars wrapped up in this. You're not physically hurt. You're going through stress. You'll be all right. You can handle it." That's the mentality of cops: You can handle anything. Don't worry about it, kid, you can handle it. I was devastated.

. . . The secrecy required for undercover work offers rich opportunities for short-cuts, financial rewards, and self-aggrandizement. Agents may learn the technical skills needed for complicated offenses. Their knowledge of how police operate lessens the likelihood of discovery, as does the usual absence of a complainant. Moral corrosion or a lowering of standards may occur when agents are granted the power to engage in conspiracies on behalf of law enforcement and are immersed in a seamy, morally relative world.

New York City's elite narcotics force, the SIU (Special Investigating Unit), illustrates many of these issues. Its members gave heroin to informants, set illegal wiretaps, committed perjury, and sometimes took bribes. They also engaged in vigilante tactics, such as seizing drugs and cash and summarily ordering foreign dealers out of the country (referred to as "taking the devil's money to do the Lord's work" or "make them bleed, bust their ass, and steal their weed").

This highly select unit (chosen from the "best guys in all the precincts") roamed the city, had no assigned precinct, and were exempt from many of the bureaucratic restrictions faced by others. Belief in the special elite character of the unit resulted in a lessening of supervision ("they supervise themselves"). The unit made major arrests and seized large quantities of drugs. Its spectacular success did not suggest corruption, but effectiveness and opportunities for corruption often go hand in hand.

The unit did not fare well: of 70 SIU detectives, 52 were indicted, 2 committed suicide, and 1 had a mental breakdown.

Undercover agents may come to have an exaggerated sense of their own power. The highly committed members of the elite San Diego decoy unit wanted no part of ordinary police duties and came to feel apart from, and superior to, other police:

> They started to come to work looking like something that fell off a boxcar or was pushed off by a railroad bull. They'd work in their yards or wash their cars or haul fertilizer or whatever, and they'd come to work rank. Unshaven . . .
>
> They'd tell their wives and friends, and fellow cops who worked patrol and detectives, that they *had* to dress and look and smell like that. That out in the canyons they had to *be* aliens. That their performances might make the difference in whether they lived or died . . .

A number of the interview, news, and nonfiction and fiction accounts in the literature suggests that some deep-cover agents undergo a striking metamorphosis. As lying becomes a way of life, the agent may become confused about his or her true identity. Familiarity can breed affection as well as contempt. This is particularly likely to the extent that the agent is cut off from friends and becomes immersed in a new life. The phenomenon of "going native" is a danger well known to social science field researchers. A few agents "cross over."

The parallel to the informer who comes to identify with police is the officer who comes to identify with criminals. In his novel *Mother Night*, Kurt Vonnegut observes that "we are what we pretend to be, so we must be careful about what we pretend to be." Or, put more prosaically by a vice-squad detective: "You're working with dope fiends and perverts all day, and a guy on the vice squad usually goes down; he deteriorates; he becomes like the people you work with." Most agents, however, do not turn into "weird guys," even though the potential for adverse effects is there.

A Connecticut officer from a conservative family background spent a year posing as a street person and riding with a motorcycle gang. He was overtaken by the role. He reports: "I knew [it] was a role-playing thing, but I became total, 100 percent involved. I became what I was trying to tell people I was, and it confused me. Believe me, it confused me a lot."

Robert Leuci, who served as the model for the book and film *Prince of the City*, noted a gradual change in himself and the officers he worked with:

> I began to wake up in the morning and look at myself in the mirror and see my reflection—and I didn't like what I saw . . . I didn't like the way I was dressing . . . We all started wearing pinkie rings. I *hated* them, but I found myself wearing one . . . spending a lot of money on shoes . . . It seemed like I was becoming like the people I was *after*. I started looking like Mafia guys. You look at those guys—they talk out of the sides of their mouths—they talk like there's a big criminal conspiracy going on, even if they're only talking

to their kids. They're never up front. They live a life of whispers. So then I found myself talking to my father in the same way.

An officer in San Jose describes how he changed after being "buried" in a deep-cover operation:

> This was really strange . . . For the first nine months I was really nervous and afraid . . . You meet a lot of bad people and you've got . . . no cover. But I still remember one day . . . something snapped. I just felt it like a jolt going through . . . and I was no longer afraid or nervous. It was like I had a handle on things . . . [and] a short time after that . . . I didn't believe I was a cop.

Most of the same social and psychological factors involving agents and targets are operating in political settings as in criminal ones. But there is an additional paradox here when an ideological issue involves matters of class, age, ethnicity, race, religion, or gender. The agent must share at least some of these attributes in order to be credible, and this common bond increases the likelihood that the agent will understand and sympathize with the group's goals . . .

An officer's personal habits may change as a result of easily accessible vice opportunities. Police may become consumers or purveyors of the very vice they set out to control. In Chicago, an officer was suspended for operating a prostitution ring. He had initially posed as a pimp and infiltrated the ring as part of a police operation. When the investigation ended, he continued in his role as a pimp. A vice detective referred to involvement with prostitutes as an "occupational habit," then corrected himself, saying, "I mean occupational hazard." . . .

With drugs the problem is more serious. Little is known about police drug use and addiction. Departments have become increasingly concerned as officers raised in a more permissive culture have entered the force. Undercover officers may be even more prone to their use than conventional officers because of greater stress, isolation, and accessibility. Drug use is frequently linked to the covert role and life-style that the agent is affecting. Its use is at least informally justified. Most drug officers certainly do not develop drug problems, but there are tragic cases, and the risk is real . . .

The strains on a marriage or a relationship are considerable: the odd hours, days, or weeks away from home; unpredictability of work schedules; concern over safety; late-night temptations and partying that the role may bring; and personality and life-style changes that the agent may undergo. The need for secrecy and the inability to share work details and problems, as well as limitations on a spouse's talking to others, can be costly. Knowledge of the agent's skill at acting, deception, and lying can increase paranoia and suspiciousness once initial doubts appear. The wife of one agent observes, "When you live under cover, you live a lie. You can't confide in friends about the pressures on your husband; you can't even tell your children what their father really does. You live under constant strain."

Although extreme, consider the case of an officer who was promoted for his outstanding work in infiltrating an international drug ring. He gained access to the ring by having an affair with one of its female leaders. His wife was proud of his heroic efforts and promotion, but, when the full details of the investigation became clear, she sought a divorce. An officer who got divorced in the middle of a three-year operation observed: "Imagine having a relationship with someone where you can't talk about what you do and where you suddenly say 'I'll see you in a week' and just disappear. There is also stress on her because you may not come back." For some agents, the "job becomes the mistress."

Should the agent be so inclined, the role is supportive of affairs. It also can offer a useful cover, as one supervisor in Los Angeles discovered. He received a call from the wife of an agent who complained that her husband's undercover assignment was keeping him away from home too many nights. The wife did not know that the operation had ended months before . . .

LEAVING THE ROLE

. . . When the investigation ends, the agent may feel relief, but he may be unable simply to return to an ordinary existence. If there is a danger of reprisals, it may be necessary for him to move to a new location and change his appearance and some customary behavior patterns. Apart from this, some agents experience subsequent personality changes and difficulties in readjustment. Ironically, some of the qualities thought to aid in effective undercover work (being outgoing, extroverted, a risk taker, adept at role playing) also may be associated with problems once the role ends.

An experienced officer observed that training a policeman to act like a criminal can be "like training a vicious dog. When you're through with him, you don't know what to do with him." Although this is certainly overstated, problems may appear in the transition from a covert deep-cover agent to a conventional police role. Like an actor caught up in a stage part, the agent may have trouble leaving the role. There are parallels to the re-entry problems sometimes faced by combat soldiers. The agent may initially find it difficult to shed fully the trappings of the caper, whether it be in language, dress, hairstyle, or conspicuous consumption. He may be hesitant to return false identification or jewelry used in the operation. The agent may miss the more freewheeling expressive life and work style and the excitement and attention associated with the role. After the high of a successful case, some agents have trouble fitting back into normal office routines. They may have discipline problems and show various neurotic responses and in a few cases appear to have a split personality.

Consider, for example, a northern California police officer who rode with the Hell's Angels for a year and a half. He was responsible for a large number of arrests, including previously almost untouchable higher-level drug dealers. He was praised for doing a "magnificent job." But this came at a cost of heavy drug use, alcoholism, brawling, the breakup of his family, and his inability to fit back into routine police work after the investigation was over. The result was resignation from the force, several bank robberies, and a prison term.

FBI agent John Livingston spent two and a half years posing as a distributor of sexually explicit materials in Operation MiPorn (Miami pornography). The operation—the largest federal pornography investigation ever undertaken—was hailed as a great success and received extensive media coverage. Livingston was praised for his excellent work, but he had trouble separating from his role. He continued to use his undercover name in situations unrelated to his FBI work and to frequent bars and places he had been during the investigation. After two brushes with the law, he was eventually arrested for shoplifting and gave his undercover alias. He split up with his wife and lost many friends. Psychiatric evaluation found that he had difficulty distinguishing his undercover from his real identity. Fourteen indictments that had resulted from his prior covert work were dropped because they were believed to be tainted by the investigator's confusion. Livingston initially demonstrated a "lack of candor" in describing his actions to his superiors. In what another former FBI agent characterized as "shooting our wounded," he was fired from the FBI after 17 years of service. He eventually obtained a disability pension.

Although not experiencing that degree of trouble, a northern California officer reports difficulty in returning to regular police work:

> At first it was really kind of strange and weird and scary and funny. I'd be riding in a patrol car, and I wouldn't be in the frame of mind of a uniformed police officer. I'd see another patrol car, and I'd tense up in knots. I really felt like the crooks. It would take me a second to realize that "hey, he's one of us." People would flag me down and I'd just wave back and keep driving. They want a cop, not me. I'd find myself answering [radio] calls and flipping back to my old [street] vocabulary. It was very embarrassing. I'm still having problems.

. . . There may be interactive effects. If the agent has changed, colleagues may perceive this and act differently toward him, which may further encourage his paranoia and estrangement. Peers and supervisors may add to the problem should they not welcome the agent back with open arms. They may look skeptically on the recently submerged agent, wondering if he or she is (or always was) a bit strange. They may be ambivalent about what the agent has done. Perhaps they respect the agent's skill and courage, but also think that the agent was out having a good time and not doing much with an expense account, a fancy car, and an apartment while they were stuck in the office working regular hours. An agent who described this asked rhetorically: "If they think it's so much fun, why don't they volunteer then?" . . .

7

A CRIME BY ANY OTHER NAME

Jeffrey Reiman

Think of a crime, any crime. Picture the first "crime" that comes into your mind. What do you see? The odds are you are not imagining a mining company executive sitting at his desk, calculating the costs of proper safety precautions and deciding not to invest in them. Probably what you do see with your mind's eye is one person physically attacking another or robbing something from another on the threat of physical attack. Look more closely. What does the attacker look like? It's a safe bet he (and it is a *he*, of course) is not wearing a suit and tie. In fact, my hunch is that you—like me, like almost anyone in America—picture a young, tough, lower-class male when the thought of crime first pops into your head. You (we) picture someone like the Typical Criminal described above. The crime itself is one in which the Typical Criminal sets out to attack or rob some specific person.

This last point is important. What it indicates is that we have a mental image not only of the Typical Criminal, but also of the Typical Crime. If the Typical Criminal is a young lower-class male, the Typical Crime is *one-on-one harm*—where harm means either physical injury or loss of something valuable or both. If you have any doubts that this is the Typical Crime, look at any random sample of police or private eye shows on television. How often do you see Jim Rockford or "The Equalizer" investigate consumer fraud or failure to remove occupational hazards? A study of TV crime shows by The Media Institute in Washington, D.C., indicates that, while the fictional criminals portrayed on television are on the average both older and wealthier than the real criminals who figure in the FBI *Uniform Crime Reports*, "TV crimes are almost 12 times as likely to be violent as crimes committed in the real world." In short, TV crime shows broadcast the double-edged message that the "one-on-one" crimes of the poor are the typical crimes of all and thus not uniquely caused by the pressures of poverty; *and* that the criminal justice system pursues rich and poor alike—thus, when the criminal justice system happens mainly to pounce on the poor in real life, it is not out of any class bias.

In addition to the steady diet of fictionalized TV violence and crime, there has been an increase in the graphic display of crime on many TV news programs. A new breed of nonfictional "tabloid" TV show has appeared in which viewers are shown films of actual violent crimes, blood and screams and all, or reenactments of actual violent crimes, sometimes using the actual victims playing themselves! An article in *The Washingtonian* says that the word around two prominent local TV news programs is, "If it bleeds, it leads." The *Wall Street Journal*, reporting on the phenomenon of tabloid TV, informs us that "Television has gone tabloid. The seamy underside of life is being bared in a new rash of true-crime series and contrived-confrontation talk shows." Is there any surprise that a survey by *McCall's* indicates that its readers have grown more afraid of crime in the past five years—even though this period has witnessed a decrease in crime rates?

It is important to identify this model of the Typical Crime because it functions like a set of blinders. It keeps us from calling a mine disaster a mass murder even if twenty-six men are killed, even if someone is responsible for the unsafe conditions in which they worked and died. In fact, I argue that this particular piece of mental furniture so blocks our view that it keeps us from using the criminal justice system to protect ourselves from the greatest threats to our persons and possessions.

What keeps a mine disaster from being a mass murder in our eyes is the fact that it is not one-on-one harm. What is important here is not the numbers but the *intent to harm someone*. An attack by a gang on one or more persons or an attack by one individual on several fits the model of one-on-one harm. That is, for each person harmed there is at least one individual who wanted to harm that person. Once he selects his victim, the rapist, the mugger, the murderer, all want this person they have selected to suffer. A mine executive, on the other hand, does not want his employees to be harmed. He would truly prefer that there be no accident, no injured or dead miners. What he does want is something legitimate. It is what he has been hired to get: maximum profits at minimum costs. If he cuts corners to save a buck, he is just doing his job. If twenty-six men die because he cut corners on safety, we may think him crude or callous but not a killer. He is, at most, responsible for an *indirect harm*, not a one-on-one harm. For this, he may even be criminally indictable for violating safety regulations—but not for murder. The twenty-six men are dead as an unwanted consequence of his (perhaps overzealous or undercautious) pursuit of a legitimate goal. So, unlike the Typical Criminal, he has not committed the Typical Crime—or so we generally believe. As a result, twenty-six men are dead who might be alive now if cutting corners of the kind that leads to loss of life, whether suffering is specifically intended or not, were treated as murder.

This is my point. Because we accept the belief—encouraged by our politicians' statements about crime and by the media's portrayal of crime—that the model for crime is one person specifically intending to harm another, we accept a legal system that leaves us unprotected against much greater dangers to our lives and well-being than those threatened by the Typical Criminal. Before developing this point further, let us anticipate and deal with a likely objection. The defender of the present legal order is likely to respond to my argument at this point with irritation. Because this will surely turn to outrage in a few pages, let us talk to him now while the possibility of rational communication still exists.

The Defender of the Present Legal Order (I'll call him "the Defender" for short whenever it is necessary to deal with his objections in the future) is neither a foolish nor an evil person. He is not a racist, nor is he oblivious to the need for reform in the criminal justice system to make it more evenhanded and for reform in the larger society to make equal opportunity a reality for all Americans. In general, his view is that—given our limited resources, particularly the resource of human altruism—the political and legal institutions we have are the best that can be. What is necessary is to make them work better and to weed out those who are intent on making them work shoddily. His response to my argument at this point is that the criminal justice system *should* occupy itself primarily with one-on-one harm. Harms of the sort exemplified in the "mine disaster" are really *not* murders and are better dealt with through stricter government enforcement of safety regulations. He would admit that this enforcement has been rather lax and recommend that it be improved. Basically, though, he thinks this division of labor is right because it fits our ordinary moral sensibilities.

The Defender maintains that, according to our ordinary moral notions, someone who wants to do another harm and does is really more evil than someone who jeopardizes others while pursuing legitimate goals but wishes no one harm. Being directly harmed by another person, he believes, is terrifying in a way that being harmed impersonally, say, by a safety hazard, is not—even if the resultant injury is the same in both cases. What's more, we should be tolerant of the one responsible for lax safety measures because he is pursuing a legitimate goal, that is, his dangerous action occurs as part of a productive activity, something that ultimately adds to social wealth and thus benefits everyone—whereas the doer of direct harm benefits no one but himself. Thus, the latter is rightfully in the province of the criminal justice system with its drastic weapons, and the former is appropriately dealt with by the milder forms of regulation.

Moreover, the Defender insists, the crimes identified as such by the criminal justice system are imposed on their victims totally against their will, whereas the victims of occupational hazards chose to accept their risky jobs and thus have in some degree consented to subject themselves to the dangers. Where dangers are consented to, the appropriate response is not blame but correction, and this is most efficiently done by regulation rather than with the guilt-seeking methods of criminal justice.

I think that the Defender's argument rests on three errors. First, he overestimates the reality of the "free consent" with which workers enter their jobs. Although no one is forced at gunpoint to accept any particular job, virtually everyone is forced by the requirements of necessity to take some job. Thus, at best, workers can choose among the dangers present at various worksites and not choose to face no danger at all. Moreover, workers can only choose jobs where there are openings, which means they cannot simply pick their place of employment at will. Consequently, for all intents and purposes, most workers *must* face the dangers of the jobs that are available to them.

Second, the Defender's argument errs by treating our ordinary notions of morality as a single consistent fabric rather than the crazy quilt of conflicting values and ideals it is. In other words, even if it fits some of our ordinary moral notions to believe that one-on-one harm is more evil than indirect harm, other aspects of our ordinary moral sensibilities lead to the opposite conclusion. For instance, it is a feature of both our moral sensibilities and our legal system that we often hold people culpable for harms they have caused through negligence or recklessness, even though they wished to harm no one—thus the kid-glove treatment meted out to those responsible for occupational hazards and the like is no simple reflection of our ordinary moral sensibilities, as the Defender claims. Moreover, compare the mine executive who cuts corners to the typical murderer. Most murders, we know, are committed in the heat of some passion like rage or jealousy. Two lovers or neighbors or relatives find themselves in a heated argument. One (usually it is a matter of chance *which* one) picks up a weapon and strikes the other a fatal blow. Such a person is clearly a murderer and rightly subject to punishment by the criminal justice system. Is this person more evil than the executive who chooses not to pay for safety equipment? I think a perfectly good case can be made that starts with our ordinary moral notions and ends up with the opposite conclusion.

The one who kills in a heated argument kills from passion. What he does he probably would not do in a cooler moment. He is likely to feel "he was not himself." The one he killed was someone he knew, a specific person who at the time seemed to him to be the embodiment of all that frustrates him, someone whose very existence makes life unbearable. I do not mean to suggest that this is true of all killers, although there is reason to believe it is true of many. Nor do I mean to suggest that such a state of mind justifies murder. What it does do, however, is suggest that the killer's action, arising out of passion, does not show general disdain for the lives of his fellows. Here is where he is different from the doer of *indirect harm.* Our absentee killer intended harm to no one in particular, but he *knew his acts were likely to harm someone*—and once someone is harmed, *he* (the victim) is someone in particular. Nor can our absentee killer claim that "he was not himself." His act is done, not out of passion, but out of cool reckoning. Precisely here his evil shows. In his willingness to jeopardize the lives of unspecified others who pose him no real or imaginary threat in order to make a few dollars, he shows his general disdain for all his fellow human beings. In this light, it is surely absurd to hold that he is less evil than one who kills from passion. My point will be made if you merely agree that both are equally wicked.

I think the Defender is right in believing that direct personal assault is terrifying in a way that impersonal harm is not. This difference is no stranger to the criminal justice system. Prosecutors, judges, and juries constantly have to consider how terrifying an attack is in determining what to charge and what to convict offenders for. This is why we allow gradations in charges of homicide or assault and allow particularly grave sentences for particularly grave attacks. In short, the difference the Defender is pointing to here might justify treating a one-on-one murder as graver than murder by lax safety, but it doesn't justify treating one as a grave crime and the other as a mere regulatory (or very minor criminal) matter. After all, although it is true that for the same level of injury it is worse to be injured with terror than without, it is still the injury that constitutes the worst part of violent crime. Given the choice, seriously injured victims of crime would surely rather have been terrorized and not injured than injured and not terrorized. If that is so, then the worst part of violent crime is still shared by the indirect harms that the Defender would relegate to regulation.

There is also something to the Defender's claim that indirect harms, such as ones that result from lax safety measures, are part of productive and thus generally beneficial activities, whereas one-on-one crimes are not. Here, too, the difference can be overstated. What the Defender calls productive is any activity that produces something that other people are willing to buy. For him, the manufacture of cancer-causing cigarettes is as much a productive activity as the manufacture of cancer-curing medicines. If that is what is meant by productive activity, then it covers a great deal of the crimes that people fear. For example, many of these crimes are committed in the course of the commerce in illicit drugs or prostitution. Moreover, even if we must or should tolerate the risks that are necessary ingredients of productive activity, that doesn't imply that we shouldn't identify those risks, or levels of danger, that are not necessary and use the law to protect innocent people from them. Needless to say, this will require identifying such risks or levels clearly in advance so that the executives who will be held responsible for them can know in advance what they may and what they may not do.

The Defender's argument errs a third time by overlooking the role of legal institutions in shaping our ordinary moral notions. Many who defend the criminal justice system do so precisely because of its function in educating the public about the difference between right and wrong. The great historian of English law, Sir James Fitzjames Stephens, held that a

> great part of the general detestation of crime which happily prevails amongst the decent part of the community in all civilized countries arises from the fact that the commission of offenses is associated in all such communities with the solemn and deliberate infliction of punishment wherever crime is proved.

In other words, one cannot simply appeal to ordinary moral notions to defend the criminal law because the criminal law has already had a hand in shaping ordinary moral notions. At least one observer has argued that making narcotics use a crime in the beginning of this century *caused* a change in the public's ordinary moral notions about drug addiction, which prior to that time had been viewed as a medical problem. It is probably safe to say that in our own time, civil rights legislation has sharpened the public's moral condemnation of racial discrimination. Hence, we might speculate that if the criminal justice system began to prosecute—and if the media began to portray—those who inflict *indirect harm* as serious criminals, our ordinary moral notions would change on this point as well.

I think this disposes of the Defender for the time being. We are left with the conclusion that there is no moral basis for treating *indirect harm* as less evil than *one-on-one harm*. What matters, then, is whether the purpose of the criminal justice system will be served by including, in the category of serious crime, actions that are predictably likely to produce serious harm, yet that are done in pursuit of otherwise legitimate goals and without the desire to harm someone. . . .

In the remainder of this section I identify some acts that are *crimes by any other name*—that is, acts that cause harm and suffering comparable to that caused by acts called crimes. My purpose is to confirm the first hypothesis: that the definitions of crime in the criminal law do not reflect the only or the most dangerous behaviors in our society. To do this, we will need some measure of the harm and suffering caused by crimes with which we can compare the harm and suffering caused by noncrimes. Our measure need not be too refined because my point can be made if I can show that there are some acts that we do not treat as crime but that cause harm *roughly comparable* to that caused by acts that we do treat as crimes. Thus, it is not necessary to compare the harm caused by noncriminal acts to the harm caused by *all* crimes. I need only show that the harm produced by some noncriminal acts is comparable to the harm produced by *any* serious crime. Because the harms caused by noncriminal acts fall into the categories of death, bodily injury (including the disabling effects of disease), and property loss, I will compare these harms to the injuries caused by the crimes of murder, aggravated assault, and theft.

According to the FBI's *Uniform Crime Reports*, in 1986 there were 20,613 murders and nonnegligent manslaughters. During that year, there were 834,322 reported cases of aggravated assault. "Murder and nonnegligent manslaughter" includes all "willful (nonnegligent) killing of one human being by another." "Aggravated assault" is defined as an "attack by one person on another for the purpose of inflicting severe or aggravated bodily harm." Thus, as a measure of the physical harm done by crime in 1986, I will assume that reported crimes led to roughly 20,000 deaths and 800,000 instances of serious bodily injury short of death. As a measure of property loss due to crime, we can use $11,583,489,000—the total value of property stolen in 1986 according to the UCR. Whatever the shortcomings of these reported crime statistics, they are the statistics upon which public policy has traditionally been based. Because it is my aim to analyze the difference between public policy regarding crime and that regarding other dangers, it is appropriate to use the reported figures. Thus, I will consider any actions that lead to loss of life, physical harm, and property loss comparable to the figures in the UCR as actions that pose grave dangers to the community comparable to the threats posed by crimes. They are surely precisely the kind of harmful actions from which a criminal justice system whose purpose is to protect our persons and property ought to protect us. *They are crimes by other names.*

WORK MAY BE DANGEROUS TO YOUR HEALTH

Since the publication of *The President's Report on Occupational Safety and Health* in 1972, numerous studies have documented both the astounding incidence of disease, injury, and death due to hazards in the workplace *and* the fact that much or most of this carnage is the consequence of the refusal of management to pay for safety measures and of government to enforce safety standards.

In that 1972 report, the government estimated the number of job-related illnesses at 390,000 per year and the number of annual deaths from industrial disease at 100,000. For 1986, the Bureau of Labor Statistics of the U.S. Department of Labor estimates 136,800 job-related illnesses and 3,610 work-related deaths. Note that the latter figure applies only to private-sector work environments with eleven or more employees. It is not limited to death from occupational disease but includes all work-related deaths, including those resulting from accidents on the job.

Before considering the significance of these figures, it should be pointed out that there is wide agreement that occupational diseases are seriously underreported. *The Report of the President to the Congress on Occupational Safety and Health* for 1980 stated that

> recording and reporting of illnesses continue to present measurement problems, since employers (and doctors) are often unable to recognize some illnesses as work-related. The annual survey includes data only on the visible illnesses of workers. To the extent that occupational illnesses are unrecognized and, therefore, not recorded or reported, the illness survey estimates may understate their occurrence.

Part of the difficulty is that there may be a substantial delay between contracting a fatal disease on the job and the appearance of symptoms, and from these to death. Moreover, OSHA (Occupational Safety and Health Administration) relies on employer reporting for its figures and there are many incentives for underreporting. Writing in the journal *Occupational Hazards*, Robert Reid states that

> OSHA concedes that many factors—including insurance rates and supervisor evaluations based on safety performance—are incentives to underreport. And the agency acknowledges that record-keeping violations have increased more than 27 percent since 1984, with most of the violations recorded for not maintaining the injuries and illnesses log examined by compliance officers and used for BLS' [Bureau of Labor Statistics'] annual survey.

A study by the National Institute for Occupational Safety and Health (NIOSH) concludes that "there may be several thousand more workplace deaths each year than
employers report."

For these reasons, plus the fact that BLS's figures on work-related deaths are only
for private workplaces with eleven or more employees, we must supplement the BLS
figures with other estimates. In 1982, then U.S. Secretary of Health and Human
Services Richard Schweiker stated that "current estimates for overall workplace-
associated cancer mortality vary within a range of five to fifteen percent." With
annual cancer deaths currently running more than 460,000, that translates into
between 23,000 and 69,000 job-related cancer deaths per year. In testimony before the
Senate Committee on Labor and Human Resources, Dr. Philip Landrigan, director of
the Division of Environmental and Occupational Medicine at the Mount Sinai School
of Medicine in New York City, stated that,

> Recent data indicate that occupationally related exposures are responsible
> each year in New York State for 5,000 to 7,000 deaths and for 35,000 new
> cases of illness (not including work-related injuries). These deaths due to
> occupational disease include 3,700 deaths from cancer. . . .
>
> Crude national estimates of the burden of occupational disease in the
> United States may be developed by multiplying the New York State data by
> a factor of 10. New York State contains slightly less than 10 percent of the
> nation's workforce, and it includes a broad mix of employment in the man-
> ufacturing, service and agricultural sectors. Thus, it may be calculated that
> occupational disease is responsible each year in the United States for 50,000
> to 70,000 deaths, and for approximately 350,000 new cases of illness.

It is some confirmation of Dr. Landrigan's estimates that they imply work-
related cancer deaths of approximately 37,000 a year—a figure that is squarely in the
middle of the range implied in Secretary Schweiker's statement on this issue. Thus,
even if we discount OSHA's 1972 estimate of 100,000 deaths a year due to occupational disease or Dr. Landrigan's estimate of between 50,000 to 70,000, we would
surely be erring in the other direction to accept the BLS figure of 3,610. We can hardly
be overestimating the actual toll if we set it at 25,000 deaths a year resulting from
occupational disease.

As for the BLS estimate of 136,800 job-related illnesses, here, too, there is reason
to assume that the figure considerably understates the real situation. Dr. Landrigan's
estimates suggest that the BLS figure represents less than half of the actual number.
However, the BLS figure is less inaccurate than its figure for job-related deaths for at
least two reasons: It is not limited to firms with eleven or more employees and symptoms of illness generally can be expected to appear sooner after contracting an illness
than does death. To stay on the conservative side, then, I shall assume that there are
annually in the United States approximately 150,000 job-related illnesses and 25,000
deaths from occupational diseases. How does this compare to the threat posed by
crime? Before jumping to any conclusions, note that the risk of occupational disease

and death falls only on members of the labor force, whereas the risk of crime falls on the whole population, from infants to the elderly. Because the labor force is less than half the total population (110,000,000 in 1986, out of a total population of 241,000,000), to get a true picture of the *relative* threat posed by occupational diseases compared to that posed by crime we should *halve* the crime statistics when comparing them to the figures for industrial disease and death. Using the 1986 statistics, this means that the comparable figures would be:

	Occupational Disease	Crime (halved)
Death	25,000	10,000
Other physical harm	150,000	400,000

If it is argued that this paints an inaccurate picture because so many crimes go unreported, my answer is this: First of all, homicides are by far the most completely reported of crimes. For obvious reasons, the general underreporting of crimes is not equal among crimes. It is much easier or tempting to avoid reporting a rape or a mugging than a corpse. Second, aggravated assaults are among the better-reported crimes, although not the best. Based on victimization studies, it is estimated that 54 percent of aggravated assaults were reported to the police in 1980, compared to 26.9 percent of thefts. On the other hand, we should expect more—not less—underreporting of industrial than criminal victims because diseases and deaths are likely to cost firms money in the form of workdays lost and insurance premiums raised, occupational diseases are frequently first seen by company physicians who have every reason to diagnose complaints as either non-job-related or malingering, and many occupationally caused diseases do not show symptoms or lead to death until after the employee has left the job.

> A survey conducted last year by the University of Washington reported that one in four Americans currently suffers an occupational disease. The report also disclosed that only one of the 10 workers with an occupational disease had been included in either OSHA statistics or in the state's workmen's compensation records.

In sum, both occupational and criminal harms are underreported. Consequently, it is reasonable to assume that the effect of underreporting is probably balanced out, and the figures that we have give as accurate a picture of the *relative* threats of each as we need.

It should be noted further that the statistics given so far are *only* for occupational *diseases* and deaths from those diseases. They do not include death and disability from work-related injuries. Here, too, the statistics are gruesome. The National Safety Council reported that in 1986, work-related accidents caused 10,700 deaths and 1.8 million disabling work injuries, at a total cost to the economy of $34.8 billion. This brings the number of occupation-related deaths to 36,700 a year. If, on the basis of these additional figures, we recalculated our chart comparing occupational to criminal dangers, it would look like this:

	Occupational Disease	Crime (halved)
Death	36,700	10,000
Other physical harm	1,950,000	400,000

Can there be any doubt that workers are more likely to stay alive and healthy in the face of the danger from the underworld than in the face of what their employers have in store for them on the job? If any doubt lingers, consider this: Lest we falter in the struggle against crime, the FBI includes in their annual *Uniform Crime Reports* a table of "crime clocks," which graphically illustrates the extent of the criminal menace. For 1986, the crime clock shows a murder occurring every 25 minutes. If a similar clock were constructed for occupational deaths—using the conservative estimate of 36,700 cited above and remembering that this clock ticks only for that half of the population that is in the labor force—this clock would show an occupational death about every 14 minutes! In other words, in roughly the time it takes for one murder on the crime clock, two workers have died *just from trying to make a living.*

To say that some of these workers died from accidents due to their own carelessness is about as helpful as saying that some of those who died at the hands of murderers asked for it. It overlooks the fact that where workers are careless, it is not because they love to live dangerously. They have production quotas to meet, quotas that they themselves do not set. If quotas were set with an eye to keeping work at a safe pace rather than to keeping the production-to-wages ratio as high as possible, it might be more reasonable to expect workers to take the time to be careful. Beyond this, we should bear in mind that the vast majority of occupational deaths result from disease, not accident, and disease is generally a function of conditions outside a worker's control. Examples of such conditions are the level of coal dust in the air (about 10 percent of all active coal miners have black lung disease) or textile dust (some 85,000 American cotton textile workers presently suffer breathing impairments caused by acute byssinosis or brown lung, and another 35,000 former mill workers are totally disabled with chronic brown lung) or asbestos fibers (a study of 632 asbestos-insulation workers between 1943 and 1971 indicates that 11 percent have died of asbestosis and 38 percent of cancer; two doctors who have studied asbestos workers conclude "we can anticipate three thousand excess respiratory, cardiopulmonary deaths and cancers of the lung—three thousand excess deaths *annually* for the next twenty or thirty years"), or coal tars ("workers who had been employed five or more years in the coke ovens died of lung cancer at a rate three and a half times that for all steelworkers"; coke oven workers also develop cancer of the scrotum at a rate five times that of the general population). Also, some 800,000 people suffer from occupationally related skin disease each year (according to a 1968 estimate by the U.S. surgeon general), and "the number of American workers experiencing noise conditions that may damage their hearing is estimated [in a 1969 Public Health Service publication of the Department of Health, Education and Welfare] to be in excess of 6 million, and may even reach 16 million."

To blame the workers for occupational disease and deaths is simply to ignore the history of governmental attempts to compel industrial firms to meet safety standards that would keep dangers (such as chemicals or fibers or dust particles in the air) that are outside of the worker's control down to a safe level. This has been a continual struggle, with firms using everything from their own "independent" research institutes to more direct and often questionable forms of political pressure to influence government in the direction of loose standards and lax enforcement. So far, industry has been winning because OSHA has been given neither the personnel nor the mandate to fulfill its purpose. It is so understaffed that, in 1973, when 1,500 federal sky marshals guarded the nation's airplanes from hijackers, only 500 OSHA inspectors toured the nation's workplaces. By 1980, OSHA employed 1,581 compliance safety and health officers, but this still enabled inspection of only roughly 2 percent of the 2.5 million establishments covered by federal OSHA. The *New York Times* reports that in 1987, the number of OSHA inspectors was down to 1,044. As might be expected, the agency performs fewer inspections than it did a dozen years ago.

> When inspectors do find violations, the penalties they can assess are severely limited by the OSHA law that Congress has not updated since it established the agency. The maximum penalty for a serious OSHA violation is $1,000; an employer who acts willfully can be fined up to $10,000 for each incident. . . .
>
> Even when the agency hits employers hard, however, the sting does not often last very long. The big proposed fines that grab headlines are seldom paid in full. The two record-breaking citations of last year, against Union Carbide Corporation for $1.37 million and Chrysler for $910,000, were each settled this year for less than a third of the original amounts.

According to *Occupational Hazards*,

> an October 1986 hearing of the House Governmental Operations Subcommittee of Intergovernmental Relations and Human Resources concluded that occupational disease surveillance had now fallen 72 years behind its counterpart for communicable disease data. Chaired by Rep. Ted Weiss (D.-N.Y.), this subcommittee noted that "The United States is the only large developed country without a national system for reporting occupational disease."
>
> The subcommittee report also pointed out that NIOSH's budget, rather than being increased, had continued to be cut—by as much as 47 percent since 1980, when adjusted for inflation. And that while nations such as Finland spend approximately $2 per worker each year on occupational disease surveillance, the United States spends about 2¢ per worker.

An editorial in the January 1983 issue of the *American Journal of Public Health,* titled "Can Reagan Be Indicted for Betraying Public Health?" answers the question in its title affirmatively by listing the Reagan administration's attempts to cut back government support for public health programs. On the issue of occupational safety and health, the editorial states:

> The Occupational Safety and Health Administration (OSHA) has delayed the cotton and lead [safe exposure level] standards. It proposes to weaken the generic carcinogen policy, the labeling standard, the access to medical and exposure records standard. Mine fatalities are rising again, but the Mine Safety and Health Administration and OSHA enforcement have been cut back. Research on occupational safety and health has been slashed more than any other research program in the Department of Health and Human Services. The National Institute for Occupational Safety and Health funding in real dollars is lower in 1983 than at any time in the 12-year history of the Institute. Reporting and data requirements have been devastated.

The editorial ends by asking rhetorically, "How can anyone believe that the Reagan Administration wishes to prevent disease or promote health or preserve public health in America?"

And so it goes on.

Is a person who kills another in a bar brawl a greater threat to society than a business executive who refuses to cut into his profits in order to make his plant a safe place to work? By any measure of death and suffering the latter is by far a greater danger than the former. Because he wishes his workers no harm, because he is only indirectly responsible for death and disability, while pursuing legitimate economic goals, his acts are not called "crimes." Once we free our imagination from the irrational shackle of the one-on-one model of crime, can there be any doubt that the criminal justice system does *not* protect us from the gravest threats to life and limb? It seeks to protect us when danger comes from a young, lower-class male in the inner city. When a threat comes from an upper-class business executive in an office, the criminal justice system looks the other way. This is in the face of growing evidence that *for every American citizen murdered by some thug, two American workers are killed by their bosses* (italics mine).

HEALTH CARE MAY BE DANGEROUS TO YOUR HEALTH

Almost twenty years ago, when the annual number of willful homicides in the nation was about 10,000, the President's Commission on Law Enforcement and Administration of Justice reported that

A recent study of emergency medical care found the quality, numbers, and distribution of ambulances and other emergency services severely deficient, and estimated that as many as 20,000 Americans die unnecessarily each year as a result of improper emergency care. The means necessary for correcting this situation are very clear and would probably yield greater immediate return in reducing death than would expenditures for reducing the incidence of crimes of violence.

On July 15, 1975, Dr. Sidney Wolfe of Ralph Nader's Public Interest Health Research Group testified before the House Commerce Oversight and Investigations Subcommittee that there "were 3.2 million cases of unnecessary surgery performed each year in the United States." These unneeded operations. Dr. Wolfe added, "cost close to $5 billion a year and kill as many as 16,000 Americans." Wolfe's estimates of unnecessary surgery were based on studies comparing the operations performed and surgery recommended by doctors who are paid for the operations they do with those performed and recommended by salaried doctors who receive no extra income from surgery.

The figure accepted by Dr. George A. Silver, professor of public health at the Yale University School of Medicine, is 15,000 deaths a year "attributable to unnecessary surgery." Dr. Silver places the annual cost of excess surgery at $4.8 billion. In an article on an experimental program by Blue Cross and Blue Shield aimed at curbing unnecessary surgery, *Newsweek* reports that

> a Congressional committee earlier this year [1976] estimated that more than 2 million of the elective operations performed in 1974 were not only unnecessary—but also killed about 12,000 patients and cost nearly $4 billion.

Because the number of surgical operations performed in the United States rose from 16.7 million in 1975 to 20.2 million in 1985, there is every reason to believe that at least somewhere between 12,000 and 16,000 people a year still die from unnecessary surgery. In 1986, the FBI reported that 3,957 murders were committed by a "cutting or stabbing instrument." Obviously, the FBI does not include the scalpel as a cutting or stabbing instrument. If they did, they would have had to report that between 15,957 and 19,957 persons were killed by "cutting or stabbing" in 1980—depending on whether you take *Newsweek*'s figure or Dr. Wolfe's. No matter how you slice it, the scalpel may be more dangerous than the switchblade.

While they are at it, the FBI should probably add the hypodermic needle and the prescription to their list of potential murder weapons. Professor Silver points out that these are also death-dealing instruments.

> Of the 6 billion doses of antibiotic medicines administered each year by injection or prescription, it is estimated that 22 percent are unnecessary. Of the doses given, 10,000 result in fatal or near-fatal reactions. Somewhere between 2,000 and 10,000 deaths probably would not have occurred if the drugs, meant for the patient's benefit, had not been given.

The danger continues. The Public Citizen Health Research Group reports in its *Health Letter* of October 1988 that

> two major U.S. drug companies—Lilly and SmithKline—have pleaded guilty to criminal charges for having withheld information from the Food and Drug Administration (FDA) about deaths and life-threatening adverse drug reactions.

The response of the Justice Department has been predictably merciful:

> SmithKline, the actions of whose executives resulted in at least ... 36 deaths, pleaded guilty to 14 criminal misdemeanor counts and was fined $34,000. Lilly and its executives, whose criminal negligence was responsible for deaths to at least 49 Americans ..., were slapped on the wrist with a total of $45,000 in fines.

In fact, if someone had the temerity to publish a *Uniform Crime Reports* that really portrayed the way Americans are murdered, the FBI's statistics on the *type of weapon used* in murder would have to be changed for 1986, from those shown in Table 2A to something like those shown in Table 2B.

The figures shown in Table 2B would give American citizens a much more honest picture of what threatens them. We are not likely to see it broadcast by the criminal justice system, however, because it would also give American citizens a more honest picture of *who* threatens them.

We should not leave this topic without noting that, aside from the other losses it imposes, unnecessary surgery was estimated to have cost between $4 and $5 billion in 1974. The price of medical care has nearly tripled between 1974 and 1986. Thus, assuming that the same number of unneeded operations were performed in 1986, the cost of unnecessary surgery would be between $12 and $15 billion. To this we should add the unnecessary 22 percent of the 6 billion administered doses of medication. Even at the extremely conservative estimate of $3 a dose, this adds about $4 billion. In short, assuming that earlier trends have continued, there is reason to believe that unnecessary surgery and medication cost the public between $16 and $19 billion annually—far outstripping the $11.6 billion taken by thieves that concern the FBI. This gives us yet another way in which we are robbed of more money by practices that are not treated as criminal than by practices that are. . . .

TABLE 1A *How Americans Are Murdered*

Total	Firearms	Knife or Other Cutting Instrument	Other Weapon: Club, Arson, Poison Strangulation, etc.	Personal Weapons Hands, Fists, etc.
19,257[a]	11,381	3,957	2,609	1,310

[a]Note that this figure diverges somewhat from the figure of 20,613 murders and nonnegligent manslaughters used elsewhere in the FBI Uniform Crime Reports, 1987.
Source: FBI *Uniform Crime Reports*, 1987: "Murder Victims: Weapons Used, 1986."

TABLE 1B *How Americans Are (Really) Murdered*

Total	Occupational Hazard & Disease	Inadequate Emergency Medical Care	Knife or Other Cutting-Instrument Including Scalpel	Firearms	Other Weapon: Club, Poison, Hypodermic, Prescription Drug	Personal Weapon: Hands, Fists, etc.
114,957	61,700	20,000	15,957	11,381	4,609	1,310

SUMMARY

Once again, our investigations lead to the same result. The criminal justice system does not protect us against the gravest threats to life, limb, or possessions. Its definitions of crime are not simply a reflection of the objective dangers that threaten us. The workplace [and] the medical profession lead to far more human suffering, far more death and disability, and take far more dollars from our pockets than the murders, aggravated assaults, and thefts reported annually by the FBI. What is more, this human suffering is preventable. A government really intent on protecting our well-being could enforce work safety regulations [or] police the medical profession but it does not. Instead we hear a lot of cant about law and order and a lot of rant about crime in the streets. It is as if our leaders were not only refusing to protect us from the major threats to our well-being but trying to cover up this refusal by diverting our attention to crime—as if this were the only real threat. As we have seen, the criminal justice system is a carnival mirror that presents a distorted image of what threatens us. The distortions do not end with the definitions of crime. As we will see in what follows, new distortions enter at every level of the system, so that in the end, when we look in our prisons to see who really threatens us, all we see are poor people. By that time, virtually all the well-to-do people who endanger us have been discreetly weeded out of the system. As we watch this process unfold in the following chapter, we should bear in mind the conclusion of the present chapter: All the mechanisms by which the criminal justice system comes down more frequently and more harshly on the poor criminal than on the well-off criminal take place *after* most of the dangerous acts of the well-to-do have been excluded from the definition of crime itself. The bias against the poor within the criminal justice system is all the more striking when we recognize that the door to that system is shaped in a way that excludes in advance the most dangerous acts of the well-to-do.

8

WEALTH AND WANT IN THE UNITED STATES

Michael Parenti

Most scholars and journalists who write about the American political system never mention capitalism. But the capitalist economy creates imperatives that bear urgently upon political life. In this chapter we will consider how wealth is distributed and used in the United States.

WEALTH AND CLASS

One should distinguish between those who own the wealth of the society, specifically the very rich families and individuals whom we might call "the owning class," and those who are dependent on that class for their employment, "the working class." The latter includes not only blue-collar workers but just about everyone else who is not independently wealthy. The distinction between owners and employees is blurred somewhat by the range of affluence within the owning and working classes. "Owners" include both the wealthy stockholders of giant corporations and the proprietors of small stores. But the latter control a relatively small portion of the wealth and hardly qualify as part of the *corporate* owning class. While glorified as the purveyors of the entrepreneurial spirit, small businesses are really just so many squirrels dancing among the elephants. Small owners often are stamped out when markets decline or bigger competitors move in. By the 1980s, over 600 small and medium-sized businesses were going bankrupt every week in the United States.

Among the employee class are professionals and middle-level executives who in income, education, and life-style tend to be identified as "middle class." Then there are some entertainment and sports figures, lawyers, doctors, and top executives who earn such lavish incomes that they become in part, or eventually in whole, members of the owning class by investing their surplus wealth and living mostly off the profits of their investments.

You are a member of the owning class when your income is very large and comes mostly from the labor of other people—that is, when others work for you, either in a company you own, or by creating the wealth that allows your money and realty investments to increase in value. Hard work seldom makes anyone rich. The secret to wealth is to have others work hard for you. This explains why workers who spend their lives toiling in factories or offices retire with little or no wealth to speak of, while the owners of these businesses, who do not work in them at all, can amass riches from such enterprises.

Wealth is created by the labor power of workers. As Adam Smith noted, "Labor . . . is alone the ultimate and real standard by which the value of all commodities can at all times and places be estimated and compared. It is their real price; money is their nominal price only." What transforms a tree into a profitable commodity such as paper or furniture is the labor that goes into harvesting the timber, cutting the lumber, and manufacturing, shipping, advertising, and selling the commodity (along with the labor that goes into making the tools, trucks, and whatever else is needed in the production process). For their efforts, workers are paid wages that represent only a portion of the wealth created by their labor. The unpaid portion is expropriated by the owners for personal consumption and further investment.

Workers endure an exploitation of their labor as certainly as do slaves and serfs. Under slavery, it is obvious that the chattel works for the enrichment of the master and receives only a bare subsistence. Under feudalism, when serfs work numerous days for the lord without compensation, again the exploitation is readily apparent. So with sharecroppers who must give a third or half their crop to the landowner. Under capitalism, however, the portion taken from the worker is not visible. All one sees is five days' pay for five days' work. If wages did represent the total value created by labor, there would be no surplus wealth, no profits for the owner, no great fortunes for those who do not labor.

But don't managers and executives make a contribution to production for which they should be compensated? Yes, if they are performing productive and useful labor for the enterprise, and usually they are paid very well indeed. But income from ownership is apart from salary and apart from labor; it is money you are paid *when not working*. The author of a book, for instance, does not make "profits" on his book; he *earns* an income from the labor of writing it, proportionately much less than the sum going to those who own the publishing house and who do none of the writing, editing, printing, and marketing of books. The sum going to the owners is profits; it is *unearned* income. Profits are what you make when not working.

While corporations are often called "producers," the truth is they produce nothing. They are organizational devices for the expropriation of labor and for the accumulation of capital. The real producers are those who apply their brawn, brains, and talents to the creation of goods and services. The primacy of labor was noted years ago by a Republican president. In a message to Congress, Abraham Lincoln stated: "Labor is prior to and independent of capital. Capital is only the fruit of labor and could not have existed had not labor first existed. Labor is the superior of capital and deserves much the higher consideration." Lincoln's words went largely unheeded. The dominance of capital over labor remains the essence of the American economic system, bringing ever greater concentrations of wealth and power into the hands of a small moneyed class.

WHO OWNS AMERICA?

Contrary to a widely propagated myth, this country's wealth does not belong to a broad middle class. The top 10 percent of American households own 98 percent of the tax-exempt state and local bonds, 94 percent of business assets, 95 percent of the value of all trusts. The richest 1 percent own 60 percent of all corporate stock, and fully 60 percent of all business assets; while 90 percent of American families have little or no net assets. The greatest source of individual wealth is inheritance. If you are not rich, it is probably because you lacked the initiative to pick the right parents at birth.

The trend is toward greater economic inequality. In the last fifteen years, income from investments and property (interest, dividends, rents, land and mineral royalties) has been growing two to three times faster than income from work (wages, salaries). By 1988, there were 65,000 millionaires in the United States with combined incomes of $173 billion. The top 800,000 people have more money and wealth than the other 184,000,000 combined (over age sixteen). The top 1 percent saw their average incomes soar by 85.4 percent after taxes in the decade up to 1990, while the incomes of the bottom fifth declined by 10 percent. Income and wealth disparities are greater today than at any time since such information was first collected in 1947. As one economist put it: "If we made an income pyramid out of a child's blocks, with each layer portraying $1,000 of income, the peak would be far higher than the Eiffel Tower, but almost all of us would be within a yard of the ground."

Less than 1 percent of all corporations account for over 80 percent of the total output of the private sector. In 1992 the combined sales of goods and services of the corporate giants totaled $4 trillion. Forty-nine of the biggest banks hold a controlling interest in the 500 largest corporations. American Express, ITT, IBM, Citicorp, and others can claim J. P. Morgan, Inc. as one of their top investors. J. P. Morgan is the nation's largest stockholder, with more than $15 billion invested in the stock market. The trend is toward ever greater concentrations of corporate wealth as giant companies are bought up by supergiants. The ten largest corporate mergers in U.S. history occurred in the last dozen years. Texaco engulfed Getty Oil; Philip Morris inhaled Miller Brewing; Coca-Cola swallowed Columbia Pictures. In 1989, Time, Inc. joined Warner Communications in a $14 billion merger, the largest in history.

The many billions spent on mergers absorb money that could be better spent on new technologies and jobs. A corporation has to procure large sums to buy a dominant share of its own stock if it wishes to ward off a hostile takeover by corporate raiders. Or if acquiring another company, it usually needs money to buy up that firm's stock. In either case, cash reserves are seldom sufficient and the company must borrow huge sums from banks. Then, to meet its debt obligations, it must lay off workers, enforce speedups, break labor unions, reduce wages and benefits, sell off productive plants for quick cash, move to cheaper labor markets abroad, and take other such measures that fail to create new assets and diminish existing ones for quick paper profits. The owner-managers borrow enormous sums not to build factories or invest in research but to merge, raid, and buy one another, issuing new stock and walking away with enormous profits for themselves, leaving the company and the community of employees in worse shape than ever. Because of leveraged buyouts and other such factors, U.S. businesses increased their borrowing 50 percent in the last decade, emerging with debts of $3.5 *trillion.* Currently, U.S. corporations expend about half their earnings just on interest payments—all of which are tax deductible. "Never before has so much money changed hands so quickly and produced so little."

We are taught that the economy consists of a wide array of independent producers. We refer to "farmers" as an interest group apart from business, at a time when Bank of America has a multimillion dollar stake in California farmlands; Beatrice Foods has absorbed more than four hundred companies; and R. J. Reynolds, with vast holdings in cigarettes, transportation, and petroleum, owns Del Monte—itself a multinational agribusiness. A handful of agribusiness firms control most of our farmland. Just 1 percent of all food corporations control 80 percent of the industry's assets and close to 90 percent of the profits. Six multinational firms handle 90 percent of all the grain shipped in the world market.

This centralized food industry represents an American success story—for the big companies. Independent family farms are going deeper into debt or completely out of business. Today, the combined farm debt is many times greater than net farm income. With the growth of corporate agribusiness, regional self-sufficiency in food has virtually vanished. The Northeast, for instance, imports more than 70 percent of its food from other regions. For every $2 spent to grow food in the United States, another $1 is spent to move it. Giant agribusiness farms rely on intensive row crop farming and heavy use of toxic spraying and artificial fertilizers, all of which cause massive damage to ecosystems. The nation's ability to feed itself is being jeopardized, as each year more and more land is eroded by large-scale, quick-profit commercial farming. This is not to mention the harmful effects on people's health resulting from the consumption of food produced by these methods.

Many corporations are owned by stockholders who have little say over the management of their holdings. From this fact, it has been incorrectly inferred that control of most firms has passed into the hands of corporate managers who run their companies with a regard for the public interest that is not shared by their profit-hungry stockholders. Since 1932, when A. A. Berle and Gardner Means first portrayed the giant firms as developing "into a purely neutral technocracy," controlled by disinterested managers who allocated resources on the basis of public need "rather than private cupidity," many observers have come to treat this fantasy as a reality. In fact, the decline of family capitalism has not led to widespread ownership among the general public. The diffusion of stock ownership has not cut across class lines but has occurred within the upper class itself. In an earlier day, three families might have owned companies A, B, and C, respectively, whereas today all three have holdings in all three companies, giving "the upper class an ever greater community of interest than they had in the past."

Some "family enterprises" are of colossal size. Indeed, a small number of the wealthiest families, such as the Mellons, Morgans, Du Ponts, and Rockefellers, dominate the American economy. The Du Ponts control ten corporations, each worth billions of dollars, including General Motors, Coca-Cola, and United Brands, along with many smaller firms. The Du Ponts serve as trustees of scores of colleges. They own about forty manorial estates and private museums in Delaware alone and have set up thirty-one tax-exempt foundations. The family is frequently the largest contributor to Republican presidential campaigns and has financed right-wing and anti-labor causes.

Another powerful family enterprise, that of the Rockefellers, extends into just about every industry in every state of the Union and every nation in the world. The Rockefellers control five of the twelve largest oil companies and four of the largest banks in the world. At one time or another, they or their close associates have occupied the offices of the president, vice-president, secretaries of state, commerce, Defense, and other cabinet posts, the Federal Reserve Board, the governorships of several states, key positions in the Central Intelligence Agency (CIA), the U.S. Senate and House, and the Council on Foreign Relations.

Whether companies are or are not under family control, their corporate heads prove to be anything but "public-minded," showing far less interest in developing new technologies and creating jobs than in feathering their own nests. During the 1990-93 recession, while corporate profits fell and workers were being laid off or were taking pay cuts, compensation for CEOs rose sharply. In 1990, the chief executive officer (CEO) of Time Warner, a company that was facing harrowing debt payments, took home $78.2 million in salary and bonuses, making more in one day than most of his employees made in five years. The ten highest paid Wall Street executives, investment bankers, and money managers were paid between $30 million to $125 million a year. In 1992, the ten top-paid corporate CEOs made from $24.6 million to $127 million in salaries, bonuses, and long-term incentive payouts. CEOs are voted sumptuous raises by their directors—most of whom are themselves CEOs for other firms. The directors thereby lift the income floor for themselves. Japanese CEOs earn only one-fifth as much as their U.S. counterparts (still outrageously high sums), yet they perform just as well—if not better.

CEO Richard Munro admitted: "Corporate managers lead just about the most privileged lives in our society." Far from being neutral technocrats dedicated to the public welfare, they are self-enriching members of the owning class. Their social and political power rests not in their personal holdings but in their corporate positions. "Not great fortunes, but great corporations are the important units of wealth, to which individuals of property are variously attached."

THE DYNAMIC OF CAPITALISM

There is something more to capitalism than just the concentration of wealth. Vast fortunes existed in ancient Egypt, feudal Europe, and other early class societies. What is unique about capitalism is its perpetual dynamic of capital accumulation and expansion—and the dominant role this process plays in the economic order.

Capitalists like to say they are "putting their money to work," but money as such cannot create more wealth. What capitalists really mean is that they are putting more human labor power to work, paying workers less in wages than they produce in value, thereby siphoning off more profit for themselves. That's how money "grows." The average private-sector employee works a little over two hours for himself or herself and almost six hours for the boss. That latter portion is the "surplus value," which Marx described as the source of the owner's wealth. Sometimes non-Marxists will acknowledge the existence of surplus value as in this advertisement to lure investments: "New York's manufacturing workers produce $4.25 in value over and above every dollar they get in wages." Workers in Texas produce $5 in surplus value for every wage dollar. The percentage is vastly higher in most Third World nations.

All of Rockefeller's capital could not build a house nor a machine, only human labor can do that. Of itself, capital cannot produce anything; it is the thing that is produced by labor. Under capitalism, the ultimate purpose of work is not to produce goods and services but to make money for the investor. Money harnesses labor in order to convert itself into goods and services that will produce still more money. Capital annexes living labor in order to create more capital.

The function of the corporation is not to perform public services or engage in philanthropy but to make as large a profit as possible. The social uses of the product and its effects upon human well-being and the natural environment win consideration in capitalist production, if at all, only to the extent that they do not violate the profit goals of the corporation. As David Roderick, the president of U.S. Steel (now USX) put it: "United States Steel Corporation is not in the business of making steel. We're in the business of making profits."

This relentless pursuit of profit results from something more than just greed—although there is enough of that. Under capitalism, enterprises must expand in order to survive. To stand still amidst growth is to decline, not only relatively but absolutely. A slow-growth firm is less able to move into new markets, hold onto old ones, command investment capital, and control suppliers. A decline in the rate of production eventually cuts into profits and leads to a company's decline. Even the biggest corporations, enjoying a relatively secure oligopolistic control over markets, are beset by a ceaseless drive to expand, to find new ways of making money. Ultimately, the only certainty, even for the giants, is uncertainty. Larger size, greater reserves, and better organizational control might bring security were it not that all other companies are pursuing these same goals. So survival can never be taken for granted.

Recession and Stagnation

Business leaders admit that they could not survive if they tried to feed or house the poor, or invested in nonprofit projects for the environment, or in something so nebulous as a desire to "get the economy moving again." Nor can they invest simply to "create more jobs." In fact, many of their labor-saving devices and overseas investments are designed to lower wages and eliminate jobs. By holding down wages capitalists increase profits, but they also reduce the buying power of the very public that consumes their services and commodities. Every owner would prefer to pay employees as little as possible while selling goods to better-paid workers from other companies. "For the system as a whole, no such solution is possible; the dilemma is basic to capitalism. Wages, a cost of production, must be kept down; wages, a source of consumer spending, must be kept up." This contradiction creates a tendency toward overproduction and stagnation.

As unemployment climbs, buying power and sales decline, inventories accumulate, investment opportunities recede, more layoffs are imposed, and the recession deepens. For the big capitalists, however, recessions are not unmitigated gloom. Weaker competitors are weeded out and business is better able to resist labor demands, forcing workers to accept wage and benefit cutbacks in order to hang onto their jobs. A reserve supply of unemployed workers helps to deflate wages further. Unions are weakened and often broken; strike activity declines, and profits rise faster than wages. The idea that all Americans are in the same boat, experiencing good and bad times together, should be put to rest. Even as the economy declines, the rich grow richer—not by producing a bigger pie but by grabbing a bigger-than-ever slice of whatever exists. Thus, during the recession of 1992, corporate profits grew to record levels, as companies squeezed more output from each employee and paid less in wages and benefits.

Inflation

A common problem of modern capitalism is inflation. The 4 to 5 percent inflation rate that has regularly plagued our economy can, in a few years, substantially reduce the buying power of wage earners and persons on fixed incomes. Corporation leaders maintain that inflation is caused by the wage demands of labor unions. In fact, wages have not kept pace with prices and profits. "Except for a few brief intervals, inflation has risen faster than wages for nearly two decades, leaving workers less well off."

Hardest hit by inflation are the four essentials, which devour 70 percent of the average family income: food, fuel, housing, and health care. But in these necessities, the share of costs going to labor has been dropping. For instance, labor costs in home construction have declined as construction unions have failed to win contracts and have been broken. Nor can the astronomical costs of the health industry be blamed on the low wages paid to health-care workers. Medical costs have been outpacing inflation not because of wage increases but as a result of price gouging by hospital corporations, insurance companies, and the drug industry. In most industries the portion of production costs going to workers over the last decade has been shrinking, while the share taken by executive salaries and interest payments to bankers has multiplied dramatically. The "wage-price" spiral is more often a profit-price spiral, with the worker more the victim than the cause of inflation.

As financial power is concentrated in fewer and fewer hands, supplies, markets—and prices—are more easily manipulated. Instead of lowering prices when sales drop, the big monopoly firms often raise them to compensate for sales losses. The same with agribusiness: whether crops are poor or plentiful, food prices tend to go only in an upward direction. Prices are pushed up also by limiting production, as when the petroleum cartels repeatedly create artificial scarcities in oil supplies, which mysteriously disappear after the companies get price increases.

Other inflationary expenditures include the billions spent on unemployment payments and welfare expenditures to assist the poor, the jobless, and others who fall by the wayside under capitalism. There are also hundreds of thousands of able-bodied adults who do not work but who consume a substantial portion of the surplus value because they are wealthy. While not all the rich are idle, practically all live parasitically, largely off their trust funds or other "private incomes."

Massive military expenditures "happen to be a particularly inflation-producing type of federal spending," admits the *Wall Street Journal*. The Civil War, the First and Second World Wars, the Korean War, and the Vietnam War all produced periods of extreme inflation. Aggregate demand—mostly government demand for military goods and payments to military personnel—far exceed supply during wartime and are not usually covered by increased taxes. Even during "peacetime," assuming that's what we have today, huge defense outlays help create inflationary scarcities, as the military consumes vast amounts of labor power and material resources. (For instance, it is the largest single consumer of fuel in the United States.) The resulting excess of demand over supply generates an upward pressure on prices, especially since the defense budget is funded mostly through deficit spending—that is, by the government's spending more than it collects in taxes.

PRODUCTIVITY AND HUMAN NEEDS

Those who insist that private enterprise can answer our needs seem to overlook the fact that private enterprise has no such interest, its function being to produce the biggest profits possible for the owners. People may need food, but they offer no market until their need (or want) is coupled with buying power to become a market demand. When asked by the Citizens Board what they were doing about the widespread hunger in the United States, one food manufacturer responded: "If we saw evidence of profitability, we might look into this."

The difference between need and demand shows up on the international market also. When buying power rather than human need determines how resources are used, poor nations feed rich ones. Much of the beef, fish, and other protein products consumed by North Americans (and their livestock and domestic pets) comes from Peru, Mexico, Panama, India, and other Third World countries. These foods find their way to profitable U.S. markets rather than feed the children in these countries who suffer from protein deficiencies. In Guatemala alone, 55,000 children die before the age of five each year because of illnesses connected to malnutrition. Yet, the dairy farmers of countries like Guatemala are converting to more profitable beef cattle for the North American market. The children *need* milk, but they lack the money; hence, there is no market. In the "free market," money is invested only where money is to be made.

Capitalism's defenders claim that the pursuit of profits is ultimately beneficial to all since corporate productivity creates prosperity. This argument overlooks several things: high productivity frequently detracts from the common prosperity even while making fortunes for the few, and it not only fails to answer to certain social needs but may generate new ones. The coal-mining companies in Appalachia, for example, created many miseries, swindling the Appalachians out of their land, forcing them to work under dangerous conditions, destroying their countryside, and refusing to pay for any of the resulting social costs.

Furthermore, an increase in productivity, as measured by a gross national product (GNP) of more than $6 trillion a year, may mean *less* efficient use of social resources and more waste. The GNP, the total value of all goods and services produced in a given year, contains some hidden values in its measurements. Important nonmarket services like housework and child rearing go uncounted, while many things of negative social value are tabulated. Thus, highway accidents, which lead to increased insurance, hospital, and police costs, add quite a bit to the GNP but take a lot out of life.

The *human* value of productivity rests in its social purpose. Is the purpose to plunder the environment without regard to ecological needs, fabricate endless consumer desires, produce shoddy goods designed to wear out quickly, create wasteful forms of consumption, pander to snobbism and acquisitiveness, squeeze as much compulsive toil as possible out of workers while paying them as little as possible, create artificial scarcities in order to jack up prices—all in order to grab as big a profit as one can? Or is productivity geared to satisfying the communal needs of the populace in an equitable manner? Is it organized to serve essential needs first and superfluous wants last, to care for the natural environment and the health and safety of citizens and workers? Is it organized to maximize the capabilities, responsibilities, and participation of its people?

Capitalist productivity-for-profit gives little consideration to the latter set of goals. What is called productivity, as measured quantitatively, may actually represent a decline in the quality of life—for example, the relationship between the increasing quantity of automotive and industrial usage and the decreasing quality of our environment. Under capitalism, there is a glut of nonessential goods and services for those with money and a shortage of essential ones for those without money. Stores groan with unsold items while millions of people are ill-housed and ill-fed.

It is argued that the accumulation of great fortunes is a necessary condition for economic growth, for only the wealthy can provide the huge sums needed for the capitalization of new enterprises. Yet in many industries, from railroads to aeronautics to nuclear energy, much of the funding has come from the government—that is, from the taxpayer—and most of the growth has come from sales to the public—from consumers and from the wealth created by the labor power of workers. It is one thing to say that large-scale production requires capital accumulation but something else to presume that the source of accumulation must be the purses of the rich.

It is also argued that the concentration of corporate wealth is a necessary condition for progress because only big companies are capable of carrying out modern technological innovations. Actually, giant companies leave a good deal of the pioneering research to smaller businesses and individual entrepreneurs. The inventiveness record of the biggest oil companies, Exxon and Shell, is strikingly undistinguished. Referring to electric appliances, one General Electric vice-president noted: "I know of no original product invention, not even electric shavers or heating pads, made by any of the giant laboratories or corporations. . . . The record of the giants is one of moving in, buying out, and absorbing the small creators."

Defenders of the present system claim that big production units are more efficient than smaller ones. In fact, huge firms tend to become less efficient and more bureaucratized with size, and after a certain point in growth there is a diminishing return in productivity. Moreover, bigness is less the result of technological advance than of profit growth. When the same corporation has holdings in manufacturing, insurance, utilities, amusement parks, and publishing, it becomes clear that giantism is not a technological necessity that brings greater efficiency but the outcome of capital concentration.

The long-term survival of an enterprise is of less concern to the investor than the margin of profit to be gained from it. Mines, factories, and housing complexes have been bought and sold like so many game pieces for the sole purpose of extracting as much profit as possible, often with little regard for maintaining their functional capacity. Railroads shipping lines, aerospace companies, and banks have often tottered on the edge of ruin, to be rescued by generous infusions of government funds—even as these enterprises were being milked for millions in profits.

When times are good, the capitalists sing praise to the wonders of their freemarket system. When times are bad, they blame labor for capitalism's ills. Inflation is supposedly labor's fault because wage demands drive up prices. If we are to believe management, recession, too, is labor's fault. Workers must learn to work harder for less in order to stay competitive in the global economy. If they did so, business would not move to cheaper labor markets in Third World countries. In fact, studies show that U.S. full-time workers were 30 percent more productive than their opposite numbers in Japan and 12 percent more than in Germany, yet they received less in wages and benefits than Japanese and German full-time workers. In the last two decades, U.S. real wages fell 19 percent, despite a 25 percent growth in productivity.

If there is low productivity, it is among U.S. corporate executives. Business administrative costs are upwards of $1 trillion, of which the lion's share goes to executives and corporate professionals. Yet as little as one-fourth of an executive's time is actually spent working, that is, developing, analyzing, or executing company policies.

Another cause of low productivity is technological obsolescence. Unwilling to spend their own money to modernize their plants, big companies cry poverty and call for federal funds to finance technological innovation—supposedly to help them compete against foreign firms. Yet, these same companies sometimes will produce huge cash reserves for mergers. For example, after laying off 20,000 workers, refusing to modernize its aging plants, and milking the government of hundreds of millions of dollars in subsidies and tax write-offs, U.S. Steel came up with $6.2 billion to purchase Marathon Oil.

Unemployment

In capitalist societies, unlike socialist ones, people have no guaranteed right to employment. If they cannot find work, that's their tough luck. No free-market economy has ever attained full employment. If anything, unemployment is functional to capitalism. Without a reserve army of unemployed to compete for jobs and deflate wages, labor would cut more deeply into profits. In recent years official unemployment has ranged above 7 percent, or over 9 million people. But this figure does not count the many who have given up looking for work or who have exhausted their unemployment compensation and left the rolls, nor the millions of part-time or reduced-time workers who want full-time jobs, nor the many forced into early retirement, nor those who have joined the armed forces because they could not find work (and who are thereby listed as "employed.")

The real unemployment figure in 1992 was over 14 percent, or more than 18 million people. In 1991, according to the Department of Labor, about 21.3 million people experienced some unemployment. Moreover, people are finding it harder to get back into the work force and are remaining unemployed for longer periods. More than in any previous recession, workers have been permanently rather than temporarily laid off.

Some conservatives say there are plenty of jobs; unemployment results because some people are just lazy. But when unemployment jumped by a half-million in the early 1990s, was it really because a mass of people suddenly found work too irksome and preferred to lose their income, homes, cars, medical coverage, and pensions? In fact, a perusal of the help wanted ads shows that the great majority of available positions require college training or special skills. For entry level openings, it is another story: in various parts of the country, thousands of people show up for a handful of job openings. Even among the more skilled positions, firms receive hundreds of applications for a few scarce openings.

Another myth is that union wages cause unemployment by pricing workers out of the market. Actually, in states where labor unions are weakest and wages lowest, like Mississippi and Alabama, unemployment is among the highest. For the country as a whole, the decline in both unions and real wages in the last decade has been accompanied by a higher, not lower, rate of unemployment.

It is corporate "restructuring," not high wages, that causes unemployment. Nowadays, unemployment and economic stagnation seem more structural than cyclical, showing no self-correcting upturn. As companies expand their productivity through computers and automation, this no longer creates a commensurate gain in jobs. In 1992 Chrysler announced an investment of $225 million for a new line of Dodge trucks that created only seventy jobs, while the company as a whole continued to lay off workers. As constant capital (machinery, technologies, fuels and the like) outstrips variable capital (labor), fixed costs become proportionately higher, creating a still greater pressure to increase productivity in order to maintain and expand profit levels. Proportionately more capital is needed to attain any given return. Thus there exists a continual tendency toward a falling rate of profit.

Unable to raise profitability rates sufficiently through capital investment, the capitalist raises it through downsizing (laying off workers), speedups (making the diminished work force toil faster and harder), downgrading (reclassifying jobs to lower-wage categories), and part-time and contract labor (hiring people who receive no benefits, seniority, or steady employment). Tens of thousands of workers have been laid off across the country in recent times, many of them from profitable companies. In the last dozen years some 14 percent of manufacturing jobs have disappeared. There also has been a substantial drop in white-collar openings and salaries for college-educated people. Between 1990 and 1992, 2.2 million jobs were lost through mergers and layoffs.

It is widely believed that the United States can compensate for losses in manufacturing by expanding its service sector. But much service production—such as construction engineering, transportation, and telecommunications—is linked to manufacturing. As the manufacturing base declines, so does the entire economy. Another cause of decline is the runaway shop; U.S. firms move to cheaper Third

World labor markets, supposedly to maintain their competitiveness in the "global economy." As one corporate executive put it: "Until we get [U.S.] real wages down much closer to those of the Brazils and South Koreas, we cannot pass along productivity gains to wages and still be competitive." In other words, working people must continue to sacrifice until they are reduced to poverty and corporate profit rates are as high as they are in the Third World.

The power of the business class is like no other group in our society. The giant corporations control the rate of technological development and the terms of production. They fix prices and determine the availability of livelihoods. They create new standards of consumption and popular taste. They decide which labor markets to explore and which to abandon, sometimes relegating whole communities to destitution in the process. They devour environmental resources, toxifying the land, water, and air. They command an enormous surplus wealth while helping to create and perpetuate conditions of scarcity for millions of people at home and abroad. And as we shall see, they enjoy a predominating voice in the highest councils of government.

THE HARDSHIPS OF WORKING AMERICA

By 1994, in the midst of a deep recession, the U.S. economy was going through what some called "a jobless recovery." Business failures and bankruptcy rates were still high; real wages had declined; consumer spending was down; over a thousand jobs were being eliminated daily; and poverty was on the rise. We were witnessing the gradual Third-Worldization of the United States, involving the abolition of high-wage jobs, a growth in low-wage and part-time employment, an increase in permanent unemployment, a shrinking middle-income population, a growing number of mortgage delinquencies, greater concentrations of wealth for the few and more poverty and privation for the many.

One hears much talk from politicians and media pundits about the middle class. In fact, most Americans are working class; their income source is hourly wages and their labor is manual, unskilled, or semiskilled. Even among white-collar service employees, 87 percent were nonsupervisory, earning less than $20,000 in 1990 in full-time jobs. Compared to twenty years earlier, U.S. workers put in an average 158 more hours in job related activities—the equivalent of an extra month of toil. They had fewer paid days off, fewer benefits, less sick leave, shorter vacations, and less discretionary income. In short, people are experiencing a declining standard of living.

Millions do not earn enough to live in any comfort or security. Almost two-thirds of the families below the government's official poverty line have a member who is fully employed. They work for a living but not for a living wage. The Census Bureau reports that some 14.4 million (18 percent) full-time, year-round workers earned wages below the poverty level in 1990—up from 6.6 million (12.3 percent) in 1974.

Two-thirds of them were high school or college educated and half were over thirty-three years old. Over a quarter of our labor force, some 30 million, are employed in part-time, temporary, and low-paid "contingent work." It is not laziness that keeps so many in poverty; it is the low wages their bosses pay them and the high prices, rents, and taxes they must pay others. Of the 13 million jobs created in the last decade, 8.2 million paid less than $7,000 annually. To make ends meet, millions are obliged to hold down two jobs. Underemployment was hurting even middle-level managers, engineers, technicians, lawyers, and other usually well-off professionals.

By 1993, the number of people living in poverty had climbed to 37 million, or 14.5 percent of the U.S. population. The Census Bureau's poverty line for a family of four in that year was $13,920, but some 26 million additional people in families that made upwards of $20,000 still lived in serious deprivation, lacking medical insurance, unable to pay utility bills or keep up car payments, even lacking sufficient funds for food during certain times in the month. They were officially above the poverty line but still poor.

Americans have been taught that they are the most prosperous and fortunate people in the world. The truth is, of twenty major industrial countries, the United States has the highest infant death rate and the highest rate of youth deaths due to accidents, homicide, and other violence. In addition, poverty is more widespread, severe, and long-lasting than in most other developed nations. Low-income communities are a source of great profit for price-gouging merchants and rent-gouging slumlords. The poor pay more for most commodities, including food. When able to find work, they often perform the toughest, grimiest, lowest-paying jobs, serving as a reserve army of underemployed labor that helps deflate wages and keeps profits up.

Especially hard hit have been people of color. In the early 1990s, African Americans had a declining life expectancy, an infant mortality rate twice as high as Whites, a school drop-out rate of more than 50 percent in some cities, a poverty rate that was 300 percent higher than Caucasians, and an unemployment rate 176 percent higher (compared to 86 percent in 1970). African Americans who were employed took home an overall income that was only 56 percent of White income. Black people continued to suffer racial discrimination in employment and other areas of life.

Women also number among the superexploited. Of the more than 53 million women who work, a disproportionately high number are concentrated in low-paying secretarial and clerking jobs. Although 20 million mothers are working, 44 percent of single mothers remain below the poverty level. Women with college degrees earn about the same as men with one to three years of high school. Two out of three adults in poverty are women.

By the mid-1990s, one out of every five children in the USA lived in poverty. Official investigations found a dramatic increase in child labor violations, with millions of minors illegally working long hours that interfere with their education or toiling at hazardous jobs in sweatshops, mills, fast food restaurants, and on farms. Employers often seek out child workers because they can pay them less and take advantage of them. The American Academy of Pediatrics estimates that 100,000 minors are injured on the job each year. At least several hundred are killed yearly; many more suffering burns, deep cuts, and amputations. The federal government had relatively few inspectors to check workplaces for child-labor violations. The average fine in cases involving death or permanent injury was $750—a measure of the value placed on the life of low-income children.

As of 1992, about thirty million Americans were not getting enough to eat—up from twenty million in 1985—as hunger spread from the inner cities to the heartland. The number of families lining up for emergency food assistance has increased sharply over the last two decades. Many of those experiencing hunger were regularly employed in the free market. The poorest households spent 60 percent of their incomes on housing, cutting deeply into food budgets. Among those below the poverty line, average outlay per individual meal was only sixty-eight cents. In major cities and small towns, there were people who picked their food out of garbage cans and dumps. As one columnist noted, "If the president on his visit to China had witnessed Chinese peasants eating from garbage cans, he almost certainly would have cited it as proof that communism doesn't work. What does it prove when it happens in the capitalist success called America?"

A team of doctors investigating rural poverty found children plagued with diseases of the heart, lungs, and kidneys, and other serious ailments that would normally warrant immediate hospitalization. One in eight children in the nation suffered from hunger, with millions more facing insufficient nutrition. Such children are preoccupied with desires for food and medical care for their illnesses. They show signs of lethargy, "stunting," "wasting," and Third World diseases such as kwashiorkor and marasmus.

One of every five American adults is functionally illiterate. One of four individuals lives in substandard housing without adequate plumbing, heat, or other facilities. Housing is the largest single expenditures for most families. Due to realty speculations, gentrification, condominium conversions, and unemployment, people of modest means have been squeezed out of the housing market in greater numbers than ever. Affordable housing has become so scarce that more and more working-class families have been forced to double- and triple-up, imposing hardships and severe strains on family relations.

Current estimates of homelessness vary from 250,000 to three million, almost a third of whom are families with children. Half the homeless in major cities are single men. Homelessness is something more than being without shelter. It is the most desperate condition of poverty, offering a life of hunger, filth, destitution, mental depression, unattended illness, and violent victimization. Even among the housed there are millions who are doubled up with family and friends or who are only a paycheck away from the streets. One study found that 20 percent to 82 percent of persons who stayed in homeless shelters held jobs (employment varying according to particular shelters). Most worked full time but with rents so high and pay so low, they could not afford a place to live.

Despite all the talk about the affluent elderly, almost half of the Americans who live below the poverty line are aged. More than three million senior citizens experienced chronic hunger in 1990. Every winter hundreds of people, mostly the very old and very young, freeze to death in unheated apartments or perish in fires caused by unsafe gas stoves (used to compensate for heat cutoffs). Not more than 3 percent of senior citizens have coverage for nursing homes or long-term care. Despite Medicare assistance, the elderly face the highest out-of-pocket health-care costs. Millions are finding that Social Security, pensions, and savings are insufficient. Almost half of all seniors have returned to work or are looking for work.

It is difficult for those who have never known serious economic want to imagine the misery and social pathology it can cause. Studies indicate that even small rises in unemployment bring noticeable increases in illness, mental problems, substance addictions, suicide, and crime. Tuberculosis, a disease much associated with poverty, has risen to a rate unseen in over half a century in the United States.

This country is beset by the greatest illegal drug epidemic in its history, with annual consumption estimated at nearly $150 *billion*. With only 6 percent of the world's population, the U.S. consumes 70 percent of the world's illicit drugs. Some 6.5 million U.S. citizens use heroin, crack, cocaine, or some other narcotic. Millions more are addicted to legal drugs such as amphetamines and barbiturates. The pushers are the doctors; the suppliers are the drug industry; the profits are stupendous. About 32 percent of Americans have experienced some form of mental "disorder" such as serious depression. One out of every four families is affected by alcohol-related problems, a 100 percent increase since 1974. An estimated four in ten Americans suffer some direct or indirect effect of alcohol abuse.

Suicide has become the third leading cause of death among U.S. youth. Each year, some 25,000 to 27,000 Americans take their own lives. Another 23,000 to 24,000 are murdered. An estimated 135,000 children take guns to school, with more than two dozen a day being killed. About 30 percent of American households experience a crime of violence or theft each year, the highest rates being in the poorest neighborhoods. Over the last two decades serious crimes almost doubled and the prison population has tripled. With more than 1.2 million people in prison, or one out of every 180 persons over the age of sixteen, the United States has the highest incarceration rate in the world. Over 40 percent of inmates have an alcohol or drug abuse problem. In an average year, almost ten million are admitted to local jails, with some people entering and getting released several times in one year. More and more prisons are being built to ease overcrowding; in the midst of recession, prison construction remains a boom industry.

With economic adversity there has come a skyrocketing increase in family violence and abuse. Millions of U.S. women are battered by men; almost five million sustain serious injury each year. Over two million children—predominantly but not exclusively from lower income families—are battered, abused, or abandoned each year. Over 30,000 children annually are left permanently physically handicapped from abuse and neglect. Child abuse kills more children than leukemia, automobile accidents, and infectious diseases combined. Every year 150,000 children are reported missing, of whom some 50,000 are never found. Ten to thirteen youngsters are stabbed, raped, beaten, or burned to death by parents or surrogates every day. One in four women and almost one in six men report having been sexually abused as children by adults. An estimated 1.5 million elderly are subjected to serious abuse, such as forced confinement and beatings. Like child abuse, the mistreatment of elderly parents increases dramatically when economic conditions worsen.

9

THE GLOBAL COLLAPSE: A NON-ORTHODOX VIEW

Walden Bello

This is the longer version of an essay by the author released by the British Broadcasting Corporation (BBC) on 6 February 2009.

Week after week, we see the global economy contracting at a pace worse than predicted by the gloomiest analysts. We are now, it is clear, in no ordinary recession but are headed for a global depression that could last for many years.

THE FUNDAMENTAL CRISIS: OVERACCUMULATION

Orthodox economics has long ceased to be of any help in understanding the crisis. Non-orthodox economics, on the other hand, provides extraordinarily powerful insights into the causes and dynamics of the current crisis. From the progressive perspective, what we are seeing is the intensification of one of the central crises or "contradictions" of global capitalism: the crisis of overproduction, also known as overaccumulation or overcapacity. This is the tendency for capitalism to build up, in the context of heightened inter-capitalist competition, tremendous productive capacity that outruns the population's capacity to consume owing to income inequalities that limit popular purchasing power. The result is an erosion of profitability, leading to an economic downspin.

To understand the current collapse, we must go back in time to the so-called Golden Age of Contemporary Capitalism, the period from 1945 to 1975. This was a period of rapid growth both in the center economies and in the underdeveloped economies—one that was partly triggered by the massive reconstruction of Europe and East Asia after the devastation of the Second World War, and partly by the new socioeconomic arrangements and instruments based on a historic class compromise between Capital and Labor that were institutionalized under the new Keynesian state.

But this period of high growth came to an end in the mid-1970s, when the center economies were seized by stagflation, meaning the coexistence of low growth with high inflation, which was not supposed to happen under neoclassical economics.

Stagflation, however, was but a symptom of a deeper cause: the reconstruction of Germany and Japan and the rapid growth of industrializing economies like Brazil, Taiwan, and South Korea added tremendous new productive capacity and increased global competition, while income inequality within countries and between countries limited the growth of purchasing power and demand, thus eroding profitability. This was aggravated by the massive oil price rises of the seventies.

The most painful expression of the crisis of overproduction was global recession of the early 1980s, which was the most serious to overtake the international economy since the Great Depression, that is, before the current crisis.

Capitalism tried three escape routes from the conundrum of overproduction: neoliberal restructuring, globalization, and financialization

ESCAPE ROUTE # 1: NEOLIBERAL RESTRUCTURING

Neoliberal restructuring took the form of Reaganism and Thatcherism in the North and Structural Adjustment in the South. The aim was to invigorate capital accumulation, and this was to be done by 1) removing state constraints on the growth, use, and flow of capital and wealth; and 2) redistributing income from the poor and middle classes to the rich on the theory that the rich would then be motivated to invest and reignite economic growth.

The problem with this formula was that in redistributing income to the rich, you were gutting the incomes of the poor and middle classes, thus restricting demand, while not necessarily inducing the rich to invest more in production. In fact, it could be more profitable to invest in speculation.

In fact, neoliberal restructuring, which was generalized in the North and south during the eighties and nineties, had a poor record in terms of growth: Global growth averaged 1.1 percent in the 1990s and 1.4 percent in the '80s, compared with 3.5 percent in the 1960s and 2.4 percent in the '70s, when state interventionist policies were dominant. Neoliberal restructuring could not shake off stagnation.

ESCAPE ROUTE # 2: GLOBALIZATION

The second escape route global capital took to counter stagnation was "extensive accumulation" or globalization, or the rapid integration of semi-capitalist, non-capitalist, or pre-capitalist areas into the global market economy. Rosa Luxemburg, the famous German radical economist, saw this long ago in her classic "The Accumulation of Capital" as necessary to shore up the rate of profit in the metropolitan economies.

How? By gaining access to cheap labor, by gaining new, albeit limited, markets, by gaining new sources of cheap agricultural and raw material products, and by bringing into being new areas for investment in infrastructure. Integration is accomplished via trade liberalization, removing barriers to the mobility of global capital, and abolishing barriers to foreign investment.

China is, of course, the most prominent case of a non-capitalist area to be integrated into the global capitalist economy over the last 25 years.

By the middle of the first decade of the 21st century, roughly 40-50 percent of the profits of US corporations came from their operations and sales abroad, especially in China.

The problem with this escape route from stagnation is that it exacerbates the problem of overproduction because it adds to productive capacity. A tremendous amount of manufacturing capacity has been added in China over the last 25 years, and this has had a depressing effect on prices and profits. Not surprisingly, by around 1997, the profits of US corporations stopped growing. According to one calculation, the profit rate of the Fortune 500 went from 7.15 in 1960-69 to 5.30 in 1980-90 to 2.29 in 1990-99 to 1.32 in 2000-2002. By the end of the 1990s, with excess capacity in almost every industry, the gap between productive capacity and sales was the largest since the Great Depression.

ESCAPE ROUTE # 3: FINANCIALIZATION

Given the limited gains in countering the depressive impact of overproduction via neoliberal restructuring and globalization, the third escape route—financialization—became very critical for maintaining and raising profitability.

With investment in industry and agriculture yielding low profits owing to overcapacity, large amounts of surplus funds have been circulating in or invested and reinvested in the financial sector—that is, the financial sector is turning on itself.

The result is an increased bifurcation between a hyperactive financial economy and a stagnant real economy. As one financial executive noted in the pages of the *Financial Times*, "there has been an increasing disconnection between the real and financial economies in the last few years. The real economy has grown . . . but nothing like that of the financial economy—until it imploded." What this observer does not tell us is that the disconnect between the real and the financial economy is not accidental—that the financial economy exploded precisely to make up for the stagnation owing to overproduction of the real economy.

One indicator of the super-profitability of the financial sector is that while profits in the US manufacturing sector came to one percent of US gross domestic product (GDP), profits in the financial sector came to two percent. Another is the fact that 40 percent of the total profits of US financial and non-financial corporations is accounted for by the financial sector although it is responsible for only five percent of US gross domestic product (and even that is likely to be an overestimate).

The problem with investing in financial sector operations is that it is tantamount to squeezing value out of already created value. It may create profit, yes, but it does not create new value—only industry, agricultural, trade, and services create new value. Because profit is not based on value that is created, investment operations become very volatile and prices of stocks, bonds, and other forms of investment can depart very radically from their real value—for instance, the stock of Internet startups may keep rising to heights unknown, driven mainly by upwardly spiraling financial valuations.

Profits then depend on taking advantage of upward price departures from the value of commodities, then selling before reality enforces a "correction," that is a crash back to real values. The radical rise of prices of an asset far beyond real values is what is called the formation of a bubble.

Profitability being dependent on speculative coups, it is not surprising that the finance sector lurches from one bubble to another, or from one speculative mania to another. Because it is driven by speculative mania, finance-driven capitalism has experienced about 100 financial crises since capital markets were deregulated and liberalized in the 1980s, the most serious before the current crisis being the Asian Financial Crisis of 1997.

DYNAMICS OF THE SUBPRIME IMPLOSION

The current Wall Street collapse has its roots in the Technology Bubble of the late 1990s, when the price of the stocks of Internet startups skyrocketed, then collapsed, resulting in the loss of $7 trillion worth of assets and the recession of 2001-2002.

The loose money policies of the Fed under Alan Greenspan had encouraged the Technology Bubble, and when it collapsed into a recession, Greenspan, trying to counter a long recession, cut the prime rate to a 45-year low of 1.0 percent in June 2003 and kept it there for over a year. This had the effect of encouraging another bubble—the real estate bubble.

As early as 2002, progressive economists were warning about the real estate bubble. However, as late as 2005, then Council of Economic Advisers Chairman and now Federal Reserve Board Chairman Ben Bernanke attributed the rise in US housing prices to "strong economic fundamentals" instead of speculative activity. Is it any wonder that he was caught completely off guard when the Subprime Crisis broke in the summer of 2007?

The subprime mortgage crisis was not a case of supply outrunning real demand. The "demand" was largely fabricated by speculative mania on the part of developers and financiers that wanted to make great profits from their access to foreign money—most of it Asian and Chinese in origin—that flooded the US in the last decade. Big ticket mortgages were aggressively sold to millions who could not normally afford them by offering low "teaser" interest rates that would later be readjusted to jack up payments from the new homeowners.

How did problematic mortgages become such a massive problem? The reason is that these assets were then "securitized"—that is converted into spectral commodities called "collateralized debt obligations" (CDOs) that enabled speculation on the odds that the mortgage would not be paid. These were then traded by the mortgage originators working with different layers of middlemen who understated risk so as to offload them as quickly as possible to other banks and institutional investors. These institutions in turn offloaded these securities onto other banks and foreign financial institutions.

The idea was to make a sale quickly, get your money upfront, and make a tidy profit, while foisting the risk on the suckers down the line—the hundreds of thousands of institutions and individual investors that bought the mortgage-tied securities. This was called "spreading the risk," and it was actually seen as a good thing because it lightened the balance sheet of financial institutions, enabling them to engage in other lending activities.

When the interest rates were raised on the subprime loans, adjustable mortgage, and other housing loans, the game was up. There are about four million subprime mortgages which will likely go into default in the next two years, and five million more defaults from adjustable rate mortgages and other "flexible loans" that were geared to snag the most reluctant potential homebuyer will occur over the next several years. But securities whose value run into as much as $2 trillion had already been injected, like virus, into the global financial system. Global capitalism's gigantic circulatory system was fatally infected. And, as with a plague, we don't know who and how many are fatally infected until they keel over because the whole financial system has become so non-transparent owing to lack of regulation.

For Lehman Brothers, Merrill Lynch, Fannie Mae, Freddie Mac, Bear Stearns, Bank of America, and Citigroup, the losses represented by these toxic securities simply overwhelmed their reserves. Iceland's banks and many European financial institutions have since joined the list of victims. Some, like Lehman Brothers, have been allowed to die, but most have been kept alive with massive injections of taxpayers' cash by governments that want the banks to lend to keep the real economy going.

COLLAPSE OF THE REAL ECONOMY

But instead of performing their primordial task of lending to facilitate productive activity, the banks are holding on to their cash or buying up rivals to strengthen their financial base. Not surprisingly, with global capitalism's circulatory system seizing up, it was only a matter of time before the real economy would contract, as it has with frightening speed in the last few weeks. Woolworth, a retail icon, has folded in Britain, the US auto industry is on emergency care, and even mighty Toyota has suffered an unprecedented decline in its profits. With American consumer demand plummeting, China and East Asia have seen their goods rotting on the docks, bringing about a sharp contraction of their economies and massive layoffs.

Globalization has ensured that economies that went up together in the boom would also go down together, with unparalleled speed, in the bust, the end of which is nowhere to be discerned.

Walden Bello is professor at the University of the Philippines, Diliman; senior analyst at Focus on the Global South; and president of the Freedom from Debt Coalition. He can be reached at <waldenbello@yahoo.com>. This article was first published by the *Philippine Daily Inquirer* on 11 February 2009, and it is reproduced here for educational purposes.

10

CLASS STRUGGLE 101

HOW CAPITALISTS ACCUMULATE WEALTH: PAY THE WORKERS LESS THAN THE VALUE OF THE WEALTH CREATED BY THE WORKERS

Chuck O'Connell

According to the labor theory of value, it is the labor of workers who extract and transform raw materials into usable things that adds value to the goods so produced. Because the workers, however, do not have ownership rights to the means of production, they cannot legally lay claim to the wealth they have created. Their wealth is seized by the capitalist class precisely because it owns the means of production. Some of the wealth does come back to the workers in the form of wages and (occasionally) in the form of benefits such as health insurance, paid medical leave, and retirement pensions. The portion of wealth that comes back to workers is a function of a struggle between the owners of the means of production and the workers. There is a conflict between the two classes because they have antagonistic interests: the capitalists desire higher profits but taking greater profits reduces the amount of money available for wages; the workers desire higher wages but receiving higher wages reduces the amount of money available for profits. The outcome of this struggle over the division of company income into profits and wages is determined by the political and economic strength of the two contending classes. The process of labor exploitation has intensified since the mid-1970s when capitalism globally entered a crisis of profitability (also called a crisis of overproduction). As the rate of profit fell, employers began to attack labor unions and restructure the job market so as to get more work from us at lower wages. Here are some of the methods of wage reduction that capitalists have used and continue to use in their efforts to acquire greater profits.

1. Don't hire all workers. This is a method that has been used in all historical periods of capitalism (except perhaps during periods of total mobilization for war). By keeping the number of jobs available at a number less than the number of workers needing jobs, capitalists put workers into competition with one another. This competition creates a downward pressure on wages as workers, desperate for jobs, continually underbid one another. There is always a pool of unemployed workers; this pool can be thought of as the *reserve army of labor* because it provides a group of "reserves" that can be called upon when the economy expands and more workers are needed. It can also be called upon (i.e. hired) whenever employed workers go out on strike; that is, the unemployed can be used as strikebreakers.

2. Prevent the minimum wage from keeping pace with inflation. Inflation is the rise in the price of goods and services. If your wage does not keep up with inflation, you lose purchasing power; in other words, expenses go up and your standard of living begins to fall as you can afford less. In 2010 the federal minimum wage was $6.55 which "is 24 percent lower than the average level of the minimum wage in the 1960s, [and] 23 percent lower than in the 1970s ..." (W. J. Wilson, 2009: 38). Adjusted for inflation the federal minimum wage should be at about $8.73. Workers receiving the minimum wage have lost substantial purchasing power. Additionally, because the minimum wage sets the official "floor" of the wage structure, the ability of the capitalist class to prevent its rise has a depressor effect on other wages in general.

3. Transform career jobs into temporary ones. This has the following effects: it lowers the wages and benefits and furthermore weakens the political solidarity of the workers because they are only temporary employees. It is often used in higher education where many professors are hired on a semester-by-semester basis. This step is often used with the next one.

4. Turn full-time jobs into part-time jobs. By reducing the number of hours per week to make jobs part-time, the bosses can put workers on lower wage and benefit scales. This method of exploiting workers is widely used in colleges and universities which have long been regarded as part of the primary labor market. Although advanced degrees are necessary for entrance into the occupation of professor, the part-time, temporary lower paid faculty at many colleges and universities now outnumber the full-time tenured higher paid faculty. For example, at CSU Chico the math department in 1990 had 32 full-time professors and only 2 part-time professors; by 2006 only 12 full-timers remained while the number of part-timers grew to more than 40.

5. Fire the workers and then rehire them from a leasing agency. This allows the capitalist firm to reduce labor costs (e.g. benefits such as medical and retirement) and add a buffer zone of management (the leasing agency) between the workers and itself. If a worker has a complaint, which is the proper authority to receive it: the leasing agency that hired him or her or the company where he or she does the actual work?

6. Fire some workers, redistribute their work to the remaining workers and thus make the company more "efficient" (i.e. profitable). Why is the company now more efficient? Because production levels have been maintained with fewer workers; fewer workers mean lower costs for the firm. By lowering costs yet producing the same amount of goods the company increases its profits. Of course, this constitutes a form of "speed-up" for the remaining workers but who are they to say anything? The owners of the firm (the investors) are happy as their stocks go up in value. If the stocks rise enough, the CEO (chief executive officer) may be rewarded at the end of the year with a generous bonus.

Sound fanciful? It's not. This practice was notoriously common in the early 1990s. In 1993 and 1994 CEO George Fisher laid off 14,100 workers at Eastman Kodak. Before doing so his salary was $1.89 million; afterwards it jumped to $3.9 million. In 1994 CEO Albert Dunlop of Scott Paper laid off 10,500 workers. Before doing so, his salary was a mere $618,000; as a result of making Scott Paper more "efficient" his compensation increased to $3.5 million. Again, in 1994 CEO Louis Gerstner at IBM fired 36,000 workers. He was earning only $2.8 million when he dumped them. His reward for "improving" IBM was a pay raise to $4.6 million.

During the current recession (or is it a *depression*?), those CEOs at the fifty firms that fired the most workers in 2009 received 42% more pay than other CEOs. On average these CEOs made $12 million compared to the $8.5 million average than their counterparts at companies not laying off as many workers. Some of these executive officers were paid well above the average. For example, William Weldon at Johnson and Johnson fired 9,000 workers and made $25.6 million in 2009. Kenneth Chenault at American Express dumped 4,000 workers *while taking federal bailout funds* (your tax dollars) in 2008 and was paid $16.8 million (of which $5 million was a cash bonus) in 2009. Mark Hurd, CEO of Hewlett-Packard, fired 6,400 employees and was paid $24.2 million in 2009; when he resigned in August 2010 he was given a severance package of $28 million. If these companies can't afford the workers, how can they afford such generous compensation for the CEOs? (For more data and analysis see the study, "CEO Pay and the Great Recession" by the Institute of Policy Studies.)

7. **Put workers on salary and thus exempt them from rules requiring payment of overtime wages.** It's a neat trick to kick workers upstairs into salaried "management" positions where they really aren't *management* but are required to put in more than forty hours a week for a pre-set salary. According the *Wall Street Journal* (a pro-business newspaper), this trick means that the workers lose about $19 billion annually in overtime wages; put another way, capitalists have increased profits by $19 billion each year (LA Times, June 8, 2003, M6). According to workers who filed class-action lawsuits to reclaim lost overtime compensation, companies engaging in such practices include Starbucks, Rite-Aid, Bank of America, U-Haul International, and Farmers Insurance Group.

8. **Layoff workers who have worked their way up the wage scale and offer to rehire them at the prevailing entry level wage.** This strategy was used by the Circuit City corporation in 2007. It fired 3,400 veteran workers who were making $18.90 per hour after putting in fifteen to twenty years of service and offered them their jobs back at the current minimum wage with no health coverage. A wage of $18.90 earned about $39,312 each year. A new wage at $7.50 reduced the earnings of the worker to about $15,600. This amounted to a savings in labor costs of $23,712 per worker. When you multiply this by the number of workers affected (3,400), you come up with the sum $80,620,800 in lost wages for workers and increased profits for the bosses annually.

9. <u>Create a two-tier workforce</u> when negotiating a new contract with the labor union. Threaten workers with a reduction of wages and benefits in the new contract. Then offer the older workers retention of their current wages and benefits in return for

their agreement to a contract that will pay new hires a lower wage and benefits for the same work. By pitting older workers against younger workers, the bosses can create a two-tier wage system that increases the rate of exploitation for new hires (not all of whom are younger workers). This tactic has been effectively used in the Southern California grocery industry and in the auto industry; it will probably be used in the field of education because the teachers union has no effective strategy to oppose it.

10. Move jobs into prisons. Writing back in the late 1990s, populist author Jim Hightower claimed:

"Since 1990 thirty states have contracted out prison labor to private companies.

JC Penney, Kmart, and Eddie Bauer are getting such products as jeans, sweatshirts, and toys made by prisoners in Tennessee and Washington State.

IBM, Texas Instruments, and Dell computer all get circuit boards made by Texas prisoners.

Honda has had car parts made in Ohio prisons, McDonald's has uniforms made in Oregon prisons, AT&T has hired telemarketers in Colorado prisons, and Spalding gets golf balls packed in Hawaii prisons.

California's correctional system has become a one-stop hiring hall for corporations: San Quentin inmates do data entry for Chevron, Macy's, and BankAmerica; Ventura inmates take telephone reservations for TWA [former airline], ...Folsom inmates work for both a plastics manufacturer and a brass faucet maker ..." (Hightower, 1998: 93).

In 1994 the State of California sent a promotional letter to a number of national corporations offering them tax incentives if they hired California prison labor. The letter read in part as follows:

"Dear Business Leader:

As you know, there are many advantages to doing business in California. I [i.e. Governor Pete Wilson] am very pleased to tell you about yet another way companies can gain a competitive edge, while helping to provide California's inmates an opportunity to rebuild their lives ...

The Joint and Free Venture Programs, sponsored by the California Department of Corrections and the California Youth authority, give businesses access to motivated employees—all volunteers—who want to become productive members of our communities. Companies which participate will be eligible for:

Cost-effective long-term leases;

A 10 percent California tax credit;

Access to 30 diverse locations throughout the state [i.e. the California prisons]."

This letter was accompanied by a color brochure with a section describing "Employer Benefits" as follows:

"Federal and State Tax Incentives.

No benefits package [i.e. no retirement pay, vacation pay, sick leave pay, or medical coverage].

Discount rates on Workers Compensation.

On call labor pool [i.e. the prisoners].

Inmates pay 20 percent of salary for room and board."

In the 1990s in Los Angeles, the MTA (Metropolitan Transit Authority) adopted a "temporary and limited" program to replace MTA workers who made $16.50 per hour plus medical benefits with inmates from the LA County work camp. The prisoners swept out the buses, wiped down the handrails, cleaned the windshields, mirrors and lights for $10 per *day*.

Although there are limits to what kind of work can be imported into prisons and thus to the number of jobs that can be transferred from the non-prison labor market, the use of low wage prisoners across the country reduces to some extent the ability of free workers to bargain for higher wages and better working conditions.

11. Move jobs overseas to regions of cheaper labor. This method of reducing wages has accelerated in the last thirty years with companies moving to Mexico, Guatemala, El Salvador, China, Korea, the Philippines, Indonesia, Sri Lanka, Viet Nam, and several other places.

12. Transform welfare into "workfare". This is the policy used since the mid-1990s to require welfare recipients to perform labor in order to receive their welfare grants. Of course, workers go on welfare because there aren't enough jobs to go around in the first place; so, where are their new jobs going to come from? The answer is this: from already existing jobs that will be transferred from high wage union work to low wage workfare labor. This is a clever strategy that allows bosses to replace unionized public sector jobs with jobs that pay minimum and sub-minimum wages thereby undermining the wages and job security of current workers. For example, in New York City in 1996 the New York City Transit Authority convinced the Transport Workers Union to allow management to use thousands of welfare recipients to clean subway cars and buses in order to "earn" their welfare grants. The union gave up 586 jobs to workfare. These cleaning jobs had paid the unionized city workers a wage of $16.62. The workfare replacements had to work 26 hours per week to receive their grants of $81.25 each. Dividing the weekly grant by the number of hours worked, you get the miserly sum of $3.12 per hour! New York City extended workfare to other areas replacing, for example, 7,000 unionized municipal parks-and-recreation employees with workfare laborers. Eventually 32,000 workfare employees of NYC sued in court claiming the right to earn the same pay and benefits as unionized workers, "But the Appellate Division of [the] state Supreme Court unanimously rejected their argument in dismissing the lawsuit" (LA Times, Sept. 19, 1998; A25; see also, Peter Dreier and Fernando Gapasin, "Treat Welfare Recipients Like Workers: Pay Them a Wage", LA Times, August 29, 1999, M6).

13. Use home labor. This involves requiring the workers to use their own residences as assembly or office sites thus saving the firm the costs of providing a physical place of employment. This practice is used for clerical work (telecommuting), garment, auto assembly, semiconductor assembly, and education (where do you think your temporary, part-time instructors do their research and prepare their lectures?). The cost of operating a production site is transferred to the worker. Also, because workers are not brought together to labor a one common place, there is little if any communication among them as to their common situation; this gives them a greater sense of political isolation and impotence and inhibits their ability to collectively struggle for higher wages.

14. Outsource some of the production process to non-union factories. For example, Boeing pays its unionized workers about $31 per hour. To reduce this labor cost it moved some production to non-union factories in Alabama where the workers made $16 per hour. Later it shifted more production to non-union factories in Southern California where workers are paid about $10 per hour thus saving Boeing more than twenty dollars per hour per worker.

15. Steal wages. This method of reducing labor costs is called *wage theft* and is quite pervasive in the secondary labor market. Bosses use it often against desperate, vulnerable workers—especially immigrants. Wage theft consists of a variety of tactics including: paying less than the minimum wage, making illegal payroll deductions for the use of tools or for damaged goods, forcing workers to labor without pay before and after regular shift hours (known as "off-the-clock" violations), stealing tips, refusing to pay overtime, and denying or reducing time for meal breaks during the shift. A UCLA study of 2010 "found that wage theft costs Los Angeles County workers $26 million a week... workers [experiencing wage theft] ...lost an average of about $40 from typical weekly earnings of $318. About three-fourths of 160,000 people who worked more than 40 hours a week did not receive overtime pay, and nearly 30% of the county's low-earning workers were paid less than the minimum wage..." (*"Stiffer Penalties Proposed for Shortchanging Workers"*, LA Times, September 17, 2010; B1, B4). One unfortunate car-washer was often paid only $35 for working a ten hour day—basically getting paid $3.50 an hour! To say that workers lose $26 million each week to wage theft is to say that the capitalist class makes $26 million each week. Over the course of a year this figure adds up to $1.35 *billion* in profits in LA County alone.

According to a 2009 study conducted by the Institute for Research on Labor and Employment at UCLA, "in a given week, approximately 1,114,074 workers in the three cities [Chicago, Los Angeles, New York] have at least one pay-based violation. Extrapolating from this figure, front-line workers in low-wage industries in Chicago, Los Angeles, and New York City lose more than $56.4 million *per week* as a result of employment and labor law violations. The largest portion of these lost wages is due to minimum wage violations (58 percent), followed by overtime violations (22 percent), rest break violations (10 percent), and off-the-clock violations (8 percent)" (Annette Bernhardt, Ruth Milkman et al, "Broken Laws, Unprotected Workers", Institute for Research on Labor and Employment, UCLA, 2009). The $56 million lost each week is an annual loss of almost 3 billion dollars for the workers in these three cities! 56 million multiplied by 52 weeks comes to $2,912,000,000. That's a hefty profit for the capitalist class and indicates that, for the bosses, crime (labor law violations) does pay.

16. Replace defined-benefit pension plans with defined-contribution plans. Market this switch to workers as "freedom to manage your own money". This is a way to cut the costs associated with paying retirement benefits to workers. Workers will no longer have a company pension but will have to rely on their own savings.

17. Incarcerate minority poor—especially young Black and Latino men. The attacks on the working class have hit the bottom forty percent of the population (the poorest sectors of the working class) especially hard. Blacks and Latinos historically have been channeled through racist practices into secondary labor markets and have been disproportionally members of the "reserve army of labor" (i.e. the unemployed). As industrial jobs declined in the cities after the 1970s and educational and social safety net benefits were drastically reduced, huge percentages of the unemployed and under-employed minority poor have been warehoused in prisons as superfluous workers. Loic Wacquant points out that at the end of World War II about 70% of the prison pop-ulation was white and 30% "other". By the end of the twentieth century the statistic had flipped so that Blacks and Latinos counted for 70% of prisoners. Their dominant char-acteristic is their position as the economically most vulnerable and expendable mem-bers of the working class: "fewer than half of inmates held a full-time job at the time of their arraignment and two-thirds issue from households with annual income amount-ing to less than *half* of the so-called poverty line." (Wacquant, in Loury, 2007: 60; empha-sis in original). About 80% of criminal defendants are indigent and thus unable to afford defense attorneys; many are high school dropouts and some are functionally illiterate.

The main effect of locking up about a million and a half minority poor is not to remove them from the labor pool temporarily but to stick them with the label "con-vict" or, worse, "felon". This label results in what can be called "civic death" since the effects minimize the ability to get a job post-prison and to participate in civic affairs. Employers are less likely to hire them, public benefits are often unavailable, and in some states they are excluded from juries and from voting—a form of politi-cal disenfranchisement. They remain economically trapped and politically excluded.

18. Harass, intimidate, and repress immigrant workers through workplace raids and deportations carried out by State authorities; reinforce this labor repression with repetition of ideologies blaming immigrants for economic problems.

The result: The end result of this class struggle is that most of the wealth created through the labor of the workers is in the hands of the capitalist class. It holds about 80-85 percent of the wealth leaving the working class with no more than 15 percent. More specifically, we can say the ruling class comprising 1% of the population holds 34.6% of the wealth. The stratum of managers, professionals, and small business owners who are the bulk of the next 19% of the population holds 50.5% of the wealth. This leaves the working class of wage and salaried workers who are the majority of the bottom 80% of the population with 15% of the wealth.

Another result of this class struggle is that between 1980 and 2007 the wages of non-supervisory production workers (who make up 80% of the workforce) have stayed flat. Workers responded by reducing their savings, taking on more debt, and relying on rising stock and housing values which have now collapsed.

A final result is that people of color and women, because they are "channeled" more into the secondary labor market with its lower wages and greater unemploy-ment, not only have lower incomes but also far less wealth than whites. Whites have about fifteen times the amount of wealth that people of color have.

We might also note that the bottom 20% of the population has zero wealth. They either have no assets or their debt exceeds their assets; they generally have no savings.

11

Testing for a Class-Dominance View of the Federal Government

G. William Domhoff

APPOINTEES TO GOVERNMENT

The first way to test a class-dominance view of the federal government is to study the social and occupational backgrounds of the people who are appointed to manage the major departments of the executive branch, such as state, treasury, defense, and justice. If pluralists are correct, these appointees should come from a wide range of interest groups. If the state autonomy theorists are correct, they should be disproportionately former elected officials or longtime government employees. If the class-dominance view is correct, they should come disproportionately from the upper class, the corporate community, and the policy-formation network.

There have been numerous studies over the years of major governmental appointees under both Republican and Democratic administrations, usually focusing on the top appointees in the departments that are represented in the president's cabinet. These studies are unanimous in their conclusion that most top appointees in both Republican and Democratic administrations are corporate executives and corporate lawyers—and hence members of the power elite. Moreover, they are often part of the policy-formation network as well, supporting the claim that the networks play a central role in preparing members of the power elite for government service.

In the most quantitative study of the factors leading to appointments, Useem showed that corporate executives from large companies who had two or more outside directorships were four times more likely to serve in a federal government advisory position than executives from smaller companies with no directorships, and that participation in at least one policy group increased the chances of an appointment for the big corporate interlockers by a factor of 1.7. In a subsequent interview study, he learned that chief executive officers often mentioned participation in a policy group as a qualification for an appointment to government.

Reflecting the different coalitions that make up the two parties, there are some differences between the second-level and third-level appointees in Republican and Democratic administrations. Republicans frequently appoint ultraconservatives to agencies that are thoroughly disliked by the appointee, such as the Environmental Protection Agency, the Occupational Safety and Health Administration, the National Highway Traffic Safety Administration, and the Office of Civil Rights. Democrats, on the other hand, often place liberals in the same agencies, creating a dramatic contrast when a Democratic administration replaces a Republican one.

To the degree that there is any disagreement with these conclusions, there are two reasons. First, the pluralists and Dye put all lawyers in a "professional" or "civic" category separate from business, even if they are corporate lawyers and sit on corporate boards. Such an approach leads Dye to say that there is relatively little corporate representation in the Clinton Administration, a claim that is refuted later in this section. Second, the pluralists and state autonomy theorists put policy experts in a "professional" category and classify them as independent of business, ignoring any corporate directorships or affiliations within the policy-formation network.

Two historical studies of cabinet appointees from the founding of the country through the Carter Administration provide relevant background information. Detailed studies of the top appointees in the Kennedy, Reagan, and Clinton Administrations provide comparisons between Democrats and Republicans that bring the information forward to 1996.

The most ambitious historical study, a three-volume work by Philip Burch that covers cabinet officers, diplomats, and Supreme Court justices from 1780 to 1980, found that (1) 96 percent of the cabinet and diplomatic appointees from 1780 to 1861 were members of the economic elite (defined as the top few percent of wealth holders), with a predominance of landowners, merchants, and lawyers; (2) from 1862 to 1933, the figure was 84 percent, with an increasing number of financiers and corporate lawyers; and (3) from 1934 to 1980, the overall percentage was 64, but with only 47 percent during the New Deal period. In a more detailed study, sociologist Beth Mintz looked at the percentage of members from the "social elite" and "business elite" for the 205 individuals who served in presidential cabinets between 1897 and 1972. She found that 60 percent were members of the upper class and 78 percent members of the corporate community. There were no differences in the overall percentages for Democrats and Republicans or for the years before and after 1933.

The way in which presidents rely on corporate leaders and experts from the policy groups in making appointments to government can be seen very dramatically in the contrasting cases of John F. Kennedy, Ronald Reagan, and Bill Clinton. After winning an election in 1960 based on promises of a "new frontier" and the image of an urbane liberalism. President-elect Kennedy called in Republican Robert Lovett, a Wall Street investment banker who was a former member of the Committee for Economic Development and the Council on Foreign Relations as well as a former secretary of defense. Kennedy wished to have Lovett's advice on possible appointments to the new administration. Lovett soon became, according to historian and Kennedy aide Arthur M. Schlesinger, Jr., the "chief agent" between Kennedy and the "American Establishment." Schlesinger defined this establishment as consisting primarily of financiers and corporate lawyers who were an "arsenal of talent which had so long furnished a steady supply of always orthodox and often able people to Democratic as well as Republican administrations." Lovett seemed to be an unusual adviser for a president-elect who had promised to "get the country moving again," but Kennedy said he needed experienced experts to run the government:

> He had spent the last five years, he said ruefully, running for office, and he did not know any real public officials, people to run a government, serious men. The only ones he knew, he admitted, were politicians, and if this seemed a denigration of his own kind, it was not altogether displeasing to the older man. Politicians did need men to serve, to run the government. The implication was obvious. Politicians could run Pennsylvania and Ohio, and if they could not run Chicago, they could at least deliver it. But could politicians run the world? What did they know about the Germans, the French, the Chinese? He needed experts for that, and now he was summoning them.

Kennedy first asked Lovett if he would be interested in serving as the secretary of state, defense, or treasury, but he gracefully declined for reasons of health. When talk then turned to possible people for these positions, Lovett named several. Among them were Dean Rusk, president of the Rockefeller Foundation and a member of the Council on Foreign Relations; Robert McNamara, president of the Ford Motor Company; and C. Douglas Dillon, head of the investment banking firm of Dillon, Read and a member of the Council on Foreign Relations. Kennedy solicited other names, and there was intense lobbying for some of the candidates, but in the end there was general consensus around Rusk for secretary of state, McNamara for secretary of defense, and Dillon for secretary of the treasury.

Many other members of the Kennedy Administration came from the policy-formation groups. In particular, they were members of the policy network who had taken part in a special set of commissions and panels sponsored by the Rockefeller

Brothers Fund in the late 1950s. These panels, whose deliberations were published as a book entitled *Prospect for America,* were designed to assess the prospects for the United States in the 1960s on such issues as foreign policy, national security, education, and the domestic economy. Among the eighty-three men who served on one or more of these panels and lived into the 1960s, twenty-six later served in the Kennedy Administration. Most were consultants or advisers, but the list also included the secretary of state, the undersecretary of state, two assistant secretaries of state, and four other State Department appointees.

Ronald Reagan came to the presidency in 1980 with a promise to do something about all the problems that allegedly were being caused by the federal government. However, as a conservative he would accomplish this feat by removing the liberal establishment figures who supposedly had caused them. Edward Meese III, who went on to serve as one of Reagan's most important White House advisers, told *Business Week* that "you will see people who have never served in Washington before and who can make a significant change in the course of government. It's like bringing a new management team to turn around a failing business."

Nonetheless, Reagan's first secretary of state was a former army officer, Alexander Haig, who had served as an aide to the secretary of defense in the 1960s and to President Nixon in the 1970s. He was president of United Technologies and a director of Chase Manhattan Bank, Crown Cork & Seal, Texas Instruments, and ConAgra, as well as being a member of the Council on Foreign Relations. Reagan's second appointment to that position, George Schultz, was president of the Bechtel Corporation, one of the largest construction firms in the world, and a director of J. P. Morgan Bank. He also was a director of the Council on Foreign Relations, a former adviser to the Committee for Economic Development, and a former secretary of both labor and the treasury in the Nixon Administration.

The secretary of defense, Caspar Weinberger, was a corporate lawyer from San Francisco who had served in three different positions in Washington between 1970 and 1975. He was a vice president and general counsel of the Bechtel Corporation, a director of Pepsico and Quaker Oats, and a member of the Trilateral Commission. As for the secretary of the treasury, Donald T. Regan, he was the chief executive officer of Merrill, Lynch, a trustee of the Committee for Economic Development, a member of the policy committee of the Business Roundtable, and a member of the Council on Foreign Relations.

The rest of the Reagan Administration also consisted of members of the corporate community who had previous government experience or visibility in the policy-formation network. To the consternation of the ultraconservatives, there were many other appointees in addition to Haig, Shultz, and Regan who were members of the Council on Foreign Relations. They included the director of the CIA, the secretary of commerce, the special trade adviser, the deputy secretary of defense, and eight top-level appointments at the State Department. According to one cataloguing of over ninety advisers, consultants, and members of the Reagan Administration in early

1981, thirty-one were members of the Council on Foreign Relations, twenty-five were associated with the American Enterprise Institute, thirteen were affiliated with the Center for Strategic and International Studies, and twelve were participants in the Trilateral Commission.

The Clinton Administration drew just as heavily from the corporate community and policy network as its predecessors. Dye stresses the legal backgrounds and governmental experience of the Clinton appointees, and the administration itself emphasized that it had a greater number of women and minorities than past administrations, but the appointees were first and foremost wealthy people with many corporate and policy network connections. Warren Christopher, the first secretary of state, was a director of Lockheed Martin, Southern California Edison, and First Interstate Bancorp, a trustee of the Carnegie Corporation, a recent vice-chair of the Council on Foreign Relations, and officially a corporate lawyer. The second secretary of state, Madeleine Albright, is from a Czechoslovakian diplomatic family, had married into wealth in the United States, and was a director of the Atlantic Council.

The first secretary of the treasury, Lloyd Bentsen, inherited millions from his rancher father and founded his own insurance company in Texas before becoming a senator and then secretary of the treasury. He was succeeded by Robert Rubin, a codirector of the Wall Street investment banking firm of Goldman, Sachs and a trustee of the Carnegie Corporation, with a net worth between $50 and $100 million and an income of $26 million in 1992. The first director of the CIA, R. James Woolsey, a corporate lawyer, was a director of Martin Marietta, a large defense contractor; the second, John Deutch, a professor and administrator at MIT, was a director of Citicorp, Perkins-Elmer, and CMS Energy.

The first secretary of agriculture, Michael Espy, is an African-American from the Mississippi Delta and a former member of Congress, but his grandfather and father were major landowners and business owners. The first secretary of commerce, Ronald Brown, also an African-American, came from a family that managed a hotel in Harlem; at the time of his appointment he was a lawyer with one of the leading corporate firms in Washington, which paid him $580,000 in 1992 even though he spent most of his time as chair of the Democratic Party. The secretary of energy, Hazel O'Leary, is both African-American and female, but she is also the daughter of two physicians and was the executive vice president of Northern States Power, a utility company in Minnesota.

The first secretary of housing and urban development, Henry Cisneros, is a Mexican-American who had been mayor of San Antonio, but at the time of his appointment he was the chair of an investment firm, the head of an air charter company, and a trustee of the Rockefeller Foundation. The least-connected major figure in the cabinet, Janet Reno, the attorney general, is the daughter of journalists in Florida and had been a state attorney in Miami.

Clinton's White House team also is tightly connected with the corporate world. His first White House chief of staff was the president of a large natural gas company in Arkansas. The legislative liaison to Congress had been the president of the Washington office of one of the biggest public relations firms in the world, Hill and Knowlton; he earned $154,943 from the firm in 1992 and another $287,377 from a Washington lobbying firm, Timmons and Co., headed by a top Republican adviser. The head of the Office of Management and Budget, a woman, sat on the boards of Union Carbide and Unisys and was a Fellow of the Brookings Institution.

The administration drew many of its key members from a small group of current or recent directors on the board of the Council on Foreign Relations. In addition to Warren Christopher, a Council director from 1982 to 1991, three other Council directors held top positions in the State Department at one point or another: Clifton Wharton, Jr., a well-to-do African-American who sat on the board of Ford Motors; Strobe Talbott, the son of an upper-class investment banker and Clinton's close friend since their years at Oxford University as Rhodes Scholars; and Peter Tarnoff, president of the council at the time of his appointment. Clinton's third secretary of defense, William S. Cohen, was a council director at the time of his appointment, as was Donna Shalala, the chancellor of the University of Wisconsin and a trustee of the Committee for Economic Development, the Brookings Institution, and the liberal Children's Defense Fund, who became secretary of health and human services. Other CFR directors who served in the Clinton Administration at one point or another were the White House special counsel, the director of the Office of Management and Budget, and the head of the Federal Reserve Board. A list of council directors and members with important positions in the two Clinton Administrations is presented in table 1.

Clinton also made liberal and nonwealthy appointments, but they tended to be in secondary positions from a power point of view. Robert Reich, a friend from their days as Rhodes Scholars together, and a liberal, was the secretary of labor in the first Clinton Administration but had little impact on major policies. The African-Americans who served as secretary of veterans affairs, Jesse Brown (1993–), as secretary of transportation, Rodney Slater (1997–), and as secretary of labor, Alexis Herman (1997–), are not from well-to-do-backgrounds or high-status universities. Ellen Haas, a consumer advocate and a longtime critic of the Department of Agriculture, was put in charge of nutrition and consumer affairs in that department. Carol Bellamy, head of the Peace Corps, is the daughter of a telephone installer and nurse, served in the Peace Corps in Guatemala in the 1960s, and worked as a waitress to put herself through law school. Such examples are few and far between in policymaking positions of concern to the power elite.

The general picture that emerges from this information is that the highest levels of the executive branch—especially in the State, Defense, and Treasury Departments—are interlocked constantly with the corporate community through the movement of executives and lawyers in and out of government. Although the same person is not in government and corporate positions at the same time, there is enough continuity for the relationship to be described as one of "revolving interlocks." Corporate leaders resign from their numerous directorships to serve in government for two or three years, then return to the corporate community. This system gives corporate officials temporary independence from the narrow concerns of their own companies and allows them to perform the more general roles they have learned in the policy-discussion groups. However, it does not give them the time or inclination to become fully independent of the corporate community or to develop a perspective that includes the interests of other classes and groups. In terms of the "Who sits?" indicator of power, then, it is clear that the power elite is the predominant voice in the top-level appointive positions in the executive branch.

TABLE 1 *Clinton Appointees Who Were Directors or Members of the Council on Foreign Relations Before Their Appointments*

Name	Dates CRF Director	Government Position
Warren Christopher	1892–1991	Secretary of State (1993–1996)
William S. Cohen	1989–1996	Secretary of Defense (1997–)
Lloyd Cutler	1977–1979	Special counsel to president (1994–1995)
Alan Greenspan	1982–1988	Chair, Federal Reserve Board (1993–)
Alice Rivlin	1989–1992	Deputy Director (1993–1994), Director (1995–1996), Office of Management and Budget
Donna Shalala	1992–1993	Secretary of health and human services (1993–)
Strobe Talbott	1988–1992	Deputy Secretary of State (1995–)
Peter Tarnoff	1986–1992	Undersecretary of state for political affairs (1995–)
Clifton Wharton, Jr.	1983–1992	Deputy Secretary of State (1993–1994)

Members

Name	Government Position
Madeleine Albright	U.S. representative to the United Nations (1993–1996); secretary of state (1997–)
Roger Altman	Deputy secretary of treasury (1993–1995)
Les Aspin	Secretary of defense (1993–1994)
Bruce Babbitt	Secretary of interior (1993–)
Reginald Bartholomew	Undersecretary of state for international security affairs (1993–1995); ambassador to Italy (1996–)
Samuel Berger	Deputy assistant to the president for national security affairs (1993–1996); assistant to the president for national security affairs (1997–)
Henry Cisneros	Secretary of housing and urban development (1993–)
Lynn Davis	Undersecretary of state for arms control and international security affairs (1994–)
John Deutch	Deputy secretary of defense (1994–1995); director, CIA (1995–1996)
Jeffrey Garten	Undersecretary of commerce for international affairs (1994–1995)
Arnold Kanter	Undersecretary of state for political affairs (1993–1996)

W. Anthony Lake	Assistant to the president for national security affairs (1993–1996)
Franklin Raines	Director, Office of Management and Budget (1997–)
Walter Slocombe	Undersecretary of defense for policy (1995–)
Joan Spero	Undersecretary of state for economic and agricultural affairs (1996–)
Lawrence Summers	Undersecretary of treasury for international affairs (1993–)
Laura Tyson	Chair, Council of Economic Advisers (1993–1996)
John P. White	Deputy secretary of defense (1995–)
Thomas S. Williamson, Jr.	Solicitor, Department of Labor (1993–)
Timothy Wirth	Undersecretary of state for global affairs (1995–)
Frank Wisner	Undersecretary of defense for policy (1993–1995); ambassador to India (1996–)
R. James Woolsey	Director, CIA (1993–1995)
Robert Zoellick	Undersecretary of state for economic and agricultural affairs (1993–1996)

12

BARACK OBAMA AS A RULING CLASS CANDIDATE

Paul Street

"This is bigger than life itself. When I was coming up, I always thought they put in who they wanted to put it. I didn't think my vote mattered. But I don't think that anymore."

The speaker of these words is Deddrick Battle, a black janitor who grew up in St. Louis's notorious Pruitt-Igoe housing projects during the 1950s and 1960s.

Battle was speaking about the presidential candidacy of Barack Obama. He was quoted on the front page of last Sunday's New York Times in a story about the pride many African Americans are naturally feeling in Obama's candidacy. The story contained numerous examples of American blacks who have been encouraged by the Obama phenomenon to think for the first time that "politics is for them, too" [1].

It is a welcome democratic development for people who previously felt disenfranchised to become engaged in the political process. And I have no doubt that expanded black turnout is going to be (I am writing on the Monday before the 2008 election) a major factor in Obama's victory, something that will remove the more viciously reactionary of the nation's two dominant business parties from executive power for at least four years.

But, as The New York Times' editors certainly know, "they" still "put in who they want to put in" to no small extent. **The predominantly white U.S. business and political establishment still makes sure that nobody who questions dominant domestic and imperial hierarchies and doctrines can make a serious ("viable") run for higher office—the presidency, above all.** It does this **by denying adequate campaign funding** (absolutely essential to success in an age of super-expensive, media-driven campaigns) and **favorable media treatment** (without which a successful campaign is unimaginable at the current stage of corporate media consolidation and power) to candidates who step beyond the narrow boundaries of elite opinion. Thanks to these **critical electoral filters** and to the legally mandated U.S. **winner-take-all "two party" system** [2], a candidate who even remotely questions corporate and imperial power is not permitted to make a strong bid for the presidency.

Barack Obama is no exception to the rule. Anyone who thinks he could have risen to power without prior and ongoing ruling class approval is living in a dream world.

AN EARLY AND "QUIETER AUDITION" WITH THE "MONEYED ESTABLISHMENT"

Conventional wisdom holds that Obama entered national politics with his instantly famous keynote address to the 2004 Democratic National Convention. But, as Ken Silverstein noted in Harper's in the fall of 2006, "If the speech was his debut to the wider American public, he had already undergone an equally successful but much quieter audition with Democratic Party leaders and fund-raisers, without whose support he would surely never have been chosen for such a prominent role at the convention.

The favorable elite assessment of Obama began in October of 2003. That's when "Vernon Jordan, the well-known power broker and corporate board-member who chaired Bill Clinton's presidential transition team after the 1992 election, placed calls to roughly twenty of his friends and invited them to a fund-raiser at his home. That event," Silverstein noted, "marked his **entry into a well-established Washington ritual—the gauntlet of fund-raising parties and meet-and-greets through which potential stars are vetted by fixers, donors, and lobbyists.**"

Drawing on his undoubted charm, wit, intelligence, and Harvard credentials, Obama passed this trial with shining colors. **At a series of social meetings with assorted big "players" from the financial, legal and lobbyist sectors, Obama impressed key establishment figures like Gregory Craig (a longtime leading attorney and former special counsel to the White House), Mike Williams (the legislative director of the Bond Market Association), Tom Quinn (a partner at the top corporate law firm Venable and a leading Democratic Party "power broker"), and Robert Harmala, another Venable partner and "a big player in Democratic circles."**

Craig liked the fact that Obama was **not a racial "polarizer"** on the model of past African-American leaders like Jesse Jackson and Al Sharpton.

Williams was soothed by Obama's reassurances that he was **not "anti-business"** and became "convinced...that the two could work together."

"There's a **reasonableness** about him," Harmala told Silverstein. "I don't see him as being on the liberal fringe."

By Silverstein's account, the good **"word about Obama spread through Washington's blue-chip law firms, lobby shops, and political offices,** and this accelerated after his win in the March [2004] Democratic primary." **Elite financial, legal, and lobbyists contributions came into Obama's coffers at a rapid and accelerating pace** [3].

The "good news" for Washington and Wall Street insiders was that Obama's "star quality" would not be directed against the elite segments of the business class. The interesting black legislator from the South Side of Chicago was "someone the rich and powerful could work with." According to Obama biographer and Chicago Tribune reporter David Mendell, in late 2003 and early 2004:

> **Word of Obama's rising star was now spreading beyond Illinois, especially through influential Washington political circles like blue chip law firms, party insiders, lobbying houses.** They were all hearing about this rare, exciting, charismatic, up-and-coming African American who unbelievably could win votes across color lines . . . [his handlers and] influential Chicago supporters and fund-raisers all vigorously worked their D.C. contacts to help Obama make the rounds with the Democrats' set of power brokers. . . . Obama . . . spent a couple of days and nights shaking hands making small talk and delivering speeches to liberal groups, national union leaders, lobbyists, fund-raisers and well-heeled money donors. In setting after setting, Obama's Harvard Law resume and his reasonable tone impressed the elite crowd

According to Mendell, **Obama now cultivated the support of the privileged few by "advocate[ing] fiscal restraint" and "calling for pay-as-you-go government" and "extol[ing] the merits of free trade and charter schools."** He "moved beyond being an obscure good-government reformer to being a candidate more than palatable to the moneyed and political establishment." [4].

"Reasonable tone" was code language with a useful translation for Obama's new business-class backers: **"friendly to capitalism and its opulent masters."**

"On condition of anonymity," Silverstesin reported two years ago, "one Washington lobbyist I spoke with was willing to point out the obvious: that big donors would not be helping out Obama if they didn't see him as a 'player.' The lobbyist added: 'What's the dollar value of a starry-eyed idealist?'"

OBAMA'S "DOLLAR VALUE"

Since his election to the U.S. Senate and through the presidential campaign, the "deeply conservative" (according to New Yorker writer Larissa MacFarquhar) **Obama has done nothing to undermine his "palatability" to concentrated economic and political power. He has made his safety to the power elite evident on matters both domestic and global, from his support for bailing out parasitic Wall Street financial firms with hundreds of billions of taxpayer dollars (while claiming to be "a free market guy" and proclaiming "love" for "capitalism") to his** refusal to question the morality of U.S. colonial wars and his strident support for maintaining a globally unmatched "defense" (empire) budget that accounts for nearly half the world's military spending. As Edward S. Herman and David Peterson note in an important recent article, "in 2007-08, Obama has placated establishment circles on virtually every front imaginable, the candidate of 'change we can believe in' has visited interest group after interest group to promise them that they needn't fear any change in the way they're familiar with doing business" [5].

It's all very consistent with Obama's history stretching back to his days as the Republican-pleasing editor of the Harvard Law Review and his climb up the corporate-friendly politics of Chicago. As Ryan Lizza noted in The New Yorker last July, **"Perhaps the greatest misconception about Barack Obama is that he is some sort of anti-establishment revolutionary. Rather, every stage of his political career has been marked by an eagerness to accommodate himself to existing institutions rather than tear them down or replace them"** [6].

Obama's business-friendly centrism has helped him garner an astonishing, record-setting stash of corporate cash. He has received more than $33 million from "FIRE," the finance-real-estate and insurance sector. His winnings include $824,202 from the leading global investment firm Goldman Sachs [7]. He has been consistently backed by the biggest and most powerful Wall Street firms.

At the same time and by more than mere coincidence, Obama has enjoyed a remarkable windfall of **favorable corporate media coverage. That media treatment is the key to Obama's success in winning support and donations from the middle-class and from non-affluent people** like Deddrick Battle.

This does not mean that the Obama phenomenon has raised no concerns among the rich and powerful. As Herman and Peterson note, "Obama's race, his background, his enthusiastic, and less predictable constituency, and the occasional slivers of populism that creep into his campaign, make the establishment nervous, whereas Hillary Clinton and John McCain clearly posed no such threat."

Still, the monied elite's most reactionary wing has used its formidable media and propaganda system to keep the Obama "movement" safely within conservative boundaries. It has employed a series of neo-McCarthyite anti-radical and related racial scare tactics including the Jeremiah Wright Affair and subsequent public relations campaigns surrounding alleged Obama links to "terrorist" charter-school advocate William Ayers and "radical professor" Rashid Khalidi. It has sought to link the openly capitalist Obama to the "anti-American" threat of "socialism," alleging that that the harbors a nefarious desire to "redistribute" wealth.

"HOLDING DOMESTIC CONSTITUENCIES IN CHECK"

At the same time, **many in the establishment sense (accurately) that Obama is particularly well-suited to the goal of wrapping corporate politics and the related American Empire Project in insurgent garb. Their profit- and empire-based system** and "leadership" has been behaving so badly that a major image makeover is required to keep the rabble (the citizenry) in line. Once he was properly "vetted" and found to be "reasonable"—to be someone who would not fundamentally question dominant power structures and doctrines—Obama's multicultural background, race, youth, charisma, and even his early opposition to the Iraq War became useful to corporate and imperial elites. His outwardly progressive "change" persona is perfectly calibrated to divert, capture, control, and contain coming popular rebellions. He is uniquely qualified to simultaneously surf, de-fang, and "manage" the U.S. and world citizenry's hopes for radical and democratic transformation in the wake of the Bush-Cheney nightmare. As John Pilger warned last May

> "What is Obama's attraction to big business? Precisely the same as Robert Kennedy's [in 1968]. By offering a 'new,' young and apparently progressive face of Democratic Party—with the bonus of being a member of the black elite—he can blunt and divert real opposition. That was Colin Powell's role as Bush's secretary of state. **An Obama victory will bring intense pressure on the US antiwar and social justice movements to accept a Democratic administration for all its faults. If that happens, domestic resistance to rapacious America will fall silent**" [8].

Obama's race is no small part of what makes him "uniquely qualified" to perform the key tasks of mass pacification for which he has been hired task in question. As Aurora Levins Morales noted in a Z Magazine essay written for left progressives last April:

> "We're far more potent as organizers and catalysts than as voters. Our ability to create a world we can thrive on does not depend on who wins this election, it depends on our ability to dismantle profit-based societies in which greed trumps ethics. **This election is about finding a CEO capable of holding domestic constituencies in check as they are furthered disenfranchised and... [about]mak[ing] them feel that they have a stake in the military aggressiveness that the ruling class believes is necessary.** Having a black man and a white woman run helps to obscure the fact that ...decline of empire is driving the political elite to the right. Both [Obama and Hillary Clinton] represent very reactionary politics...**Part of the cleverness of having such candidates is the fact that they will be attacked in ways that make oppressed people feel compelled to protect them**" [9].

IMPERIAL "REBRANDING"

The logic works at the global as well as the domestic level. A considerable segment of the U.S. foreign policy establishment thinks that Obama's race, name (technically Islamic), experience living (Muslim Indonesia, as a child) in and visiting (chiefly his father's homeland Kenya) poor nations and his nominally anti-Iraq War history will help them repackage the U.S. imperial project (replete with more than 730 military bases located in nearly every nation on Earth) in softer and more politically correct cover [10]. John Kerry, who ran for the presidency four years earlier largely on the claim that he would be a more effective manager of empire (and the Iraq War) than George W. Bush [11], was certainly thinking of these critical imperial "soft power" assets when he praised Obama as someone who could "reinvent America's image abroad" [11A]. So was Obama himself when he said the following to reporters aboard his campaign plane in the fall of 2007:

> "If I am the face of American foreign policy and American power, as long as we are making prudent strategic decisions, handling emergences, crises, and opportunities in the world in an intelligent and sober way. . . . I think that if you can tell people, 'We have a president in the White House who still has a grandmother living in a hut on the shores of Lake Victoria and has a sister who's half-Indonesian, married to a Chinese-Canadian,' then they're going to think that he may have a better sense of what's going on in our lives and country. And they'd be right" [12].

What Obama didn't tell reporters was that his idea of "prudent" and "intelligent" foreign policy is strongly committed to U.S. global hyper-militarism and world supremacy, including unilateral action whenever "we" deem it necessary to "protect the American people and their vital interests" [13].

Obama's distinctive biography is one of his great attractions to the mostly white U.S. foreign policy elite in a majority non-white world that has been deeply provoked and disgusted by U.S. behavior in the post-9/11 era (and truthfully before). He is a perfect symbol of deceptive imperial "re-branding." According to the unconsciously power-worshipping and imperialist New York Times columnist Nicholas Kristof two weeks ago, **the election of a black president "could change global perceptions of the United States, redefining the American 'brand' to be less about Guantanamo and more about equality"[14].** Never mind that the U.S. remains the most unequal and wealth-top-heavy country in the industrialized world by far, strongly dedicated to maintaining steep socioeconomic and disparity within and between nations and scarred by a domestic racial wealth gap of seven black cents on the white dollar.

Call it "the identity politics of foreign policy." The Empire wants new clothes and Obama is just the man to wear them.

Such is the dark authoritarian reality lurking behind the pride and excitement felt by Deddrick Battle and many other poor and black voters who have been inspired by the Obama phenomenon to think that "politics is for them too." President Obama can be counted on to use their new faith in reactionary and imperial ways reflecting hidden allegiance to the timeworn elite principle that really big matters of politics and policy are for the rich and powerful—not ordinary citizens—at the end of the day Obama's job is to keep the restless poor, working class, and global

Many safely pacified while serving the needs of the wealthy and imperial Few. It's a deadly juggling act that could have terrible consequences. **How long he can maintain the illusion of serving the interests of the people and the elite at one and the same time is an open question.**

The sooner seriously left agitators and activists can expose the corporate-imperial truth behind the progressive façade to disenfranchised people at home and abroad, the quicker we can get to real social and democratic change beyond the ruling class's latest quadrennial candidate-centered electoral extravaganza.

Paul Street's books include Empire and Inequality: America and the World Since 9/11 (Boulder, CO: Paradigm, 2004); Racial Oppression in the Global Metropolis (New York, 2007), and most recently Barack Obama and the Future of American Politics (Boulder, CO: Paradigm, September 2008). Paul can be reached at paulstreet99@yahoo.com.

NOTES

1. Susan Saulny, "Obama-Inspired Black Voters Find Politics is For Them Too," New York Times, November 2, 2008, sec.1, p. 1.
2. In deciding against "fusion" electoral options (which would allow a voter to select Obama [or McCain] in the name of the Green Party or any other non-mainstream party). The U.S. Supreme Court has ruled that the nation has an interest in restricting the number of viable political parties to just two.
3. Ken Silverstein, "Barack Obama, Inc.: The Birth of a Washington Machine," Harper's (November 2006).
4. David Mendell, Obama: From Promise to Power (New York: HarperCollins, 2007), pp. 248-49.
5. E.S. Herman and D. Peterson, "Jeremiah Wright in the Propaganda System," Monthly Review, September 2008, pp. 3-4; Paul Street, Barack Obama and the Future of American Politics (Boulder, CO: Paradigm, 2008). For Obama as "deeply conservative," see Larissa MacFarquhar, "The Conciliator: Where is Barack Obama Coming From?" The New Yorker (May 7, 2007). According to MacFarquhar, "In his view of history, in his respect for tradition, in his skepticism that the world can be changed any way but very, very slowly, Obama is deeply conservative."
6. Ryan Lizza, "Making It: How Chicago Shaped Obama," The New Yorker, (July 21, 2008).
7. Center for Responsive Politics, "Open Secrets," Barack Obama's Campaign Finance Profile, read at www.opensecetrs.org (accessed on November 2, 2008).
8. John Pilger, "After Bobby Kennedy There Was Barack Obama," Common Dreams, May 31, 2008, read at www.commondreams.org/archive/2008/05/31/9327/.
9. Aurora Levins Morales, "Thinking Outside the Ballot Box," Z Magazine (April 2008).

10. James Traub 2007. "Is (His) Biography (Our) Destiny?" New York Times Magazine (November 4, 2007). See also Liza Mundy, "A Series of Fortunate Events: Barack Obama Needed More Than Talent and Ambition to Rocket From Obscure State Senator to Presidential Contender in Three Years," Washington Post Magazine (August 12, 2007).

11. See Paul Street, "Bush, Kerry, and 'Body Language' v. 'Message': Notes on Race, Gender, Empire and Mass Infantilization," ZNet Magazine (October 12, 2004).

11A. John F. Kerry, "Truly Transformative," Newsweek (April 28, 2008): 34.

12. Quoted in Traub, "Is (His) Biography (Our) Destiny?"

13. For truly ugly details, please see the fourth chapter—titled "How 'Antiwar?' Obama, Iraq, and the Audacity of Empire"—in my book Barack Obama and the Future of American Politics.

14. Nicholas Kristof, "Rebranding the U.S. With Obama," The New York Times, October 23, 2008, p. A27.

13

A PROPAGANDA MODEL

Edward Herman & Noam Chomsky

The mass media serve as a system for communicating messages and symbols to the general populace. It is their function to amuse, entertain, and inform, and to inculcate individuals with the values, beliefs, and codes of behavior that will integrate them into the institutional structures of the larger society. In a world of concentrated wealth and major conflicts of class interest, to fulfil this role requires systematic propaganda.

In countries where the levers of power are in the hands of a state bureaucracy, the monopolistic control over the media, often supplemented by official censorship, makes it clear that the media serve the ends of a dominant elite. It is much more difficult to see a propaganda system at work where the media are private and formal censorship is absent. This is especially true where the media actively compete, periodically attack and expose corporate and governmental malfeasance, and aggressively portray themselves as spokesmen for free speech and the general community interest. What is not evident (and remains undiscussed in the media) is the limited nature of such critiques, as well as the huge inequality in command of resources, and its effect both on access to a private media system and on its behavior and performance.

A propaganda model focuses on this inequality of wealth and power and its multilevel effects on mass-media interests and choices. It traces the routes by which money and power are able to filter out the news fit to print, marginalize dissent, and allow the government and dominant private interests to get their messages across to the public. The essential ingredients of our propaganda model, or set of news "filters," fall under the following headings: (1) the size, concentrated ownership, owner wealth, and profit orientation of the dominant mass-media firms; (2) advertising as the primary income source of the mass media; (3) the reliance of the media on information provided by government, business, and "experts" funded and approved by these primary sources and agents of power; (4) "flak" as a means of disciplining the media; and (5) "anticommunism" as a national religion and control mechanism. These elements interact with and reinforce one another. The raw material of news must pass through successive filters, leaving only the cleansed residue fit to print. They fix the premises of discourse and interpretation, and the definition of what is newsworthy in the first place, and they explain the basis and operations of what amount to propaganda campaigns.

The elite domination of the media and marginalization of dissidents that results from the operation of these filters occurs so naturally that media news people, frequently operating with complete integrity and goodwill, are able to convince themselves that they choose and interpret the news "objectively" and on the basis of professional news values. Within the limits of the filter constraints they often are objective; the constraints are so powerful, and are built into the system in such a fundamental way, that alternative bases of news choices are hardly imaginable. In assessing the newsworthiness of the U.S. government's urgent claims of a shipment of MIGs to Nicaragua on November 5, 1984, the media do not stop to ponder the bias that is inherent in the priority assigned to government-supplied raw material, or the possibility that the government might be manipulating the news, imposing its own agenda, and deliberately diverting attention from other material. It requires a macro, alongside a micro- (story-by-story), view of media operations, to see the pattern of manipulation and systematic bias.

Let us turn now to a more detailed examination of the main constituents of the propaganda model, which will be applied and tested in the sections that follow.

SIZE, OWNERSHIP, AND PROFIT ORIENTATION OF THE MASS MEDIA: THE FIRST FILTER

In their analysis of the evolution of the media in Great Britain, James Curran and Jean Seaton describe how, in the first half of the nineteenth century, a radical press emerged that reached a national working-class audience. This alternative press was effective in reinforcing class consciousness: it unified the workers because it fostered an alternative value system and framework for looking at the world, and because it "promoted a greater collective confidence by repeatedly emphasizing the potential power of working people to effect social change through the force of 'combination' and organized action." This was deemed a major threat by the ruling elites. One MP asserted that the working-class newspapers "inflame passions and awaken their selfishness, contrasting their current condition with what they contend to be their future condition—a condition incompatible with human nature, and those immutable laws which Providence has established for the regulation of civil society." The result was an attempt to squelch the working-class media by libel laws and prosecutions, by requiring an expensive security bond as a condition for publication, and by imposing various taxes designed to drive out radical media by raising their costs. These coercive efforts were not effective, and by mid-century they had been abandoned in favor of the liberal view that the market would enforce responsibility.

Curran and Seaton show that the market *did* successfully accomplish what state intervention failed to do. Following the repeal of the punitive taxes on newspapers between 1853 and 1869, a new daily local press came into existence, but not one new local working-class daily was established through the rest of the nineteenth century. Curran and Seaton note that

> Indeed, the eclipse of the national radical press was so total that when the Labour Party developed out of the working-class movement in the first decade of the twentieth century, it did not obtain the exclusive backing of a single national daily or Sunday paper.

One important reason for this was the rise in scale of newspaper enterprise and the associated increase in capital costs from the mid-nineteenth century onward, which was based on technological improvements along with the owners' increased stress on reaching large audiences. The expansion of the free market was accompanied by an "industrialization of the press." The total cost of establishing a national weekly on a profitable basis in 1837 was under a thousand pounds, with a break-even circulation of 6,200 copies. By 1867, the estimated start-up cost of a new London daily was 50,000 pounds. The *Sunday Express,* launched in 1918, spent over two million pounds before it broke even with a circulation of over 250,000.

Similar processes were at work in the United States, where the start-up cost of a new paper in New York City in 1851 was $69,000; the public sale of the *St. Louis Democrat* in 1872 yielded $456,000; and city newspapers were selling at from $6 to $18 million in the 1920s. The cost of machinery alone, of even very small newspapers, has for many decades run into the hundreds of thousands of dollars; in 1945 it could be said that "Even small-newspaper publishing is big business . . . [and] is no longer a trade one takes up lightly even if he has substantial cash—or takes up at all if he doesn't."

Thus the first filter—the limitation on ownership of media with any substantial outreach by the requisite large size of investment—was applicable a century or more ago, and it has become increasingly effective over time. In 1986 there were some 1,500 daily newspapers, 11,000 magazines, 9,000 radio and 1,500 TV stations, 2,400 book publishers, and seven movie studios in the United States—over 25,000 media entities in all. But a large proportion of those among this set who were news dispensers were very small and local, dependent on the large national companies and wire services for all but local news. Many more were subject to common ownership, sometimes extending through virtually the entire set of media variants.

Ben Bagdikian stresses the fact that despite the large media numbers, the twenty-nine largest media systems account for over half of the output of newspapers, and most of the sales and audiences in magazines, broadcasting, books, and movies. He contends that these "constitute a new Private Ministry of Information and Culture" that can set the national agenda.

Actually, while suggesting a media autonomy from corporate and government power that we believe to be incompatible with structural facts (as we describe below), Bagdikian also may be understating the degree of effective concentration in news manufacture. It has long been noted that the media are tiered, with the top tier—as measured by prestige, resources, and outreach—comprising somewhere between ten and twenty-four systems. It is this top tier, along with the government and wire services, that defines the news agenda and supplies much of the national and international news to the lower tiers of the media, and thus for the general public. Centralization within the top tier was substantially increased by the post-World War II rise of television and the national networking of this important medium. Pre-television news markets were local, even if heavily dependent on the higher tiers and a narrow set of sources for national and international news; the networks provide national and international news from three national sources, and television is now the principal source of news for the public. The maturing of cable, however, has resulted in a fragmentation of television audiences and a slow erosion of the market share and power of the networks.

Table I provides some basic financial data for the twenty-four media giants (or their controlling parent companies) that make up the top tier of media companies in the United States. This compilation includes: (1) the three television networks: ABC (through its parent, Capital Cities), CBS, and NBC (through its ultimate parent, General Electric [GE]); (2) the leading newspaper empires: *New York Times, Washington Post, Los Angeles Times* (Times-Mirror), *Wall Street Journal* (Dow Jones), Knight-Ridder, Gannett, Hearst, Scripps-Howard, Newhouse (Advance Publications), and the Tribune Company; (3) the major news and general-interest magazines: *Time, Newsweek* (subsumed under *Washington Post*), *Reader's Digest, TV Guide* (Triangle), and *U.S. News & World Report*; (4) a major book publisher (McGraw-Hill); and (5) other cable-TV systems of large and growing importance: those of Murdoch, Turner, Cox, General Corp., Taft, Storer, and Group W (Westinghouse). Many of these systems are prominent in more than one field and are only arbitrarily placed in a particular category (Time, Inc., is very important in cable as well as magazines; McGraw-Hill is a major publisher of magazines; the Tribune Company has become a large force in television as well as newspapers; Hearst is important in magazines as well as newspapers; and Murdoch has significant newspaper interests as well as television and movie holdings).

These twenty-four companies are large, profit-seeking corporations, owned and controlled by quite wealthy people. It can be seen in table I that all but one of the top companies for whom data are available have assets in excess of $1 billion, and the median size (middle item by size) is $2.6 billion. It can also be seen in the table that approximately three-quarters of these media giants had after-tax profits in excess of $100 million, with the median at $183 million.

TABLE I *Financial data for twenty-four large media corporations (or their parent firms), December 1986*

Company	Total Assets ($ Millions)	Profits Before Taxes ($ Millions)	Profits After Taxes ($ Millions)	Total Revenue ($ Millions)
Advance Publications (Newhouse)[1]	2,500	NA	NA	2,200
Capital Cities/ABC	5,191	688	448	4,124
CBS	3,370	470	370	4,754
Cox Communications[2]	1,111	170	87	743
Dow Jones & Co.	1,236	331	183	1,135
Gannett	3,365	540	276	2,801
General Electric (NBC)	34,591	3,689	2,492	36,725
Hearst[3]	4,040	NA	215	2,100
Knight-Ridder	1,947	267	140	1,911
McGraw-Hill	1,463	296	154	1,577
News Corp (Murdoch)[4]	8,460	377	170	3,822
New York Times	1,405	256	132	1,565
Reader's Digest[5]	NA	75–110 (1985)	NA	1,400 (1985)
Scripps-Howard[6]	NA	NA	NA	1,062
Storer[7]	1,242	68	(-17)	537
Taft	1,257	(-11)	(-53)	500
Time, Inc.	4,230	626	376	3,762
Times-Mirror	2,929	680	408	2,948
Triangle[8]	NA	NA	NA	730
Tribune Co.	2,589	523	293	2,030
Turner Broadcasting	1,904	(-185)	(-187)	570
U.S. News & World Report[9]	200+	NA	NA	140
Washington Post	1,145	205	100	1,215
Westinghouse	8,482	801	670	10,731

NA = not available

1. The asset total is taken from *Forbes* magazine's wealth total for the Newhouse family for 1985; the total revenue is for media sales only, as reported in *Advertising Age,* June 29, 1987.
2. Cox Communications was publicly owned until 1985, when it was merged into another Cox family company, Cox Enterprises. The data presented here are for year-end 1984, the last year of public ownership and disclosure of substantial financial information.
3. Data compiled in William Bairett, "Citizens Rich," *Forbes,* Dec. 14, 1987.
4. These data are in Australian dollars and are for June 30, 1986; at that date the Australian dollar was worth $^{68}/_{100}$ of a U.S. dollar.
5. Data for 1985, as presented in the *New York Times,* Feb. 9, 1986.
6. Total revenue for media sales only, as reported in *Advertising Age,* June 29, 1987.
7. Storer came under the control of the Wall Street firm Kohlberg Kravis Roberts & Co. in 1985; the data here are for December 1984, the last period of Storer autonomy and publicly available information.
8. Total revenue for media sales only; from *Advertising Age,* June 29, 1987.
9. Total assets as of 1984–85, based on "Mort Zuckerman, Media's New Mogul," *Fortune,* Oct. 14, 1985; total revenue from *Advertising Age,* June 29, 1987.

Many of the large media companies are fully integrated into the market, and for the others, too, the pressures of stockholders, directors, and bankers to focus on the bottom line are powerful. These pressures have intensified in recent years as media stocks have become market favorites, and actual or prospective owners of newspapers and television properties have found it possible to capitalize increased audience size and advertising revenues into multiplied values of the media franchises—and great wealth. This has encouraged the entry of speculators and increased the pressure and temptation to focus more intensively on profitability. Family owners have been increasingly divided between those wanting to take advantage of the new opportunities and those desiring a continuation of family control, and their splits have often precipitated crises leading finally to the sale of the family interest.

This trend toward greater integration of the media into the market system has been accelerated by the loosening of rules limiting media concentration, cross-ownership, and control by non-media companies. There has also been an abandonment of restrictions—previously quite feeble anyway—on radio-TV commercials, entertainment-mayhem programming, and "fairness doctrine" threats, opening the door to the unrestrained commercial use of the airwaves.

The greater profitability of the media in a deregulated environment has also led to an increase in takeovers and takeover threats, with even giants like CBS and Time, Inc., directly attacked or threatened. This has forced the managements of the media giants to incur greater debt and to focus ever more aggressively and unequivocally on profitability, in order to placate owners and reduce the attractiveness of their properties to outsiders. They have lost some of their limited autonomy to bankers, institutional investors, and large individual investors whom they have had to solicit as potential "white knights."

While the stock of the great majority of large media firms is traded in the securities markets, approximately two-thirds of these companies are either closely held or still controlled by members of the originating family who retain large blocks of stock. This situation is changing as family ownership becomes diffused among larger numbers of heirs and the market opportunities for selling media properties continue to improve, but the persistence of family control is evident in the data shown in table II. Also evident in the table is the enormous wealth possessed by the controlling families of the top media firms.

For seven of the twenty-four, the market value of the media properties owned by the controlling families in the mid-1980s exceeded a billion dollars, and the median value was close to half a billion dollars. These control groups obviously have a special stake in the status quo by virtue of their wealth and their strategic position in one of the great institutions of society. And they exercise the power of this strategic position, if only by establishing the general aims of the company and choosing its top management.

The control groups of the media giants are also brought into close relationships with the mainstream of the corporate community through boards of directors and social links. In the cases of NBC and the Group W television and cable systems, their

TABLE II *Wealth of the control groups of twenty-four large media corporations (or their parent companies), February 1986*

Company	Controlling Family or Group	% of Voting Stock Held by Control Group	Value of Controlling Stock Interest ($ Millions)
Advance Publications	Newhouse family	Closely held	2,200[F]
Capital Cities	Officers and directors (ODS)	20.7 (Warren Buffett, 17.8)	711[P]
CBS	ODs	20.6[1]	551[P]
Cox Communications	Cox family	36	1,900[F]
Dow Jones & Co.	Bancroft-Cox families	54	1,500[P]
Gannett	ODs	1.9	95[P]
General Electric	ODs	Under 1	171[P]
Hearst	Hearst family	33	1,500[F]
Knight-Ridder	Knight and Ridder families	18	447[P]
McGraw-Hill	McGraw family	c.20	450[F]
News Corp.	Murdoch family	49	300[F]
New York Times	Sulzberger family	80	450[F]
Reader's Digest	Wallace estate managed by trustees; no personal beneficiaries	NA	NA
Scripps-Howard	Scripps heirs	NA	1,400[F]
Storer	ODs	8.4	143[P]
Taft	ODs	4.8	37[P]
Time, Inc.	ODs	10.7 (Luce 4.6, Temple 3.2)	406[P]
Times-Mirror	Chandlers	35	1,200[P]
Triangle	Annenbergs	Closely held	1,600[F]
Tribune Co.	McCormick heirs	16.6	273[P]
Turner Broadcasting	Turner	80	222[P]
U.S. News & World Report	Zuckerman	Closely held	176[2]
Washington Post	Graham family	50+	350[F]
Westinghouse	ODs	Under 1	42[P]

Sources: P means taken from proxy statements and computed from stock values as of February 1986; F means taken from *Forbes* magazine's annual estimate of wealth holdings of the very rich.

1. These holdings include William Paley's 8.1 percent and a 12.2 percent holding of Laurence Tisch through an investment by Loews. Later in the year, Loews increased its investment to 24.9 percent, and Laurence Tisch soon thereafter became acting chief executive officer.
2. This is the price paid by Zuckerman when he bought *U.S. News* in 1984. See Gwen Kinkead, "Mort Zuckerman, Media's New Mogul," *Fortune*, Oct. 14, 1985, p. 196.

respective parents, GE and Westinghouse, are themselves mainstream corporate giants, with boards of directors that are dominated by corporate and banking executives. Many of the other large media firms have boards made up predominantly of insiders, a general characteristic of relatively small and owner-dominated companies. The larger the firm and the more widely distributed the stock, the larger the number and proportion of outside directors. The composition of the outside directors of the media giants is very similar to that of large non-media corporations. Table III shows that active corporate executives and bankers together account for a little over half the total of the outside directors of ten media giants; and the lawyers and corporate-banker retirees (who account for nine of the thirteen under "Retired") push the corporate total to about two-thirds of the outside-director aggregate. These 95 outside directors had directorships in an additional 36 banks and 255 other companies (aside from the media company and their own firm of primary affiliation).

TABLE III *Affiliations of the outside directors of ten large media companies (or their parents) in 1986**

Primary Affiliation	Number	Percent
Corporate executive	39	41.1
Lawyer	8	8.4
Retired (former corporate executive or banker)	13 (9)	13.7 (9.5)
Banker	8	8.4
Consultant	4	4.2
Nonprofit organization	15	15.8
Other	8	8.4
Total	95	100.0
OTHER RELATIONSHIPS		
Other directorships (bank directorships)	255 (36)	
Former government officials	15	
Member of Council on Foreign Relations	20	

* Dow Jones & Co.; Washington Post; New York Times; Time, Inc.; CBS; Times-Mirror; Capital Cities; General Electric; Gannett; and Knight-Ridder.

In addition to these board linkages, the large media companies all do business with commercial and investment bankers, obtaining lines of credit and loans, and receiving advice and service in selling stock and bond issues and in dealing with acquisition opportunities and takeover threats. Banks and other institutional investors are also large owners of media stock. In the early 1980s, such institutions held 44 percent of the stock of publicly owned newspapers and 35 percent of the stock of publicly owned broadcasting companies. These investors are also frequently among the largest stockholders of individual companies. For example, in 1980–81, the Capital Group, an investment company system, held 7.1 percent of the stock of ABC, 6.6 percent of Knight-Ridder, 6 percent of Time, Inc., and 2.8 percent of Westinghouse. These holdings, individually and collectively, do not convey control, but these large investors can make themselves heard, and their actions can affect the welfare of the companies and their managers. If the managers fail to pursue actions that favor shareholder returns, institutional investors will be inclined to sell the stock (depressing its price), or to listen sympathetically to outsiders contemplating takeovers. These investors are a force helping press media companies toward strictly market (profitability) objectives.

So is the diversification and geographic spread of the great media companies. Many of them have diversified out of particular media fields into others that seemed like growth areas. Many older newspaper-based media companies, fearful of the power of television and its effects on advertising revenue, moved as rapidly as they could into broadcasting and cable TV. Time, Inc., also, made a major diversification move into cable TV, which now accounts for more than half its profits. Only a small minority of the twenty-four largest media giants remain in a single media sector.

The large media companies have also diversified beyond the media field, and non-media companies have established a strong presence in the mass media. The most important cases of the latter are GE, owning RCA, which owns the NBC network, and Westinghouse, which owns major television-broadcasting stations, a cable network, and a radio-station network. GE and Westinghouse are both huge, diversified multinational companies heavily involved in the controversial areas of weapons production and nuclear power. It may be recalled that from 1965 to 1967, an attempt by International Telephone and Telegraph (ITT) to acquire ABC was frustrated following a huge outcry that focused on the dangers of allowing a great multinational corporation with extensive foreign investments and business activities to control a major media outlet. The fear was that ITT control "could compromise the independence of ABC's news coverage of political events in countries where ITT has interests." The soundness of the decision disallowing the acquisition seemed to have been vindicated by the later revelations of ITT's political bribery and involvement in attempts to overthrow the government of Chile. RCA and Westinghouse, however, had been permitted to control media companies long before the ITT case, although some of the objections applicable to ITT would seem to apply to them as well. GE is a more powerful company than ITT, with an extensive international reach, deeply involved in the nuclear power business, and far more important than ITT in the arms industry. It is a highly centralized and quite secretive organization, but one with a vast stake in "political" decisions. GE has contributed to the funding of the American Enterprise Institute, a right-wing think tank that supports intellectuals who will get the business message across. With the acquisition of ABC, GE should be in a far better position to assure that sound views are given proper attention. The lack of outcry over its takeover of RCA and NBC resulted in part from the fact that RCA control over NBC had already breached the gate of separateness, but it also reflected the more pro-business and *laissez-faire* environment of the Reagan era.

The non-media interests of most of the media giants are not large, and, excluding the GE and Westinghouse systems, they account for only a small fraction of their total revenue. Their multinational outreach, however, is more significant. The television networks, television syndicators, major news magazines, and motion-picture studios all do extensive business abroad, and they derive a substantial fraction of their revenues from foreign sales and the operation of foreign affiliates. *Reader's Digest* is printed in seventeen languages and is available in over 160 countries. The Murdoch empire was originally based in Australia, and the controlling parent company is still an Australian corporation; its expansion in the United States is funded by profits from Australian and British affiliates.

Another structural relationship of importance is the media companies' dependence on and ties with government. The radio-TV companies and networks all require government licenses and franchises and are thus potentially subject to government control or harassment. This technical legal dependency has been used as a club to discipline the media, and media policies that stray too often from an establishment orientation could activate this threat. The media protect themselves from this contingency by lobbying and other political expenditures, the cultivation of political relationships, and care in policy. The political ties of the media have been impressive. Table III shows that fifteen of ninety-five outside directors of ten of the media giants are former government officials, and Peter Dreier gives a similar proportion in his study of large newspapers. In television, the revolving-door flow of personnel between regulators and the regulated firms was massive during the years when the oligopolistic structure of the media and networks was being established.

The great media also depend on the government for more general policy support. All business firms are interested in business taxes, interest rates, labor policies, and enforcement and nonenforcement of the antitrust laws. GE and Westinghouse depend on the government to subsidize their nuclear power and military research and development, and to create a favorable climate for their overseas sales. The *Reader's Digest, Time, Newsweek,* and movie- and television-syndication sellers also depend on diplomatic support for their rights to penetrate foreign cultures with U.S. commercial and value messages and interpretations of current affairs. The media giants, advertising agencies, and great multinational corporations have a joint and close interest in a favorable climate of investment in the Third World, and their interconnections and relationships with the government in these policies are symbiotic.

In sum, the dominant media firms are quite large businesses; they are controlled by very wealthy people or by managers who are subject to sharp constraints by owners and other market-profit-oriented forces; and they are closely interlocked, and have important common interests, with other major corporations, banks, and government. This is the first powerful filter that will affect news choices.

THE ADVERTISING LICENSE TO DO BUSINESS: THE SECOND FILTER

In arguing for the benefits of the free market as a means of controlling dissident opinion in the mid-nineteenth century, the Liberal chancellor of the British exchequer, Sir George Lewis, noted that the market would promote those papers "enjoying the preference of the advertising public." Advertising did, in fact, serve as a powerful mechanism weakening the working-class press. Curran and Seaton give the growth of advertising a status comparable with the increase in capital costs as a factor allowing the market to accomplish what state taxes and harassment failed to do, noting that these "advertisers thus acquired a de facto licensing authority since, without their support, newspapers ceased to be economically viable."

Before advertising became prominent, the price of a newspaper had to cover the costs of doing business. With the growth of advertising, papers that attracted ads could afford a copy price well below production costs. This put papers lacking in advertising at a serious disadvantage: their prices would tend to be higher, curtailing sales, and they would have less surplus to invest in improving the salability of the paper (features, attractive format, promotion, etc.). For this reason, an advertising-based system will tend to drive out of existence or into marginality the media companies and types that depend on revenue from sales alone. With advertising, the free market does not yield a neutral system in which final buyer choice decides. The *advertisers'* choices influence media prosperity and survival. The ad-based media receive an advertising subsidy that gives them a price-marketing-quality edge, which allows them to encroach on and further weaken their ad-free (or ad-disadvantaged) rivals. Even if ad-based media cater to an affluent ("upscale") audience, they easily pick up a large part of the "downscale" audience, and their rivals lose market share and are eventually driven out or marginalized.

In fact, advertising has played a potent role in increasing concentration even among rivals that focus with equal energy on seeking advertising revenue. A market share and advertising edge on the part of one paper or television station will give it additional revenue to compete more effectively—promote more aggressively, buy more salable features and programs—and the disadvantaged rival must add expenses it cannot afford to try to stem the cumulative process of dwindling market (and revenue) share. The crunch is often fatal, and it helps explain the death of many large-circulation papers and magazines and the attrition in the number of newspapers.

From the time of the introduction of press advertising, therefore, working-class and radical papers have been at a serious disadvantage. Their readers have tended to be of modest means, a factor that has always affected advertiser interest. One advertising executive stated in 1856 that some journals are poor vehicles because "their readers are not purchasers, and any money thrown upon them is so much thrown away." The same force took a heavy toll of the post-World War II social-democratic press in Great Britain, with the *Daily Herald, News Chronicle,* and *Sunday Citizen* failing or absorbed into establishment systems between 1960 and 1967, despite a collective average daily readership of 9.3 million. As James Curran points out, with 4.7 million readers in its last year, "the *Daily Herald* actually had almost double the readership of *The Times,* the *Financial Times* and the *Guardian* combined." What is more, surveys showed that its readers "thought more highly of their paper than the regular readers of any other popular newspaper," and "they also read more in their paper than the readers of other popular papers despite being overwhelmingly working class. . . ." The death of the *Herald,* as well as of the *News Chronicle* and *Sunday Citizen,* was in large measure a result of progressive strangulation by lack of advertising support. The *Herald,* with 8.1 percent of national daily circulation, got 3.5 percent of net advertising revenue; the *Sunday Citizen* got one-tenth of the net advertising revenue of the *Sunday Times* and one-seventh that of the *Observer* (on a per-thousand-copies basis). Curran argues persuasively that the loss of these three papers was an important contribution to the declining fortunes of the Labor party, in the case of the *Herald* specifically removing a mass-circulation institution that provided "an alternative framework of analysis and understanding that contested the dominant systems of representation in both broadcasting and the mainstream press." A mass movement without any major media support, and subject to a great deal of active press hostility, suffers a serious disability, and struggles against grave odds.

The successful media today are fully attuned to the crucial importance of audience "quality": CBS proudly tells its shareholders that while it "continuously seeks to maximize audience delivery," it has developed a new "sales tool" with which it approaches advertisers: "Client Audience Profile, or CAP, will help advertisers optimize the effectiveness of their network television schedules by evaluating audience segments in proportion to usage levels of advertisers' products and services." In short, the mass media are interested in attracting audiences with buying power, not audiences per se; it is affluent audiences that spark advertiser interest today, as in the nineteenth century. The idea that the drive for large audiences makes the mass media "democratic" thus suffers from the initial weakness that its political analogue is a voting system weighted by income!

The power of advertisers over television programming stems from the simple fact that they buy and pay for the programs—they are the "patrons" who provide the media subsidy. As such, the media compete for their patronage, developing specialized staff to solicit advertisers and necessarily having to explain how their programs serve advertisers' needs. The choices of these patrons greatly affect the welfare of the media, and the patrons become what William Evan calls "normative reference organizations," whose requirements and demands the media must accommodate if they are to succeed.

For a television network, an audience gain or loss of one percentage point in the Nielsen ratings translates into a change in advertising revenue of from $80 to $100 million a year, with some variation depending on measures of audience "quality." The stakes in audience size and affluence are thus extremely large, and in a market system there is a strong tendency for such considerations to affect policy profoundly. This is partly a matter of institutional pressures to focus on the bottom line, partly a matter of the continuous interaction of the media organization with patrons who supply the revenue dollars. As Grant Tinker, then head of NBC-TV, observed, television "is an advertising-supported medium, and to the extent that support falls out, programming will change."

Working-class and radical media also suffer from the political discrimination of advertisers. Political discrimination is structured into advertising allocations by the stress on people with money to buy. But many firms will always refuse to patronize ideological enemies and those whom they perceive as damaging their interests, and cases of overt discrimination add to the force of the voting system weighted by income. Public-television station WNET lost its corporate funding from Gulf + Western in 1985 after the station showed the documentary "Hungry for Profit," which contains material critical of multinational corporate activities in the Third World. Even before the program was shown, in anticipation of negative corporate reaction, station officials "did all we could to get the program sanitized" (according to one station source). The chief executive of Gulf + Western complained to the station that the program was "virulently anti-business if not anti-American," and that the station's carrying the program was not the behavior "of a friend" of the corporation. The London *Economist* says that "Most people believe that WNET would not make the same mistake again."

In addition to discrimination against unfriendly media institutions, advertisers also choose selectively among programs on the basis of their own principles. With rare exceptions these are culturally and politically conservative. Large corporate advertisers on television will rarely sponsor programs that engage in serious criticisms of corporate activities, such as the problem of environmental degradation, the workings of the military-industrial complex, or corporate support of and benefits from Third World tyrannies. Erik Barnouw recounts the history of a proposed documentary series on environmental problems by NBC at a time of great interest in these issues. Barnouw notes that although at that time a great many large companies were spending money on commercials and other publicity regarding environmental problems, the documentary series failed for want of sponsors. The problem was one of excessive objectivity in the series, which included suggestions of corporate or systemic failure, whereas the corporate message "was one of reassurance."

Television networks learn over time that such programs will not sell and would have to be carried at a financial sacrifice, and that, in addition, they may offend powerful advertisers. With the rise in the price of advertising spots, the forgone revenue increases; and with increasing market pressure for financial performance and the diminishing constraints from regulation, an advertising-based media system will gradually increase advertising time and marginalize or eliminate altogether programming that has significant public-affairs content.

Advertisers will want, more generally, to avoid programs with serious complexities and disturbing controversies that interfere with the "buying mood." They seek

programs that will lightly entertain and thus fit in with the spirit of the primary purpose of program purchases—the dissemination of a selling message. Thus over time,
instead of programs like "The Selling of the Pentagon," it is a natural evolution of a
market seeking sponsor dollars to offer programs such as "A Bird's-Eye View of Scot-
land," "Barry Goldwater's Arizona," "An Essay on Hotels," and "Mr. Rooney Goes
to Dinner"—a CBS program on "how Americans eat when they dine out, where they
go and why." There are exceptional cases of companies willing to sponsor serious
programs, sometimes a result of recent embarrassments that call for a public-
relations offset. But even in these cases the companies will usually not want to sponsor close examination of sensitive and divisive issues—they prefer programs on
Greek antiquities, the ballet, and items of cultural and national history and nostalgia.
Barnouw points out an interesting contrast: commercial-television drama "deals
almost wholly with the here and now, as processed via advertising budgets," but on
public television, culture "has come to mean 'other cultures.' . . . American civilization, here and now, is excluded from consideration."

Television stations and networks are also concerned to maintain audience "flow"
levels, i.e., to keep people watching from program to program, in order to sustain
advertising ratings and revenue. Airing program interludes of documentary-cultural
matter that cause station switching is costly, and over time a "free" (i.e., ad-based)
commercial system will tend to excise it. Such documentary-cultural-critical materials will be driven out of secondary media vehicles as well, as these companies
strive to qualify for advertiser interest, although there will always be some cultural-
political programming trying to come into being or surviving on the periphery of the
mainstream media.

SOURCING MASS-MEDIA NEWS: THE THIRD FILTER

The mass media are drawn into a symbiotic relationship with powerful sources
of information by economic necessity and reciprocity of interest. The media need a
steady, reliable flow of the raw material of news. They have daily news demands and
imperative news schedules that they must meet. They cannot afford to have
reporters and cameras at all places where important stories may break. Economics
dictates that they concentrate their resources where significant news often occurs,
where important rumors and leaks abound, and where regular press conferences are
held. The White House, the Pentagon, and the State Department, in Washington,
D.C., are central nodes of such news activity. On a local basis, city hall and the police
department are the subject of regular news "beats" for reporters. Business corporations and trade groups are also regular and credible purveyors of stories deemed
newsworthy. These bureaucracies turn out a large volume of material that meets the
demands of news organizations for reliable, scheduled flows. Mark Fishman calls
this "the principle of bureaucratic affinity: only other bureaucracies can satisfy the
input needs of a news bureaucracy."

Government and corporate sources also have the great merit of being recognizable and credible by their status and prestige. This is important to the mass media. As Fishman notes,

> Newsworkers are predisposed to treat bureaucratic accounts as factual because news personnel participate in upholding a normative order of authorized knowers in the society. Reporters operate with the attitude that officials ought to know what it is their job to know. . . . In particular, a newsworker will recognize an official's claim to knowledge not merely as a claim, but as a credible, competent piece of knowledge. This amounts to a moral division of labor: officials have and give the facts; reporters merely get them.

Another reason for the heavy weight given to official sources is that the mass media claim to be "objective" dispensers of the news. Partly to maintain the image of objectivity, but also to protect themselves from criticisms of bias and the threat of libel suits, they need material that can be portrayed as presumptively accurate. This is also partly a matter of cost: taking information from sources that may be presumed credible reduces investigative expense, whereas material from sources that are not prima facie credible, or that will elicit criticism and threats, requires careful checking and costly research.

The magnitude of the public-information operations of large government and corporate bureaucracies that constitute the primary news sources is vast and ensures special access to the media. The Pentagon, for example, has a public-information service that involves many thousands of employees, spending hundreds of millions of dollars every year and dwarfing not only the public-information resources of any dissenting individual or group but the *aggregate* of such groups. In 1979 and 1980, during a brief interlude of relative openness (since closed down), the U.S. Air Force revealed that its public-information outreach included the following:

140 newspapers, 690,000 copies per week
Airman magazine, monthly circulation 125,000
34 radio and 17 TV stations, primarily overseas
45,000 headquarters and unit news releases
615,000 hometown news releases
6,600 interviews with news media
3,200 news conferences
500 news media orientation flights
50 meetings with editorial boards
11,000 speeches

This excludes vast areas of the air force's public-information effort. Writing back in 1970, Senator J. W. Fulbright had found that the air force public-relations effort in 1968 involved 1,305 full-time employees, exclusive of additional thousands that "have public functions collateral to other duties." The air force at that time offered a weekly film-clip service for TV and a taped features program for use three times a week, sent to 1,139 radio stations; it also produced 148 motion pictures, of which 24 were released for public consumption. There is no reason to believe that the air force public-relations effort has diminished since the 1960s.

Note that this is just the air force. There are three other branches with massive programs, and there is a separate, overall public-information program under an assistant secretary of defense for public affairs in the Pentagon. In 1971, an *Armed Forces Journal* survey revealed that the Pentagon was publishing a total of 371 magazines at an annual cost of some $57 million, an operation sixteen times larger than the nation's biggest publisher. In an update in 1982, the *Air Force Journal International* indicated that the Pentagon was publishing 1,203 periodicals. To put this into perspective, we may note the scope of public-information operations of the American Friends Service Committee (AFSC) and the National Council of the Churches of Christ (NCC), two of the largest of the nonprofit organizations that offer a consistently challenging voice to the views of the Pentagon. The AFSC's main office information-services budget in 1984–85 was under $500,000, with eleven staff people. Its institution-wide press releases run at about two hundred per year, its press conferences thirty a year, and it produces about one film and two or three slide shows a year. It does not offer film clips, photos, or taped radio programs to the media. The NCC Office of Information has an annual budget of some $350,000, issues about a hundred news releases per year, and holds four press conferences annually. The ratio of air force news releases and press conferences to those of the AFSC and NCC taken together are 150 to 1 (or 2,200 to 1 if we count hometown news releases of the air force), and 94 to 1 respectively. Aggregating the other services would increase the differential by a large factor.

Only the corporate sector has the resources to produce public information and propaganda on the scale of the Pentagon and other government bodies. The AFSC and NCC cannot duplicate the Mobil Oil company's multimillion-dollar purchase of newspaper space and other corporate investments to get its viewpoint across. The number of individual corporations with budgets for public information and lobbying in excess of those of the AFSC and NCC runs into the hundreds, perhaps even the thousands. A corporate *collective* like the U.S. Chamber of Commerce had a 1983 budget for research, communications, and political activities of $65 million. By 1980, the chamber was publishing a business magazine (*Nation's Business*) with a circulation of 1.3 million and a weekly newspaper with 740,000 subscribers, and it was producing a weekly panel show distributed to 400 radio stations, as well as its own weekly panel-discussion programs carried by 128 commercial television stations.

Besides the U.S. Chamber, there are thousands of state and local chambers of commerce and trade associations also engaged in public-relations and lobbying activities. The corporate and trade-association lobbying network community is "a network of well over 150,000 professionals," and its resources are related to corporate income, profits, and the protective value of public-relations and lobbying outlays. Corporate profits before taxes in 1985 were $295.5 billion. When the corporate community gets agitated about the political environment, as it did in the 1970s, it obviously has the wherewithal to meet the perceived threat. Corporate and trade-association image and issues advertising increased from $305 million in 1975 to $650 million in 1980. So did direct-mail campaigns through dividend and other mail stuffers, the distribution of educational films, booklets and pamphlets, and outlays on initiatives and referendums, lobbying, and political and think-tank contributions. Aggregate corporate and trade-association political advertising and grass-roots out-lays were estimated to have reached the billion-dollar-a-year level by 1978, and to have grown to $1.6 billion by 1984.

To consolidate their preeminent position as sources, government and business-news promoters go to great pains to make things easy for news organizations. They provide the media organizations with facilities in which to gather; they give journal-ists advance copies of speeches and forthcoming reports; they schedule press con-ferences at hours well-geared to news deadlines; they write press releases in usable language; and they carefully organize their press conferences and "photo opportu-nity" sessions. It is the job of news officers "to meet the journalist's scheduled needs with material that their beat agency has generated at its own pace."

In effect, the large bureaucracies of the powerful *subsidize* the mass media, and gain special access by their contribution to reducing the media's costs of acquiring the raw materials of, and producing, news. The large entities that provide this subsidy become "routine" news sources and have privileged access to the gates. Non-routine sources must struggle for access, and may be ignored by the arbitrary decision of the gatekeepers. It should also be noted that in the case of the largesse of the Pentagon and the State Department's Office of Public Diplomacy, the subsidy is at the taxpayers' expense, so that, in effect, the citizenry pays to be propagandized in the interest of powerful groups such as military contractors and other sponsors of state terrorism.

Because of their services, continuous contact on the beat, and mutual depen-dency, the powerful can use personal relationships, threats, and rewards to further influence and coerce the media. The media may feel obligated to carry extremely dubious stories and mute criticism in order not to offend their sources and disturb a close relationship. It is very difficult to call authorities on whom one depends for daily news liars, even if they tell whoppers. Critical sources may be avoided not only because of their lesser availability and higher cost of establishing credibility, but also because the primary sources may be offended and may even threaten the media using them.

Powerful sources may also use their prestige and importance to the media as a lever to deny critics access to the media: the Defense Department, for example, refused to participate in National Public Radio discussions of defense issues if experts from the Center for Defense Information were on the program; Elliott Abrams refused to appear on a program on human rights in Central America at the Kennedy School of Government, at Harvard University, unless the former ambassador, Robert White, was excluded as a participant; Claire Sterling refused to participate in television-network shows on the Bulgarian Connection where her critics would appear. In the last two of these cases, the authorities and brand-name experts were successful in monopolizing access by coercive threats.

Perhaps more important, powerful sources regularly take advantage of media routines and dependency to "manage" the media, to manipulate them into following a special agenda and framework. Part of this management process consists of inundating the media with stories, which serve sometimes to foist a particular line and frame on the media (e.g., Nicaragua as illicitly supplying arms to the Salvadoran rebels), and at other times to help chase unwanted stories off the front page or out of the media altogether (the alleged delivery of MIGs to Nicaragua during the week of the 1984 Nicaraguan election). This strategy can be traced back at least as far as the Committee on Public Information, established to coordinate propaganda during World War I, which "discovered in 1917–18 that one of the best means of controlling news was flooding news channels with 'facts,' or what amounted to official information."

The relation between power and sourcing extends beyond official and corporate provision of day-to-day news to shaping the supply of "experts." The dominance of official sources is weakened by the existence of highly respectable unofficial sources that give dissident views with great authority. This problem is alleviated by "co-opting the experts"—i.e., putting them on the payroll as consultants, funding their research, and organizing think tanks that will hire them directly and help disseminate their messages. In this way bias may be structured, and the supply of experts may be skewed in the direction desired by the government and "the market." As Henry Kissinger has pointed out, in this "age of the expert," the "constituency" of the expert is "those who have a vested interest in commonly held opinions; elaborating and defining its consensus at a high level has, after all, made him an expert." It is therefore appropriate that this restructuring has taken place to allow the commonly held opinions (meaning those that are functional for elite interests) to continue to prevail.

"This process of creating the needed body of experts has been carried out on a deliberate basis and a massive scale. Back in 1972, Judge Lewis Powell (later elevated to the Supreme Court) wrote a memo to the U.S. Chamber of Commerce urging business "to buy the top academic reputations in the country to add credibility to corporate studies and give business a stronger voice on the campuses." One buys them, and assures that—in the words of Dr. Edwin Feulner, of the Heritage Foundation—the public-policy area "is awash with in-depth academic studies" that have the proper conclusions. Using the analogy of Procter & Gamble selling toothpaste, Feulner explained that "They sell it and resell it every day by keeping the product fresh in the consumer's mind." By the sales effort, including the dissemination of the correct ideas to "thousands of newspapers," it is possible to keep debate "within its proper perspective."

In accordance with this formula, during the 1970s and early 1980s a string of institutions was created and old ones were activated to the end of propagandizing the corporate viewpoint. Many hundreds of intellectuals were brought to these institutions, where their work was funded and their outputs were disseminated to the media by a sophisticated propaganda effort. The corporate funding and clear ideological purpose in the overall effort had no discernible effect on the credibility of the intellectuals so mobilized; on the contrary, the funding and pushing of their ideas catapaulted them into the press.

As an illustration of how the funded experts preempt space in the media, table IV describes the "experts" on terrorism and defense issues who appeared on the "McNeil-Lehrer News Hour" in the course of a year in the mid-1980s. We can see that, excluding journalists, a majority of the participants (54 percent) were present or former government officials, and that the next highest category (15.7 percent) was drawn from conservative think tanks. The largest number of appearances in the latter category was supplied by the Georgetown Center for Strategic and International Studies (CSIS), an organization funded by conservative foundations and corporations, and providing a revolving door between the State Department and CIA and a nominally private organization. On such issues as terrorism and the Bulgarian Connection, the CSIS has occupied space in the media that otherwise might have been filled by independent voices.

TABLE IV *Experts on terrorism and defense on the "McNeil-Lehrer News Hour," January 14, 1985, to January 27, 1986**

Category of Expert	Number	Percent	Number Excluding Journalists	Percent Excluding Journalists
Government official	24	20	24	27
Former government official	24	20	24	27
Conservative think tank	14	11.7	14	15.7
Academic	12	10	12	13.5
Journalist	31	25.8	—	—
Consultant	3	2.5	3	3.4
Foreign government official	5	4.2	5	5.6
Other	7	5.8	7	7.8
Totals	120	100	89	100

* This is a compilation of all appearances on the news hour concerning the Bulgarian Connection (3), the shooting down of the Korean airliner KAL 007 (5), and terrorism, defense, and arms control (33), from January 14, 1985, through January 27, 1986.

The mass media themselves also provide "experts" who regularly echo the official view. John Barron and Claire Sterling are household names as authorities on the KGB and terrorism because the *Reader's Digest* has funded, published, and publicized their work; the Soviet defector Arkady Shevchenko became an expert on Soviet arms and intelligence because *Time,* ABC-TV, and the *New York Times* chose to feature him (despite his badly tarnished credentials). By giving these purveyors of the preferred view a great deal of exposure, the media confer status and make them the obvious candidates for opinion and analysis.

Another class of experts whose prominence is largely a function of serviceability to power is former radicals who have come to "see the light." The motives that cause these individuals to switch gods, from Stalin (or Mao) to Reagan and free enterprise, is varied, but for the establishment media the reason for the change is simply that the ex-radicals have finally seen the error of their ways. In a country whose citizenry values acknowledgement of sin and repentance, the turncoats are an important class of repentant sinners. It is interesting to observe how the former sinners, whose previous work was of little interest or an object of ridicule to the mass media, are suddenly elevated to prominence and become authentic experts. We may recall how, during the McCarthy era, defectors and ex-Communists vied with one another in tales of the imminence of a Soviet invasion and other lurid stories. They found that news coverage was a function of their trimming their accounts to the prevailing demand. The steady flow of ex-radicals from marginality to media attention shows that we are witnessing a durable method of providing experts who will say what the establishment wants said.

FLAK AND THE ENFORCERS: THE FOURTH FILTER

"Flak" refers to negative responses to a media statement or program. It may take the form of letters, telegrams, phone calls, petitions, lawsuits, speeches and bills before Congress, and other modes of complaint, threat, and punitive action. It may be organized centrally or locally, or it may consist of the entirely independent actions of individuals.

If flak is produced on a large scale, or by individuals or groups with substantial resources, it can be both uncomfortable and costly to the media. Positions have to be defended within the organization and without, sometimes before legislatures and possibly even in courts. Advertisers may withdraw patronage. Television advertising is mainly of consumer goods that are readily subject to organized boycott. During the McCarthy years, many advertisers and radio and television stations were effectively coerced into quiescence and blacklisting of employees by the threats of determined Red hunters to boycott products. Advertisers are still concerned to avoid offending constituencies that might produce flak, and their demand for suitable programming is a continuing feature of the media environment. If certain kinds of fact, position, or program are thought likely to elicit flak, this prospect can be a deterrent.

The ability to produce flak, and especially flak that is costly and threatening, is related to power. Serious flak has increased in close parallel with business's growing resentment of media criticism and the corporate offensive of the 1970s and 1980s. Flak from the powerful can be either direct or indirect. The direct would include letters or phone calls from the White House to Dan Rather or William Paley, or from the FCC to the television networks asking for documents used in putting together a program, or from irate officials of ad agencies or corporate sponsors to media officials asking for reply time or threatening retaliation. The powerful can also work on the media indirectly by complaining to their own constituencies (stockholders, employees) about the media, by generating institutional advertising that does the same, and by funding right-wing monitoring or think-tank operations designed to attack the media. They may also fund political campaigns and help put into power conservative politicians who will more directly serve the interests of private power in curbing any deviationism in the media.

Along with its other political investments of the 1970s and 1980s, the corporate community sponsored the growth of institutions such as the American Legal Foundation, the Capital Legal Foundation, the Media Institute, the Center for Media and Public Affairs, and Accuracy in Media (AIM). These may be regarded as institutions organized for the specific purpose of producing flak. Another and older flak-producing machine with a broader design is Freedom House. The American Legal Foundation, organized in 1980, has specialized in Fairness Doctrine complaints and libel suits to aid "media victims." The Capital Legal Foundation, incorporated in 1977, was the Scaife vehicle for Westmoreland's $120-million libel suit against CBS.

The Media Institute, organized in 1972 and funded by corporate-wealthy patrons, sponsors monitoring projects, conferences, and studies of the media. It has focused less heavily on media failings in foreign policy, concentrating more on media portrayals of economic issues and the business community, but its range of interests is broad. The main theme of its sponsored studies and conferences has been the failure of the media to portray business accurately and to give adequate weight to the business point of view, but it underwrites works such as John Corry's exposé of the alleged left-wing bias of the mass media. The chairman of the board of trustees of the institute in 1985 was Steven V. Seekins, the top public-relations officer of the American Medical Association; chairman of the National Advisory Council was Herbert Schmertz, of the Mobil Oil Corporation.

The Center for Media and Public Affairs, run by Linda and Robert Lichter, came into existence in the mid-1980s as a "non-profit, nonpartisan" research institute, with warm accolades from Patrick Buchanan, Faith Whittlesey, and Ronald Reagan himself, who recognized the need for an objective and fair press. Their *Media Monitor* and research studies continue their earlier efforts to demonstrate the liberal bias and anti-business propensities of the mass media.

AIM was formed in 1969, and it grew spectacularly in the 1970s. Its annual income rose from $5,000 in 1971 to $1.5 million in the early 1980s, with funding mainly from large corporations and the wealthy heirs and foundations of the corporate system. At least eight separate oil companies were contributors to AIM in the early 1980s, but the wide representation in sponsors from the corporate community is impressive. The function of AIM is to harass the media and put pressure on them to follow the corporate agenda and a hard-line, right-wing foreign policy. It presses the media to join more enthusiastically in Red-scare bandwagons, and attacks them for alleged deficiencies whenever they fail to toe the line on foreign policy. It conditions the media to expect trouble (and cost increases) for violating right-wing standards of bias.

Freedom House, which dates back to the early 1940s, has had interlocks with AIM, the World Anticommunist League, Resistance International, and U.S. government bodies such as Radio Free Europe and the CIA, and has long served as a virtual propaganda arm of the government and international right wing. It sent election monitors to the Rhodesian elections staged by Ian Smith in 1979 and found them "fair," whereas the 1980 elections won by Mugabe under British supervision it found dubious. Its election monitors also found the Salvadoran elections of 1982 admirable. It has expended substantial resources in criticizing the media for insufficient sympathy with U.S. foreign-policy ventures and excessively harsh criticism of U.S. client states. Its most notable publication of this genre was Peter Braestrup's *Big Story*, which contended that the media's negative portrayal of the Tet offensive helped lose the war. The work is a travesty of scholarship, but more interesting is its premise: that the mass media not only should support any national venture abroad, but should do so with enthusiasm, such enterprises being by definition noble. In 1982, when the Reagan administration was having trouble containing media reporting of the systematic killing of civilians by the Salvadoran army, Freedom House came through with a denunciation of the "imbalance" in media reporting from El Salvador.

Although the flak machines steadily attack the mass media, the media treat them well. They receive respectful attention, and their propagandistic role and links to a larger corporate program are rarely mentioned or analyzed. AIM head, Reed Irvine's diatribes are frequently published, and right-wing network flacks who regularly assail the "liberal media," such as Michael Ledeen, are given Op-Ed column space, sympathetic reviewers, and a regular place on talk shows as experts. This reflects the power of the sponsors, including the well-entrenched position of the right wing in the mass media themselves.

The producers of flak add to one another's strength and reinforce the command of political authority in its news-management activities. The government is a major producer of flak, regularly assailing, threatening, and "correcting" the media, trying to contain any deviations from the established line. News management itself is designed to produce flak. In the Reagan years, Mr. Reagan was put on television to exude charm to millions, many of whom berated the media when they dared to criticize the "Great Communicator."

ANTICOMMUNISM AS A CONTROL MECHANISM

A final filter is the ideology of anticommunism. Communism as the ultimate evil has always been the specter haunting property owners, as it threatens the very root of their class position and superior status. The Soviet, Chinese, and Cuban revolutions were traumas to Western elites, and the ongoing conflicts and the well-publicized abuses of Communist states have contributed to elevating opposition to communism to a first principle of Western ideology and politics. This ideology helps mobilize the populace against an enemy, and because the concept is fuzzy it can be used against anybody advocating policies that threaten property interests or support accommodation with Communist states and radicalism. It therefore helps fragment the left and labor movements and serves as a political-control mechanism. If the triumph of communism is the worst imaginable result, the support of fascism abroad is justified as a lesser evil. Opposition to social democrats who are too soft on Communists and "play into their hands" is rationalized in similar terms.

Liberals at home, often accused of being pro-Communist or insufficiently anti-Communist, are kept continuously on the defensive in a cultural milieu in which anticommunism is the dominant religion. If they allow communism, or something that can be labeled communism, to triumph in the provinces while they are in office, the political costs are heavy. Most of them have fully internalized the religion anyway, but they are all under great pressure to demonstrate their anti-Communist credentials. This causes them to behave very much like reactionaries. Their occasional support of social democrats often breaks down where the latter are insufficiently harsh on their own indigenous radicals or on popular groups that are organizing among generally marginalized sectors. In his brief tenure in the Dominican Republic, Juan Bosch attacked corruption in the armed forces and government, began a land-reform program, undertook a major project for mass education of the populace, and maintained a remarkably open government and system of effective civil liberties. These policies threatened powerful internal vested interests, and the United States resented his independence and the extension of civil liberties to Communists and radicals. This was carrying democracy and pluralism too far. Kennedy was "extremely disappointed" in Bosch's rule, and the State Department "quickly soured on the first democratically elected Dominican President in over thirty years." Bosch's overthrow by the military after nine months in office had at least the tacit support of the United States. Two years later, by contrast, the Johnson administration invaded the Dominican Republic to make sure that Bosch did not resume power.

The Kennedy liberals were enthusiastic about the military coup and displacement of a populist government in Brazil in 1964. A major spurt in the growth of neo-Fascist national-security states took place under Kennedy and Johnson. In the cases of the U.S. subversion of Guatemala, 1947–54, and the military attacks on Nicaragua, 1981–87, allegations of Communist links and a Communist threat caused many liberals to support counterrevolutionary intervention, while others lapsed into silence, paralyzed by the fear of being tarred with charges of infidelity to the national religion.

It should be noted that when anti-Communist fervor is aroused, the demand for serious evidence in support of claims of "communist" abuses is suspended, and charlatans can thrive as evidential sources. Defectors, informers, and assorted other opportunists move to center stage as "experts," and they remain there even after exposure as highly unreliable, if not downright liars. Pascal Delwit and Jean-Michel Dewaele point out that in France, too, the ideologues of anticommunism "can do and say anything." Analyzing the new status of Annie Kriegel and Pierre Daix, two former passionate Stalinists now possessed of a large and uncritical audience in France, Delwit and Dewaele note:

> If we analyse their writings, we find all the classic reactions of people who have been disappointed in love. But no one dreams of criticising them for their past, even though it has marked them forever. They may well have been converted, but they have not changed. . . . no one notices the constants, even though they are glaringly obvious. Their best sellers prove, thanks to the support of the most indulgent and slothful critics anyone could hope for, that the public can be fooled. No one denounces or even notices the arrogance of both yesterday's eulogies and today's diatribes; no one cares that there is never any proof and that invective is used in place of analysis. Their inverted hyper-Stalinism—which takes the usual form of total manicheanism—is whitewashed simply because it is directed against Communism. The hysteria has not changed, but it gets a better welcome in its present guise.

The anti-Communist control mechanism reaches through the system to exercise a profound influence on the mass media. In normal times as well as in periods of Red scares, issues tend to be framed in terms of a dichotomized world of Communist and anti-Communist powers, with gains and losses allocated to contesting sides, and rooting for "our side" considered an entirely legitimate news practice. It is the mass media that identify, create, and push into the limelight a Joe McCarthy, Arkady Shevehenko, and Claire Sterling and Robert Leiken, or an Annie Kriegel and Pierre Daix. The ideology and religion of anticommunism is a potent filter.

DICHOTOMIZATION AND PROPAGANDA CAMPAIGNS

The five filters narrow the range of news that passes through the gates, and even more sharply limit what can become "big news," subject to sustained news campaigns. By definition, news from primary establishment sources meets one major filter requirement and is readily accommodated by the mass media. Messages from and about dissidents and weak, unorganized individuals and groups, domestic and foreign, are at an initial disadvantage in sourcing costs and credibility, and they often do not comport with the ideology or interests of the gatekeepers and other powerful parties that influence the filtering process.

Thus, for example, the torture of political prisoners and the attack on trade unions in Turkey will be pressed on the media only by human-rights activists and groups that have little political leverage. The U.S. government supported the Turkish martial-law government from its inception in 1980, and the U.S. business community has been warm toward regimes that profess fervent anticommunism, encourage foreign investment, repress unions, and loyally support U.S. foreign policy (a set of virtues that are frequently closely linked). Media that chose to feature Turkish violence against their own citizenry would have had to go to extra expense to find and check out information sources; they would elicit flak from government, business, and organized right-wing flak machines, and they might be looked upon with disfavor by the corporate community (including advertisers) for indulging in such a quixotic interest and crusade. They would tend to stand alone in focusing on victims that from the standpoint of dominant American interests were *unworthy*.

In marked contrast, protest over political prisoners and the violation of the rights of trade unions in Poland was seen by the Reagan administration and business elites in 1981 as a noble cause, and, not coincidentally, as an opportunity to score political points. Many media leaders and syndicated columnists felt the same way. Thus information and strong opinions on human-rights violations in Poland could be obtained from official sources in Washington, and reliance on Polish dissidents would not elicit flak from the U.S. government or the flak machines. These victims would be generally acknowledged by the managers of the filters to be *worthy*. The mass media never explain *why* Andrei Sakharov is worthy and José Luis Massera, in Uruguay, is unworthy—the attention and general dichotomization occur "naturally" as a result of the working of the filters, but the result is the same as if a commissar had instructed the media: "Concentrate on the victims of enemy powers and forget about the victims of friends."

Reports of the abuses of worthy victims not only pass through the filters; they may also become the basis of sustained propaganda campaigns. If the government or corporate community and the media feel that a story is useful as well as dramatic, they focus on it intensively and use it to enlighten the public. This was true, for example, of the shooting down by the Soviets of the Korean airliner KAL 007 in early September 1983, which permitted an extended campaign of denigration of an official enemy and greatly advanced Reagan administration arms plans. As Bernard Gwertzman noted complacently in the *New York Times* of August 31, 1984, U.S. officials "assert that worldwide criticism of the Soviet handling of the crisis has strengthened the United States in its relations with Moscow." In sharp contrast, the shooting down by Israel of a Libyan civilian airliner in February 1973 led to no outcry in the West, no denunciations for "cold-blooded murder," and no boycott. This difference in treatment was explained by the *New York Times* precisely on the grounds of utility: "No useful purpose is served by an acrimonious debate over the assignment of blame for the downing of a Libyan airliner in the Sinai peninsula last week." There was a very "useful purpose" served by focusing on the Soviet act, and a massive propaganda campaign ensued.

Propaganda campaigns in general have been closely attuned to elite interests. The Red scare of 1919–20 served well to abort the union-organizing drive that followed World War I in the steel and other industries. The Truman-McCarthy Red scare helped inaugurate the Cold War and the permanent war economy, and it also served to weaken the progressive coalition of the New Deal years. The chronic focus on the plight of Soviet dissidents, on enemy killings in Cambodia, and on the Bulgarian Connection helped weaken the Vietnam syndrome, justify a huge arms buildup and a more aggressive foreign policy, and divert attention from the upward redistribution of income that was the heart of Reagan's domestic economic program. The recent propaganda-disinformation attacks on Nicaragua have been needed to avert eyes from the savagery of the war in El Salvador and to justify the escalating U.S. investment in counterrevolution in Central America.

Conversely, propaganda campaigns will *not* be mobilized where victimization, even though massive, sustained, and dramatic, fails to meet the test of utility to elite interests. Thus, while the focus on Cambodia in the Pol Pot era (and thereafter) was exceedingly serviceable, as Cambodia had fallen to the Communists and useful lessons could be drawn by attention to their victims, the numerous victims of the U.S. bombing *before* the Communist takeover were scrupulously ignored by the U.S. elite press. After Pol Pot's ouster by the Vietnamese, the United States quietly shifted support to this "worse than Hitler" villain, with little notice in the press, which adjusted once again to the national political agenda. Attention to the Indonesian massacres of 1965–66, or the victims of the Indonesian invasion of East Timor from 1975 onward, would also be distinctly unhelpful as bases of media campaigns, because Indonesia is a U.S. ally and client that maintains an open door to Western investment, and because, in the case of East Timor, the United States bears major responsibility for the slaughter. The same is true of the victims of state terror in Chile and Guatemala, U.S. clients whose basic institutional structures, including the state terror system, were put in place and maintained by, or with crucial assistance from, U.S. power, and who remain U.S. client states. Propaganda campaigns on behalf of these victims would conflict with government-business-military interests and, in our model, would not be able to pass through the filtering system.

Propaganda campaigns may be instituted either by the government or by one or more of the top media firms. The campaigns to discredit the government of Nicaragua, to support the Salvadoran elections as an exercise in legitimizing democracy, and to use the Soviet shooting down of the Korean airliner KAL 007 as a means of mobilizing public support for the arms buildup, were instituted and propelled by the government. The campaigns to publicize the crimes of Pol Pot and the alleged KGB plot to assassinate the pope were initiated by the *Reader's Digest*, with strong follow-up support from NBC-TV, the *New York Times*, and other major media companies. Some propaganda campaigns are jointly initiated by government and media; all of them require the collaboration of the mass media. The secret of the unidirectionality of the politics of media propaganda campaigns is the multiple filter system discussed above: the mass media will allow any stories that are hurtful to large interests to peter out quickly, if they surface at all.

For stories that are *useful*, the process will get under way with a series of government leaks, press conferences, white papers, etc., or with one or more of the mass media starting the ball rolling with such articles as Barron and Paul's "Murder of a Gentle Land" (Cambodia), or Claire Sterling's "The Plot to Kill the Pope," both in the *Reader's Digest*. If the other major media like the story, they will follow it up with their own versions, and the matter quickly becomes newsworthy by familiarity. If the articles are written in an assured and convincing style, are subject to no criticisms or alternative interpretations in the mass media, and command support by authority figures, the propaganda themes quickly become established as true even without real evidence. This tends to close out dissenting views even more comprehensively, as they would now conflict with an already established popular belief. This in turn opens up further opportunities for still more inflated claims, as these can be made without fear of serious repercussions. Similar wild assertions made in contradiction of official views would elicit powerful flak, so that such an inflation process would be controlled by the government and the market. No such protections exist with system-supportive claims; there, flak will tend to press the media to greater hysteria in the face of enemy evil. The media not only suspend critical judgment and investigative zeal, they compete to find ways of putting the newly established truth in a supportive light. Themes and facts—even careful and well-documented analyses—that are incompatible with the now institutionalized theme are suppressed or ignored. If the theme collapses of its own burden of fabrications, the mass media will quietly fold their tents and move on to another topic.

Using a propaganda model, we would not only anticipate definitions of worth based on utility, and dichotomous attention based on the same criterion, we would also expect the news stories about worthy and unworthy victims (or enemy and friendly states) to differ in *quality*. That is, we would expect official sources of the United States and its client regimes to be used heavily—and uncritically—in connection with one's own abuses and those of friendly governments, while refugees and other dissident sources will be used in dealing with enemies. We would anticipate the uncritical acceptance of certain premises in dealing with self and friends— such as that one's own state and leaders seek peace and democracy, oppose terrorism, and tell the truth—premises which will not be applied in treating enemy states. We would expect different criteria of evaluation to be employed, so that what is villainy in enemy states will be presented as an incidental background fact in the case of oneself and friends. What is on the agenda in treating one case will be off the agenda in discussing the other. We would also expect great investigatory zeal in the search for enemy villainy and the responsibility of high officials for abuses in enemy states, but diminished enterprise in examining such matters in connection with one's own and friendly states.

The quality of coverage should also be displayed more directly and crudely in placement, headlining, word usage, and other modes of mobilizing interest and outrage. In the opinion columns, we would anticipate sharp restraints on the range of opinion allowed expression. Our hypothesis is that worthy victims will be featured prominently and dramatically, that they will be humanized, and that their victimization will receive the detail and context in story construction that will generate reader interest and sympathetic emotion. In contrast, unworthy victims will merit only slight detail, minimal humanization, and little context that will excite and enrage.

Meanwhile, because of the power of establishment sources, the flak machines, and anti-Communist ideology, we would anticipate outcries that the worthy victims are being sorely neglected, that the unworthy are treated with excessive and uncritical generosity, that the media's liberal, adversarial (if not subversive) hostility to government explains our difficulties in mustering support for the latest national venture in counterrevolutionary intervention.

In sum, a propaganda approach to media coverage suggests a systematic and highly political dichotomization in news coverage based on serviceability to important domestic power interests. This should be observable in dichotomized choices of story and in the volume and quality of coverage. In the chapters that follow we will see that such dichotomization in the mass media is massive and systematic: not only are choices for publicity and suppression comprehensible in terms of system advantage, but the modes of handling favored and inconvenient materials (placement, tone, context, fullness of treatment) differ in ways that serve political ends.

14

"BLACK HAWK DOWN"—
HOLLYWOOD DRAGS BLOODY CORPSE OF TRUTH ACROSS MOVIE SCREENS

Larry Chin

January 3, 2002—True to its post-9/11 government-sanctioned role as US war propaganda headquarters, Hollywood has released "Black Hawk Down," a fictionalized account of the tragic 1993 US raid in Somalia. The Pentagon assisted with the production, pleased for an opportunity to "set the record straight." The film is a lie that compounds the original lie that was the operation itself.

SOMALIA: THE FACTS

According to the myth, the Somalia operation of 1993 was a humanitarian mission, and a shining example of New World Order morality and altruism. In fact, United States and UN troops waged an undeclared war against an Islamic African populace that was hostile to foreign interests.

Also contrary to the legend, the 1993 Somalia raid was not a "Clinton foreign policy bungle." In fact, the incoming Clinton administration inherited an operation that was already in full swing—planned and begun by outgoing President George Herbert Walker Bush, spearheaded by deputy national security adviser Jonathan Howe (who remained in charge of the UN operation after Clinton took office), and approved by Colin Powell, then head of the Joint Chiefs.

The operation had nothing to do with humanitarianism or Africa-love on the part of Bush or Clinton. Several US oil companies, including Conoco, Amoco, Chevron and Phillips were positioned to exploit Somalia's rich oil reserves. The companies had secured billion-dollar concessions to explore and drill large portions of the Somali countryside during the reign of pro-US President Mohamed Siad Barre. (In fact, Conoco's Mogadishu office housed the US embassy and military headquarters.) A "secure" Somalia also provided the West with strategic location on the coast of the Arabian Sea. UN military became necessary when Barre was overthrown by warlord Mohammed Farrah Aidid, suddenly rendering Somalia inhospitable to US corporate interests.

Although the pretext for the mission was to safeguard food shipments, and stop the "evil Aidid" from stealing the food, the true UN goal was to remove Aidid from the political equation, and form a pro-Western coalition government out of the nation's warring clans. The US operation was met with "surprisingly fierce resistance"—surprising to US officials who underestimated Somalian resolve, and even more surprising to US troops who were victims and pawns of UN policy makers.

The highly documented series by Mark Bowden of the *Philadelphia Inquirer* on which the film is based focuses on the participants, and the "untenable" situation in which troops were placed. But even Bowden's gung-ho account makes no bones about provocative American attacks that ultimately led to the decisive defeat in Mogadishu.

Bowden writes: "Task Force Ranger was not in Mogadishu to feed the hungry. Over six weeks, from late August to Oct. 3, it conducted six missions, raiding locations where either Aidid or his lieutenants were believed to be meeting. The mission that resulted in the Battle of Mogadishu came less than three months after a surprise missile attack by U.S. helicopters (acting on behalf of the UN) on a meeting of Aidid clansmen. Prompted by a Somalian ambush on June 5 that killed more than 20 Pakistani soldiers, the missile attack killed 50 to 70 clan elders and intellectuals, many of them moderates seeking to reach a peaceful settlement with the United Nations. After that July 12 helicopter attack, Aidid's clan was officially at war with America—a fact many Americans never realized."

Hundreds, perhaps thousands, of Somalis were killed in the course of US incursions that took place over three months. In his book *The New Military Humanism*, Noam Chomsky cites other under-reported facts. "In October 1993, criminal incompetence by the US military led to the slaughter of 1,000 Somalis by American firepower," Chomsky writes. "The official estimate was 6–10,000 Somali casualties in the summer of 1993 alone, two-thirds women and children. Marine Lt. Gen. Anthony Zinni, who commanded the operation, informed the press that 'I'm not counting bodies . . . I'm not interested.' Specific war crimes of US forces included direct military attacks on a hospital and on civilian gatherings. Other Western armies were implicated in serious crimes as well. Some of these were revealed at an official Canadian inquiry, not duplicated by the US or other governments."

Bowden's more forgiving account does not contradict Chomsky's in this regard:

> "Official U.S. estimates of Somalian casualties at the time numbered 350 dead and 500 injured. Somalian clan leaders made claims of more than 1,000

deaths. The United Nations placed the number of dead at "between 300 to 500." Doctors and intellectuals in Mogadishu not aligned with the feuding clans say that 500 dead is probably accurate.

The attack on Mogadishu was particularly vicious. Quoting Bowden: "The Task Force Ranger commander, Maj. Gen. William F. Garrison, testifying before the Senate, said that if his men had put any more ammunition into the city 'we would have sunk it.' Most soldiers interviewed said that through most of the fight they fired on crowds and eventually at anyone and anything they saw."

After 18 US Special Forces soldiers were killed in the final Mogadishu firefight, which included the downing of a US helicopter, television screens filled with the scene of a dead US soldier being dragged through the streets by jubilant Somalis. Clinton immediately called off the operation. US forces left Somalia in disgrace. Some 19,000 UN troops remained for a short period, but eventually left in futility. The Somalia defeat elicited howls of protest and rage from the military brass, congressional hawks, and right-wing provocateurs itching for an excuse to declare political war on the "liberal" Clinton administration.

The "Somalia syndrome" would dog Clinton throughout his presidency, and mar every military mission during his tenure. Today, as right-wing extremist George W. Bush occupies the White House, surrounded by his father's operatives, and many of the architects of the original raid, military fanaticism is all the rage. A global war "without end" has just begun.

What a perfect moment to "clean up" the past.

HOLLYWOOD TO THE RESCUE

In promoting the film, producer Jerry Bruckheimer (who rewrote another humiliating episode of US military history with "Pearl Harbor") is seeking to convince Americans that the Somalia operation was "not America's darkest hour, but America's brightest hour;" that a bungled imperialist intervention was a noble incident of grand moral magnificence.

CNN film reviewer Paul Tatara describes "Black Hawk Down" as "pound for pound, one of the most violent films ever released by a major studio," from "two of the most pandering, tactless filmmakers in Hollywood history (Jerry Bruckheimer and Ridley Scott)" who are attempting to "teach us about honor among soldiers."

More important are the film's true subtexts, and the likely emotional reaction of viewers.

What viewers see is "brave and innocent young American boys" getting shot at and killed for "no reason" by "crazy black Islamists" that the Americans are "just trying to help." (Subtext one: America is good, and it is impossible to understand why "they hate us." Subtext two: "Those damned ungrateful foreigners." Subtext three: "Those damned blacks." Subtext four: "Kill Arabs.")

What viewers will remember is a line spoken by one of the "brave soldiers" about how, in the heat of combat, "politics goes out the window." (Subtext one: there is no need for thought: shoot first, talk later. Subtext two: it is right to abandon one's sanity, morality and ethics when faced with chaos. Subtext three: when the Twin Towers went down on 9/11, America was right in embracing radical militarism and extreme violence, throwing all else "out the window.")

In the currently lethal political climate, in which testosterone rage, mob mentality, and love of war pass for normal behavior (while reason, critical thinking, and tolerance are considered treasonous), "Black Hawk Down" will appeal to the most violent elements of American society. Many who have seen the film report leaving the theater feeling angry, itching to "kick some ass." In short, the film is dangerous. And those who "love" it are dangerous.

Considering the fact that Somalia is one of the targets in the next phase of the Bush administration's "war on terrorism," the timing of the film is no coincidence.

As Herbert London of the Hudson Institute said of 'Black Hawk Down,' "I would never deny the importance of heroism in battle, but just as we should recognize and honor heroes, we should also respect the truthfulness of the events surrounding their heroic acts. In the case of 'Black Hawk Down,' we get a lot of the former and almost nothing of the latter."

15

IMPERIALISM

Markar Melkonian

> *Lenin was virtually prophetic, because as the colonial age advanced it became more and more obvious that those who stood to benefit most were the monopoly concerns, and especially those involved in finance.*
>
> *—Walter Rodney*

Capitalism today is very different from what it was two hundred years ago. In this chapter we'll take a look at some of the most important differences.

THE MONOPOLY STAGE OF CAPITALISM

Ever since there have been capitalists, they have competed with each other for buyers. One of the chief ways to attract buyers is to offer commodities for sale at a lower price than one's rivals. For obvious reasons, large-scale producers can sell more cheaply than small-scale producers. Bigger producers can purchase raw materials more cheaply by buying in bulk, of course. And because they have more capital at their disposal to update machinery and invest in new production techniques than do their smaller rivals, large-scale producers can increase the productivity of labor, enabling fewer workers to produce more in less time. Big capitalists can also get credit more easily and on better terms than their smaller rivals, and they enjoy a number of other advantages including the ability to capture a larger share of the market through extensive advertising. Furthermore, some fields of modern industry—steel production, the construction of locomotives, shipbuilding, and so on—are quite impossible for small manufacturers to compete in.

As we can see, then, competition among industrial capitalists favors large producers over smaller ones. The same thing holds for agriculture, although at a much slower pace than in heavy industry. Many small farmers cannot afford to invest in heavy machinery, irrigation systems, fertilizers, pesticides, and improved seed stock. Furthermore, heavy machinery and other innovations can be put to use most efficiently when large areas of land are under cultivation. As a result, agricultural production has become more capital intensive—that is, the expenditure for constant capital (capital expended for the means of production) has increased greatly relative to variable capital (capital expended for labor-power).

As large-scale machine production has been introduced into industry and agriculture to reduce the cost of production, more and more workers and small farmers have been replaced by labor-saving machinery. They, together with smaller capitalists who have been ruined by larger capitalists, have been pushed down into the ranks of wage earners. Small-business owners, highly paid professionals, self-employed artisans, and other members of the middle classes continue to make up an important part of industrialized capitalist societies, of course. This is why an analysis of the class makeup of these societies is not a simple matter and must be undertaken carefully, in detail and on a case-by-case basis. Nevertheless, there has been a marked tendency for these societies to "shake out" into a big working class and a much smaller capitalist class.

Over the years, the scale of production in one branch of industry after another has grown larger and larger, as big capitalists have ruined small ones. Hundreds and sometimes even thousands of workers in England, the United States, Germany, Japan, France, and elsewhere were brought together under one roof in steel foundries, coal mines, textile mills, and shipbuilding yards to operate larger and ever more complicated machines. The division of labor within a factory became much more complicated, as each step in the production process was undertaken by a different worker. Moreover, the division of labor within society as a whole also became much more complicated, as raw materials and parts were produced in one place and worked up or assembled hundreds, or even thousands of miles away. As a result, larger numbers of workers were brought into connection and interdependence with one another. In this sense, capitalism collectivized production.

Capitalism has also collectivized the task of directing large capitalist firms. Increasingly, management responsibilities have been taken out of the hands of individual capitalists and put in the hands of highly paid professional management teams.

Meanwhile, in one branch of industry after another we have seen fewer and fewer capitalist firms producing on an ever-larger scale. The process that leads to an ever-larger scale of industry in fewer and fewer hands is called *concentration of production*. The growth of industry has gone hand in hand with concentration of production.

Technical innovations such as the steam engine, the cotton gin, and more recently, electronics, computers, and telecommunications technologies have made it possible to greatly increase the productivity of labor. Contrary to the technological determinists' view of things, however, the relationship between technological innovation and economic development is not a one-way street running from the former to the latter. Improved technology is both a cause of concentration of production and a result of it. In an effort to increase the productivity of labor and in that way to increase the rate of exploitation, for instance, capitalist firms bought patents for new inventions and founded laboratories and research institutes. In this way, technological innovation and improvement have also been collectivized, along with other fields of economic production.

In one branch of industry after another competition has taken place among fewer but larger competitors. In conformity with the profit motive, capitalists strive to increase their capital, to add to existing capital part of the surplus value they have extracted from workers. As capital increases, production must extend. At the same time, bigger capitalists also increase their capital by wrenching capital from the hands of smaller capitalists. As a result, more and more capital ends up in the hands of fewer and fewer big capitalists. The process whereby ever-larger sums of capital come to be held in an ever-smaller number of hands is termed *concentration of capital*.

If a company is to survive in a field of large-scale production, it needs to control or command a lot of capital, to expand production, hold goods off the market for the best prices, improve machinery, and so on. Without command of ever-larger amounts of capital, a company would be one of the doomed small fish. Because of this need for ever more capital, individually owned capitalist companies have given way more and more to joint-stock companies, or corporations. As we might have suspected, this system allowed the biggest capitalists efficiently to collect large amounts of money capital under their control, making it possible for them to make a larger number of investments. One way this is done is by means of holding companies— that is, companies holding large blocks of shares in a number of different corporations.

As Marx foresaw in *Capital*, the concentration of production and capital has proceeded on an enormous scale in one branch of industry after another. In the last decades of the nineteenth century, concentration developed to such a degree that it resulted in the formation of monopolies, which began to play a decisive role in the economic life of the most highly industrialized societies. (By the way, when we speak of the formation of monopolies, we do not usually mean the domination of a market or branch of industry by just one company, but by a small number of companies or groups of companies.) Concentration of production leads to the formation of monopolies in whole spheres of industry. For example, as early as 1900, monopolies in the United States already held 50 percent of textile production in their hands, 54 percent of glass production, 60 percent of paper production, 84 percent of iron and steel production, and 81 percent of chemical production. Ever since then these percentages have steadily risen. Taking these trends into account, Lenin concluded that the turn of the twentieth century marked a breaking point between two very different forms of capitalism: the older competitive or free exchange capitalism and a new form of capitalism, which he called *monopoly capitalism*.

Once a few big companies dominate a particular branch of industry, they are in a position to fix production quotas, divide the market among themselves, and set prices above levels that would prevail under conditions of free competition. Throughout the twentieth century we have seen that companies have come together to form cartels and trusts to do just this. Other ways in which a group of capitalists may succeed in establishing a monopoly include combines, trade associations, and price agreements. Monopolies suppress competition in a number of ways including stopping supplies of raw materials, agreeing with unions to stop the supply of labor, cutting off deliveries, closing trade outlets, entering into exclusive purchase agreements with buyers, stopping credit, and selling below production costs to force competitors out of business.

Increasingly, monopolies expand vertically, to several related branches of production at once, in order to control the whole process of production of a line of goods, from the source of raw materials to the display shelf. Thus, a tire manufacturer may acquire chemical factories and rubber tree groves as well as retail tire stores. Other monopolies expand horizontally, to any of a number of unrelated fields of economic activity.

To get an idea of the scale of monopolies today, let's take a quick look at International Telephone and Telegraph (or ITT). This single diversified corporation, or conglomerate, owns firms that produce electronic components, lighting fixtures, microwave equipment, and semiconductors as well as aerospace, avionics, and navigations systems. ITT also owns companies that produce frozen foods, baked goods, candies, processed meat, silica, glass, tools and machine parts, heating and air conditioning systems, pumps, and fire protection equipment. ITT owns insurance companies, real estate and development companies, trade schools, research facilities, marketing and advertising companies, data services, credit and securities corporations, financial services, cable television systems, radio, telephone and telecommunications systems, restaurants, vending machine companies, shopping centers, wood preserves, mines, automobile and truck rental companies, parking garages, hotels, motels, and lots and lots of other companies in over fifty countries, from Argentina to Zambia.

This scale of concentration could never have taken place if capitalists allowed their money to lie idle until they had need of it, say for expansion of a plant or upgrading facilities. Capitalists must find sellers for their commodities quickly, they must have money capital ready at hand for the purchase of new raw materials at the right time, they must invest promptly and profitably the money they receive from sales, and they must keep abreast of technological innovations. If capitalists fail to do these things, they risk falling behind their competitors or being driven out of business. Furthermore, capitalists must respond quickly to changing market conditions to produce commodities for which there is an effective demand or for which a need can be produced by expanding the market through advertising or in some other way. Otherwise, the surplus value contained in the unsold commodities will be lost. From this review we can see that capitalists have a constant need for capital in the form of money.

Responding to this need, individual capitalists join together, thanks to the credit system and the banks, to advance each other the money they need to ensure that production and sale of commodities take place without interruption. Capitalists put their money in banks, and banks invest capital in industry.

In the course of running a current account for a company, however, a bank finds itself in a position to keep track of the company and control it by selectively extending or denying loans, lending at high or low interest rates, and so forth. As a result, industry has become dependent on the banks, which in many cases can make or break a company. Eventually, the banks' agents are appointed directors of trusts, corporations, and other companies. In this way one large bank may unite many companies by supplying them all with money capital to convert into industrial capital. As a result, banks today have at their command most of the money capital of all capitalists.

When banking capital merges with industrial capital and dominates it in this manner, the result is *finance capital*. During the course of the past hundred years, as I have indicated, and as Lenin observed as early as 1916, a small group of finance capitalists have concentrated control over much of the economic system in their hands and in this way have come to dominate society as a whole. It would be more accurate, therefore, to describe the ruling class of the United States and other highly industrialized capitalist societies as the finance capitalist class or monopoly capital, rather than big business, as we have been calling it so far.

THE INTERNATIONAL CAPITALIST SYSTEM

We have already seen that competition among capitalists leads to monopoly. As we will see somewhat later on, monopolies tend to spill over the borders of any single state. Let's back up for a moment to see how this tendency developed.

Throughout most of the eighteenth and nineteenth centuries, Great Britain was the undisputed industrial power, the "workshop of the world." Moreover, with its colonies in North America, India, Africa, Australia, and elsewhere, Great Britain was a colonial power without rivals. By the late nineteenth century, however, this situation began to change. Protecting themselves with tariff walls against British imports, Germany, the United States, and France developed into major capitalist powers in their own right. As the younger capitalist powers began to challenge Great Britain's leadership in industry, they also began to challenge it as the leading colonial power. Great Britain and the other "Great Powers" became locked in a fierce competition for cheap sources of raw materials, new opportunities for capital investment, and new markets for manufactured goods.

For Great Britain, the most extensive colonial conquests in the period of monopoly capitalism took place between 1860 and 1880. For France and Germany, the main grab for colonies took place between 1880 and 1900. These and the other "Great Powers" shuffled and reshuffled alliances, carved up whole continents and skirmished with each other over economic spheres of interest. Between 1870 and 1890, for example, what has been called the "Scramble for Africa" reached its peak: In 1876 one-tenth of African territory was colonized by European powers; by 1900 nine-tenths of the continent had been colonized. In order to safeguard their domination over colonial lands, the "Great Powers" built up their armies and navies and set up military bases to watch over trade routes, force open new markets, and grab up new colonial lands. In the course of doing this they destroyed native societies, stripped the land of raw materials, imposed regimes of mass terror, and reduced tens of millions of people to worse misery than they had ever known.

In trade, the "Great Powers" were (and still are) able to exchange the products of a few hours of labor-time for the products of many more hours of labor-time in less industrialized societies of Asia, Africa, Latin America, and elsewhere. Recognizing the advantages, the "Great Powers" grabbed up territories not already colonized and set up huge plantations, farms, mines, railroads, harbors, and drilling rigs throughout these lands. By exporting the building materials, machinery, parts, and other capital necessary to set production into motion and keep it in motion, the colonial powers could then recruit local workers to perform the dirtiest, hardest, and most dangerous work at wages far below those of the home country. And to ensure that labor-power remained cheap in these lands, these same "Great Powers" kept wages and standards of living low. In some cases, as we know, workers in the colonized lands were (and still are) paid little more than enough to keep them alive. In this way, exporting capital to colonies allowed the "Great Power" capitalists to reap superprofits, or profits over and above what capitalists squeeze out of workers in the wealthier capitalist societies.

This was the background for a new form of colonialism that relied on the export of capital, rather than just commodities, as in the past. As it turned out, however, the export of capital brought along its own problems. Capital exported obviously creates more capital. Exported capital in the form of mining equipment, for example, enables capitalists to turn coal into capital. This new capital then seeks profitable new investment, as fuel for steam engines, furnaces, and so forth. At the same time, however, the field for such investment is narrowed, because competition among the "Great Powers" narrows effective demand: Major markets, for instance, may be closed off to coal from competing monopoly groups, while at the same time the home market is glutted.

With more and more capital and fewer opportunities to invest it, the struggle among groups of monopolies seeking to extend their markets and spheres of operation took a fierce turn at the beginning of the twentieth century. These monopoly groups used the machinery of the state, including navies, armies, and administrative staff, to achieve their ends. And in the course of doing this, they have provided us with yet another example of the identity of purpose uniting ruling classes with the state.

When Lenin wrote his book *Imperialism: The Highest Stage of Capitalism* at the height of World War I, even self-described socialists in Europe criticized him for insisting that the war was one of imperialists plunder. Far from being the "war to end all wars" as many politicians proclaimed, Lenin saw it as just one of the bloodier conflicts into which monopoly capitalism was driving humanity. Lenin's view, which was angrily denounced on all sides during the war, hardly strikes even bourgeois historians as controversial in the final decades of the twentieth century. The slaughter of millions of human beings for the sake of conquering and redividing ever-larger spheres of interest for monopoly capital; the wholesale massacre of civilians; the profitable arms sales; the secret agreements for division of spoils by the victors; the emotional appeals to national honor, freedom, self-determination, and democracy—all of these features of World War I have been features of imperialist wars ever since.

Domination of the global market by monopoly groupings using the state machinery of a handful of "Great Powers" to achieve their goals is the defining characteristic of the *imperialist* stage of capitalism. The leaders of the "Great Powers" typically have described their motives with lofty slogans. However, their actions have spoken louder then their words. One unusually honest foot soldier of monopoly capital, Major General Smedley D. Butler of the United States Marine Corps, summed up his contribution to U.S. foreign policy as follows:

> I spent thirty-three years and four months in active service as a member of our country's most agile military force—the Marine Corps. I served in all commissioned ranks from a second lieutenant to major-general. And during that period I spent most of my time being a high-class muscle man for Big Business, for Wall Street, and for the bankers. In short, I was a racketeer for capitalism. . . .
>
> Thus I helped make Mexico and especially Tampico safe for American oil interests in 1914. I helped make Haiti and Cuba a decent place for the National City Bank boys to collect revenues in. . . . I helped purify Nicaragua for the international banking house of Brown Brothers in 1909–1912. I brought light to the Dominican Republic for American sugar interests in 1916. I helped make Honduras "right" for American fruit companies in 1903. In China in 1927 I helped see to it Standard Oil went its way unmolested. During those years I had, as the boys in the back room would say, a swell racket. I was rewarded with honors, medals, promotion. Looking back on it, I feel I might have given Al Capone a few hints. The best he could do was operate his racket in three city districts. We marines operated on three continents.

Lenin emphasized that the sort of aggression Major General Butler described was not the result of state policies that the "Great Powers" could just as well have refused to adopt. On the contrary, in the era of monopoly capitalism, states that were not in a position to pursue imperialist policies simply did not become "Great Powers" in the first place.

With some exceptions, the era of direct colonial domination has passed. After World War II, colonialism proved to be too difficult to defend in the face of mounting nationalist pressure and rising Marxist influence in Asia, Africa, and Latin America.

Moreover, it has become possible to maintain imperialist domination without direct colonial domination. Evidently, monopoly capitalists made a calculation similar to Joseph Kennedy's, and they, like him, concluded that it would be better to give a few "middlemen" in the colonized territories "a piece" rather than to risk losing the "whole pie." By the early 1960s the old colonial powers had lost most of their colonies in Asia, Africa, and elsewhere. One after another, the colonies officially became independent states, some after valiant and terribly costly armed struggles, others after a more or less peaceful changing of the guard.

Although new flags were run up flagpoles with great fanfare, the end of direct colonial domination did not result in a real improvement in the lives of most people in the officially independent states emerging from colonial domination. Many of the new regimes were little more than tools of what has come to be known as *neocolonialism*. Neocolonialism is the indirect exploitation of ex-colonized peoples by means of entirely unbalanced trade relations, the export of capital on terms unfavorable to those on the receiving end, manipulation of the terms of trade, and "development aid." What makes neocolonialism an indirect form of imperialist control is that the local managers for the imperialist powers—the highest ranking political leaders and administrators as well as the army and police personnel—are usually members of the very groups of people they help to keep under foreign economic and political domination.

In spite of the fact that foreign control is indirect, however, imperialist domination and exploitation has become more efficient in the postcolonial era. As early as 1965, Ghanaian leader Kwame Nkrumah summed up the new reality of neocolonialism as follows: "For those who practice it, it means power without responsibility, and for those who suffer from it, it means exploitation without redress."

Even leaders of newly independent states who have sincerely wanted to build independent economies have found themselves in tight binds. Since the poorest states of Asia, Africa, and Latin America do not generate enough savings to finance their own capital formation, they have been unable to compete economically with the ex-colonial powers that were responsible in large part for "underdeveloping" them. Therefore, they must acquire the needed capital from abroad by obtaining foreign investments or loans. To attract foreign investors, however, the leaders of these states must promote the construction of roads, telephone systems, power plants, technical schools, and other infrastructural facilities foreign investors require to make acceptably high profits. New leaders might also have to offer tax breaks, insurance protection, guarantees of profits, and other guarantees, to reduce risks to prospective foreign investors and "sweeten the deals."

It is easy to see, then, that creating a favorable climate for foreign investment requires obtaining large amounts of exported capital in the form of loans. In view of this reality, it is not surprising that even leaders in Asia, Africa, and Latin America who sincerely would have preferred to follow a more independent path have been forced into the familiar pattern of domination by the International Monetary Fund

(IMF), the World Bank, and other agencies representing the interests of imperialist states and finance capital.

Peoples under neo-colonial domination are caught in a trap of ever deeper national debt. Imperialist lending institutions and states siphon off most of the economic surplus produced in the societies they dominate, which then must seek further aid and credits from the imperialist states. As a result, states under neo-colonial domination need more exports to service their larger debts. As more value is transferred through this kind of export policy, however, less surplus product remains, and there is consequently a greater need for loans to subsidize state expenditures. By 1990 Africa's debt alone was 272 billion dollars—two and one half times greater than Africa's debt in 1980. For sub-Saharan Africa, the debt was 174 billion dollars in 1990, as compared to 56 billion dollars in 1980, and its ratio of debt to gross national product was a staggering 112 percent. Debt servicing takes over 30 percent of Africa's total export earnings, and countries on that continent have been sending 4 percent of their gross domestic product to the wealthiest capitalist states, as interest on its debts alone. Thus, what are misleadingly called "developing countries" find themselves locked in a downward spiral of greater exploitation, indebtedness, and poverty.

It should be clear that lower standards of living mean cheaper labor-power and lower prices for raw materials and other commodities. As long as imports from imperialist-dominated regions continue to fetch low prices, these products of highly exploited labor help to keep profits in the advanced capitalist societies from falling. This, in large part, is what has been behind the prosperity of the advanced capitalist societies, their political stability, and the relatively high standard of living enjoyed by many workers in these societies.

We've seen that the burden of economic crisis in the advanced capitalist societies has been displaced onto workers and peasants in Asia, Africa, Latin America, and elsewhere. In fact, if we recall that many workers in imperialist countries receive dividends from corporate stock and other investments, it could be argued that these profits make it possible for some workers to become partial capitalists themselves. Lenin called the section of a working class that has received the "crumbs" of imperialist superprofits the *aristocracy of labor.* Imperialist superprofits and the existence of an aristocracy of labor help to account for the fact that a minority of monopoly capitalists have been able to maintain overwhelming political and ideological hegemony in the richest capitalist societies for decades.

Despite the well-financed propaganda abut the benefits to everyone of "free trade," the gap between rich countries and poor ones has grown. In 1890, for example, Europe was twice as wealthy per capita as China or India. By 1940, it was forty times richer; in 1990, it was seventy times richer. Each year since 1986, at least 43 billion dollars more has flowed from the "South" (that is, the poorer regions of Asia, Africa, Latin America, and elsewhere) to the "North" (that is, the wealthiest countries of Europe, North America, Japan, and elsewhere) than vice versa. Together, states in Latin America, Africa, and Asia pay about three times more every year just to service their foreign debts than the total they receive in development assistance through all channels. These debt payments are, in essence, a forced contribution by the poorest people of the poorest societies to the richest people of the richest societies.

Recognizing this, it should not have come as a surprise when a U.N. study released in 1992 reported that the global gap between rich and poor has doubled since 1960. Fully half of the population of Asia, Africa, and Latin America does not have safe drinking water. In these regions, nearly 1 billion people cannot read or write; every night, billions of people go to bed hungry; and 700 million people, mostly women and children, suffer from malnutrition. After hopeful signs in the 1980s, the World Health Organization (WHO) now reports that in those regions smallpox, HIV, tuberculosis, cancer, heart disease, malaria, and other diseases connected with poverty are on the rise again. According to WHO, 14 million children under five years of age die every year from diarrhea and other easily preventable diseases.

To make prospects for the future even more desperate, a brain drain is in full swing throughout the South, as highly skilled and educated people migrate to the North. A United Nations report estimated that in 1989 there were eighty-one scientists and technicians per thousand people in the richest countries of the North, as opposed to nine per thousand in the South. Africa has lost one-third of its skilled workers to European immigration. In Ghana, for example, 60 percent of the doctors trained in the early 1980s now work abroad. The result is an increasing dependency of the South on the North and an even deeper downward spiral of poverty.

A society that is economically dependent is also politically dependent. We can illustrate this point by taking a quick look at the World Bank, with its 170 or so member states. According to Martin Kore, a representative from the Philippines to an international conference on the IMF, the World Bank is

> continuing the patterns that were developed during the colonial period...
> and even though our countries in the "South" have gained political inde-
> pendence that independence to a large degree is empty because economi-
> cally speaking, we are even more dependent on the ex-colonial countries
> than we ever were and the World Bank and the IMF are playing the role of
> ex-colonial masters.

This sort of domination is now being extended to post-Cold War eastern Europe and what used to be the Soviet Union.

Fidel Castro has argued that the poorest countries should organize themselves into a cartel to collectively renegotiate their debts from a position of strength. It is not surprising that lender banks have threatened countries with financial boycott if they attempt to take Castro's advice.

16

A WARNING TO AFRICA: THE NEW U.S. IMPERIAL GRAND STRATEGY

John Bellamy Foster

Imperialism is constant for capitalism. But it passes through various phases as the system evolves. At present the world is experiencing a new age of imperialism marked by a U.S. grand strategy of global domination. One indication of how things have changed is that the U.S. military is now truly global in its operations with permanent bases on every continent, including Africa, where a new scramble for control is taking place focused on oil.

Elite opinion in the United States in the decade immediately following the collapse of the Soviet Union often decried the absence of a U.S. grand strategy comparable to what George Kennan labeled "containment," under the mantle of which the United States intervened throughout the Cold War years. The key question, as posed in November 2000 by national-security analyst Richard Haass, was that of determining how the United States should utilize its current "surplus of power" to reshape the world. Haass's answer, which doubtless contributed to his being hired immediately after as director of policy planning for Colin Powell's State Department in the new Bush administration, was to promote an "Imperial America" strategy aimed at securing U.S. global dominance for decades to come. Only months before, a similar, if even more nakedly militaristic, grand strategy had been presented by the Project for the New American Century, in a report authored by future top Bush-administration figures Donald Rumsfeld, Paul Wolfowitz, and Lewis Libby, among others.[1]

This new imperial grand strategy became a reality, following the attacks of September 11, 2001, in the U.S. invasions of Afghanistan and Iraq—and was soon officially enshrined in the White House's *National Security Strategy* statement of 2002. Summing up the new imperial thrust in *Harvard Magazine*, Stephen Peter Rosen, director of the Olin Institute for Strategic Studies at Harvard and a founding member of the Project for the New American Century, wrote:

A political unit that has overwhelming superiority in military power, and uses that power to influence the internal behavior of other states, is called an empire. Because the United States does not seek to control territory or govern the overseas citizens of the empire, we are an indirect empire, to be sure, but an empire nonetheless. If this is correct, our goal is not combating a rival, but maintaining our imperial position, and maintaining imperial order. Planning for imperial wars is different from planning for conventional international wars. . . . Imperial wars to restore order are not so constrained [by deterrence considerations]. The maximum amount of force can and should be used as quickly as possible for psychological impact—to demonstrate that the empire cannot be challenged with impunity. . . . [I]mperial strategy focuses on preventing the emergence of powerful, hostile challengers to the empire: by war if necessary, but by imperial assimilation if possible.[2]

Commenting in late 2002 in *Foreign Policy*, John Lewis Gaddis, professor of military and naval history at Yale, stated that the goal of the impending war on Iraq was one of inflicting an "Agincourt on the banks of the Euphrates." This would be a demonstration of power so great that, as in Henry V's famous fifteenth-century victory in France, the geopolitical landscape would be changed for decades to come. What was ultimately at issue, according to Gaddis, was "the management of the international system by a single hegemon"—the United States. This securing of hegemony over the entire world by the United States by means of preemptive actions was, he contended, nothing less than "a new grand strategy of transformation."[3]

THE NATURE OF GRAND STRATEGY

Since the time of Clausewitz, tactics has been designated in military circles as "the art of using troops in battle"; strategy as "the art of using battles to win the war."[4] In contrast, the idea of "grand strategy" as classically promoted by military strategists and historians, such as Edward Meade Earle and B. H. Liddell Hart, refers to the integration of the war-making potential of a state with its larger political-economic ends. As historian Paul Kennedy observed in *Grand Strategies in War and Peace* (1991): "a true grand strategy" is "concerned with peace as much as (perhaps even more than) with war . . . . about the evolution or integration of policies that should operate for decades, or even for centuries."[5]

Grand strategies are geopolitical in orientation, geared to domination of whole geographical regions—including strategic resources such as minerals and waterways, economic assets, populations, and vital military positions. The most successful grand strategies of the past are seen as those of long-standing empires, which have been able to maintain their power over large geographical expanses for extended periods of time. Hence, historians of grand strategy commonly focus on the nineteenth-century British Empire (Pax Britannica) and even the ancient Roman Empire (Pax Romana).

For the United States today what is at stake is no longer control of a mere portion of the globe, but a truly global Pax Americana. Although some commentators have seen the latest U.S. imperial thrust as the work of a small cabal of neoconservatives within the Bush administration, the reality is one of broad concurrence within the U.S. power structure on the necessity of expanding the U.S. empire. One recent collection, including contributions by administration critics, is entitled *The Obligation of Empire: United States' Grand Strategy for a New Century*.[6]

Ivo. H. Daalder (senior fellow at the Brookings Institution and former foreign policy advisor to Howard Dean) and James M. Lindsay (vice president of the Council on Foreign Relations, previously employed by Clinton's National Security Council) argue in their book *America Unbound* that the United States has long had a "secret empire," disguised by multilateralism. The Bush White House's unilateral policy of building "empire on American power alone" has changed things only to the extent that it has stripped away the empire's hidden character and reduced its overall force by relying less on vassal states. According to Daalder and Lindsay, the United States is now under the command of "hegemonist" thinkers who want to ensure that the United States dominates the entire globe—both in its own national self-interest and in order to reshape the world in tune with "democratic imperialism." But such an aggressive posture, they point out, is not outside the historic range of U.S. policy. A unilateralist imperial thrust can be traced back to Theodore Roosevelt and was present from the beginning of the Cold War era in the Truman and Eisenhower administrations. Still, Daalder and Lindsay hold out the possibility of a more cooperative strategy, with the other great powers falling in behind the United States, as a superior approach to running an empire.[7]

Such cooperative imperialism, however, becomes more difficult to achieve once the hegemon's power begins to wane. Not only is the United States suffering increased economic competition, but with the demise of the Soviet Union the NATO alliance has weakened: Washington's European vassals do not always follow its lead, even though they are unable to challenge it directly. The temptation facing a waning hegemonic power—still armed and dangerous—caught in such circumstances is to attempt to rebuild and even expand its power by acting unilaterally and monopolizing the spoils.

The War for the 'New American Century'

Capitalism is a system that is worldwide in its economic scope but divided politically into competing states that develop economically at different rates. The contradiction of uneven capitalist development was classically expressed by Lenin in 1916 in *Imperialism, the Highest Stage of Capitalism*:

> There can be *no* other conceivable basis under capitalism for the division of spheres of influence, of interests, of colonies, etc., than a calculation of the *strength* of the participants in the division, their general economic, financial, military strength, etc. And the strength of these participants in the division does not change to an equal degree, for under capitalism the development of different undertakings, trusts, branches of industry, or countries cannot be *even*. Half a century ago, Germany was a miserable, insignificant country, as far as its capitalist strength was concerned, compared with the strength of England at that time. Japan was similarly insignificant compared with Russia. Is it "conceivable" that in ten or twenty years' time the relative strength of the imperialist powers will have remained *un*changed? Absolutely inconceivable.[8]

It is now widely acknowledged that the world is undergoing a global economic transformation. Not only is the growth rate of the world economy as a whole slowing, but the relative economic strength of the United States is continuing to weaken. In 1950 the United States accounted for about half of world GDP, falling to a little over a fifth by 2003. Likewise it accounted for almost half of the world's stock of global foreign direct investment in 1960, compared to a little over 20 percent at the beginning of this century. According to projections of Goldman Sachs, China could overtake the United States as the world's largest economy by 2039.[9]

This growing threat to U.S. power is fueling Washington's obsession with laying the groundwork for a "New American Century." Its current interventionism is aimed at taking advantage of its present short-term economic and military primacy to secure strategic assets that will provide long-term guarantees of global supremacy. The goal is to extend U.S. power directly while depriving potential competitors of those vital strategic assets that might allow them eventually to challenge it globally or even within particular regions.

The National Security Strategy of the United States of 2002 gave notice that "Our forces will be strong enough to dissuade potential adversaries from pursuing a military build-up in hopes of surpassing, or equaling, the power of the United States." But grand strategy extends beyond mere military power. Economic advantages vis-à-vis potential rivals are the real coin of intercapitalist competition. Hence, U.S. grand strategy integrates military power with the struggle to control capital, trade, the value of the dollar, and strategic raw materials.

Perhaps the clearest ordering of U.S. strategic objectives has been provided by Robert J. Art, professor of international relations at Brandeis and a research associate of the Olin Institute, in *A Grand Strategy for America*. "A grand strategy," he writes, "tells a nation's leaders what goals they should aim for and how best they can use their country's military power to attain these goals." In conceptualizing such a grand strategy for the Untied States, Art presents six "overarching national interests" in order of importance:

- First, prevent an attack on the American homeland;
- Second, prevent great-power Eurasian wars and, if possible, the intense security competitions that make them more likely;
- Third, preserve access to a reasonably priced and secure supply of oil;
  Fourth, preserve an open international economic order;
- Fifth, foster the spread of democracy and respect for human rights abroad, and prevent genocide or mass murder in civil wars;
- Sixth, protect the global environment, especially from the adverse effects of global warming and severe climate change.

After national defense proper, i.e., defense of "the homeland" against external attack, the next three highest strategic priorities are thus: (1) the traditional geopolitical goal of hegemony over the Eurasian heartland seen as the key to world power, (2) securing control over world oil supplies, and (3) promoting global-capitalist economic relations.

In order to meet these objectives, Art contends, Washington should "maintain forward-based forces" in Europe and East Asia (the two rimlands of Eurasia with great power concentrations) and in the Persian Gulf (containing the bulk of world oil reserves). "Eurasia is home to most of the world's people, most of its proven oil reserves, and most of its military powers, as well as a large share of its economic growth." It is therefore crucial that the U.S. imperial grand strategy be aimed at strengthening its hegemony in this region, beginning with the key oil regions of South-Central Asia.[10]

With the wars on and occupations of Afghanistan and Iraq still unresolved, Washington has been stepping-up its threats of a "preemptive" attack on these states' more powerful neighbor, Iran. The main justification offered for this is Iran's uranium-enrichment program, which could eventually allow it to develop nuclear weapons capabilities. Yet, there are other reasons that the United States is interested in Iran. Like Iraq before it, Iran is a leading oil power, now with the second largest proven oil reserves behind Saudi Arabia and ahead of Iraq. Control of Iran is thus crucial to Washington's goal of dominating the Persian Gulf and its oil.

Iran's geopolitical importance, moreover, stretches far beyond the Middle East. It is a key prize (as in the case also of Afghanistan) in the New Great Game for control of all of South-Central Asia, including the Caspian Sea Basin with its enormous fossil fuel reserves. U.S. strategic planners are obsessed with fears of an Asian energy-security grid, in which Russia, China, Iran, and the Central Asian countries (possibly also including Japan) would come together economically and in an energy accord to break the U.S. and Western stranglehold on the world oil and gas market—creating the basis for a general shift of world power to the East. At present China, the world's fastest growing economy, lacks energy security even as its demand for fossil fuels is rapidly mounting. It is attempting to solve this partly through greater access to the energy resources of Iran and the Central Asian states. Recent U.S. attempts to establish a stronger alliance with India, with Washington bolstering India's status as a nuclear power, are clearly part of this New Great Game for control of South-Central Asia—reminiscent of the nineteenth-century Great Game between Britain and Russia for control of this part of Asia.[11]

THE NEW SCRAMBLE FOR AFRICA

If there is a New Great Game afoot in Asia there is also a "New Scramble for Africa" on the part of the great powers.[12] *The National Security Strategy of the United States* of 2002 declared that "combating global terror" and ensuring U.S. energy security required that the United States increase its commitments to Africa and called upon "coalitions of the willing" to generate regional security arrangements on that continent. Soon after the U.S. European Command, based in Stuttgart, Germany—in charge of U.S. military operations in Sub-Saharan Africa—increased its activities in West Africa, centering on those states with substantial oil production and/or reserves in or around the Gulf of Guinea (stretching roughly from the Ivory Coast to Angola). The U.S. military's European Command now devotes 70 percent of its time to African affairs, up from almost nothing as recently as 2003.[13]

As pointed out by Richard Haass, now president of the Council on Foreign Relations, in his foreword to the 2005 council report entitled *More Than Humanitarianism: A Strategic U.S. Approach Toward Afric*a: "By the end of the decade sub-Saharan Africa is likely to become as important as a source of U.S. energy imports as the Middle East."[14] West Africa has some 60 billion barrels of proven oil reserves. Its oil is the low sulfur, sweet crude prized by the U.S. economy. U.S. agencies and think tanks project that one in every five new barrels of oil entering the global economy in the latter half of this decade will come from the Gulf of Guinea, raising its share of U.S. oil imports from 15 to over 20 percent by 2010, and 25 percent by 2015. Nigeria already supplies the United States with 10 percent of its imported oil. Angola provides 4 percent of U.S. oil imports, which could double by the end of the decade. The discovery of new reserves and the expansion of oil production are turning other states in the region into major oil exporters, including Equatorial Guinea, São Tomé and Principe, Gabon, Cameroon, and Chad. Mauritania is scheduled to emerge as an oil exporter by 2007. Sudan, bordering the Red Sea in the east and Chad to the west, is an important oil producer.

At present the main, permanent U.S. military base in Africa is the one established in 2002 in Djibouti in the Horn of Africa, giving the United States strategic control of the maritime zone through which a quarter of the world's oil production passes. The Djibouti base is also in close proximity to the Sudanese oil pipeline. (The French military has long had a major presence in Djibouti and also has an air base at Abeche, Chad on the Sudanese border.) The Djibouti base allows the United States to dominate the eastern end of the broad oil swath cutting across Africa that it now considers vital to its strategic interests—a vast strip running southwest from the 994-mile Higleig-Port Sudan oil pipeline in the east to the 640-mile Chad-Cameroon pipeline and the Gulf of Guinea in the West. A new U.S. forward-operating location in Uganda gives the United States the potential of dominating southern Sudan, where most of that country's oil is to be found.

In West Africa, the U.S. military's European Command has now established forward-operating locations in Senegal, Mali, Ghana, and Gabon—as well as Namibia, bordering Angola on the south—involving the upgrading of airfields, the pre-positioning of critical supplies and fuel, and access agreements for swift deployment of U.S. troops.[15] In 2003 it launched a counterterrorism program in West Africa, and in March 2004 U.S. Special Forces were directly involved in a military operation with Sahel countries against the Salafist Group for Preaching and Combat—on Washington's list of terrorist organizations. The U.S. European Command is developing a coastal security system in the Gulf of Guinea called the Gulf of Guinea Guard. It has also been planning the construction of a U.S. naval base in São Tomé and Principe, which the European Command has intimated could rival the U.S. naval base at Diego Garcia in the Indian Ocean. The Pentagon is thus moving aggressively to establish a military presence in the Gulf of Guinea that will allow it to control the western part of the broad trans-Africa oil strip and the vital oil reserves now being discovered there. Operation Flintlock, a start-up U.S. military exercise in West Africa in 2005, incorporated 1,000 U.S. Special Forces. The U.S. European Command will be conducting exercises for its new rapid-reaction force for the Gulf of Guinea this summer.

Here the flag is following trade: the major U.S. and Western oil corporations are all scrambling for West African oil and demanding security. The U.S. military's European Command, the *Wall Street Journal* reported in its April 25th issue, is also working with the U.S. Chamber of Commerce to expand the role of U.S. corporations in Africa as part of an "integrated U.S. response." In this economic scramble for Africa's petroleum resources the old colonial powers, Britain and France, are in competition with the United States. Militarily, however, they are working closely with the United States to secure Western imperial control of the region.

The U.S. military buildup in Africa is frequently justified as necessary both to fight terrorism and to counter growing instability in the oil region of Sub-Saharan Africa. Since 2003 Sudan has been torn by civil war and ethnic conflict focused on its southwestern Darfur region (where much of the country's oil is located), resulting in innumerable human rights violations and mass killings by government-linked militia forces against the population of the region. Attempted coups recently occurred in the new petrostates of São Tomé and Principe (2003) and Equatorial Guinea (2004). Chad, which is run by a brutally oppressive regime shielded by a security and intelligence apparatus backed by the United States, also experienced an attempted coup in 2004. A successful coup took place in Mauritania in 2005 against U.S.-supported strongman Ely Ould Mohamed Taya. Angola's three-decade-long civil war—instigated and fueled by the United States, which together with South Africa organized the terrorist army under Jonas Savimbi's UNITA—lasted until the ceasefire following Savimbi's death in 2002. Nigeria, the regional hegemon, is rife with corruption, revolts, and organized oil theft, with considerable portions of oil production in the Niger Delta region being siphoned off—up to 300,000 barrels a day in early 2004.[16] The rise of armed insurgency in the Niger Delta and the potential of conflict between the Islamic north and non-Islamic south of the country are major U.S. concerns.

Hence there are incessant calls and no lack of seeming justifications for U.S. "humanitarian interventions" in Africa. The Council on Foreign Relations report *More than Humanitarianism* insists that "the United States and its allies must be ready to take appropriate action" in Darfur in Sudan "including sanctions and, if necessary, military intervention, if the Security Council is blocked from doing so." Meanwhile the notion that the U.S. military might before long need to intervene in Nigeria is being widely floated among pundits and in policy circles. *Atlantic Monthly* correspondent Jeffrey Taylor wrote in April 2006 that Nigeria has become "the largest failed state on earth," and that a further destabilization of that state, or its takeover by radical Islamic forces, would endanger "the abundant oil reserves that America has vowed to protect. Should that day come, it would herald a military intervention far more massive than the Iraqi campaign."[17]

Still, U.S. grand strategists are clear that the real issues are not the African states themselves and the welfare of their populations but oil and China's growing presence in Africa. As the *Wall Street Journal* noted in "Africa Emerges as a Strategic Battlefield," "China has made Africa a front line in its pursuit of more global influence, tripling trade with the continent to some $37 billion over the last five years and locking up energy assets, closing trade deals with regimes like Sudan's and educating Africa's future elites at Chinese universities and military schools." In *More than Humanitarianism*, the Council on Foreign Relations likewise depicts the leading threat as coming from China: "China has altered the strategic context in Africa. All across Africa today, China is acquiring control of natural resource assets, outbidding Western contractors on major infrastructure projects, and providing soft loans and other incentives to bolster its competitive advantage."[18] China imports more than a quarter of its oil from Africa, primarily Angola, Sudan, and Congo. It is Sudan's largest foreign investor. It has provided heavy subsidies to Nigeria to increase its influence and has been selling fighter jets there. Most threatening from the standpoint of U.S. grand strategists is China's $2 billion low-interest loan to Angola in 2004, which has allowed Angola to withstand IMF demands to reshape its economy and society along neoliberal lines.

For the Council on Foreign Relations, all of this adds up to nothing less than a threat to Western imperialist control of Africa. Given China's role, the council report says, "the United States and Europe cannot consider Africa their chasse gardé [private hunting ground], as the French once saw francophone Africa. The rules are changing as China seeks not only to gain access to resources, but also to control resource production and distribution, perhaps positioning itself for priority access as these resources become scarcer." The council report on Africa is so concerned with combating China through the expansion of U.S. military operations in the region, that none other than Chester Crocker, former assistant secretary of state for African affairs in the Reagan administration, charges it with sounding "wistfully nostalgic for an era when the United States or the West was the only major influence and could pursue its . . . objectives with a free hand."[19]

What is certain is that the U.S empire is being enlarged to encompass parts of Africa in the rapacious search for oil. The results could be devastating for Africa's peoples. Like the old scramble for Africa this new one is a struggle among great powers for resources and plunder—not for the development of Africa or the welfare of its population.

A GRAND STRATEGY OF ENLARGEMENT

Despite the rapidly evolving strategic context and the shift to a more naked imperialism in recent years, there is a consistency in U.S. imperial grand strategy, which derives from the broad agreement at the very top of the U.S. power structure that the United States should seek "global supremacy," as President Jimmy Carter's former National Security Advisor, Zbigniew Brzezinski put it.[20]

The Council on Foreign Relations' 2006 report on More Than Humanitarianism, which supports the enlargement of U.S. grand strategy to take in Africa, was cochaired by Anthony Lake, National Security Advisor to Clinton from 1993–1997 and Christine Todd Whitman, former head of the Environmental Protection Agency under Bush. As Clinton's National Security Advisor, Lake played a leading role in defining the U.S. grand strategy in the Clinton administration. In a speech entitled "From Containment to Enlargement," delivered to the School of Advanced International Studies at Johns Hopkins University on September 21, 2003, he declared that with the collapse of the Soviet Union the United States was the world's "dominant power...we have the world's strongest military, its largest economy and its most dynamic, multiethnic society. . . . We contained a global threat to market democracies; now we should seek to enlarge, their reach. The successor to a doctrine of containment must be a strategy of enlargement." Translated this meant an expansion of the sphere of world capitalism under the U.S. military-strategic umbrella. The chief enemies of this new world order were characterized by Lake as the "backlash states," especially Iraq and Iran. Lake's insistence, in the early Clinton era, on a grand "strategy of enlargement" for the United States is being realized today in the enlargement of the U.S. military role not only in Central Asia and the Middle East, but also in Africa.[21]

U.S. imperial grand strategy is less a product of policies generated in Washington by this or that wing of the ruling class, than an inevitable result of the power position that U.S. capitalism finds itself in at the commencement of the twenty-first century. U.S. economic strength (along with that of its closest allies) has been ebbing fairly steadily. The great powers are not likely to stand in the same relation to each other economically two decades hence. At the same time U.S. world military power has increased relatively with the demise of the Soviet Union. The United States now accounts for about half of all of the world's military spending—a proportion two or more times its share of world output.

The goal of the new U.S. imperial grand strategy is to use this unprecedented military strength to preempt emerging historical forces by creating a sphere of full-spectrum dominance so vast, now encompassing every continent, that no potential rivals will be able to challenge the United States decades down the line. This is a war against the peoples of the periphery of the capitalist world and for the expansion of world capitalism, particularly U.S. capitalism. But it is also a war to secure a "New American Century" in which third world nations are viewed as "strategic assets" within a larger global geopolitical struggle

The lessons of history are clear: attempts to gain world dominance by military means, though inevitable under capitalism, are destined to fail and can only lead to new and greater wars. It is the responsibility of those committed to world peace to resist the new U.S. imperial grand strategy by calling into question imperialism and its economic taproot: capitalism itself.

NOTES

1. Haass's views are explored in John Bellamy Foster, "'Imperial America' and War," *Monthly Review* 55, no. 1 (May 2003): 1–10; Project for the New American Century, *Rebuilding America's Defenses* (September 2000), http://www.newamericancentury.org/.

2. Stephen Peter Rosen, "The Future of War and the American Military," *Harvard Magazine* 104, no. 5 (May–June 2002): 29–31.

3. John Lewis Gaddis, "A Grand Strategy of Transformation," *Foreign Policy* (November/December 2002): 50–57.

4. Clausewitz quoted in Paul Kennedy, ed., *Grand Strategies in War and Peace* (New Haven: Yale University Press, 1991), 1.

5. Edwin R. Earle, ed., *Makers of Modern Strategy* (Princeton: Princeton University Press, 1948); B. H. Liddel Hart, *Strategy* (New York: Praeger, 1967); Kennedy, ed., Grand *Strategies*, 1–4.

6. James J. Hentz, ed., *The Obligation of Empire: United States' Grand Strategy for a New Century* (Lexington, Kentucky: University of Kentucky Press, 2004).

7. Ivo H. Daalder & James M. Lindsay, *America Unbound* (Hoboken, New Jersey: John Wiley and Sons, 2005), 4–5, 40–41, 194.

8. V. I. Lenin, *Imperialism, the Highest Stage of Capitalism* (New York: International Publishers, 1939), 119.

9. Richard B. Du Boff, "U.S Empire," *Monthly Review* 55, no. 7 (December 2003): 1–2; Dominic Wilson & Roopa Purshothaman, "Dreaming with BRICs," *Goldman Sachs Global Economics Paper*, no. 99 (October 1, 2003), 4, http://www.gs.com/

10. Robert J. Art, *A Grand Strategy for America* (Ithaca: Cornell University Press, 2003), 1–11.

11. Noam Chomsky, *Failed States* (New York: Metropolitan Books, 2006), 254–55; Lutz Kleveman, *The New Great Game* (New York: Grove Press, 2004).

12. See Pierre Abramovici, "United States: The New Scramble for Africa," *Le Monde Diplomatique* (Engish edition), July 2004; "Revealed: The New Scramble for Africa," *The Guardian*, June 1, 2005.

13. Fred Kempe, "Africa Emerges as a Strategic Battlefield," *Wall Street Journal*, April 25, 2006.

14. Council on Foreign Relations, *More Than Humanitarianism: A Strategic U.S. Approach Toward Africa*, 2006, xiii.

15. Council on Foreign Relations, *More Than Humanitarianism*, 59.

16. Center for Strategic and International Studies, *A Strategic U.S. Approach to Governance and Security in the Gulf of Guinea*, July 2005, 3.

17. Council on Foreign Relations, *More Than Humanitarianism*, 24, 133; Jeffrey Taylor, "Worse Than Iraq?," *Atlantic*, April 2006, 33–34.

18. Council on Foreign Relations, *More Than Humanitarianism*, 40.

19. Council on Foreign Relations, *More Than Humanitarianism*, 52–53, 131.

20. Zbigniew Brzezinski, *The Grand Chessboard* (New York: Basic Books, 1997), 3.

21. Anthony Lake, "From Containment to Enlargement," speech to School of Advanced International Studies, Johns Hopkins University, September 21, 2003, http://www.mtholyoke.ed/.

17

A New Silk Road: Proposed Petroleum Pipeline in Afghanistan

John Maresca

The following testimony by John J. Maresca, a vice president of Unocal Corporation, was presented to a Congressional Committee on February 12, 1998. The hearings were held before a subcommittee of the House Committee on International Relations that was concerned with Asia and the Pacific. The subcommittee dealt extensively with Central Asia oil and gas reserves and the shaping of U.S. policy.

It has not been our practice to publish documents. Given the size of MR, we need to stick to our last. We felt, however, that an exception had to be made in this case. We think you will understand why.—The Editors.

Mr. Chairman, I am John Maresca, Vice President, International Relations, of Unocal Corporation. Unocal is one of the world's leading energy resource and project development companies. Our activities are focused on three major regions—Asia, Latin America, and the U.S. Gulf of Mexico. In Asia and the U.S. Gulf of Mexico, we are a major oil and gas producer. I appreciate your invitation to speak here today. I believe these hearings are important and timely, and I congratulate you for focusing on Central Asia oil and gas reserves and the role they play in shaping U.S. policy.

Today we would like to focus on three issues concerning this region, its resources and U.S. policy:

The need for multiple pipeline routes for Central Asian oil and gas.
The need for U.S. support for international and regional efforts to achieve balanced and lasting political settlements within Russia, other newly independent states, and in Afghanistan.

The need for structured assistance to encourage economic reforms and the
development of appropriate investment climates in the region. In this
regard, we specifically support repeal or removal of Section 907 of the Freedom Support Act.

For more than two thousand years, Central Asia has been a meeting ground
between Europe and Asia, the site of ancient east-west trade routes collectively called
the Silk Road and, at various points in history, a cradle of scholarship, culture and
power. It is also a region of truly enormous natural resources, which are revitalizing
cross-border trade, creating positive political interaction and stimulating regional
cooperation. These resources have the potential to recharge the economies of neighboring countries and put entire regions on the road to prosperity.

About one hundred years ago, the international oil industry was born in the
Caspian/Central Asian region with the discovery of oil. In the intervening years,
under Soviet rule, the existence of the region's oil and gas resources was generally
known, but only partially or poorly developed.

As we near the end of the twentieth century, history brings us full circle. With
political barriers falling, Central Asia and the Caspian are once again attracting
people from around the globe who are seeking ways to develop and deliver its boun-
tiful energy resources to the markets of the world.

The Caspian region contains tremendous untapped hydrocarbon reserves, much
of them located in the Caspian Sea basin itself. Proven natural gas reserves within
Azerbaijan, Uzbekistan, Turkmenistan and Kazakhstan equal more than 236 trillion
cubic feet. The region's total oil reserves may reach more than 60 billion barrels of
oil—enough to service Europe's oil needs for eleven years. Some estimates are as
high as 200 billion barrels. In 1995, the region was producing only 870,000 barrels per
day (44 million tons per year [Mt/y]).

By 2010, Western companies could increase production to about 4.5 million barrels a day (Mb/d)—an increase of more than 500 percent in only fifteen years. If this
occurs, the region would represent about 5 percent of the world's total oil production, and almost 20 percent of oil produced among non-OPEC countries.

One major problem has yet to be resolved: how to get the region's vast energy
resources to the markets where they are needed. There are few, if any, other areas of the
world where there can be such a dramatic increase in the supply of oil and gas to the
world market. The solution seems simple: build a "new" Silk Road. Implementing this
solution, however, is far from simple. The risks are high, but so are the rewards.

Finding and Building Routes to World Markets

One of the main problems is that Central Asia is isolated. The region is bounded
on the north by the Arctic Circle, on the east and west by vast land distances, and on

the south by a series of natural obstacles—mountains and seas—as well as political obstacles, such as conflict zones or sanctioned countries.

This means that the area's natural resources are landlocked, both geographically and politically. Each of the countries in the Caucasus and Central Asia faces difficult political challenges. Some have unsettled wars or latent conflicts. Others have evolving systems where the laws—and even the courts—are dynamic and changing. Business commitments can be rescinded without warning, or they can be displaced by new geopolitical realities.

In addition, a chief technical obstacle we face in transporting oil is the region's existing pipeline infrastructure. Because the region's pipelines were constructed during the Moscow-centered Soviet period, they tend to head north and west toward Russia. There are no connections to the south and east.

Depending wholly on this infrastructure to export Central Asia oil is not practical. Russia currently is unlikely to absorb large new quantities of "foreign" oil, is unlikely to be a significant market for energy in the next decade, and lacks the capacity to deliver it to other markets.

Certainly there is no easy way out of Central Asia. If there are to be other routes, in other directions, they must be built.

Two major energy infrastructure projects are seeking to meet this challenge. One, under the aegis of the Caspian Pipeline Consortium, or CPC, plans to build a pipeline west from the Northern Caspian to the Russian Black Sea port of Novorossisk. From Novorossisk, oil from this line would be transported by tanker through the Bosphorus to the Mediterranean and world markets.

The other project is sponsored by the Azerbaijan International Operating Company (AIOC), a consortium of eleven foreign oil companies including four American companies—Unocal, Amoco, Exxon and Pennzoil. It will follow one or both of two routes west from Baku. One line will angle north and cross the North Caucasus to Novorossisk. The other route would cross Georgia and extend to a shipping terminal on the Black Sea port of Supsa. This second route may be extended west and south across Turkey to the Mediterranean port of Ceyhan.

But even if both pipelines were built, they would not have enough total capacity to transport all the oil expected to flow from the region in the future; nor would they have the capability to move it to the right markets. Other export pipelines must be built.

Unocal believes that the central factor in planning these pipelines should be the location of the future energy markets that are most likely to need these new supplies. Just as Central Asia was the meeting ground between Europe and Asia in centuries past, it is again in a unique position to potentially service markets in both of these regions—if export routes to these markets can be built. Let's take a look at some of the potential markets.

Western Europe

Western Europe is a tough market. It is characterized by high prices for oil products, an aging population, and increasing competition from natural gas. Between

1995 and 2010, we estimate that demand for oil will increase from 14.1 Mb/d (705 Mt/y) to 15.0 Mb/d (750 Mt/y), an average growth rate of only 0.5 percent annually. Furthermore, the region is already amply supplied from fields in the Middle East, North Sea, Scandinavia and Russia. Although there is perhaps room for some of Central Asia's oil, the Western European market is unlikely to be able to absorb all of the production from the Caspian region.

Central and Eastern Europe

Central and Eastern Europe markets do not look any better. Although there is increased demand for oil in the region's transport sector, natural gas is gaining strength as a competitor. Between 1995 and 2010, demand for oil is expected to increase by only half a million barrels per day, from 1.3 Mb/d (67 Mt/y) to 1.8 Mb/d (91.5 Mt/y). Like Western Europe, this market is also very competitive. In addition to supplies of oil from the North Sea, Africa and the Middle East, Russia supplies the majority of the oil to this region.

The Domestic NIS Market

The growth in demand for oil also will be weak in the Newly Independent States (NIS). We expect Russian and other NIS markets to increase demand by only 1.2 percent annually between 1997 and 2010.

Asia/Pacific

In stark contrast to the other three markets, the Asia/Pacific region has a rapidly increasing demand for oil and an expected significant increase in population. Prior to the recent turbulence in the various Asian/Pacific economies, we anticipated that this region's demand for oil would almost double by 2010. Although the short-term increase in demand will probably not meet these expectations, Unocal stands behind its long-term estimates.

Energy demand growth will remain strong for one key reason: the region's population is expected to grow by 700 million people by 2010.

It is in everyone's interests that there be adequate supplies for Asia's increasing energy requirements. If Asia's energy needs are not satisfied, they will simply put pressure on all world markets, driving prices upwards everywhere.

The key question is how the energy resources of Central Asia can be made available to satisfy the energy needs of nearby Asian markets. There are two possible solutions—with several variations.

EXPORT ROUTES

East to China: Prohibitively Long?

One option is to go east across China. But this would mean constructing a pipeline of more than 3,000 kilometers to central China—as well as a 2,000-kilometer connection to reach the main population centers along the coast. Even with these formidable challenges, China National Petroleum Corporation is considering building a pipeline east from Kazakhstan to Chinese markets.

Unocal had a team in Beijing just last week for consultations with the Chinese. Given China's long-range outlook and its ability to concentrate resources to meet its own needs, China is almost certain to build such a line. The question is what will the costs of transporting oil through this pipeline be and what netback will the producers receive.

South to the Indian Ocean:
A Shorter Distance to Growing Markets

A second option is to build a pipeline south from Central Asia to the Indian Ocean.

One obvious potential route south would be across Iran. However, this option is foreclosed for American companies because of U.S. sanctions legislation. The only other possible route option is across Afghanistan, which has its own unique challenges.

The country has been involved in bitter warfare for almost two decades. The territory across which the pipeline would extend is controlled by the Taliban, an Islamic movement that is not recognized as a government by most other nations. From the outset, we have made it clear that construction of our proposed pipeline cannot begin until a recognized government is in place that has the confidence of governments, lenders, and our company.

In spite of this, a route through Afghanistan appears to be the best option with the fewest technical obstacles. It is the shortest route to the sea and has relatively favorable terrain for a pipeline. The route through Afghanistan is the one that would bring Central Asian oil closest to Asian markets and thus would be the cheapest in terms of transporting the oil.

Unocal envisions the creation of a Central Asian Oil Pipeline Consortium. The pipeline would become an integral part of a regional oil pipeline system that will utilize and gather oil from existing pipeline infrastructure in Turkmenistan, Uzbekistan, Kazakhstan, and Russia.

The 1,040-mile-long oil pipeline would begin near the town of Chardzhou, in northern Turkmenistan, and extend southeasterly through Afghanistan to an export terminal that would be constructed on the Pakistan coast on the Arabian Sea. Only about 440 miles of the pipeline would be in Afghanistan.

This forty-two-inch-diameter pipeline will have a shipping capacity of one million barrels of oil per day. Estimated cost of the project—which is similar in scope to the Trans Alaska Pipeline—is about US$2.5 billion.

There is considerable international and regional political interest in this pipeline. Asian crude oil importers, particularly from Japan, are looking to Central Asia and the Caspian as a new strategic source of supply to satisfy their desire for resource diversity. The pipeline benefits Central Asian countries because it would allow them to sell their oil in expanding and highly prospective hard currency markets. The pipeline would benefit Afghanistan, which would receive revenues from transport tariffs, and would promote stability and encourage trade and economic development. Although Unocal has not negotiated with any one group, and does not favor any group, we have had contacts with and briefings for all of them. We know that the different factions in Afghanistan understand the importance of the pipeline project for their country, and have expressed their support of it.

A recent study for the World Bank states that the proposed pipeline from Central Asia across Afghanistan and Pakistan to the Arabian Sea would provide more favorable netbacks to oil producers through access to higher value markets than those currently being accessed through the traditional Baltic and Black Sea export routes.

This is evidenced by the netback values producers will receive as determined by the World Bank study. For West Siberian crude, the netback value will increase by nearly $2.00 per barrel by going south to Asia. For a producer in western Kazakhstan, the netback value will increase by more than $1 per barrel by going south to Asia as compared to west to the Mediterranean via the Black Sea.

Natural Gas Export

Given the plentiful natural gas supplies of Central Asia, our aim is to link a specific natural resource with the nearest viable market. This is basic for the commercial viability of any gas project. As with all projects being considered in this region, the following projects face geo-political challenges, as well as market issues.

Unocal and the Turkish company, Koc Holding A.S., are interested in bringing competitive gas supplies to the Turkey market. The proposed Eurasia Natural Gas Pipeline would transport gas from Turkmenistan directly across the Caspian Sea through Azerbaijan and Georgia to Turkey. Sixty percent of this proposed gas pipeline would follow the same route as the oil pipeline proposed to run from Baku to Ceyhan. Of course, the demarcation of the Caspian remains an issue.

Last October, the Central Asia Pipeline, Ltd. (CentGas) consortium, in which Unocal holds an interest, was formed to develop a gas pipeline that will link Turkmenistan's vast natural gas reserves in the Dauletabad Field with markets in Pakistan and possibly India. An independent evaluation shows that the field's resources are adequate for the project's needs, assuming production rates rising over time to 2 billion cubic feet of gas per day for thirty years or more.

In production since 1983, the Dauletabad Field's natural gas has been delivered north via Uzbekistan, Kazakhstan and Russia to markets in the Caspian and Black Sea areas. The proposed 790-mile pipeline will open up new markets for this gas, travelling from Turkmenistan through Afghanistan to Multan, Pakistan. A proposed extension would link with the existing Sui pipeline system, moving gas to near New Delhi, where it would connect with the existing HBJ pipeline. By serving these additional volumes, the extension would enhance the economics of the project, leading to overall reductions in delivered natural gas costs for all users and better margins. As currently planned, the CentGas pipeline would cost approximately $2 billion. A 400-mile extension into India could add $600 million to the overall project cost.

As with the proposed Central Asia Oil Pipeline, CentGas cannot begin construction until an internationally recognized Afghanistan government is in place. For the project to advance, it must have international financing, government-to-government agreements and government-to-consortium agreements.

CONCLUSION

The Central Asia and Caspian region is blessed with abundant oil and gas that can enhance the lives of the region's residents and provide energy for growth for Europe and Asia.

The impact of these resources on U.S. commercial interests and U.S. foreign policy is also significant and intertwined. Without peaceful settlement of conflicts within the region, cross-border oil and gas pipelines are not likely to be built. We urge the Administration and the Congress to give strong support to the United Nations-led peace process in Afghanistan.

U.S. assistance in developing these new economies will be crucial to business' success. We encourage strong technical assistance programs throughout the region. We also urge repeal or removal of Section 907 of the Freedom Support Act. This section unfairly restricts U.S. government assistance to the government of Azerbaijan and limits U.S. influence in the region.

Developing cost-effective, profitable and efficient export routes for Central Asia resources is a formidable, but not impossible, task. It has been accomplished before. A commercial corridor, a "new" Silk Road, can link the Central Asia supply with the demand—once again making Central Asia the crossroads between Europe and Asia.

Thank you.

> Even their own people are aware of the admission by the Saudi Ambassador in Washington, Bandar bin Sultan, that corrupt Saudis may have siphoned off as much as $50 billion of the $400 billion spent on development.
> —*Business Week*, October 29, 2001, p. 34.

18

BLUE GOLD, TURKMEN BASHES, AND ASIAN GRIDS: PIPELINEISTAN IN CONFLICT

Pepe Escobar

As Barack Obama heads into his second hundred days in office, let's head for the big picture ourselves, the ultimate global plot line, the tumultuous rush towards a new, polycentric world order. In its first hundred days, the Obama presidency introduced us to a brand new acronym, OCO for Overseas Contingency Operations, formerly known as GWOT (as in Global War on Terror). Use either name, or anything else you want, and what you're really talking about is what's happening on the immense energy battlefield that extends from Iran to the Pacific Ocean. It's there that the Liquid War for the control of Eurasia takes place.

Yep, it all comes down to black gold and "blue gold" (natural gas), hydrocarbon wealth beyond compare, and so it's time to trek back to that ever-flowing wonderland—Pipelineistan. It's time to dust off the acronyms, especially the SCO or Shanghai Cooperative Organization, the Asian response to NATO, and learn a few new ones like IPI and TAPI. Above all, it's time to check out the most recent moves on the giant chessboard of Eurasia, where Washington wants to be a crucial, if not dominant, player.

We've already seen Pipelineistan wars in Kosovo and Georgia, and we've followed Washington's favorite pipeline, the BTC, which was supposed to tilt the flow of energy westward, sending oil coursing past both Iran and Russia. Things didn't quite turn out that way, but we've got to move on, the New Great Game never stops. Now, it's time to grasp just what the Asian Energy Security Grid is all about, visit a surreal natural gas republic, and understand why that Grid is so deeply implicated in the Af-Pak war.

Every time I've visited Iran, energy analysts stress the total "interdependence of Asia and Persian Gulf geo-ecopolitics." What they mean is the ultimate importance to various great and regional powers of Asian integration via a sprawling mass of energy pipelines that will someday, somehow, link the Persian Gulf, Central Asia, South Asia, Russia, and China. The major Iranian card in the Asian integration game is the gigantic South Pars natural gas field (which Iran shares with Qatar). It is estimated to hold at least 9% of the world's proven natural gas reserves.

As much as Washington may live in perpetual denial, Russia and Iran together control roughly 20% of the world's oil reserves and nearly 50% of its gas reserves. Think about that for a moment. It's little wonder that, for the leadership of both countries as well as China's, the idea of Asian integration, of the Grid, is sacrosanct.

If it ever gets built, a major node on that Grid will surely be the prospective $7.6 billion Iran-Pakistan-India (IPI) pipeline, also known as the "peace pipeline." After years of wrangling, a nearly miraculous agreement for its construction was initialed in 2008. At least in this rare case, both Pakistan and India stood shoulder to shoulder in rejecting relentless pressure from the Bush administration to scotch the deal.

It couldn't be otherwise. Pakistan, after all, is an energy-poor, desperate customer of the Grid. One year ago, in a speech at Beijing's Tsinghua University, then-President Pervez Musharraf did everything but drop to his knees and beg China to dump money into pipelines linking the Persian Gulf and Pakistan with China's Far West. If this were to happen, it might help transform Pakistan from a near-failed state into a mighty "energy corridor" to the Middle East. If you think of a pipeline as an umbilical cord, it goes without saying that IPI, far more than any form of U.S. aid (or outright interference), would go the extra mile in stabilizing the Pak half of Obama's Af-Pak theater of operations, and even possibly relieve it of its India obsession.

If Pakistan's fate is in question, Iran's is another matter. Though currently only holding "observer" status in the Shanghai Cooperation Organization (SCO), sooner or later it will inevitably become a full member and so enjoy NATO-style, an-attack-on-one-of-us-is-an-attack-on-all-of-us protection. Imagine, then, the cataclysmic consequences of an Israeli preemptive strike (backed by Washington or not) on Iran's nuclear facilities. The SCO will tackle this knotty issue at its next summit in June, in Yekaterinburg, Russia.

Iran's relations with both Russia and China are swell—and will remain so no matter who is elected the new Iranian president next month. China desperately needs Iranian oil and gas, has already clinched a $100 billion gas "deal of the century" with the Iranians, and has loads of weapons and cheap consumer goods to sell. No less close to Iran, Russia wants to sell them even more weapons, as well as nuclear energy technology.

And then, moving ever eastward on the great Grid, there's Turkmenistan, lodged deep in Central Asia, which, unlike Iran, you may never have heard a thing about. Let's correct that now.

GURBANGULY IS THE MAN

Alas, the sun-king of Turkmenistan, the wily, wacky Saparmurat "Turkmenbashi" Nyazov, "the father of all Turkmen" (descendants of a formidable race of nomadic horseback warriors who used to attack Silk Road caravans) is now dead. But far from forgotten.

The Chinese were huge fans of the Turkmenbashi. And the joy was mutual. One key reason the Central Asians love to do business with China is that the Middle Kingdom, unlike both Russia and the United States, carries little modern imperial baggage. And of course, China will never carp about human rights or foment a color-coded revolution of any sort.

The Chinese are already moving to successfully lobby the new Turkmen president, the spectacularly named Gurbanguly Berdymukhamedov, to speed up the construction of the Mother of All Pipelines. This Turkmen-Kazakh-China Pipelineistan corridor from eastern Turkmenistan to China's Guangdong province will be the longest and most expensive pipeline in the world, 7,000 kilometers of steel pipe at a staggering cost of $26 billion. When China signed the agreement to build it in 2007, they made sure to add a clever little geopolitical kicker. The agreement explicitly states that "Chinese interests" will not be "threatened from [Turkmenistan's] territory by third parties." In translation: no Pentagon bases allowed in that country.

China's deft energy diplomacy game plan in the former Soviet republics of Central Asia is a pure winner. In the case of Turkmenistan, lucrative deals are offered and partnerships with Russia are encouraged to boost Turkmen gas production. There are to be no Russian-Chinese antagonisms, as befits the main partners in the SCO, because the Asian Energy Security Grid story is really and truly about them.

By the way, elsewhere on the Grid, those two countries recently agreed to extend the East Siberian-Pacific Ocean oil pipeline to China by the end of 2010. After all, energy-ravenous China badly needs not just Turkmen gas, but Russia's liquefied natural gas (LNG).

With energy prices low and the global economy melting down, times are sure to be tough for the Kremlin through at least 2010, but this won't derail its push to forge a Central Asian energy club within the SCO. Think of all this as essentially an energy *entente cordiale* with China. Russian Deputy Industry and Energy Minister Ivan Materov has been among those insistently swearing that this will *not* someday lead to a "gas OPEC" within the SCO. It remains to be seen how the Obama national security team decides to counteract the successful Russian strategy of undermining by all possible means a U.S.-promoted East-West Caspian Sea energy corridor, while solidifying a Russian-controlled Pipelineistan stretching from Kazakhstan to Greece that will monopolize the flow of energy to Western Europe.

THE REAL AFGHAN WAR

In the ever-shifting New Great Game in Eurasia, a key question—why Afghanistan matters—is simply not part of the discussion in the United States. (Hint: It has nothing to do with the liberation of Afghan women.) In part, this is because the idea that energy and Afghanistan might have anything in common is *verboten*.

And yet, rest assured, nothing of significance takes place in Eurasia without an energy angle. In the case of Afghanistan, keep in mind that Central and South Asia have been considered by American strategists crucial places to plant the flag; and once the Soviet Union collapsed, control of the energy-rich former Soviet republics in the region was quickly seen as essential to future U.S. global power. It would be there, as they imagined it, that the U.S. Empire of Bases would intersect crucially with Pipelineistan in a way that would leave both Russia and China on the defensive.

Think of Afghanistan, then, as an overlooked subplot in the ongoing Liquid War. After all, an overarching goal of U.S. foreign policy since President Richard Nixon's era in the early 1970s has been to split Russia and China. The leadership of the SCO has been focused on this since the U.S. Congress passed the Silk Road Strategy Act five days before beginning the bombing of Serbia in March 1999. That act clearly identified American geo-strategic interests from the Black Sea to western China with building a mosaic of American protectorates in Central Asia and militarizing the Eurasian energy corridor.

Afghanistan, as it happens, sits conveniently at the crossroads of any new Silk Road linking the Caucasus to western China, and four nuclear powers (China, Russia, Pakistan, and India) lurk in the vicinity. "Losing" Afghanistan and its key network of U.S. military bases would, from the Pentagon's point of view, be a disaster, and though it may be a secondary matter in the New Great Game of the moment, it's worth remembering that the country itself is a lot more than the towering mountains of the Hindu Kush and immense deserts: it's believed to be rich in unexplored deposits of natural gas, petroleum, coal, copper, chrome, talc, barites, sulfur, lead, zinc, and iron ore, as well as precious and semiprecious stones.

And there's something highly toxic to be added to this already lethal mix: don't forget the narco-dollar angle—the fact that the global heroin cartels that feast on Afghanistan only work with U.S. dollars, not euros. For the SCO, the top security threat in Afghanistan isn't the Taliban, but the drug business. Russia's anti-drug czar Viktor Ivanov routinely blasts the disaster that passes for a U.S./NATO anti-drug war there, stressing that Afghan heroin now kills 30,000 Russians annually, twice as many as were killed during the decade-long U.S.-supported anti-Soviet Afghan *jihad* of the 1980s.

And then, of course, there are those competing pipelines that, if ever built, either would or wouldn't exclude Iran and Russia from the action to their south. In April 2008, Turkmenistan, Afghanistan, Pakistan, and India actually signed an agreement to build a long-dreamt-about $7.6 billion (and counting) pipeline, whose acronym TAPI combines the first letters of their names and would also someday deliver natural gas from Turkmenistan to Pakistan and India without the involvement of either Iran or Russia. It would cut right through the heart of Western Afghanistan, in Herat, and head south across lightly populated Nimruz and Helmand provinces, where the Taliban, various Pashtun guerrillas and assorted highway robbers now merrily run rings around U.S. and NATO forces and where—surprise!—the U.S. is now building in Dasht-e-Margo ("the Desert of Death") a new mega-base to host President Obama's surge troops.

TAPI's rival is the already mentioned IPI, also theoretically underway and widely derided by Heritage Foundation types in the U.S., who regularly launch blasts of angry prose at the nefarious idea of India and Pakistan importing gas from "evil" Iran. Theoretically, TAPI's construction will start in 2010 and the gas would begin flowing by 2015. (Don't hold your breath.) Embattled Afghan President Hamid Karzai, who can hardly secure a few square blocks of central Kabul, even with the help of international forces, nonetheless offered assurances last year that he would not only rid his country of millions of land mines along TAPI's route, but somehow get rid of the Taliban in the bargain.

Should there be investors (nursed by Afghan opium dreams) delirious enough to sink their money into such a pipeline—and that's a monumental *if*—Afghanistan would collect only $160 million a year in transit fees, a mere bagatelle even if it does represent a big chunk of the embattled Karzai's current annual revenue. Count on one thing though, if it ever happened, the Taliban and assorted warlords/highway robbers would be sure to get a cut of the action.

A CLINTON-BUSH-OBAMA GREAT GAME

TAPI's roller-coaster history actually begins in the mid-1990s, the Clinton era, when the Taliban were dined (but not wined) by the California-based energy company Unocal and the Clinton machine. In 1995, Unocal first came up with the pipeline idea, even then a product of Washington's fatal urge to bypass both Iran and Russia. Next, Unocal talked to the Turkmenbashi, then to the Taliban, and so launched a classic New Great Game gambit that has yet to end and without which you can't understand the Afghan war Obama has inherited.

A Taliban delegation, thanks to Unocal, enjoyed Houston's hospitality in early 1997 and then Washington's in December of that year. When it came to energy negotiations, the Taliban's leadership was anything but medieval. They were tough bargainers, also cannily courting the Argentinean private oil company Bridas, which had secured the right to explore and exploit oil reserves in eastern Turkmenistan.

In August 1997, financially unstable Bridas sold 60% of its stock to Amoco, which merged the next year with British Petroleum. A key Amoco consultant happened to be that ubiquitous Eurasian player, former national security advisor Zbig Brzezinski, while another such luminary, Henry Kissinger, just happened to be a consultant for Unocal. BP-Amoco, already developing the Baku-Tblisi-Ceyhan (BTC) pipeline, now became the major player in what had already been dubbed the Trans-Afghan Pipeline or TAP. Inevitably, Unocal and BP-Amoco went to war and let the lawyers settle things in a Texas court, where, in October 1998 as the Clinton years drew to an end, BP-Amoco seemed to emerge with the upper hand.

Under newly elected president George W. Bush, however, Unocal snuck back into the game and, as early as January 2001, was cozying up to the Taliban yet again, this time supported by a star-studded governmental cast of characters, including Undersecretary of State Richard Armitage, himself a former Unocal lobbyist. The Taliban were duly invited back to Washington in March 2001 via Rahmatullah Hashimi, a top aide to "The Shadow," the movement's leader Mullah Omar.

Negotiations eventually broke down because of those pesky transit fees the Taliban demanded. Beware the Empire's fury. At a Group of Eight summit meeting in Genoa in July 2001, Western diplomats indicated that the Bush administration had decided to take the Taliban down before year's end. (Pakistani diplomats in Islamabad would later confirm this to me.) The attacks of September 11, 2001 just slightly accelerated the schedule. Nicknamed "the kebab seller" in Kabul, Hamid Karzai, a former CIA asset and Unocal representative, who had entertained visiting Taliban members at barbecues in Houston, was soon forced down Afghan throats as the country's new leader.

Among the first fruits of Donald Rumsfeld's bombing and invasion of Afghanistan in the fall of 2001 was the signing by Karzai, Pakistani President Musharraf and Turkmenistan's Nyazov of an agreement committing themselves to build TAP, and so was formally launched a Pipelineistan extension from Central to South Asia with brand USA stamped all over it.

Russian President Vladimir Putin did nothing—until September 2006, that is, when he delivered his counterpunch with panache. That's when Russian energy behemoth Gazprom agreed to buy Nyazov's natural gas at the 40% mark-up the dictator demanded. In return, the Russians received priceless gifts (and the Bush administration a pricey kick in the face). Nyazov turned over control of Turkmenistan's entire gas surplus to the Russian company through 2009, indicated a preference for letting Russia explore the country's new gas fields, and stated that Turkmenistan was bowing out of any U.S.-backed Trans-Caspian pipeline project. (And while he was at it, Putin also cornered much of the gas exports of Kazakhstan and Uzbekistan as well.)

Thus, almost five years later, with occupied Afghanistan in increasingly deadly chaos, TAP seemed dead-on-arrival. The (invisible) star of what would later turn into Obama's "good" war was already a corpse.

But here's the beauty of Pipelineistan: like zombies, dead deals always seem to return and so the game goes on forever.

Just when Russia thought it had Turkmenistan locked in . . .

A TURKMEN BASH

They don't call Turkmenistan a "gas republic" for nothing. I've crossed it from the Uzbek border to a Caspian Sea port named—what else—Turkmenbashi where you can purchase one kilo of fresh Beluga for $100 and a camel for $200. That's where the gigantic gas fields are, and it's obvious that most have not been fully explored. When, in October 2008, the British consultancy firm GCA confirmed that the Yolotan-Osman gas fields in southwest Turkmenistan were among the world's four largest, holding up to a staggering 14 trillion cubic meters of natural gas, Turkmenistan promptly grabbed second place in the global gas reserves sweepstakes, way ahead of Iran and only 20% below Russia. With that news, the earth shook seismically across Pipelineistan.

Just before he died in December 2006, the flamboyant Turkmenbashi boasted that his country held enough reserves to export 150 billion cubic meters of gas annually for the next 250 years. Given his notorious megalomania, nobody took him seriously. So in March 2008, our man Gurbanguly ordered a GCA audit to dispel any doubts. After all, in pure Asian Energy Security Grid mode, Turkmenistan had already signed contracts to supply Russia with about 50 billion cubic meters annually, China with 40 billion cubic meters, and Iran with 8 billion cubic meters.

And yet, none of this turns out to be quite as monumental or settled as it may look. In fact, Turkmenistan and Russia may be playing the energy equivalent of Russian roulette. After all, virtually all of Turkmenistani gas exports flow north through an old, crumbling Soviet system of pipelines, largely built in the 1960s. Add to this a Turkmeni knack for raising the stakes non-stop at a time when Gazprom has little choice but to put up with it: without Turkmen gas, it simply can't export all it needs to Europe, the source of 70% of Gazprom's profits.

Worse yet, according to a Gazprom source quoted in the Russian business daily *Kommersant*, the stark fact is that the company only thought it controlled all of Turkmenistan's gas exports; the newly discovered gas mega-fields turn out not to be part of the deal. As my *Asia Times* colleague, former ambassador M.K. Bhadrakumar put the matter, Gazprom's mistake "is proving to be a misconception of Himalayan proportions."

In fact, it's as if the New Great Gamesters had just discovered another Everest. This year, Obama's national security strategists lost no time unleashing a no-holds-barred diplomatic campaign to court Turkmenistan. The goal? To accelerate possible ways for all that new Turkmeni gas to flow through the *right* pipes, and create quite a different energy map and future. Apart from TAPI, another key objective is to make the prospective $5.8 billion Turkey-to-Austria Nabucco pipeline become viable and thus, of course, trump the Russians. In that way, a key long-term U.S. strategic objective would be fulfilled: Austria, Italy, and Greece, as well as the Balkan and various Central European countries, would be at least partially pulled from Gazprom's orbit. (Await my next "postcard" from Pipelineistan for more on this.)

IPI OR TAPI?

Gurbanguly is proving an even more riotous player than the Turkmenbashi. A year ago he said he was going to hedge his bets, that he was willing to export the bulk of the eight trillion cubic meters of gas reserves he now claims for his country to virtually anyone. Washington was—and remains—ecstatic. At an international conference last month in Ashgabat ("the city of love"), the Las Vegas of Central Asia, Gurbanguly told a hall packed with Americans, Europeans, and Russians that "diversification of energy flows and inclusion of new countries into the geography of export routes can help the global economy gain stability."

Inevitably, behind closed doors, the TAPI maze came up and TAPI executives once again began discussing pricing and transit fees. Of course, hard as that may be to settle, it's the easy part of the deal. After all, there's that Everest of Afghan security to climb, and someone still has to confirm that Turkmenistan's gas reserves are really as fabulous as claimed.

Imperceptible jiggles in Pipelineistan's tectonic plates can shake half the world. Take, for example, an obscure March report in the *Balochistan Times*: a little noticed pipeline supplying gas to parts of Sindh province in Pakistan, including Karachi, was blown up. It got next to no media attention, but all across Eurasia and in Washington, those analyzing the comparative advantages of TAPI vs. IPI had to wonder just how risky it might be for India to buy future Iranian gas via increasingly volatile Balochistan.

And then in early April came another mysterious pipeline explosion, this one in Turkmenistan, compromising exports to Russia. The Turkmens promptly blamed the Russians (and TAPI advocates cheered), but nothing in Afghanistan itself could have left them cheering very loudly. Right now, Dick Cheney's master plan to get those blue rivers of Turkmeni gas flowing southwards via a future TAPI as part of a U.S. grand strategy for a "Greater Central Asia" lies in tatters.

Still, Zbig Brzezinski might disagree, and as he commands Obama's attention, he may try to convince the new president that the world needs a $7.6-plus billion, 1,600-km steel serpent winding through a horribly dangerous war zone. That's certainly the gist of what Brzezinski said immediately after the 2008 Russia-Georgia war, stressing once again that "the construction of a pipeline from Central Asia via Afghanistan to the south . . . will maximally expand world society's access to the Central Asian energy market."

WASHINGTON OR BEIJING?

Still, give credit where it's due. For the time being, our man Gurbanguly may have snatched the leading role in the New Great Game in this part of Eurasia. He's already signed a groundbreaking gas agreement with RWE from Germany and sent the Russians scrambling.

If, one of these days, the Turkmenistani leader opts for TAPI as well, it will open Washington to an ultimate historical irony. After so much death and destruction, Washington would undoubtedly have to sit down once again with—yes—the Taliban! And we'd be back to July 2001 and those pesky pipeline transit fees.

As it stands at the moment, however, Russia still dominates Pipelineistan, ensuring Central Asian gas flows across Russia's network and not through the Trans-Caspian networks privileged by the U.S. and the European Union. This virtually guarantees Russia's crucial geopolitical status as the top gas supplier to Europe and a crucial supplier to Asia as well.

Meanwhile, in "transit corridor" Pakistan, where Predator drones soaring over Pashtun tribal villages monopolize the headlines, the shady New Great Game slouches in under-the-radar mode toward the immense, under-populated southern Pakistani province of Balochistan. The future of the epic IPI vs. TAPI battle may hinge on a single, magic word: Gwadar.

Essentially a fishing village, Gwadar is an Arabian Sea port in that province. The port was built by China. In Washington's dream scenario, Gwadar becomes the new Dubai of South Asia. This implies the success of TAPI. For its part, China badly needs Gwadar as a node for yet another long pipeline to be built to western China. And where would the gas flowing in that line come from? Iran, of course.

Whoever "wins," if Gwadar really becomes part of the Liquid War, Pakistan will finally become a key transit corridor for either Iranian gas from the monster South Pars field heading for China, or a great deal of the Caspian gas from Turkmenistan heading Europe-wards. To make the scenario even more locally mouth-watering, Pakistan would then be a pivotal place for both NATO and the SCO (in which it is already an official "observer").

Now that's as classic as the New Great Game in Eurasia can get. There's NATO vs. the SCO. With either IPI or TAPI, Turkmenistan wins. With either IPI or TAPI, Russia loses. With either IPI or TAPI, Pakistan wins. With TAPI, Iran loses. With IPI, Afghanistan loses. In the end, however, as in any game of high stakes Pipelineistan poker, it all comes down to the top two global players. Ladies and gentlemen, place your bets: will the winner be Washington or Beijing?

Pepe Escobar is the roving correspondent for Asia Times and an analyst for the Real News. Parts of this article draw on his new book, Obama Does Globalistan. His first "post-card" from Pipelineistan, "Liquid War," was posted at TomDispatch.com in March. He may be reached at pepeasia@yahoo.com.

Copyright 2009 Pepe Escobar

19

THE POLITICAL ECONOMY OF IMPERIALISM: THE INTERLOCKS BETWEEN THE OIL INDUSTRY AND THE STATE

Chuck O'Connell

". . . the highest levels of the executive branch, especially in the State, defense, and Treasury Departments, are interlocked constantly with the corporate community through the movement of executives and corporate lawyers in and out of government. Although the same person is not in governmental and corporate positions at the same time, there is enough continuity for the relationship to be described as one of *revolving interlocks*. Corporate leaders resign from their numerous directorships to serve in government for two or three years, then return to the corporate community."—G. William Domhoff, **Who Rules America?** (2006: 171)

State Office	Capitalist Class (corporation, foundation, policy discussion group)
Secretary of State	
John Foster Dulles 1953–1959	Legal counsel to Standard Oil; trustee of Rockefeller Foundation
Christian A. Herter 1959–1961	Linked to Rockefellers through the World Peace Foundation
Dean Rusk 1961–1969	Former head of the Rockefeller Foundation
Henry A. Kissinger 1973–1977	Council on Foreign Relations; Rockefeller Brothers Fund; Consultant to Unocal

Cyrus A. Vance 1977–1980	Trustee, Rockefeller Foundation Director, Council on Foreign Relations Member, Trilateral Commission
Alexander Haig 1981–1982	Director, Chase Manhattan Bank
George P. Schultz 1982–1989	Director, Bechtel Corp—Interlocked w/Chevron & Gulf Oil Member, Trilateral Commission
James A. Baker 1989–1992	Family holdings in Exxon, Mobil, Arco, Standard Oil of California, Standard Oil of Indiana
Condoleeza Rice 2005–2009	Director of Chevron Corporation
Casper Weinberger Sec of Defense under Reagan	Attorney for Bechtel and co-author of *The Next War* (1997) which argued for greater U.S. presence in the Caspian Basin.
Zbigniew Brezezinski former National SecurityAdvisor	Retained by Amoco (a major shareholder in two Azerbaijani oil consortia) as a consultant and author of *The Grand Chessboard* (1997) which argued for U.S. primacy over the Eurasian landmass.
Brent Scowcroft former National Security Advisor	Retained by Pennzoil as a consultant
Arthur Hartman former U.S. Ambassador to Moscow	Chairman of a company that buys oil from Turkmenistan
Richard Holbrooke former Assistant Secretary of State	Employed by Credit Suisse First Boston—a potential participant in pipeline financing.
Condoleeza Rice National Security Advisor Secretary of State	Director of Chevron Corporation
George Bush, Jr. President 2001–2009	Former Director of Harken Energy Corporation (Dallas) which obtained (1990) exclusive oil concession in Bahrain (200 mi SE of Kuwait)
George H.W. Bush Former U.S. President	Founder of Zapata Oil Co. which built Kuwait's first offshore oil well

Dick Cheney Vice-President 2001–2009	While CEO of Halliburton, Cheney served on the board of advisors for the state oil company of Kazakhstan along with executives from Chevron and Texaco.
Zalmay Khalilzad National Security Council member U.S. ambassador to the UN	Employed in the mid-1990s as a risk assessor for Unocal looking at the feasibility of a gas pipeline across Afghanistan

U.S. policy in the Middle East and Central Asia is shaped by the class perspective of those men and women of the capitalist class who develop their understanding of the problems of foreign relations and possible solutions to those problems through their general education in elite schools, membership in the corporate community as executives and attorneys of firms and foundations , and participation in policy discussion groups such as the Council on Foreign Relations. They are able to develop and execute policy favoring their class interests because they staff the key executive offices of the State either as elected officials or as appointed officials.

Why would Barack Obama's administration break from this pattern? (It hasn't.)

20

NONDEMOCRATIC REGIMES OF MIDEAST SUPPORTED BY THE U.S.A.

Deborah J. Gerner and Jillian Schwedler

Natural Resources	Country	Executive System	Legality of Political Parties	Notes
Oil	Bahrain	Absolute monarchy	No	
Oil	Egypt	Formally democratic	Yes	Formerly ruled by Hosni Mubarak, Egypt's corrupt, autocratic govt is second largest recipient of US military and economic aid.
Oil	Iran	Dictatorship-the Shah concentrated power in his hands at expense of landlords, merchants, and the ulama.	?	USA brought Shah to power in 1953 and supported him until his overthrow in 1979.
Oil	Iraq	Ba'athist dictatorship prior to March 2003	Yes	U.S. supported Ba'athist coup in 1963. Recognized Hussein 1982 and supported Iraq's war of aggression versus Iran.
Oil	Kuwait	Emir	No	
Oil	Oman	Absolute monarchy	No	
Oil	Qatar	Emir	No	
Oil	Saudi Arabia	Absolute monarchy	No	No constitution. No legislature. No free press.
Oil	U.A.E	Federation of emirates	No	

Adapted from Deborah J. Gerner (ed.), **Understanding the Contemporary Middle East** (2000, p. 101)

21

HART/RUDMAN—21ST CENTURY COMMISSION RECOMMENDS NEW ANTI-TERROR CABINET AGENCY

A bipartisan panel led by former US senators Warren B. Rudman and Gary Hart on Wednesday *called for the creation of a Cabinet-level agency to assume responsibility for defending the United States against the increasing likelihood of terrorist attacks in the country.* The commission making the recommendation included high-ranking military and former Cabinet secretaries. *Their report warned bluntly that terrorists probably will attack the United States* with nuclear, chemical or biological weapons at some point within the next 25 years.

The commission proposed a complete redesign of the National Guard to provide the *proposed new "Homeland Security Agency"* with U.S.-based troops to combat those who threaten a nation that for more than two centuries was isolated from attack by two oceans. The panel outlined a far-reaching reorganization of the Pentagon, State Department, National Security Council and other agencies, saying that they have become bloated and unfocused. The report even urged Congress to streamline its own committee structure to keep interference in national security matters at a minimum.

The commission acknowledged that implementing the recommendations would be difficult. Congress would have to pass legislation authorizing the changes. If all of the recommendations were to become law, it would mark the most sweeping renovation of United States defense and foreign policy operations since approval of the landmark National Security Act of 1947. Like that measure, which refocused World War II–era agencies on the challenges of the Cold War, the commission's plan is intended to ready the nation for starkly different threats in a new century.

The panel, in what many are calling a radical departure from "conventional wisdom," *recommended folding the Federal Emergency Management Agency, Customs Service,*

Border Patrol and Coast Guard into the new "Homeland Security Agency." It said that the National Guard should be "reorganized, properly trained and adequately equipped" to cope with natural disasters and attacks on U.S. targets by weapons of mass destruction. *The commission said that the National Guard should be relieved of the responsibility of participating in overseas deployments and concentrate on security at home.*

The report said: "The combination of unconventional weapons proliferation with the persistence of international terrorism will end the relative invulnerability of the US homeland to catastrophic attack. *A direct attack against American citizens on American soil is likely* over the next quarter century. The risk is not only death and destruction but also a demoralization that could undermine US global leadership. In the face of this threat, our nation has no coherent or integrated governmental structures."

US armed forces now are organized and trained to have the capability to fight two major overseas wars at the same time, a contingency the commission called "very remote." The report recommended abandoning the two-war strategy to permit the Pentagon to prepare for situations like the recent wars in Bosnia-Herzegovina and Kosovo, which it characterized as far more likely. The panel said that both the State Department and the Pentagon "need substantial bureaucratic remodeling."

22

STRAIGHT TALK ON TERRORISM

Eqbal Ahmad (1933–1999)

Eqbal Ahmad first wrote for MR *in 1968, and was a valued friend and contributor over the years, writing articles on a number of occasions on topics related to the third world, including his important article "From Potato Sack to Potato Mash: On the Contemporary Crisis of the Third World" (March 1981). For many years he was managing editor of the important journal* Race and Class. *This article is taken from a speech he delivered at the University of Colorado at Boulder on October 12, 1998, the year before his death. It is part of* Terrorism, Theirs & Ours, *a book of Ahmad's writings with a foreward and interview by David Barsamian, recently published by Seven Stories Press. It is reprinted here by permission.—the Editors*

Until the 1930s and early 1940s, the Jewish underground in Palestine was described as "terrorist." Then something happened: around 1942, as news of the Holocaust was spreading, a certain liberal sympathy with the Jewish people began to emerge in the Western world. By 1944, the terrorists of Palestine, who were Zionists, suddenly began being described as "freedom fighters." If you look in history books you can find at least two Israeli Prime Ministers, including Menachem Begin, appearing in "Wanted" posters saying, "Terrorists, reward this much." The highest reward I have seen offered was 100,000 British pounds for the head of Menachem Begin, the terrorist.

From 1969 to 1990, the Palestine Liberation Organization (PLO) occupied center stage as the terrorist organization. Yasir Arafat has been repeatedly described as the "chief of terrorism" by the great sage of American journalism, William Safire of the

New York Times. On September 29, 1998, I was rather amused to notice a picture of Yasir Arafat and Israeli Prime Minister Benjamin Netanyahu standing on either side of President Bill Clinton. Clinton was looking toward Arafat who looked meek as a mouse. Just a few years earlier, Arafat would appear in photos with a very menacing look, a gun holstered to his belt. That's Yasir Arafat. You remember those pictures, and you'll remember the next one.

In 1985, President Ronald Reagan received a group of ferocious-looking, turban-wearing men who looked like they came from another century. I had been writing about the very same men for *The New Yorker.* After receiving them in the White House, Reagan spoke to the press, referring to his foreign guests as "freedom fighters." These were the Afghan *mujahideen.* They were at the time, guns in hand, battling the "Evil Empire." For Reagan, they were the moral equivalent of our Founding Fathers.

In August 1998, another American President ordered missile strikes to kill Osama bin Laden and his men in Afghanistan-based camps. Mr. Bin Laden, at whom [. . .] American missiles were fired [. . .] was only a few years earlier the moral equivalent of George Washington and Thomas Jefferson. I'll return to the subject of bin Laden later.

I am recalling these stories to point out that the official approach to terrorism is rather complicated, but not without characteristics. To begin with, terrorists change. The terrorist of yesterday is the hero of today, and the hero of yesterday becomes the terrorist of today. In a constantly changing world of images, we have to keep our heads straight to know what terrorism is and what is not. Even more importantly, we need to know what causes terrorism and how to stop it.

Secondly, the official approach to terrorism is a posture of inconsistency, one which evades definition. I have examined at least twenty official documents on terrorism. Not one offers a definition. All of them explain it polemically in order to arouse our emotions, rather than exercise our intelligence. I'll give you an example which is representative. On October 25, 1984, Secretary of State George Shultz gave a long speech on terrorism at the Park Avenue Synagogue in New York City. In the State Department Bulletin of seven single-spaced pages, there is not a single clear definition of terrorism. What we get instead are the following statements. Number one: "Terrorism is a modern barbarism that we call terrorism." Number two is even more brilliant: "Terrorism is a form of political violence." Number three: "Terrorism is a threat to Western civilization." Number four: "Terrorism is a menace to Western moral values." Do these accomplish anything other than arouse emotions? This is typical.

Officials don't define terrorism because definitions involve a commitment to analysis, comprehension and adherence to some norms of consistency. That's the second characteristic of the official approach to terrorism. The third characteristic is that the absence of definition does not prevent officials from being globalistic. They may not define terrorism, but they can call it a menace to good order, a menace to the moral values of Western civilization, a menace to humankind. Therefore, they can call for it to be stamped out worldwide. Anti-terrorist policies therefore, must be global. In the same speech [. . .] Schultz also said: "There is no question about our ability to use force where and when it is needed to counter terrorism." There is no geographical limit. On the same day, U.S. missiles struck Afghanistan and Sudan. Those two countries are 2,300 miles apart, and they were hit by missiles belonging to a country roughly 8,000 miles away. Reach is global.

A fourth characteristic is that the official approach to terrorism claims not only global reach, but also a certain omniscient knowledge. They claim to know where terrorists are, and therefore, where to hit. To quote George Schultz again, "We know the difference between terrorists and freedom fighters, and as we look around, we have no trouble telling one from the other." Only Osama bin Laden doesn't know that he was an ally one day and an enemy another. That's very confusing for Osama bin Laden. I'll come back to him toward the end; it's a real story.

Fifth, the official approach eschews causation. They don't look at why people resort to terrorism. Cause? What cause? Another example: on December 18, 1985, the *New York Times* reported that the foreign minister of Yugoslavia—you remember the days when there was a Yugoslavia—requested the Secretary of State of the U.S. to consider the causes of Palestinian terrorism. The Secretary of State, George Shultz, and I'm quoting from the *New York Times,* "went a bit red in the face. He pounded the table and told the visiting foreign minister, There is no connection with any cause. Period." Why look for causes?

A sixth characteristic of the official approach to terrorism is the need for the moral revulsion we feel against terror to be selective. We are to denounce the terror of those groups which are officially disapproved. But we are to applaud the terror of those groups of whom officials do approve. Hence, President Reagan's statement, "I am a contra." We know that the contras of Nicaragua were by any definition terrorists, but the media heed the dominant view.

More importantly to me, the dominant approach also excludes from consideration the terrorism of friendly governments. Thus, the United States excused, among others, the terrorism of Pinochet, who killed one of my closest friends, Orlando Letelier, one of Chilean president Salvador Allende's top diplomats, killed in a car bombing in Washington D.C. in 1976. And it excused the terror of Zia ul-Haq, the military dictator of Pakistan, who killed many of my friends there. All I want to tell you is that according to my ignorant calculations, the ratio of people killed by the state terror of Zia ul-Haq, Pinochet, [and dictatorships of the] Argentinean, Brazilian, Indonesian type, versus the killing of the PLO and other organizations is literally, conservatively, 1,000 to 1. That's the ratio.

History unfortunately recognizes and accords visibility to power, not to weakness. Therefore, visibility has been accorded historically to dominant groups. Our time—the time that begins with Columbus—has been one of extraordinary unrecorded holocausts. Great civilizations have been wiped out. The Mayas, the Incas, the Aztecs, the

American Indians, the Canadian Indians were all wiped out. Their voices have not been heard, even to this day. They are heard, yes, but only when the dominant power suffers, only when resistance has a semblance of costing, of exacting a price, when a Custer is killed or when a Gordon is besieged. That's when you know that there were Indians or Arabs fighting and dying.

My last point on this subject is that during the Cold War period, the United States sponsored terrorist regimes like Somoza in Nicaragua and Batista in Cuba, one after another. All kinds of tyrants have been America's friends. In Nicaragua it was the *contra*, in Afghanistan, the *mujahideen*.

Now, what about the other side? What is terrorism? Our first job should be to define the damn thing, name it, give it a description other than "moral equivalent of founding fathers" or "a moral outrage to Western civilization." This is what Webster's Collegiate Dictionary says: "Terror is an intense, overpowering fear." Terrorism is "the use of terrorizing methods of governing or resisting a government." This simple definition has one great virtue: it's fair. It focuses on the use of violence that is used illegally, extra-constitutionally, to coerce. And this definition is correct because it treats terror for what it is, whether a government or private group commits it.

Have you noticed something? Motivation is omitted. We're not talking about whether the cause is just or unjust. We're talking about consensus, consent, absence of consent, legality, absence of legality, constitutionality, absence of constitutionality. Why do we keep motives out? Because motives make no difference. In the course of my work I have identified five types of terrorism; state terrorism, religious terrorism, (Catholics killing Protestants, Sunnis killing Shiites, Shiites killing Sunnis), criminal terrorism, political terrorism, and oppositional terrorism. Sometimes these five can converge and overlap. Oppositional protest terrorism can become pathological criminal terrorism. State terror can take the form of private terror. For example, we're all familiar with the death squads in Latin America or in Pakistan where the government has employed private people to kill its opponents. It's not quite official. It's privatized. In Afghanistan, Central America, and Southeast Asia, the CIA employed in its covert operations drug pushers. Drugs and guns often go together. The categories often overlap.

Of the five types of terror, the official approach is to focus on only one form—political terrorism—which claims the least in terms of loss of human lives and property. The form that exacts the highest loss is state terrorism. The second highest loss is created by religious terrorism, although religious terror has, relatively speaking, declined. If you are looking historically, however, religious terrorism has caused massive loss. The next highest loss is caused by criminal terrorism. A Rand Corporation study by Brian Jenkins examining a ten-year period (1978 to 1988) showed 50 percent of terrorism was committed without any political cause. No politics. Simply crime and pathology. So the focus is on only one, the political terrorist—the PLO, the bin Laden, whoever you want to take.

WHY DO THEY DO IT? WHAT MAKES TERRORISTS TICK?

I would like to knock out some quick answers. First, the need to be heard. Remember, we are dealing with a minority group, the political, private terrorist. Normally, and there are exceptions, there is an effort to be heard, to get their grievances recognized and addressed by people. The Palestinians, for example, the superterrorists of our time, were dispossessed in 1948. From 1948 to 1968 they went to every court in the world. They knocked on every door. They had been completely deprived of their land, their country, and nobody was listening. In desperation, they invented a new form of terror: the airplane hijacking. Between 1968 and 1975 they pulled the world up by its ears. That kind of terror is a violent way of expressing long-felt grievances. It makes the world hear. It's normally undertaken by small, helpless groupings that feel powerless. We still haven't done the Palestinians justice, but at least we all know they exist. Now, even the Israelis acknowledge. Remember what Golda Meir, Prime Minister of Israel, said in 1970: There are no Palestinians. They do not exist. They damn well exist now.

Secondly, terrorism is an expression of anger, of feeling helpless, angry, alone. You feel like you have to hit back. Wrong has been done to you, so you do it. During the hijacking of the TWA jet in Beirut, Judy Brown of Belmar, New Jersey, said that she kept hearing them yell, "New Jersey, New Jersey." What did they have in mind? She thought that they were gong after her. Later on it turned out that the terrorists were referring to the U.S. battleship New Jersey, which had heavily shelled the Lebanese civilian population in 1983.

Another factor is a sense of betrayal, which is connected to that tribal ethic of revenge. It comes into the picture in the case of people like bin Laden. Here is a man who was an ally of the United States, who saw America as a friend; then he sees his country being occupied by the United States and feels betrayal. Whether there is a sense of right and wrong is not what I'm saying. I'm describing what's behind this kind of extreme violence.

Sometimes, it's the fact that you have experienced violence at other people's hands. Victims of violent abuse often became violent people. The only time when Jews produced terrorists in organized fashion was during and after the Holocaust. It is rather remarkable that Jewish terrorists hit largely innocent people or UN peacemakers like Count Bernadotte of Sweden, whose country had a better record on the Holocaust. The men of Irgun, the Stern Gang, and the Hagannah terrorist groups came in the wake of the Holocaust. The experience of victimhood itself produces a violent reaction.

In modern times, with modern technology and means of communications, the targets have been globalized. Therefore, globalization of violence is an aspect of what we call globalization of the economy and culture in the world as a whole. We can't expect everything else to be globalized and violence not to be. We do have visible targets. Airplane hijacking is something new because international travel is relatively new, too. Everybody now is in your gunsight. Therefore the globe is within the gunsight. That has globalized terror.

Finally, the absence of revolutionary ideology has been central to the spread of terror in our time. One of the points in the big debate between Marxism and anarchism in the nineteenth century was the use of terror. The Marxists argued that the true revolutionary does not assassinate. You do not solve social problems by individual acts of violence. Social problems require social and political mobilization, and thus wars of liberation are to be distinguished from terrorist organizations. The revolutionaries didn't reject violence, but they rejected terror as a viable tactic of revolution. That revolutionary ideology has gone out at the moment. In the 1980s and 1990s, revolutionary ideology receded, giving in to the globalized individual. In general terms, these are among the many forces that are behind modern terrorism.

To this challenge rulers from one country after another have been responding with traditional methods. The traditional method of shooting it out, whether it's with missiles or some other means. The Israelis are very proud of it. The Americans are very proud of it. The French became very proud of it. Now the Pakistanis are very proud of it. The Pakistanis say, Our commandos are the best. Frankly, it won't work. A central problem of our time: political minds rooted in the past at odds with modern times, producing new realities.

Let's turn back for a moment to Osama bin Laden, *Jihad*, which has been translated a thousand times as "holy war," is not quite that. *Jihad* in Arabic means "to struggle." It could be struggle by violence or struggle by non-violent means. There are two forms, the small *jihad* and the big *jihad*. The small *jihad* involves external violence. The big *jihad* involves a struggle within oneself. Those are the concepts. The reason I mention it is that in Islamic history, *jihad* as an international violent phenomenon had for all practical purposes disappeared in the last four hundred years. It was revived suddenly with American help in the 1980s. When the Soviet Union intervened in Afghanistan, which borders Pakistan, Zia ul-Haq saw an opportunity and launched a *jihad* there against godless communism. The U.S. saw a God-sent opportunity to mobilize one billion Muslims against what Reagan called the Evil Empire. Money started pouring in. CIA agents starting going all over the Muslim world recruiting people to fight in the great *jihad*. Bin Laden was one of the early prize recruits. He was not only an Arab, he was a Saudi multimillionaire willing to put his own money into the matter. Bin Laden went around recruiting people for the *jihad* against communism.

I first met Osama bin Laden in 1986. He was recommended to me by an American official who may have been an agent. I was talking to the American and asked him who were the Arabs there that would be very interesting to talk with. By *there* I meant in Afghanistan and Pakistan. The American official told me, "You must meet Osama." I went to see Osama. There he was, rich, bringing in recruits from Algeria, from Sudan, from Egypt, just like Sheikh Abdul Rahman, an Egyptian cleric who was among those convicted for the 1993 World Trade Center bombing. At that moment,

Osama bin Laden was a U.S. ally. He remained an ally. He turned at a particular moment. In 1990 the U.S. went into Saudi Arabia with military forces. Saudi Arabia is the holy place of Muslims, home of Mecca and Medina. There had never been foreign troops there. In 1990, during the build-up to the Gulf War, they went in in the name of helping Saudi Arabia defend itself. Osama bin Laden remained quiet. Saddam was defeated, but the American's foreign troops stayed on in the land of the kaba (the sacred site of Islam in Mecca). Bin Laden wrote letter after letter saying, Why are you here? Get out! You came to help but you have stayed on. Finally he started a *jihad* against the other occupiers. His mission is to get American troops out of Saudi Arabia. His earlier mission was to get Russian troops out of Afghanistan. See what I was saying earlier about covert operations?

A second point to be made about him is that he come from a tribal people. Being a millionaire doesn't matter. His code of ethics is tribal. The tribal code of ethics consists of two words: loyalty and revenge. You are my friend. You keep your word. I am loyal to you. You break your word, I go on my path of revenge. For him, America has broken its word. The loyal friend has betrayed him. Now they're going to go for you. They're going to do a lot more. These are the chickens of the Afghanistan war coming home to roost.

What is my Recommendation to America?

First, avoid extremes of double standards. If you're going to practice double standards, you will be paid with double standards. Don't use it. Don't condone Israeli terror, Pakistani terror, Nicaraguan terror, El Salvadoran terror, on the one hand, and then complain about Afghan terror or Palestinian terror. It doesn't work. Try to be even-handed. A superpower cannot promote terror in one place and reasonably expect to discourage terrorism in another place. It won't work in this shrunken world.

Do not condone the terror of your allies. Condemn them. Fight them. Punish them. Avoid covert operations and low-intensity warfare. These are breeding grounds for terrorism and drugs. In the Australian documentary about covert operations, Dealing with the Demon, I say that wherever covert operations have been, there is a drug problem. Because of the structure of covert operations, Afghanistan, Vietnam, Nicaragua, Central America, etc, have been very hospitable to the drug trade. Avoid covert operations. It doesn't help.

Also, focus on causes and help ameliorate them. Try to look at causes and solve problems. Avoid military solutions. Terrorism is a political problem. Seek political solutions. Diplomacy works. Take the example of President Clinton's attack on bin Laden. Did they know what they were attacking? They say they know, but they don't know. At another point, they were trying to kill Qadaffi. Instead, they killed his young daughter. The poor child hadn't done anything. Qadaffi is still alive. They tried to kill Saddam Hussein. Instead they killed Laila bin Attar, a prominent artist, an innocent woman. They tried to kill bin Laden and his men. Twenty-five other people died. They tried to destroy a chemical factory in Sudan. Now they are admitting that they destroyed a pharmaceutical plant that produced half the medicine for Sudan.

Four of the missiles intended for Afghanistan fell in Pakistan. One was slightly damaged, two were totally damaged, one was totally intact. For ten years the American government has kept an embargo on Pakistan because Pakistan was trying, stupidly, to build nuclear weapons and missiles. So the U.S. has a technology embargo on my country. One of the missiles was intact. What do you think the Pakistani official told the *Washington Post?* He said it was a gift from Allah. Pakistan wanted U.S. technology. Now they have the technology, and Pakistan's scientists are examining this missile very carefully. It fell into the wrong hands. Look for political solutions. Military solutions cause more problems than they solve.

Finally, please help reinforce and strengthen the framework of international law. There was a criminal court in Rome. Why didn't the U.S. go there first to get a warrant against bin Laden, if they have some evidence? Enforce the United Nations. Enforce the International Court of Justice. Get a warrant, then go after him internationally.

> Gallup International Association and its member companies have conducted a survey in 30 [plus] countries around the world about the potential implications of the recent terrorist attacks in the United States. 14 Western European countries [. . .] [and] the USA, Israel and Pakistan [together with other countries] interviewed their citizens between 14th and 17th September. Only in Israel and the US do a majority of citizens agree that a military attack is the preferred option—in all other countries, extradition of the terrorists to stand trial is favored.
>
> —Gallup International Poll on Terrorism in the United States

23

VIETNAM: THE ANTIWAR MOVEMENT WE ARE SUPPOSED TO FORGET

H. Bruce Franklin

VISUALIZE THE movement against the Vietnam War. What do you see? Hippies with daisies in their long, unwashed hair yelling "Baby killers!" as they spit on clean-cut, bemedaled veterans just back from Vietnam? College students in tattered jeans (their pockets bulging with credit cards) staging a sit-in to avoid the draft? A mob of chanting demonstrators burning an American flag (maybe with a bra or two thrown in)? That's what we're supposed to see, and that's what Americans today probably do see—if they visualize the antiwar movement at all.

We are thus depriving ourselves—or are being deprived—of one legitimate source of great national pride about American culture and behavior during the war. In most wars, a nation dehumanizes and demonizes the people on the other side. Almost the opposite happened during the Vietnam war. Countless Americans came to see the people of Vietnam fighting against U.S. forces as anything but an enemy to be feared and hated. Tens of millions sympathized with their suffering, many came to identify with their 2,000-year struggle for independence, and some even found them an inspiraion for their own lives.

But in the decades since the war's official conclusion, American consciousness of the Vietnamese people, with all its potential for healing and redemption, has been deliberately and systematically obliterated. During the first few years after the war, while the White House and Congress were reneging on aid promised to Vietnam, they were not expressing the feelings of most Americans. For example, a *New York Times*/CBS News poll, published in July 1977, asked this question: "Suppose the President recommended giving assistance to Vietnam. Would you want your Congressman to approve giving Vietnam food or medicine?" Sixty-six percent said yes,

29 percent said no. Ironically, it was only *after* the war was over that demonization of the Vietnamese began to succeed. And soon those tens of millions of Americans who had fought against the war themselves became, as a corollary, a truly hateful enemy as envisioned by the dominant American culture.

The antiwar movement has been so thoroughly discredited that many of the people who were the movement now feel embarrassed or ashamed of their participation—even such prudent and peripheral participants as William Jefferson Clinton. One would never be able to guess from public discourse that for every American veteran of combat in Vietnam, there must be 20 veterans of the antiwar movement. And there seems to be almost total amnesia about the crucial role that many of those combat veterans played in the movement to stop the war.

When did Americans actually begin to oppose U.S. warfare against Vietnam? As soon as the first U.S. act of war was committed. And when was that? In 1965, when President Johnson ordered the Marines to land at Da Nang and began the nonstop bombing of North Vietnam? In 1964, when Johnson launched "retaliatory" bombing of North Vietnam after a series of covert U.S. air, sea, and land attacks? In 1963, when 19,000 U.S. combat troops were participating in the conflict and Washington arranged the overthrow of the puppet ruler it had installed in Saigon in 1954? In 1961, when President Kennedy began Operation Hades, a large-scale campaign of chemical warfare? In 1954, when U.S. combat teams organized covert warfare to support the man Washington had selected to rule South Vietnam? Americans did oppose all of those acts of war, but **the first American opposition came as soon as Washington began warfare against the Vietnamese people by equipping and transporting a foreign army to invade their country in 1945.**

Those Americans who knew anything about Vietnam during World War II knew that the United States had been allied with the Viet Minh, the Vietnamese liberation movement led by Ho Chi Minh, and had actually provided some arms to their guerrilla forces, commanded by Vo Nguyen Giap. American fliers rescued by Giap's guerrillas testified to the rural population's enthusiasm for both the Viet Minh and the United States, which they saw as the champion of democracy, anti-fascism, and anti-imperialism. American officials and officers who had contact with Ho and the Viet Minh were virtually unanimous in their support and admiration. The admiration was mutual. In September 1945 the Viet Minh issued the Vietnamese Declaration of Independence, which began with a long quotation from the U.S. Declaration of Independence, proclaiming the establishment of the Democratic Republic of Vietnam. The regional leaders of the OSS (predecessor of the CIA) and U.S. military forces joined in the celebration, with General Philip Gallagher, chief of the U.S. Military Advisory and Assistance Group, singing the Viet Minh's national anthem on Hanoi radio.

But in the following two months, the United States committed its first act of warfare against the Democratic Republic of Vietnam. At least eight and possibly twelve U.S. troopships were diverted from their task of bringing American troops home from World War II and instead began transporting U.S.-armed French troops and Foreign Legionnaires from France to re-colonize Vietnam. The enlisted crewmen of these ships, all members of the U.S. Merchant Marine, immediately began organized protests. **On arriving in Vietnam, for example, the entire crews of four troopships met together in Saigon and drew up a resolution condemning the U.S. government for using American ships to transport troops "to subjugate the native population" of Vietnam.**

The full-scale invasion of Vietnam by French forces, once again equipped and ferried by the United States, began in 1946. An American movement against the war started to coalesce as soon as significant numbers of Americans realized that Washington was supporting France's war against the Democratic Republic of Vietnam.

The years when the United States was steadily escalating its military presence and combat role in Vietnam—1954 to 1963—were also years when fundamental critiques of U.S. foreign policy had become marginalized. Outspoken domestic opposition to Cold War assumptions had been eviscerated by the purges, witch-hunts, and everyday repression (misleadingly labeled "McCarthyism") conducted under the Truman and Eisenhower administrations. The main targets of that repression had been carefully selected to include anyone in a position to communicate radically dissenting ideas to a large audience: teachers, union leaders, screenwriters, movie directors, radio and print journalists. So by the early 1960s, the aftershocks of that earlier political hammering, combined with the stifling of foreign-policy debate by "bipartisanship" between the two ruling political parties and the supersaturation of Cold War culture, had stripped the American people of any dissenting political consciousness or even a vocabulary capable of accurately describing the global political reality.

As the antiwar movement was becoming a mass movement, in 1965, it was fundamentally aimed at achieving peace through education, and it was based on what now seem incredibly naive assumptions about the causes and purposes of the war. We tend to forget that this phase of the antiwar movement began as an attempt to educate the government and the nation. Most of us opposed to the war in those relatively early days believed—and this is embarrassing to confess—that the government had somehow blundered into the war, maybe because our leaders were simply ignorant about Vietnamese history. Perhaps they didn't remember the events of 1940 to 1954. Maybe they hadn't read the Geneva Agreements. So if we had teach-ins and wrote letters to editors and Congress and the president, the government would say, "Gosh! We didn't realize that Vietnam was a single nation. Did the Geneva Agreements really say that? And we had told Ho Chi Minh we'd probably support his claims for Vietnamese independence? Golly gee, we had better put a stop to this foolish war."

Experience was the great teacher for those who were trying to teach, a lesson lost in the miasma of so-called theory that helped to paralyze activism in the 1990s. **Teaching the Vietnam War during the 1960s and early 1970s meant giving speeches at teach-ins and rallies; getting on talk shows; writing pamphlets, articles, and books; painting banners, picket signs, and graffiti; circulating petitions and leaflets; coining slogans; marching; sitting in; demonstrating at army bases; lobbying Congress; testifying before war-crimes hearings and congressional investigations; researching corporate and university complicity; harboring**

deserters; organizing strikes; heckling generals and politicians; blocking induction centers and napalm plants; and going to prison for defying the draft. It is hard to convey the emotions that inspired those actions. Probably the most widely shared was outrage, a feeling that many came to consider outdated in the cool 1990s.

While the repression of the late 1940s and 1950s helped create the embarrassing naiveté and innocence of the early 1960s, these very qualities fueled the movement's fervor. **People believed that the government would respond to them because they believed in American democracy and rectitude. Then, when the government did respond—with disinformation and new waves of repression—the fervor turned to rage.**

Back in December 1964, an obscure little organization called Students for a Democratic Society issued a call for people to go to Washington on April 17, 1965, to march against the war. Only a few thousand were expected. But when the march took place, it turned out to be the largest antiwar demonstration in Washington's history so far—25,000 people, most neatly dressed in jackets and ties or skirts and dresses.

What seemed at the time very large demonstrations continued throughout 1965, with 15,000 marching in Berkeley on October 15, 20,000 marching in Manhattan the same day, and 25,000 marching again in Washington on November 27. Those early crowds would have been imperceptible amid such later protests as the April 1967 demonstration of 300,000 to 500,000 people in New York, or the half-million or more who converged on Washington in November 1969, and again in the spring of 1971. In the nationwide Moratorium, of October 15, 1969, millions of Americans—at least 10 times the half-million then stationed in Indochina—demonstrated against the war.

Demonstrations were one form of the attempt to go beyond mere words. Other forms appeared as early as 1965. **Many of the activists were veterans of the civil rights movement, who now began to apply its use of civil disobedience and moral witness.** That summer, the Vietnam Day Committee in northern California attempted to block munitions trains by lying on the tracks; hundreds of people were arrested for civil disobedience in Washington; and public burnings of draft cards began. Moral witness was taken to its ultimate by Norman Morrison, a 32-year-old Quaker who drenched himself with gasoline and set himself on fire outside the Pentagon; the pacifist Roger La Porte, who immolated himself at the United Nations; and 82-year-old Alice Herz, who burned herself to death in Detroit to protest against the war. By 1971, civil disobedience was so widespread that the number arrested in that spring's demonstration in Washington—14,000—would have been considered a good-size march in 1965.

Whether the majority of Americans at any point supported the government's policies in Vietnam (or even knew what they were) is a matter of debate. Certainly most Americans never supported the war strongly enough to agree to pay for it with increased taxes, or even to demonstrate for it in significant numbers, much less to go willingly to fight in it. Nor were they ever willing to vote for any national candidate who pledged to fight until "victory." In fact, except for Barry Goldwater in 1964, every nominee for president of both major parties after the 1960 elections through the end of the war ran as some kind of self-professed peace candidate.

Who opposed the war? **Contrary to the impression promulgated by the media then, and overwhelmingly prevalent today, opposition to the war was not concentrated among affluent college students. In fact, opposition to the war was inversely proportional to both wealth and education.** Blue-collar workers generally considered themselves "doves" and tended to favor withdrawal from Vietnam, while those who considered themselves "hawks" and supported participation in the war were concentrated among the college-educated, high-income strata.

For example, a Gallup poll in January 1971 showed that 60 percent of those with a college education favored withdrawal of U.S. troops from Vietnam, 75 percent of those with a high-school education favored withdrawal, and 80 percent of those with only a grade-school education favored withdrawal. In *Lies My Teacher Told Me*, James Loewen reports a revealing experiment he conducted repeatedly in the 1990s. When he asked audiences to estimate the educational level of those who favored U.S. withdrawal back in 1971, by an almost 10-to-1 margin they believed that college-educated people were the most antiwar. In fact, they estimated that 90 percent of those with a college education favored withdrawal, scaling down to 60 percent of those with a grade-school education.

Opposition to the war was especially intense among people of color, though they tended not to participate heavily in the demonstrations called by student and pacifist organizations. One reason for their caution was that people of color often had to pay a heavy price for protesting the war. For speaking out in 1966 against drafting Black men to fight in Vietnam, Julian Bond was denied his seat in the Georgia legislature. Muhammad Ali was stripped of his title as heavyweight boxing champion and was criminally prosecuted for draft resistance. When 25,000 Mexican Americans staged the Chicano Moratorium, the largest antiwar demonstration held in Los Angeles, police officers attacked not just with clubs, but with guns, killing three people, including the popular television news director and Los Angeles Times reporter Rubén Salazar.

Certainly the campus antiwar movement was spectacular. The teach-ins in the spring of 1965 swept hundreds of campuses and involved probably hundreds of thousands of students. By the late 1960s, millions of students were intermittently involved in antiwar activities, ranging from petitions and candlelight marches to burning down ROTC buildings and going to prison for draft resistance. In May 1970, the invasion of Cambodia was met by the largest student-protest movement in American history, a strike that led to the shutdown of hundreds of campuses and the gunning down of students by National Guardsmen at Kent State University in Ohio (where four were killed and nine wounded) and by state troopers at Jackson State College in Mississippi (where two were killed and at least twelve wounded).

There are three principal misconceptions about the college antiwar movement. First, it was not motivated by students' selfish desire to avoid the draft, which was relatively easy for most college men to do and automatic for women. In fact, one of the earliest militant activities on campus was physical disruption of the Selective Service tests that were the basis of draft deferments for college students; the student demonstrators thus jeopardized their own deferments in protesting against them as privileges that were unfair to young men unable to attend college. (The demonstrators also risked punishment by the college authorities and, sometimes, physical attacks by men taking the tests.) **Second, most college students were not affluent (indeed, most came from the working class), and some of the largest and most militant demonstrations were at public universities that could hardly be labeled sanctuaries of the rich,** like Kent State, San Francisco State, and the state universities of Michigan, Maryland, and Wisconsin. **Third, although college antiwar activism did hamper those in Washington who were trying to conduct the war without hindrance, the most decisive opposition to the war came ultimately not from the campuses but from within the cities and the Army itself.**

To understand the antiwar movement, one must perceive its relationship with that other powerful mass movement hamstringing the Pentagon: the uprising of the African American people.

The African American movement had been helping to energize the antiwar movement since at least 1965, when a number of leading Black activists and organizations condemned the war as an assault on another people of color while articulating an anti-imperialist consciousness that would not be common in the broader antiwar movement until 1968. In January 1965, the month before he was assassinated, Malcolm X denounced the Vietnam War, placed Africans and African Americans on the same side as "those little rice farmers" who had defeated French colonialism, and predicted a similar defeat for "Sam." That July, the Mississippi Freedom Democratic Party called on African Americans not to participate in the Vietnam War and implied that their war was closer to home: "No one has a right to ask us to risk our lives and kill other Colored People in Santo Domingo and Vietnam, so that the White American can get richer. We will be looked upon as traitors by all the Colored People of the world if the Negro people continue to fight and die without a cause." In January 1966, the Student Nonviolent Coordinating Committee explained why it was taking a stand against the Vietnam War: "We believe the United States government has been deceptive in claims of concern for the freedom of the Vietnamese people, just as the government has been deceptive in claiming concern for the freedom of the colored people in such other countries as the Dominican Republic, the Congo, South Africa, Rhodesia, and in the United States itself." Stokely Carmichael was the main speaker at the first rally against napalm, in 1966. In 1968, dozens of Black soldiers, many of them Vietnam veterans, were arrested and court-martialed for refusing to mobilize against antiwar demonstrators outside the Chicago Amphitheater during the Democratic National Convention.

What made the convergence of the Black and antiwar movements explosively dangerous for those trying to maintain order and sustain the war was the disintegrating and volatile situation within the armed forces, as pointed out by an alarming article published in the January 1970 *Naval War College Review*. Very little awareness of resistance to the war inside the military survives today. But without this awareness, it is impossible to understand not just the antiwar movement, but also the military history of the war from 1968 to 1973, not to mention the end of the draft and the creation of a permanent "volunteer" army to fight America's subsequent wars. **To begin to get some sense of the relative scale and effects of civilian and active-duty war resistance, compare the widely publicized activity of draft avoidance with some little-known facts about desertion** (a serious military crime, defined by being away without leave for more than 30 days and having the intention never to return). Although draft evasion and refusal certainly posed problems for the war effort, desertion was much more common and far more threatening.

The number of draft evaders and resisters was dwarfed by the number of deserters from the active-duty armed forces. During the 1971 fiscal year alone, 98,324 servicemen deserted, an astonishing rate of 142.2 for every 1,000 men on duty. Revealing statistics flashed to light briefly as President Ford was pondering the amnesty he declared in September 1974 (at the same time he also pardoned ex-President Nixon for all federal crimes he may have committed while in office). According to the Department of Defense, there were **503,926 "incidents of desertion"** between July 1, 1966, and December 31, 1973. From 1963 through 1973 (a period almost half again as long), **only 13,518 men were prosecuted for draft evasion or resistance.** The admitted total of deserters still officially "at large" at the time was 28,661—six and a half times the 4,400 draft evaders or resisters still "at large." These numbers only begin to tell the story.

Thousands of veterans who had fought in Vietnam moved to the forefront of the antiwar movement after they returned to the United States, and they—together with thousands of active-duty GIs—soon began to play a crucial role in the domestic movement. Dozens of teach-ins on college campuses were led by Vietnam veterans, who spoke at hundreds of rallies. **More and more demonstrations were led by large contingents of veterans and active-duty service-people, who often participated under risk of grave punishment.** The vanguard of that Washington demonstration by half a million people in the spring of 1971 was a contingent of a thousand Vietnam veterans, many in wheelchairs and on crutches, who then conducted "a limited incursion into the country of Congress," which they called Dewey Canyon III (Dewey Canyon I was a 1969 covert "incursion" into Laos; Dewey Canyon II was the disastrous February 1971 invasion of Laos). About 800 marched up to a barricade hastily erected to keep them away from the Capitol and hurled back their Purple Hearts, Bronze Stars, Silver Stars, and campaign ribbons at the government that had bestowed them.

The antiwar movement initiated back in 1945 by those hundreds of merchant seamen protesting U.S. participation in the French attempt to reconquer Vietnam was thus consummated in a movement of tens of millions of ordinary American citizens spearheaded by soldiers, sailors, fliers, and veterans, which finally ended the war with a recognition that Vietnam could be neither divided nor conquered by the United States.

No, it was not Vietnam but the United States that ended up divided by America's war. And the division cut even deeper than the armed forces, biting down into the core of the secret government itself. When members of the intelligence establishment joined the antiwar movement, they had the potential to inflict even greater damage than mutinous soldiers and sailors. The perfidy of the Central Intelligence Agency in Vietnam was revealed by one of its highest-level agents in South Vietnam, Ralph McGhee, author of *Deadly Deceits: My Twenty-Five Years in the CIA*. Philip Agee decided in 1971 to publish what eventually became *Inside the Company: CIA Diary* because of "the continuation of the Vietnam war and the Vietnamization programme," writing, "Now more than ever exposure of CIA methods could help American people understand how we got into Vietnam and how our other Vietnams are germinating wherever the CIA is at work." In that same year, two of the authors of the Pentagon's own supersecret history of the war, Anthony Russo and Daniel Ellsberg, exposed it to the American people and the world.

Interviewed three years after the release of the Pentagon Papers, Ellsberg outlined the history of the Vietnam War by tracing the "lies" told by Presidents Truman, Eisenhower, Kennedy, Johnson, and Nixon. "The American public was lied to month by month by each of these five administrations," he declared. And then he added, "It's a tribute to the American public that their leaders perceived they had to be lied to."

The end of the war did not end the lies. Since then, both the war and the antiwar movement have been falsified so grossly that we risk forfeiting the most valuable knowledge we gained at such great cost to the peoples of Southeast Asia and to ourselves. Nor can we understand what America is becoming if we fail to comprehend how the same nation and its culture could have produced an abomination as shameful as the Vietnam War and a campaign as admirable as the 30-year movement that helped defeat it.

H. Bruce Franklin is a professor of English and American Studies at Rutgers University. He is the author of numerous books on American history and literature, including The Vietnam War in American Stories, Songs & Poems *(Bedford/St. Martin's Press). This article is excerpted from* Vietnam and Other American Fantasies *(University of Massachusetts Press); originally reprinted in the Chronicle of Higher Education. Copyright H. Bruce Franklin, all rights reserved. Reprinted with permission.*

24

WHY SOCIALISM?

Albert Einstein

Is it advisable for one who is not an expert on economic and social issues to express views on the subject of socialism? I believe for a number of reasons that it is.

Let us first consider the question from the point of view of scientific knowledge. It might appear that there are no essential methodological differences between astronomy and economics: scientists in both fields attempt to discover laws of general acceptability for a circumscribed group of phenomena in order to make the interconnection of these phenomena as clearly understandable as possible. But in reality such methodological differences do exist. The discovery of general laws in the field of economics is made difficult by the circumstance that observed economic phenomena are often affected by many factors which are very hard to evaluate separately. In addition, the experience which has accumulated since the beginning of the so-called civilized period of human history has—as is well known—been largely influenced and limited by causes which are by no means exclusively economic in nature. For example, most of the major states of history owed their existence to conquest. The conquering peoples established themselves, legally and economically, as the privileged class of the conquered country. They seized for themselves a monopoly of the land ownership and appointed a priesthood from among their own ranks. The priests, in control of education, made the class division of society into a permanent institution and created a system of values by which the people were thenceforth, to a large extent unconsciously, guided in their social behavior.

But historic tradition is, so to speak, of yesterday; nowhere have we really overcome what Thorstein Veblen called "the predatory phase" of human development. The observable economic facts belong to that phase and even such laws as we can derive from them are not applicable to other phases. Since the real purpose of socialism is precisely to overcome and advance beyond the predatory phase of human development, economic science in its present state can throw little light on the socialist society of the future.

Second, socialism is directed towards a social-ethical end. Science, however, cannot create ends and, even less, instill them in human beings; science, at most, can supply the means by which to attain certain ends. But the ends themselves are conceived by personalities with lofty ethical ideals and—if these ends are not stillborn, but vital and vigorous—are adopted and carried forward by those many human beings who, half unconsciously, determine the slow evolution of society.

For these reasons, we should be on our guard not to overestimate science and scientific methods when it is a question of human problems; and we should not assume that experts are the only ones who have a right to express themselves on questions affecting the organization of society.

Innumerable voices have been asserting for some time now that human society is passing through a crisis, that its stability has been gravely shattered. It is characteristic of such a situation that individuals feel indifferent or even hostile toward the group, small or large, to which they belong. In order to illustrate my meaning, let me record here a personal experience. I recently discussed with an intelligent and well-disposed man the threat of another war, which in my opinion would seriously endanger the existence of mankind, and I remarked that only a supra-national organization would offer protection from that danger. Thereupon my visitor, very calmly and coolly, said to me: "Why are you so deeply opposed to the disappearance of the human race?"

I am sure that as little as a century ago no one would have so lightly made a statement of this kind. It is the statement of a man who has striven in vain to attain an equilibrium within himself and has more or less lost hope of succeeding. It is the expression of a painful solitude and isolation from which so many people are suffering in these days. What is the cause? Is there a way out?

It is easy to raise such questions, but difficult to answer them with any degree of assurance. I must try, however, as best I can, although I am very conscious of the fact that our feelings and strivings are often contradictory and obscure and that they cannot be expressed in easy and simple formulas.

Man is, at one and the same time, a solitary being and a social being. As a solitary being, he attempts to protect his own existence and that of those who are closest to him, to satisfy his personal desires, and to develop his innate abilities. As a social being, he seeks to gain the recognition and affection of his fellow human beings, to share in their pleasures, to comfort them in their sorrows, and to improve their conditions of life. Only the existence of these varied, frequently conflicting, strivings accounts for the special character of a man, and their specific combination determines the extent to which an individual can achieve an inner equilibrium and can contribute to the well-being of society. It is quite possible that the relative strength of these two drives is, in the main, fixed by inheritance. But the personality that finally emerges is largely formed by the environment in which a man happens to find himself during his development, by the structure of the society in which he grows up, by the tradition of that society, and by its appraisal of particular types of behavior. The abstract concept "society" means to the individual human being the sum total of his direct and indirect relations to his contemporaries and to all the people of earlier generations. The individual is able to think, feel, strive, and work by himself; but he depends so much upon society—in his physical, intellectual, and emotional existence—that it is impossible to think of him, or to understand him, outside the framework of society. It is "society" which provides man with food, clothing, a home, the tools of work, language, the forms of thought, and most of the content of thought; his life is made possible through the labor and the accomplishments of the many millions past and present who are all hidden behind the small word "society."

It is evident, therefore, that the dependence of the individual upon society is a fact of nature which cannot be abolished—just as in the case of ants and bees. However, while the whole life process of ants and bees is fixed down to the smallest detail by rigid, hereditary instincts, the social pattern and interrelationships of human beings are very variable and susceptible to change. Memory, the capacity to make new combinations, the gift of oral communication have made possible developments among human beings which are not dictated by biological necessities. Such developments manifest themselves in traditions, institutions, and organizations; in literature; in scientific and engineering accomplishments; in works of art. This explains how it happens that, in a certain sense, man can influence his life through his own conduct, and that in this process conscious thinking and wanting can play a part.

Man acquires at birth, through heredity, a biological constitution which we must consider fixed and unalterable, including the natural urges which are characteristic of the human species. In addition, during his lifetime, he acquires a cultural constitution which he adopts from society through communication and through many other types of influences. It is this cultural constitution which, with the passage of time, is subject to change and which determines to a very large extent the relationship between the individual and society. Modern anthropology has taught us, through comparative investigation of so-called primitive cultures, that the social behavior of human beings may differ greatly, depending upon prevailing cultural patterns and the types of organization which predominate in society. It is on this that those who are striving to improve the lot of man may ground their hopes: human beings are not condemned, because of their biological constitution, to annihilate each other or to be at the mercy of a cruel, self-inflicted fate.

If we ask ourselves how the structure of society and the cultural attitude of man should be changed in order to make human life as satisfying as possible, we should constantly be conscious of the fact that there are certain conditions which we are unable to modify. As mentioned before, the biological nature of man is, for all practical purposes, not subject to change. Furthermore, technological and demographic developments of the last few centuries have created conditions which are here to stay. In relatively densely settled populations with the goods which are indispensable to their continued existence, an extreme division of labor and a highly-centralized productive apparatus are absolutely necessary. The time—which, looking back, seems so idyllic—is gone forever when individuals or relatively small groups could be completely self-sufficient. It is only a slight exaggeration to say that mankind constitutes even now a planetary community of production and consumption.

I have now reached the point where I may indicate briefly what to me constitutes the essence of the crisis of our time. It concerns the relationship of the individual to society. The individual has become more conscious than ever of his dependence upon society. But he does not experience this dependence as a positive asset, as an organic tie, as a protective force, but rather as a threat to his natural rights, or even to his economic existence. Moreover, his position in society is such that the egotistical drives of his make-up are constantly being accentuated, while his social drives, which are by nature weaker, progressively deteriorate. All human beings, whatever their position in society, are suffering from this process of deterioration. Unknowingly prisoners of their own egotism, they feel insecure, lonely, and deprived of the naive, simple, and unsophisticated enjoyment of life. Man can find meaning in life, short and perilous as it is, only through devoting himself to society.

The economic anarchy of capitalist society as it exists today is, in my opinion, the real source of the evil. We see before us a huge community of producers the members of which are unceasingly striving to deprive each other of the fruits of their collective labor—not by force, but on the whole in faithful compliance with legally established rules. In this respect, it is important to realize that the means of production—that is to say, the entire productive capacity that is needed for producing consumer goods as well as additional capital goods—may legally be, and for the most part are, the private property of individuals.

For the sake of simplicity, in the discussion that follows I shall call "workers" all those who do not share in the ownership of the means of production—although this does not quite correspond to the customary use of the term. The owner of the means of production is in a position to purchase the labor power of the worker. By using the means of production, the worker produces new goods which become the property of the capitalist. The essential point about this process is the relation between what the worker produces and what he is paid, both measured in terms of real value. Insofar as the labor contract is "free," what the worker receives is determined not by the real value of the goods he produces, but by his minimum needs and by the capitalists' requirements for labor power in relation to the number of workers competing for jobs. It is important to understand that even in theory the payment of the worker is not determined by the value of his product.

Private capital tends to become concentrated in few hands, partly because of competition among the capitalists, and partly because technological development and the increasing division of labor encourage the formation of larger units of production at the expense of smaller ones. The result of these developments is an oligarchy of private capital the enormous power of which cannot be effectively checked even by a democratically organized political society. This is true since the members of legislative bodies are selected by political parties, largely financed or otherwise influenced by private capitalists who, for all practical purposes, separate the electorate from the legislature. The consequence is that the representatives of the people do not in fact sufficiently protect the interests of the underprivileged sections of the population. Moreover, under existing conditions, private capitalists inevitably control, directly or indirectly, the main sources of information (press, radio, education). It is thus extremely difficult, and indeed in most cases quite impossible, for the individual citizen to come to objective conclusions and to make intelligent use of his political rights.

The situation prevailing in an economy based on the private ownership of capital is thus characterized by two main principles: first, means of production (capital) are privately owned and the owners dispose of them as they see fit; second, the labor contract is free. Of course, there is no such thing as a *pure* capitalist society in this sense. In particular, it should be noted that the workers, through long and bitter political struggles, have succeeded in securing a somewhat improved form of the "free labor contract" for certain categories of workers. But taken as a whole, the present day economy does not differ much from "pure" capitalism.

Production is carried on for profit, not for use. There is no provision that all those able and willing to work will always be in a position to find employment; an "army of unemployed" almost always exists. The worker is constantly in fear of losing his job. Since unemployed and poorly paid workers do not provide a profitable market, the production of consumers' goods is restricted, and great hardship is the consequence. Technological progress frequently results in more unemployment rather than in an easing of the burden of work for all. The profit motive, in conjunction with competition among capitalists, is responsible for an instability in the accumulation and utilization of capital which leads to increasingly severe depressions. Unlimited competition leads to a huge waste of labor, and to that crippling of the social consciousness of individuals which I mentioned before.

This crippling of individuals I consider the worst evil of capitalism. Our whole educational system suffers from this evil. An exaggerated competitive attitude is inculcated into the student, who is trained to worship acquisitive success as a preparation for his future career.

I am convinced that there is only *one* way to eliminate these grave evils, namely through the establishment of a socialist economy, accompanied by an educational system which would be oriented toward social goals. In such an economy, the means of production are owned by society itself and are utilized in a planned fashion. A planned economy, which adjusts production to the needs of the community, would distribute the work to be done among all those able to work and would guarantee a livelihood to every man, woman, and child. The education of the individual, in addition to promoting his own innate abilities, would attempt to develop in him a sense of responsibility for his fellow men in place of the glorification of power and success in our present society.

Nevertheless, it is necessary to remember that a planned economy is not yet socialism. A planned economy as such may be accompanied by the complete enslavement of the individual. The achievement of socialism requires the solution of some extremely difficult socio-political problems: how is it possible, in view of the far-reaching centralization of political and economic power, to prevent bureaucracy from becoming all-powerful and overweening? How can the rights of the individual be protected and therewith a democratic counterweight to the power of bureaucracy be assured?

Clarity about the aims and problems of socialism is of greatest significance in our age of transition. Since, under present circumstances, free and unhindered discussion of these problems has come under a powerful taboo, I consider the foundation of this magazine to be an important public service.

25

ARGENTINA: WHERE JOBLESS RUN FACTORIES

Naomi Klein and Avi Lewis

On March 19, 2003, we were on the roof of the Zanón ceramic tile factory, filming an interview with Cepillo. He was showing us how the workers fended off eviction by armed police, defending their democratic workplace with slingshots and the little ceramic balls normally used to pound the patagonian clay into raw material for tiles. His aim was impressive. It was the day the bombs started falling on Baghdad.

As journalists, we had to ask ourselves what we were doing there. what possible relevance could there be in this one factory at the southernmost tip of our continent, with its band of radical workers and its David and Goliath narrative, when bunker-busting apocalypse was descending on Iraq?

But we, like so many others, had been drawn to Argentina to witness firsthand an explosion of activism in the wake of its 2001 crisis—a host of dynamic new social movements that were not only advancing a bitter critique of the economic model that had destroyed their country, but were busily building local alternatives in the rubble.

There were many popular responses to the crisis, from neighborhood assemblies and barter clubs, to resurgent left-wing parties and mass movements of the unemployed but we spent most of our year in Argentina with workers in "recovered companies." Almost entirely under the media radar, workers in Argentina have been responding to rampant unemployment and capital flight by taking over traditional businesses that have gone bankrupt and are reopening them under democratic worker management. It's an old idea reclaimed and retrofitted for a brutal new time. The principles are so simple, so elementally fair, that they seem more self-evident than radical when articulated by one of the workers in this book: "We formed the cooperative with the criteria of equal wages and making basic decisions by assembly; we are against the separation of manual and intellectual work; we want a rotation of position and, above all, the ability to recall our elected leaders."

The movement of recovered companies is not epic in scale—some 170 companies, around 10,000 workers in Argentina. But six years on, and unlike some of the country's other new movements, it has survived and continues to build quiet strength in the midst of the country's deeply unequal "recovery." Its tenacity is a function of its pragmatism: This is a movement that is based on action, not talk. And its defining action, reawakening the means of production under worker control, while loaded with potent symbolism, is anything but symbolic. It is feeding families, rebuilding shattered pride, and opening a window of powerful possibility.

Like a number of other emerging social movements around the world, the workers in the recovered companies are rewriting the traditional script for how change is supposed to happen. Rather than following anyone's ten-point plan for revolution, the workers are darting ahead of the theory—at least, straight to the part where they get their jobs back. In Argentina, the theorists are chasing after the factory workers, trying to analyze what is already in noisy production.

These struggles have had a tremendous impact on the imaginations of activists around the world. At this point there are many more starry-eyed grad papers on the phenomenon than there are recovered companies. But there is also a renewed interest in democratic workplaces from Durban to Melbourne to New Orleans.

That said, the movement in Argentina is as much a product of the globalization of alternatives as it is one of its most contagious stories. Argentine workers borrowed the slogan, "Occupy, Resist, Produce" from Latin America's largest social movement, Brazil's **Movimento dos Trabalhadores Rurais Sem Terra,** in which more than a million people have reclaimed unused land and put it back into community production. One worker told us that what the movement in Argentina is doing is "MST for the cities." In South Africa, we saw a protester's T-shirt with an even more succinct summary of this new impatience: *Stop Asking, Start Taking.*

But as much as these similar sentiments are blossoming in different parts of the world for the same reasons, there is an urgent need to share these stories and tools of resistance even more widely. For that reason, the translation of *Sin Patrón: Argentina's Worker-Run Factories* is of tremendous importance: It's the first comprehensive portrait of Argentina's famous movement of recovered companies in English.

THE LAVACA COLLECTIVE

The book's author is the Lavaca Collective, itself a worker cooperative. While we were in Argentina filming our documentary, *The Take,* we ran into Lavaca members wherever the workers' struggles led—the courts, the legislature, the streets, the factory floor. They do some of the most sophisticated and engaged journalism in the world today.

And this book is classic Lavaca. That means it starts with a montage—a theoretical framework that is unabashedly poetic. Then it cuts to a fight scene of the hard facts: the names, the numbers, and the m.o. behind the armed robbery that was Argentina's crisis. With the scene set, the book then zooms in to the stories of individual struggles, told almost entirely through the testimony of the workers themselves.

This approach is deeply respectful of the voices of the protagonists, while still leaving plenty of room for the authors' observations, at once playful and scathing. In this interplay between the cooperatives that inhabit the book and the one that produced it, there are a number of themes that bear mention.

First of all, there is the question of ideology. This movement is frustrating to some on the left who feel it is not clearly anti-capitalist, those who chafe at how comfortably it exists within the market economy and see worker management as merely a new form of auto-exploitation. Others see the project of cooperativism, the legal form chosen by the vast majority of the recovered companies, as a capitulation in itself—insisting that only full nationalization by the state can bring worker democracy into a broader socialist project.

In the words of the workers, and between the lines, you get a sense of these tensions and the complex relationship between various struggles and parties of the left in Argentina. Workers in the movement are generally suspicious of being co-opted to anyone's political agenda, but at the same time cannot afford to turn down any support. More interesting by far is to see how workers in this movement are politicized by the struggle, which begins with the most basic imperative: Workers want to work, to feed their families. You can see in this book how some of the most powerful new working-class leaders in Argentina today discovered solidarity on a path that started from that essentially apolitical point.

Whether you think the movement's lack of a leading ideology is a tragic weakness or a refreshing strength, this book makes clear precisely how the recovered companies challenge capitalism's most cherished ideal: the sanctity of private property.

The legal and political case for worker control in Argentina does not only rest on the unpaid wages, evaporated benefits, and emptied-out pension funds. The workers make a sophisticated case for their moral right to property—in this case, the machines and physical premises—based not just on what they're owed personally, but what society is owed. The recovered companies propose themselves as an explicit remedy to all the corporate welfare, corruption, and other forms of public subsidy the owners enjoyed in the process of bankrupting their firms and moving their wealth to safety, abandoning whole communities to the twilight of economic exclusion.

LESSONS FOR AMERICA

This argument is, of course, available for immediate use in the United States. But this story goes much deeper than corporate welfare, and that's where the Argentine experience will really resonate with North Americans. It's become axiomatic on the left to say that Argentina's crash was a direct result of the IMF orthodoxy imposed on the country with such enthusiasm in the neoliberal 1990s. What this book makes clear is that in Argentina, just as in the US occupation of Iraq, those bromides about private sector efficiency were nothing more than a cover story for an explosion of frontier-style plunder—looting on a massive scale by a small group of elites. Privatization, deregulation, labor flexibility: These were the tools to facilitate a massive transfer of public wealth to private hands, not to mention private debts to the public purse. Like Enron traders, the businessmen who haunt the pages of this book learned the first lesson of capitalism and stopped there: Greed is good, and more greed is better. As one worker says in the book, "There are guys that wake up in the morning thinking about how to screw people, and others who think, how do we rebuild this Argentina that they have torn apart?"

In the answer to that question, you can read a powerful story of transformation. This book takes as a key premise that capitalism produces and distributes not just goods and services, but identities. When the capital and its carpetbaggers had flown, what was left was not only companies that had been emptied, but a whole hollowed-out country filled with people whose identities—as workers—had been stripped away too.

As one of the organizers in the movement wrote to us, "It is a huge amount of work to recover a company. But the real work is to recover a worker and that is the task that we have just begun."

On April 17, 2003, we were on Avenida Jujuy in Buenos Aires, standing with the Brukman workers and a huge crowd of their supporters in front of a fence, behind which was a small army of police guarding the Brukman factory. After a brutal eviction, the workers were determined to get back to work at their sewing machines.

In Washington, DC, that day, USAID announced that it had chosen Bechtel Corporation as the prime contractor for the reconstruction of Iraq's architecture. The heist was about to begin in earnest, both in the United States and in Iraq. Deliberately induced crisis was providing the cover for the transfer of billions of tax dollars to a handful of politically connected corporations.

In Argentina, they'd already seen this movie—the wholesale plunder of public wealth, the explosion of unemployment, the shredding of the social fabric, the staggering human consequences. And fifty-two seamstresses were in the street, backed by thousands of others, trying to take back what was already theirs. It was definitely the place to be.

26

CAPITALIST RESTORATION IN SOCIALIST SOCIETY

John G. Gurley

CHINESE CRITICISMS OF THE SOVIETS

The Chinese critics of the Soviet Union first point to some early difficulties encountered by the Bolsheviks, which compelled them eventually to overstress the productive forces to the neglect of production relations and the superstructure; they put heavy industry before light industry and agriculture, investment ahead of consumption, urban before rural areas. In overemphasizing technology, Stalin had to promote bourgeois incentives with large wage differentials, piece-rate wage systems, and generous bonuses, which resulted in marked economic and social inequalities within the working class. This led to the playing down of class struggle and the rejection of a dialectical outlook.

According to Mao Tse-tung, the restoration of capitalism did not occur under Stalin. Stalin maintained socialist forms by "clearing out quite a gang of counterrevolutionary representatives of the bourgeoisie who had wormed their way into the Party." Hence, Mao implied, Stalin's policies tended both to revitalize the bourgeoisie, through the use of capitalist incentives, and to eliminate them, through purges. Considering everything, Stalin was a staunch revolutionary who fought for the proletariat and who created the first Marxist-socialist state.

After Stalin's death, the Chinese say, Khrushchev and his supporters usurped party and state power (in 1956) on behalf of a bureaucrat-monopoly-bourgeoisie that now runs the country as a fascist dictatorship. The restoration of capitalism occurred at that time. This clique no longer believes in class struggle and revolution and has espoused peaceful coexistence with imperialism (belief in the peaceful intentions of imperialists), peaceful transition from capitalism to socialism (opposition to armed revolution), peaceful transition from socialism to communism (opposition to the dictatorship of the proletariat and to class struggle), and economism (opposition to bold measures for social transformation).

The restoration of capitalism in the U.S.S.R., according to the Chinese, has seriously disrupted the development of Soviet productive forces, and has opened the door to graft, theft, depraved social morals, alcoholism and drugs, and juvenile delinquency. The new capitalist class controls all monopoly capital in the country and obtains much surplus value through its exploitation of the Soviet and other working peoples. This is the economic base of Soviet social-imperialism, the Chinese allege, which seeks world hegemony and "is the most dangerous source of war."

SOVIET AND OTHER RESPONSES

The Soviets and their supporters, of course, deny all of these claims. To begin with, they point to their revolution, during which the proletariat captured political power. They then direct attention to their establishment of the very foundations of a socialist society—national planning and the social ownership of the means of production. Next, they say, with this much accomplished, they pursued the correct path of gradually and steadily building up their productive forces, which is the only method of guaranteeing further changes in the relations of production. Socialism can be built only through resolute long-range planning and a continuous development that emphasizes large-scale, heavy industry and utilizes the advantages of building on the progressive forces inherent in urban areas and the industrial working class. Moreover, the correct socialist principle is payment according to work, and significant wage differentials are needed as incentives for hard and better work. Piece-rate payments and bonuses contribute to this end.

The Soviets also believe that in this new nuclear age war would devastate everyone, comrades and enemies alike; furthermore, the socialist bloc is now strong enough to begin to attract third-world countries into its camp. It is now likely that gradually, peacefully, through economic competition, the vigorous growth of the socialist camp's productive forces will win the day against imperialism and allow a peaceful transition to socialism by increasing numbers of underdeveloped countries.

The Soviets have also alleged that continuing class struggle is necessary only in the transition period between capitalism and socialism, when the dictatorship of the proletariat is required, but that the socialist period itself is classless, as is the next stage to full communism. In these final two stages, therefore, the state represents all the people and there is no need for the dictatorship of one class over another. Thus, the Chinese preoccupation with the dictatorship of the proletariat and with class struggle during the socialist phase is unwarranted.

AN ASSESSMENT

Most Marxists agree that the restoration of capitalism is possible in a country that has previously achieved socialism. Such a country either progresses towards communism or retrogresses back to capitalism. There is no standing still. If it retrogresses, the capitalism that is restored is not competitive or even private monopoly capitalism but state-bureaucratic monopoly capitalism.

An underdeveloped country starting out to attain socialism will ordinarily commence from some combination of feudal and capitalist relations of production and superstructural elements. During the course of economic development, the feudal elements become weaker, the capitalist elements become potentially stronger (though perhaps actually weaker), and the socialist elements gain dominance. If the transition is successful, socialism will be reached, despite the growing potential strength of bourgeois components within the socialist society.

The class basis for the restoration of capitalism consists of various groups left over from the old regime and enlarged by the program for the development of the country's productive forces. The groups consist of enterprise managers, industrial technicians and experts, engineers, planners, scientists, and in general the intelligentsia. Under certain circumstances, they will be joined by small-scale producers, speculators, and traders. *All of these strata will be aided by bourgeois ideology* that hangs on and is daily recreated, and by imperialism—by the weight of the world capitalist system. The forces on the side of capitalist restoration are potentially powerful.

However, *restoration can be successful only when this bourgeoisie is adequately represented in the state and party bureaucracies, where the restoration has to be organized and implemented.* If restoration occurs, the social property of the working class becomes the collective property of the state bourgeoisie. That is, *the bourgeoisie recapture the power to control and profit from the means of production, through the state and party bureaucracies.* The bourgeoisie link up with the bureaucracies to take political power away from the proletariat. The monopoly bourgeoisie and the bureaucrats then share in the spoils.

Capitalist restoration apparently can be averted by a socialist country only if class struggle by the proletariat against the bourgeoisie is continued and carried out in such a way as to enhance the political power of the proletariat and to strengthen and extend socialist relations while weakening bourgeois ones—both in the economic base and in the superstructure.

If capitalism has been restored in an erstwhile socialist country, one would expect to observe the reappearance of capitalist economic crises (Marx's "capital accumulation crises"), accompanied by periodic widespread unemployment and an enduring reserve army of labor. These capitalist features would be revived through the debilitation of centralized planning and the transfer of planning powers to enterprise managers operating with profit incentives and through a widening network of commodity markets. One would also expect to find increasing economic inequalities within the working class, and increasing hierarchical arrangements within the work-places, brought on by the resuscitation of labor-power as a commodity and the extension of material incentives. The restoration of a type of monopoly capitalism and its capital accumulation crises should lead to imperialist behavior and the militarism required to support it. One would also look for the revival of the ideology opposing class struggle and advocating the primacy of productive forces. Finally, many bourgeois superstructural elements would be restored, such as bourgeois art, literature, and education, and the values of individualism and consumerism.

When these criteria are applied to the Soviet Union, the picture is seen to be somewhat mixed. On the one side, capitalist crises have definitely not reappeared there, for Soviet real GNP has increased every year since 1950. Of even more significance, over that same period there has not been one year of downturn of fixed-capital investment expenditures; they have risen steadily for 27 years, in sharp contrast to investment performance in the advanced capitalist countries. This is clear indication that the central planning system is intact and that the capital-accumulation process has not been subject to swings by enterprise managers operating in terms of the profit motive. Adding to this strong evidence is the absence of deep unemployment problems; there is in the Soviet Union nothing like the capitalist reserve army of labor. It is also true, as we have seen, that since Stalin's death income inequalities have been reduced substantially, and workers' real wages and living standards have risen markedly, which is evidence (though not conclusive) against the view that labor-power has become a commodity and material work incentives and capitalist work relations have spread without restraint.

On the other side, critics point to the superpower and imperialist behavior of the Soviets as evidence that monopoly capitalism has been restored there. That the Soviet Union is a superpower is beyond dispute. However, "superpower behavior" implies that the U.S.S.R. is primarily interested in the division of the world between itself and the United States, and in maximizing its share for its own benefit. Its recent behavior is ambiguous here. Some observers interpret its actions this way, but others believe that it is principally concerned with proletarian internationalism—that is, with the worldwide diffusion of Marxism. Either way, the Soviet Union is an expanding military power, coming into collision with the United States wherever vital resources are at stake.

Properly speaking, capitalist-imperialist actions mean that capital is being exported for the purpose of generating surplus value out of the exploitation of the working classes of other lands. Even if the U.S.S.R. is acting out of self-interest, and has little or no concern to spread proletarian revolutions, applying this definition of capitalist imperialism to it would be difficult, for it has exported very little capital to other countries, and then mainly through foreign-aid programs with fairly generous terms. Generally speaking, the Soviet Union does not build *Soviet* factories in foreign countries. The very basis for imperialism—surplus capital that cannot find profitable employment at home—does not appear to exist there. Furthermore, some evidence exists—from southern Africa, Ethiopia, Vietnam, Cuba—that it is on the revolutionary side, that it is willing to upset the status quo and thus endanger itself in the interest of extending Marxism. However, there is also evidence pointing in the other direction—from India, Egypt, Iraq, and elsewhere, where anti-Marxist regimes have been handsomely supported.

Some critics further contend that the restoration of capitalism in the Soviet Union is indicated by its full retreat from class struggle at home, its acceptance of the overriding importance of productive forces (to the neglect of the transformation of its relations of production and its superstructure), the alarming diffusion of bourgeois values and institutions throughout Soviet society, and the degeneration of socialist morality among the population. There is much evidence in support of these arguments and very little on the other side. The problem is to judge how important these arguments are compared with the others previously discussed.

Looking back, we can see that Stalin, in subordinating almost everything else to the rapid growth of his country's productive forces (which he narrowly interpreted to exclude human agents), fostered growing inequalities in wealth and status, inflicted brutalities on many of the people, and allowed the erection of a huge bureaucracy and the fashioning of a labor aristocracy and a managerial elite. Stalin failed to rely on the working classes and the masses generally in the struggle against the forces of capitalism, and in effect he depoliticized the masses. As a consequence, workers' and peasants' concerns and motivations were turned inward, and private affairs came to rule the daily lives of the people. Without a high level of political and class consciousness among the workers, without their continuing participation in the building of a socialist society, the planning mechanism went awry and work incentives increasingly had to take compensating capitalist forms. In the process, the working class lost much direct political power and came to be represented more and more by an expanding state bureaucracy.

Stalin's successors set out to reverse some of the developments associated with his name—income inequalities, geographical imbalances, urban-rural disparities, and lopsided priorities. However, the Stalinist era had generated so many bourgeois tendencies within the economy that they came to be represented by growing numbers of Soviet leaders. After Stalin's death, these tendencies coalesced into a revisionist Marxism, akin to Bernstein revisionism. The tenets of original Marxism, however, continued to coexist with, and stand in opposition to, revisionism—an ideological opposition reflecting the enduring struggle between the new bourgeoisie and the proletariat. This struggle has generated both revisionist and revolutionary actions by the Soviet leadership.

Although it is doubtful that a conclusive answer can be given, I believe that the evidence against capitalist restoration is weightier than the evidence for it—in other words, that the Soviet Union is still a socialist country. But there is also sufficient evidence to suggest that its socialism falls far short of traditional Marxian standards and that it may currently be in a process of transition from socialism to capitalism. This issue is particularly difficult to resolve because, as we now know, Marxian socialism, wherever it has appeared, has taken strong national forms, each differing significantly from the others. A single set of fixed standards cannot be used to judge the purity of all these forms of socialism. What are needed are flexible standards that reflect the historical process of world-wide socialist development and the different national traditions within which the global movement occurs. But these still remain to be worked out.

> *The third edition of Gurley's book is dated 1988 which is two years before Gorbachev publicly embraced capitalism. If Gurley were to rewrite his book today, he probably would agree with the thesis of capitalist restoration.*

27

GENDER, RELATIONSHIPS, AND COMMUNICATION

Julia T. Wood

Not long ago, I was playing a question game with my 4-year-old niece Michelle. When I asked her who she was, she immediately replied, "I'm a girl." Only after declaring her sex did she proceed to describe her likes and dislikes, family, and so forth. In focusing on being a girl, Michelle underlined the centrality of sex to personal identity.

If asked to describe yourself, like Michelle, you would probably note that you are a woman or a man before describing your personality, background, hobbies, ambitions, and appearance. According to historian Elizabeth Fox-Genovese (1991, p. 20), "To be an 'I' at all means to be gendered."

In Western society, gender is fundamental to social life and to individuals' identities, roles, and options. The influence of gender is evident in everything from social policies and laws to intimate interaction. What gender means and how we embody it depend directly on communication that expresses, sustains, and changes views of women and men. As we communicate in families, schools, playgrounds, media, offices, and Congress, we continuously re-create our understandings of cultural life, our relations with others, and ourselves as women and men.

Of the many contexts in which gender is defined and enacted, a particularly important one is our relationships with others. Our earliest relationships in nuclear families weave gender into our basic self-concepts. Later in life, we form friendships and romantic relationships in which we express our gendered identities, and we participate in professional associations in which gender may affect how we act and how others perceive and treat us. Relationships and gender influence each other, so that relationships define gender, and gender, in turn, sculpts the character of relationships. Thus, gender is both created by and creative of relationships.

This chapter traces connections among gender, our identities as women and men, communication, and relationships. We'll begin by defining gender and its impact on our lives. Next, we'll explore gender as a personal, social, and relational phenomenon. Finally, we'll highlight the formative role of communication in creating, sustaining, and revising social understandings and expectations of men and women.

UNDERSTANDING GENDER

Although *sex* and *gender* are often used as synonyms, actually they are distinct concepts (Epstein, 1988; Scott, 1986; West & Zimmerman, 1987; Wood, 1994b, 1994c, 1995a). Sex is innate, but gender is socially created and learned by individuals. Being born male or female does not necessarily lead to thinking, acting, and feeling in ways a culture prescribes for men or women. Instead, biological sex is transformed into culturally constructed gender as we interact with social structures and practices that express, uphold, and encourage individuals to embody prevailing views of women or men. As we communicate with others, we learn how society defines the sexes, and we craft our personal identities to reflect or resist social expectations. For example, society encourages women to be sensitive to relationships and to others' feelings, and many women reflect these feminine prescriptions in their concrete behaviors. Men are generally urged to be competitive and emotionally controlled, and these learnings surface in how many men communicate.

Sex

Sex is a biological quality that is determined by genetics and hormones. The terms *male* and *female, woman* and *man, girl* and *boy* refer to biological sex. Even before birth, sex is established, and, short of radical procedures, it remains stable through-out our lives. Of the 23 pairs of chromosomes that provide the blueprint for human identity, one pair controls sex. The usual chromosome patterns are XX for females and XY for males. (Less standard patterns are XO or XXX for females and XXY or XYY for males.) Both before and after birth, hormones govern secondary sexual characteristics such as facial hair, menstruation, and proportion of muscle and fat tissue (Jacklin, 1989).

Recent research also suggests that biological sex may influence tendencies toward specialization in the human brain. In general, females are more adept in using the right brain lobe, which controls creative abilities and intuitive, holistic thinking. Men are generally more skilled in the left brain functions, which govern linear thinking and abstract, analytic thought (Hartlage, 1980). Females typically have more developed corpora callosa, which are the bundles of nerves connecting brain lobes. Thus, females may have an advantage in crossing from one side of the brain to the other and in using both brain hemispheres (Hines, 1992). Research linking sex and hemispheric brain specialization, however, doesn't prove that sex determines brain activity. It is equally possible that males and females are socialized in ways that lead to differential development of ability in the distinct lobes of the brain (Breedlove, 1994).

Currently there is no conclusive evidence of sex differences beyond those associated with physiology, hormonal activity, and brain specialization. Perhaps you're thinking that these limited differences don't explain the extensive distinctions in how men and women act, perceive themselves, and are seen and treated by others. If so, you're perceptive. To make sense of pronounced and numerous dissimilarities in how the sexes act and are perceived, we need to understand gender.

Gender

Unlike sex, which is innate and stable, gender is learned, and it varies in response to experiences over a lifetime. We acquire gender as we interact with others and our social world. As we enter diverse situations and relationships during our lives, our understandings of gender continuously evolve. Gender terms such as *feminine* and *masculine* and *womanly* and *manly* reflect socially constructed views of women and men.

Gender consists of meanings and expectations of men and women that are created and upheld by social processes and structures. For example, women are expected to be sensitive to others, nurturing, and emotional, and men are expected to be independent, assertive, and emotionally reserved (Doyle, 1989; Tavris & Baumgartner, 1983). This gendered aspect of identity is particularly evident in patterns of caregiving. Although sex determines that women and not men carry fetuses, give birth, and lactate, gender accounts for the expectation that women will assume primary responsibility for caring for children and others.

Studies (Risman, 1987, 1989) have shown that men can be as loving, nurturing, and responsive to children as women, yet our society continues to expect women to be more involved than men in parenting (Okin, 1989). Likewise, women are expected to care for elderly individuals, so daughters generally assume greater responsibility than sons in caring for parents, and wives typically provide more care to in-laws than married sons do (Aronson, 1992; Wood, 1994e). Social expectations that women should care for others are reflected in and perpetuated by practices such as maternity leave and schools' tendencies to call mothers before fathers about children. It is gender, not sex, that explains why caring is expected of and assigned to women more than men.

Because gender surpasses sex in explaining patterned differences in social life and the roles, status, rights, activities, and self-concepts of individual women and men, the remainder of this chapter focuses on gender.

SOCIAL CONSTRUCTION OF GENDER

We are sexed beings even before birth, but we acquire gender in the process of social interaction. As we communicate with others, we learn the meanings and values of our culture (G. H. Mead, 1934). In particular, we learn how our culture defines women and men and what it regards as appropriate roles, activities, and identities for each.

Gender Is Variable

What gender means is not universal across time and social groups. In fact, views of men and women vary from culture to culture and at different times within a single culture. The rugged, physically strong exemplar of manhood that held sway in the U.S. in the 1700s was replaced when the Industrial Revolution created a paid labor force in which a man's worth was measured by what he earned. (Cancian, 1987; Wood, 1994b). The European American model of women as dainty decorations was displaced by a view of them as hardworking partners in the family livelihood during the agrarian era in the United States. When European American men were redefined as primary breadwinners in the public sphere, the Western ideal of womanhood was revised to that of homemaker (Cancian, 1987).

Gender also varies across cultures. For instance, in Nepal, both sexes are expected to be nurturing, and men are as likely as women to take care of children and elderly people. In other societies, men are more emotional and concerned with appearance than women, while women are more independent and emotionally restrained than men (M. Mead, 1934/1968). In still other cultures, more than two genders are recognized and celebrated, and individuals sometimes change their gender (Kessler & McKenna, 1978; Olien, 1978).

Even within the United States, gender varies among social groups. Because gender is socially created, it makes sense that different social circumstances would cultivate dissimilar views of the sexes (Haraway, 1988; Harding, 1991). For example, Gaines (1995) has shown that among blacks and Hispanics, both sexes have strongly communal orientations. As a group, African American women are also less deferential than white women and, thus, less inclined to smile and defer to men (Halberstadt & Saitta, 1987) and less likely to tolerate abuse passively (Uzzell & Peebles-Wilkins, 1989). Research indicates that lesbians tend to be somewhat more autonomous than their heterosexual sisters (Huston & Schwartz, 1995).

Gender also intersects with other social categories such as race, class, age, and affectional preference (Spelman, 1988). Thus, a heterosexual black attorney will understand and enact gender (as well as class, race, and sexuality) differently than a white working-class man or a gay accountant in Germany. Because gender varies across time and social groups and in relation to other socially constructed categories, it's a mistake to regard women and men as homogeneous groups. Among members of each sex there is substantial variation due to diverse social circumstances that contour the lives of individual women and men.

Normalizing Masculinity and Men

To create and sustain the meaning of gender, social processes and structures normalize arbitrary and often limiting views of the sexes. We thus come to take for granted the "reality" of social views that have been made to seem so natural that we seldom notice or critically evaluate them. Although *gender* is often misunderstood as a synonym for *women*, men are also gendered, since society imposes expectations on both sexes. Just as heterosexuals, as well as lesbians, gays, and bisexuals, have affectional preferences, and Caucasians, as well as people of color, have racial identity, men, as well as women, are gendered.

We tend to think of race as referring to non-Anglos, sexuality as indicating gays, lesbians, and bisexuals, and gender as describing women because whites, heterosexuality, and men have been normalized in Western culture (Wood, 1995a, 1995c). They are the standard against which all others are measured. Heterosexual patterns and activities are the assumed norms for romantic relationships, which invites us to perceive lesbian, gay, and bisexual relationships as abnormal. Similarly, in professional contexts, the behaviors and orientations of white men are the model against which the conduct of women and people of color is judged. By designating one group as *the* standard, we implicitly define everyone outside of that group as deviant, nonstandard, or other. In this manner, cultures construct a narrow vision of what or who is normal (Harding, 1991; Wood & Duck, 1995) and, also, of what or who is abnormal.

Like whiteness and heterosexuality, masculinity is not an absolute standard, but one that is socially constructed as normative. This implies that it is open to critique and change. More complete views of sexuality, professionalism, and other aspects of life would reflect all those who make up the human community and who participate in social life.

PERVASIVENESS OF GENDER

Because gender infuses the entire social order, it is difficult to notice, much less question, prevailing views of women and men. Becoming aware of how society creates and sustains gender enables social progress and personal change.

Gender Is a Pervasive Aspect of Cultural Life

Gender shapes and is evident in everything from personal relationships to public life. Families often divide labor along gendered lines so that boys are assigned independent, outdoor chores such as mowing the lawn, while girls are expected to participate in cooking and cleaning to provide comfort to others (Burns & Homel, 1989; McHale, Bartko, Crouter, & Perry-Jenkins, 1990). These different chores inscribe gender by encouraging boys to be independent and adventurous and girls to respond to others. Public policies, too, bespeak cultural views of women and men (Okin, 1989). Despite some changes, our laws still grant substantial presumption to women in child custody cases, which reflects gendered views of women as caregivers and men as detached from family ties (Coleman & Ganong, 1995).

Gender is Difficult to Notice

Even though gender pervades our lives, its character and effects are difficult to perceive. Just as we seldom notice air and fish are unaware of water, for the most part we do not realize the myriad ways in which gender infuses our everyday lives as individuals and our collective life as a culture. This is because the meanings of gender that our society has constructed are normalized, making them a constant taken-for-granted background that can easily escape notice. It's difficult to grasp the ways in which gender is normalized when so many aspects of ordinary life make arbitrary views of women and men seem natural: From pink and blue blankets in hospital delivery rooms, to dolls advertised for girls and trains for boys, to guidance counselors who advise women to enter caring professions and men to pursue high-powered careers (Spender, 1989), social constructions of gender surround us at every turn, and they work together to naturalize arbitrary social meanings.

Developing a critical awareness of processes that naturalize views of women and men empowers us to make informed, deliberate choices about how we will embody gender and how we will support or resist prevailing views of women and men. Wise choices about personal identity and social impact begin with recognizing the scope of gender in life.

SCOPE OF GENDER

Gender is a facet of individual identity, a primary principle of social life, and a powerful dynamic in relationships.

Gender as Personal Identity

For most of us, gender is concretely experienced as part of personal identity. We think of ourselves and others as more or less masculine and feminine. Perceiving yourself as feminine or masculine affects the clothes you wear, what and how much you eat, whether you feel safe walking alone at night, and how closely your self-esteem is tied to success in a career and/or relationships. You may feel it is unfeminine to curse or be insensitive to others, or unmasculine to cry or show weakness. In these and other ways, we experience gender as part of personal identity, and it guides how we think, feel and act.

Gender as a Principle of Social Life

Yet gender is more than personal. It is also a system of social meanings that is constructed and sustained by a variety of cultural structures and practices. Families, schools, laws, the military, professions, religious orders, and businesses are social structures that reflect and reproduce the gender ideology of a culture. Patterns of interacting and roles are social practices that sustain gender ideology. For example, research indicates that parents tend to encourage daughters to be cooperative and attentive to others' needs, and encourage sons to be competitive and assertive of their individual rights (Fagot, Hagan, Leinbach, & Kronsberg, 1985). Many workplaces allow maternity but not paternity leaves, an inequity that reflects and sustains views of women as caregivers. The still-prevalent tendency of women to assume the names of their husbands is a practice that reflects the belief that a woman's identity is based on her relationship to a man.

Another illustration of social practices that prescribe and sustain gender comes from West's (1995) in-depth study of battered women. He reports that many women who are brutalized by their intimate partners seek support from clergy only to be told that they should stay in the their marriages, regardless of the danger to their well-being and perhaps their lives. Multiple social structures and practices establish and sustain society's gender ideology.

Gender and Relational Concepts

Social expectations of women and men are realized in particular relationships (Wood, 1994b). Elizabeth Fox-Genovese (1991, p.120) notes that "in practice gender exists not as an abstraction, but as a system of relations . . . the specific roles that [societies] assign to women and to men." As we interact with others, we discover how they see us and what they expect of us (G. H. Mead, 1934). We assess our feelings, thoughts, actions, and appearances by comparing ourselves to others. Thus, gender is both taught and concretely embodied in relationships. Consider a few examples:

- For 20 years in a row, a national survey has found that the linchpin of manhood is being a good breadwinner (Faludi, 1991). The link between manhood and professional success (Doyle, 1989; Wood, 1994c) surfaces concretely in relationships. In a study of wives who outearned husbands, Hochschild (1989) found that both spouses were ashamed of her higher salary, and they worked together to sustain a private understanding of their relationship that portrayed the husband as the leader and the wife as dependent on him.
- In heterosexual couples, both women and men continue to assume women should and will do most of the child care and homemaking (Wood, 1994b, 1994e). Even when both partners work outside of the home, only 20% of men assume half of home responsibilities (Hochschild with Manchung, 1989).
- In professional contexts, women and men are perceived and treated differently, regardless of their formal titles. For example, women flight attendants are subjected to more abuse from passengers than their male peers. Further, male attendants demand deference from females of equivalent rank and resist women's authority (Hochschild, 1983). Because women are expected to be sensitive to others, working women are assumed to be more open to and interested than men in peers' and subordinates' personal problems (Wood, 1994d).
- Even in the 1990s, men are expected to be sexually aggressive and women to be sexually available. Television shows, films, magazines, and music videos

normalize men's sexual aggression, which sheds light on the prevalence of sexual harassment and the still widespread belief that it is normal and acceptable to treat women as sexual objects (Bingham, 1995; Strine, 1992; Wood, 1992, 1995b).

Masculinity and femininity are themselves relational concepts, because the meaning of each is tied to the other. The deference widely associated with femininity requires someone to whom to defer. Likewise, the assertiveness generally associated with masculinity is not an absolute quality, but depends on others who yield. Softness exists in relation to hardness; emotional restraint is meaningful in juxtaposition to emotional expressiveness; independence gains its character in contrast to dependence. It is virtually impossible to conceive of masculinity and femininity apart from one another. In the daily life of relationships, abstract social meanings of gender are transformed into the concrete realities of individual thoughts, feelings, and actions.

DISCURSIVE (RE)CONSTRUCTION OF GENDER

Communication is the most fundamental process that creates, upholds, and alters gender (Bingham, 1995; Weedon, 1987). From public discourse to mediated messages to private talk between intimates, communication reflects social understandings of gender and expresses how individual men and women embody it in their personal identities. For instance, research indicates that men interrupt women more often than women interrupt men (Beck, 1988; DeFrancisco, 1991; Mulac, Wiemann, Widenmann, & Gibson, 1998). When we observe a specific man interrupt a particular woman and see her allow it, we are witnessing a concrete performance of gender. He assumes he should assert and dominate, which is consistent with social prescriptions for masculinity. She displays deference in keeping with social views of women.

Communication Creates and Sustains Gender

The philosopher Michael Foucault realized that communication is a pivotal force in establishing and regulating social life and personal identity. According to Foucault (1978, p. 18), communication is the primary process through which social reality is created because in communication "something is formed." This implies that communication defines experience and establishes meaning. As Spender (1984) has pointed out, language shapes what we perceive. Words confer social existence on what a culture considers important. For instance, the term *date rape* was only recently coined. Before the term entered our language, many women whose dates forced them into sexual activity had no socially authorized way to describe what had happened or to label it as wrong and a violation (Wood, 1992). In like manner, all meanings of ourselves and our world are formed in and fortified by communication on playgrounds, over the breakfast table, in congressional debates, and in schools.

Social views of women and men are established and normalized through ongoing symbolic interaction in society. From family conversations to political discourse to intimate dialogues, communication constructs perspectives of men and women, and at the same time, individuals use communication to embody or resist social meanings. As children, we learned that boys are made of "snakes and snails and puppy dog tails," and girls are made of "sugar and spice and everything nice." Gendered expectations are further communicated through parents' distinctive treatment of daughters and sons. Despite convincing evidence of the detrimental effects of sex-stereotyped childrearing (Morrow, 1990), many parents still perceive and treat boys and girls differently. Parents tend to expect and encourage sons to be independent, active, and tough and daughters to be social and interpersonally sensitive (Jones & Dembo, 1989; Safilios-Rothschild, 1979; Stern & Karraker, 1989; Thompson & Walker, 1989; Thorbecke & Grotevant, 1982). From nursery rhymes to parental instruction, family communication teaches children society's expectations of women and men.

Peers' communication reinforces parental messages about gender. Boys learn early that being afraid will earn them epithets of *sissy, wimp,* and *mama's boy,* and girls discover peers will reject them if they aren't nice to others (Maccoby & Jacklin, 1987; Martin, 1989). Gender is also reinforced in childhood games. Football, for instance, teaches boys to compete, assert themselves, and focus on achieving clearcut goals. Games that girls typically play (jump rope and house) encourage and reward cooperation and responsiveness to others (Maltz & Borker, 1982).

Communication in schools further fortifies social views of the sexes by rewarding girls for being cooperative and quiet and boys for competing and asserting themselves (Epperson, 1988; Sadker & Sadker, 1986; Wood & Lenze, 1991). A survey of over 1,300 studies revealed that teachers give males more attention and encouragement than females ("Sexism in the Schoolhouse," 1992). Thus, communication in schools echoes the meanings of gender expressed in other contexts.

As individuals enter into adult romantic relationships, social views of the sexes surface in communication between partners, especially heterosexuals. For instance, female and male college students share gender stereotypes about appropriate dating scripts. Both sexes think men should initiate relationships and plan activities other than sex (Rose & Frieze, 1989). Both sexes also expect women to be relationship experts (Tavris, 1992; Wood, 1994b) and men to be more powerful (Anderson & Leslie, 1991; Reissman, 1990). Further, an alarming number of college men and women perceive abuse, including physical violence, as a male prerogative in romantic relationships (Goldner, Penn, Sheinberg, & Walker, 1990).

Communication upholds cultural values by reinscribing and naturalizing socially constructed patterns of meaning, perception, and sense making. Also, most of us internalize prevailing social values in the process of communicating. Referring to this as "governance," Foucault (1982) asserts that we learn cultural values in the process of learning language, and this predisposes us to think and act in ways that affirm and reproduce the existing social order. Thus, as we interact with others throughout life, we learn society's meanings for gender, and we are encouraged to accept and embody them in our own lives (Wood, 1994a).

Communication Changes Gender

As we've seen, gender is not static, but consists of fluid social meanings that vary across time and social groups and in relation to other aspects of identity. Social views of men and women change as a result of communication by and between individuals. In other words, individuals can and often do use communication to reform understandings of what it means to be feminine or masculine. The athletic woman of the 1990s would have been disparaged as unfeminine in 1950, and women's participation in professional life was not widely accepted even two decades ago. Hillary Rodham Clinton embodies a new vision of women, one that could not have been attempted in the 1970s. Likewise, Bill Clinton's sensitivity to others and his personal comfort with a strong wife would have been unacceptable in the era dominated by John Wayne as the male ideal.

We notice public figures who offer new models of men and women because they are in the limelight. Yet, less famous people also resist constraining definitions of the sexes and usher in alternative visions. For example, career women become more assertive, ambitious, and comfortable using power the longer they participate in professional life (Epstein, 1981; McGowen & Hart, 1990). As women inhabit professional roles, they alter how they conceive and enact their gender. In turn, this influences how others view men and women and relations between them.

In ordinary family life, too, communication instigates changes in how women and men define themselves and each other. For example, Kay and Applegate (1990) reported that men who take care of elderly people become more aware of others' feelings and more generous in responding to others' needs than men who are less involved in caregiving. Many modern men, who are more actively involved with children than their own fathers were, communicate an alternative definition of manhood and fatherhood.

Children of today who see mothers who are assertive as well as nurturing and fathers who provide personal care as well as financial support develop broader understandings of gender than those learned by many members of previous generations. Thus, much of the communication that creates, sustains, and challenges socially prescribed meanings of gender occurs in the private sphere of relationships.

SUMMARY

In this chapter, we have seen that gender is a social construction. It consists of the meanings culture attributes to men and women and the personal and social effects of those meanings on individuals' concrete lives. Abstract social meanings of gender are learned through social interaction and realized in daily life as we communicate with others in our social and personal relationships. As we interact with family members, friends, intimates, and work associates, we participate in the ongoing cultural creation of gender. Both in accepting or rejecting prevailing views of women and men and in the ways we personally embody gender, each of us influences the continuous (re)construction of gender.

Although gender is normalized through numerous and intricately entwined social structures and practices, we can choose to become critically aware of how arbitrary views of the sexes are naturalized and to take an active role in shaping the impact of gender on our personal and collective lives. It takes courage to question prevailing values and to resist social expectations of how we should be. The easy course is to accept current prescriptions for gender without question or challenge.

Yet, in every generation, individuals take issue with prevailing views of men and women and change social understandings of who they are and should be. For example, from 1848 until 1920, a number of women and a few men challenged then-prevalent views that women were not entitled to own property, pursue higher education, or vote. Resistance to social views of women in that era led to substantial changes in women's rights and opportunities. Similarly, men's movements have contested the macho John Wayne view of manhood and have provided an alternative vision of masculinity as both sensitive and strong, both individualistic and committed to others. As agents of social change, each of us has the capacity to affect what gender will mean in our society. Cultivating and acting on critical consciousness of gender empowers us to influence our personal destinies and the life of our culture.

Perhaps communication as a fulcrum of changing gender is best illustrated in a conversation I overheard between my niece and her playmate Steven. He announced, "I am the father so I get to go to work each day and you have to stay home." Michelle's response was swift and sure: "I don't want to stay home. You do that. I'm going to work." Regardless of how these two 4-year-olds work out roles in their make-believe family, they are engaged in constructing the meaning of gender and what it implies for their personal identities and their relationship with each other. Like Michelle and Steven, each of us is engaged in the social construction of gender and, thus, the continuous creation of our relationships, our society, and ourselves.

QUESTIONS FOR REFLECTION AND DISCUSSION

1. Think about the ways in which masculinity and male patterns are normalized in contexts such as professions, athletics, and media. How are norms and standards of male athletes made to seem appropriate for all athletes? How are masculine modes of doing business represented as natural and right?
2. How do media reproduce cultural views of women and men? Watch children's programs on Saturday morning and notice the roles of characters of each sex. Which sex is more active, adventurous, and successful? Which is more dependent, quiet, and unsuccessful?
3. Examine science texts used in courses for any grade level. Notice the number of women and men scientists who are mentioned. Notice pictures used to illustrate

scientific work. What view of scientists is normalized by communication in textbooks?

4. Interview a local attorney, preferably the district attorney for your area. Ask her or him to describe trial strategies used by lawyers and assumptions held by jurors that affect verdicts in rape and sexual assault cases. With others in your class, discuss how the information you gain for the interview sheds light on gender ideology.

28

DOING IT FOR OURSELVES
FROM: *IN THESE TIMES*

Barbara Ehrenreich

CAN FEMINISM SURVIVE CLASS POLARIZATION?

Here's a scene from feminist ancient history: It's 1972 and about 20 of us are gathered in somebody's living room for our weekly "women's support group" meeting. We're all associated, in one way or another, with a small public college catering mostly to "nontraditional" students, meaning those who are older, poorer and more likely to be black or Latina than typical college students in this suburban area. Almost every level of the college hierarchy is represented—students of all ages, clerical workers, junior faculty members and even one or two full professors. There are acknowledged differences among us—race and sexual preference, for example—which we examine eagerly and a little anxiously. But we are comfortable together, and excited to have a chance to discuss everything from the administration's sexist policies to our personal struggles with husbands and lovers. Whatever may divide us, we are all women, and we understand this to be one of the great defining qualities of our lives and politics.

Could a group so diverse happily convene today? Please let me know if you can offer a present day parallel, but I tend to suspect the answer is "very seldom" or "not at all." Perhaps the biggest social and economic trend of the past three decades has been class polarization—the expanding inequality in income and wealth. As United for a Fair Economy's excellent book, *Shifting Fortunes: The Perils of the Growing American Wealth Gap,* points out, the most glaring polarization has occurred between those at the very top of the income distribution—the upper 1 to 5 percent—and those who occupy the bottom 30 to 40 percent. Less striking, but more ominous for the future of feminism, is the growing gap between those in the top 40 percent and those in the bottom 40. One chart in *Shifting Fortunes* shows that the net worth of households in the bottom 40 percent declined by nearly 80 percent between 1983 and 1995. Except for the top 1 percent, the top 40 percent lost ground too—but much less. Today's college teacher, if she is not an adjunct, occupies that relatively lucky top 40 group, while today's clerical worker is in the rapidly sinking bottom 40. Could they still gather comfortably in each other's living rooms to discuss common issues? Do they still have common issues to discuss?

Numbers hardly begin to tell the story. The '80s brought sharp changes in lifestyle and consumption habits between the lower 40 percent—which is roughly what we call the "working class"—and the upper 20 to 30, which is populated by professors, administrators, executives, doctors, lawyers and other "professionals." "Mass markets" became "segmented markets," with different consumer trends signaling differences in status. In 1972, a junior faculty member's living room looked much like that of a departmental secretary—only, in most cases, messier. Today, the secretary is likely to accessorize her home at Kmart; the professor at Pottery Barn. Three decades ago, we all enjoyed sugary, refined-flour treats at our meetings (not to mention Maxwell House coffee and cigarettes!) Today, the upper-middle class grinds its own beans, insists on the whole grain, organic snacks, and vehemently eschews hot dogs and meatloaf. In the '70s, conspicuous, or even just overly enthusiastic, consumption was considered gauche—and not only by leftists and feminists. Today, professors, including quite liberal ones, are likely to have made a deep emotional investment in their houses, their furniture and their pewter ware. It shows how tasteful they are, meaning—when we cut through the garbage about aesthetics—how distinct they are from the "lower" classes.

In the case of women, there is an additional factor compounding the division wrought by class polarization: In the '60s, only about 30 percent of American women worked outside their homes; today, the proportion is reversed, with more than 70 percent of women in the work force. This represents a great advance, since women who earn their own way are of course more able to avoid male domination in their personal lives. But women's influx into the work force also means that fewer and fewer women share the common occupational experience once defined by the word "housewife." I don't want to exaggerate this commonality as it existed in the '60s and '70s; obviously the stay-at-home wife of an executive led a very different life from that of the stay-at-home wife of a blue-collar man. But they did perform similar daily tasks—housecleaning, childcare, shopping, cooking. Today, in contrast, the majority of women fan out every morning to face vastly different work experiences, from manual labor to positions of power. Like men, women are now spread throughout the occupational hierarchy (though not at the very top), where they encounter each other daily as unequals—bosses vs. clerical workers, givers of orders vs. those who are ordered around, etc.

Class was always an issue. Even before polarization set in, some of us lived on the statistical hilltops, others deep in the valleys. But today we are distributed on what looks less like a mountain range and more like a cliff-face. Gender, race and sexual preference still define compelling commonalities, but the sense of a shared condition necessarily weakens as we separate into frequent-flying female executives on the one hand and airport cleaning women on the other. Can feminism or, for that matter, any cross-class social movement, survive as class polarization spreads Americans further and further apart?

For all the ardent egalitarianism of the early movement, feminism had the unforeseen consequence of heightening the class differences between women. It was educated, middle-class women who most successfully used feminist ideology and solidarity to advance themselves professionally. Feminism has played a role in working-class women's struggles too—for example, in the union organizing drives of university clerical workers—but probably its greatest single economic effect was to open up the formerly male-dominated professions to women. Between the '70s and the '90s, the percentage of female students in business, medical and law schools shot up from less than 10 percent to more than 40 percent.

There have been, however, no comparable gains for young women who cannot afford higher degrees, and most of these women remain in the same low-paid occupations that have been "women's work" for decades. All in all, feminism has had little impact on the status or pay of traditional female occupations like clerical, retail, health care and light assembly line work. While middle-class women gained MBAs, working-class women won the right not to be called "honey"—and not a whole lot more than that.

Secondly, since people tend to marry within their own class, the gains made by women in the professions added to the growing economic gap between the working class and the professional-managerial class. Working-class families gained too, as wives went to work. But, as I argued in *Fear of Falling: The Inner Life of the Middle Class*, the most striking gains have accrued to couples consisting of two well-paid professionals or managers. The doctor/lawyer household zoomed well ahead of the truck driver/typist combination.

So how well has feminism managed to maintain its stance as the ground shifts beneath its feet? Here are some brief observations of the impact of class polarization on a few issues once central to the feminist project:

Welfare. This has to be the most tragic case. In the '70s, feminists hewed to the slogan, "Every woman is just one man away from welfare." This was an exaggeration of course; even then, there were plenty of self-supporting and independently wealthy women. But it was true enough to resonate with the large numbers of women who worked outside their homes part time or not at all. We recognized our commonality as home-makers and mothers and we considered this kind of work to be important enough to be paid for—even when there was no husband on the scene. Welfare, in other words, was potentially every woman's concern.

Flash forward to 1996, when Clinton signed the odious Republican welfare reform bill, and you find only the weakest and most tokenistic protests from groups bearing the label "feminist." The core problem, as those of us who were pro-welfare advocates found, was that many middle- and upper-middle class women could no longer see why a woman should be subsidized to raise her children. "Well, I work and raise my kids—why shouldn't they?" was a common response, as if poor women could command wages that would enable them to purchase reliable child-care. As for that other classic feminist slogan—"every mother is a working mother"— no one seems to remember it anymore.

Health care.   Our bodies, after all, are what we have most in common as women, and the women's health movement of the '70s and early '80s probably brought together as diverse a constituency—at least in terms of class—as any other component of feminism. We worked to legalize abortion and to stop the involuntary sterilization of poor women of color, to challenge the sexism of medical care faced by all women consumers and to expand low-income women's access to care.

In many ways, we were successful: Abortion is legal, if not always accessible; the kinds of health information once available only in underground publications like the original *Our Bodies, Ourselves* can now be found in *Mademoiselle*; the medical profession is no longer an all-male bastion of patriarchy. We were not so successful, however, in increasing low-income women's access to health care—in fact, the number of the uninsured is far larger than it used to be, and poor women still get second-class health care when they get any at all. Yet the only women's health issue that seems to generate any kind of broad, cross-class participation today is breast cancer, at least if wearing a pink ribbon counts as "participation."

Even the nature of medical care is increasingly different for women of different classes. While lower-income women worry about paying for abortions or their children's care, many in the upper-middle class are far more concerned with such medical luxuries as high-tech infertility treatments and cosmetic surgery. Young college women get bulimia; less affluent young women are more likely to suffer from toxemia of pregnancy, which is basically a consequence of malnutrition.

Housework.   In the '70s, housework was a hot feminist issue and a major theme of consciousness-raising groups. After all, whatever else women did, we did housework; it was the nearly universal female occupation. We debated Pat Mainardi's famous essay on "The Politics of Housework," which focused on the private struggles to get men to pick up their own socks. We argued bitterly about the "wages for housework" movement's proposal that women working at home should be paid by the state. We studied the Cuban legal code, with its intriguing provision that males do their share or face jail time.

Thirty years later, the feminist silence on the issue of housework is nearly absolute. Not, I think, because men are at last doing their share, but because so many women of the upper-middle class now pay other women to do their housework for them. Bring up the subject among affluent feminists today, and you get a guilty silence, followed by defensive patter about how well they pay and treat their cleaning women.

In fact, the $15 an hour commonly earned by freelance maids is not so generous at all, when you consider that it has to cover cleaning equipment, transportation to various cleaning sites throughout the day, as well as any benefits, like health insurance, the cleaning person might choose to purchase for herself. The fast-growing corporate cleaning services like Merry Maids and The Maids International are far worse, offering (at least in the northeastern urban area I looked into) their workers between $5 (yes, that's below the minimum wage) and $7 an hour.

In a particularly bitter irony, many of the women employed by the corporate cleaning services are former welfare recipients bumped off the rolls by the welfare reform bill so feebly resisted by organized feminists. One could conclude, if one was in a very bad mood, that it is not in the interests of affluent feminists to see the wages of working class women improve. As for the prospects of "sisterhood" between affluent women and the women who scrub their toilets—forget about it, even at a "generous" $15 an hour.

The issues that have most successfully weathered class polarization are sexual harassment and male violence against women. These may be the last concerns that potentially unite all women; and they are of course crucial. But there is a danger in letting these issues virtually define feminism, as seems to be the case in some campus women's centers today: Poor and working-class women (and men) face forms of harassment and violence on the job that are not sexual or even clearly gender-related. Being reamed out repeatedly by an obnoxious supervisor of either sex can lead to depression and stress-related disorders. Being forced to work long hours of overtime, or under ergonomically or chemically hazardous conditions, can make a person physically sick. Yet feminism has yet to recognize such routine workplace experiences as forms of "violence against women."

When posing the question—"can feminism survive class polarization?"—to middle-class feminist acquaintances, I sometimes get the response: "Well, you're right—we have to confront our classism." But the problem is not classism, the problem is class itself: the existence of grave inequalities among women, as well as between women and men.

We should recall that the original radical—and yes, utopian—feminist vision was of a society without hierarchies of any kind. This of course means equality among the races and the genders, but class is different: There can be no such thing as "equality among the classes." The abolition of hierarchy demands not only racial and gender equality, but the abolition of class. For a start, let's put that outrageous aim back into the long-range feminist agenda and mention it as loudly and often as we can.

In the shorter term, there's plenty to do, and the burden necessarily falls on the more privileged among us: to support working-class women's workplace struggles, to advocate for expanded social services (like childcare and health care) for all women, to push for greater educational access for low-income women and so on and so forth. I'm not telling you anything new here, sisters—you know what to do.

But there's something else, too, in the spirit of another ancient slogan that is usually either forgotten or misinterpreted today: "The personal is the political." Those of us who are fortunate enough to have assets and income beyond our immediate needs need to take a hard look at how we're spending our money. New furniture—and please, I don't want to hear about how tastefully funky or antique-y it is—or a donation to a homeless shelter? A chic outfit or a check written to an organization fighting sweatshop conditions in the garment industry? A maid or a contribution to a clinic serving low-income women?

I know it sounds scary, but it will be a lot less so if we can make sharing stylish again and excess consumption look as ugly as it actually is. Better yet, give some of your time and your energy too. But if all you can do is write a check, that's fine: Since Congress will never redistribute the wealth (downward, anyway), we may just have to do it ourselves.

29

GENDERED VIOLENCE IN INTIMATE RELATIONSHIPS

Jacquelyn W. White & Barrie Bondurant

They had grown up together, and now they were college roommates. Very distraught, Janet revealed that Rob, they guy she had been dating for the last 3 weeks had raped her. She kept blaming herself, wondering what she did wrong, and chastising herself for not being able to tell what he was really like. Sue, in seeking to comfort Janet, confided that the same thing had happened to her in high school. Her boyfriend, whom they all knew and believed to be a nice guy, had forced her to have sex with him. Until this moment, she had never told anyone, sure no one would believe her. She understood just what Janet was feeling. Sara then spoke up, assuring both that she understood, because she had been sexually victimized by her step-father when she was 8 years old. In sharing their experiences, these friends came to see that what had happened to them was not unique. Girls and women of different ages are the victims of violence committed by men they thought they could trust.

In spite of images of loving, supportive families and caring, protective lovers, intimate relationships often are plagued by alarming levels of aggression and violence. In a wide array of nonintimate crimes, adult men are usually the perpetrators and the victims. In families, however, girls are more likely to be victims of sexual abuse than boys, and boys are more likely to be victims of physical abuse than girls (youth is defined as 0–18 years). In play groups, boys encounter more opportunities for physical aggression than girls. In intimate relationships, women are much more likely than men to be the victims of both emotionally and physically damaging violence at the hands of men they know and frequently trust. Women too commit acts of aggression and violence toward intimate partners, often as frequently as men, but usually with less serious consequences and for different reasons (Straus & Gelles,

1990; White & Koss, 1991). In this chapter, we explore the character of gendered violence. We first discuss historical and research influences on what is known about gendered violence and then trace the pattern of its occurrence from childhood through adulthood. Although the research discussed in this chapter focuses primarily on violence in relationships in the United States, violence against women is recognized as a worldwide problem (French, 1992).

THE CONTEXT OF RESEARCH ON GENDERED VIOLENCE

Research Biases

Most of the research in this chapter focuses on intimate heterosexual relationships for several reasons. First, strong emphasis is placed on heterosexuality in our culture. Friends, family, acquaintances, movies, and television programs all usually assume and expect individuals to have heterosexual interests. Researchers mirror this cultural prejudice by studying male-female intimate relationships, often assuming that "couple" refers to a man and a woman. This heterosexist bias has slowed research on violence in lesbian and gay relationships. A second reason for concentrating on heterosexual relationships is the low number of lesbian and gay male relationships. Although research indicates that 20 to 37% of men and 13 to 20% of women have had homosexual experiences (Hunt, 1974), the actual number of long-term homosexual relationships is lower. Even researchers who want to study lesbian and gay couples have difficulty locating research participants.

Along with heterosexist bias, research on violence in relationships is limited by ethnic and class assumptions. Frequently, research is done on college students. As with heterosexual relationships, middle-class, white behavior has been assumed to characterize all human behavior or to represent "normal" behavior. Because people tend to study people with whom they are familiar, ethnic minorities are more likely to study ethnic minorities (Reid, 1993). However, few researchers belong to ethnic minorities. Furthermore, white, middle-class researchers have more difficulty assessing and gaining the confidence of poor or minority populations. These biases shape the nature of our knowledge just as other cultural factors shape our attitudes. Even though knowledge of violence in minority and gay and lesbian relationships is limited, we will discuss the information that is available.

Historical Setting

One cultural factor that may be important for intimate relationships is Americans' preoccupation with obsessive love and violent love. Violence is romanticized, as in Harlequin-type novels where the rugged, mysterious stranger simultaneously frightens and intrigues, then violently "seduces" (that is, rapes), the innocent young heroine. Violent relationships also are romanticized in film, with Scarlett O'Hara and Rhett Butler in *Gone with the Wind* being but one of many examples. Unfortunately, examples of violent relationships throughout history are not limited to fiction. The violent control of women has existed since the beginning of recorded history. In *The Creation of Patriarchy*, Gerda Lerner (1986) asserts that because of biological vulnerability in childbearing, more men than women filled the role of warrior. When neighboring tribes were conquered, the defeated men were killed, and their wives and children were enslaved. Rape was the most powerful mechanism to enforce the subjugation of the captured women. Thus, these women became property. Ironically, women of the victorious tribes also came to be viewed as property. Women and men began to realize that if their tribe were defeated, the women would become the property of the enemy. Hence, the women turned to their own men for protection from captivity by warring forces. Over time, men's power extended from controlling the strategies and tools of war to controlling most aspects of public and private life, including the treatment of women as men's possessions. Today, many feminists argue that fear of rape remains a powerful social tool that maintains men's control of women (Koss et al., 1994).

THE PERVASIVENESS OF GENDERED VIOLENCE

Women state that rape is a crime they most fear (Warr, 1985). The notion of a stranger lurking in shadows, poised to attack the unsuspecting victim, is a continuing fear of many women. However, as devastating as stranger rape is, it is not the most common crime women experience. Research has established that women are more likely to be the victims of violence committed by male acquaintances and intimates (Koss et al., 1994). This violence takes many forms, including incest, sexual abuse outside the family, emotional and physical abuse, dating violence, acquaintance rape, and marital abuse. All these forms of violence share in common the fact that they frequently are committed by men known to the girls and women. Unlike other crimes, they are crimes in which others, as well as the victim herself, tend to blame the victim for what happened. Thus, the social support that most victims of crime receive is missing for victims of gendered violence. Additionally, the consequences of sexual violence extend beyond the immediate violation and can be severe and long-lasting.

Gendered Violence in Childhood

The gendered nature of violence is evident early in childhood and establishes a framework for patterns of interactions between adult women and men. Children are at great risk for victimization because of their small physical stature and dependency on adults; they have little choice over with whom they live, and few opportunities to leave an abusive home. During childhood, boys have more experience with physical aggression and girls have more experience with sexual aggression (Finkelhor & Dziuba-Leatherman, 1994). Among older children, girls are at greater risk than boys, presumably because they are less physically able to defend themselves.

The types of messages about aggression and violence that children receive in the home are gender-specific. This is true in both normal and abusive homes. The majority of parents in American homes use verbal and physical aggression as disciplinary tactics, inadvertently teaching children that "might makes right." Murray Straus and Richard Gelles (1990) report that over 90% of children are spanked sometime in their youth, with many parents (62%) reporting physical aggression against their children; this aggression includes pushing, shoving, and slapping. Fewer parents (11%) reported using severe aggression, including hitting, kicking, beating, threatening, and using weapons against their children.

Punishment does not appear to be uniform, however; the sex of the child and the parent affect the pattern and the outcome (Strassberg, Dodge, Pettit, & Bates, 1994), as does the particular type of punishment used (Eron, 1992). Punishment can take many forms, some physical, such as spanking, and some psychological, such as withdrawal of love and approval. This distinction is important because research results may suggest different conclusions depending on what type of punishment or which aspect of child aggression is studied.

In a 22-year longitudinal study of 632 children, followed from the third grade to age 30, Eron (1992) reported conflicting tendencies in parents' attitudes and behaviors toward aggression. The parents generally saw aggression as an undesirable attribute for children, but viewed it as a desirable *masculine* behavior; this was in spite of the fact that they physically punished boys more harshly than girls for aggression (a result confirmed by Perry, Perry, & Weiss, 1989). Girls, in contrast, were more likely to receive psychological punishment from their parents (Eron, 1992). These gender-related patterns of punishment were associated with boys being more aggressive than girls. Apparently, parents' behaviors teach boys to be more physically aggressive than girls, though giving mixed messages about the desirability of aggression in boys.

In a review of socialization practices, Lytton and Romney (1991) found that, at least in North American homes, parents are as likely to spank girls as boys. However, the effects of the spanking may be different (Strassberg et al., 1994). On the one hand, paternal spanking has been shown to lead to reactive aggression in both girls and boys (that is, angry retaliation in reaction to a peer's behavior); on the other hand, spanking by fathers has been associated with bullying aggression (unprovoked attacks on peers). Strassberg and his colleagues (1994) conclude that fathers' spanking of boys communicates a "gender-based approach to interpersonal disagreements, that of physical dominance . . . explicitly transmitting gender-stereotypic notions" (p. 457). Such conclusions are consistent with social learning theory, which argues that male authority figures are modeled more than are female authority figures, and that within-gender modeling is more powerful that between-gender modeling (Hicks, 1968).

With regard to more severe punishment (that is, child abuse), at younger ages boys are at greater risk than girls, but the risk for girls increases during preadolescence and adolescence (Straus, Gelles & Steinmetz, 1980). This is presumably because of boys' increased ability to inflict harm as they physically mature. Children, especially those from abusive homes, have many opportunities to learn that the more powerful person in a relationship can use aggression to successfully control the less powerful person.

This lesson is also learned in a sexual context for a minority of girls and boys. It has been estimated that 10 to 30% of women and 2 to 9% of men are victims of child sexual abuse (Finkelhor, 1984), with approximately 95% of the abuse of girls and 80% of the abuse of boys being perpetrated by men (Russell, 1982). Boys are more likely to be sexually abused by someone outside the family; girls are more likely to be sexually abused by a family member or a man known to the family. Within the family, father-daughter incest (which includes stepfathers) is the most common form of sexual abuse (Russell, 1984).

Just as sexual abuse teaches children about the gendered nature of power, so do children's play experiences. Given that children often play in same-sex groups, it is not surprising that the forms of aggression expressed in these groups differ. For example, boys are more likely than girls to establish dominance physically (for example, by shouldering), whereas girls are more likely to use verbal persuasion (Charlesworth & Dzur, 1987). This leads boys to be the targets of physical aggression in play situations more often than girls. When children attempt to influence the other sex, boys are more successful than girls. Jean Block Miller (1986) has suggested that girls learn to protect themselves from boys' physical aggression by avoiding them. They develop a wariness that they carry into adolescence. Cultural prescriptions for gender also teach girls to be less direct in expressing aggression (Lagerspetz, Bjorkqvist, & Peltonen, 1988). Thus, women come to experience aggressive behavior as a loss of emotional control, whereas men find aggression rewarding and an effective way to control others (Campbell, 1993). These patterns explain why girls and women develop greater anxiety and feelings of guilt regarding aggressive behavior.

By the age of 6 or 7, boys and girls show definite preferences for gender-segregated play. The pressure for young boys to differentiate themselves from girls is strong at this age. Boys run from girls, tease each other about girls, and chase girls. In these ways, boys define girls as different and inferior, scorn girl-type activities, and exclude girls from their play. Girls do many of the same teasing and chasing behaviors as boys, but do not see boys as being as polluted or inferior (Thorne & Luria, 1986).

As studies of parenting styles, childhood sexual abuse, and play patterns of boys and girls suggest, boys receive numerous messages that encourage them to use aggression to establish interpersonal control, and they have many opportunities to engage in aggressive interactions. Girls, on the other hand, receive messages to be submissive and apprehensive of men. Additionally, some girls learn that their bodies are not their own, and that the people who are supposed to care about them sometimes take sexual liberties. These experiences set the stage for patterns of behavior that emerge during adolescence when intimate, heterosexual interactions develop. Boys have learned, though observations in the home, from peer interactions, and from media depictions of male-female relationships, that they are dominant and entitled to female submission. Boys are more likely to develop a sense of "entitlement," a component of which is the right to dominate girls. Girls, too, learn that men are entitled, and they learn role prescriptions that push them to be submissive.

Gendered Violence in Adolescence

The gender-related patterns learned in childhood are played out in adolescent dating and committed relationships. It is not unusual for young dating couples in high school and college to act aggressively toward each other. Young people report that their most frequent conflicts with dating partners are over jealousy, sexual behavior, and alcohol use. A recent national survey of college students found that women and men reported directing various forms of verbal and physical aggression toward their dating partners with equal frequency (White & Koss, 1991), though many more students (80 to 88%) reported being verbally aggressive than physically aggressive (35 to 39%). Other studies have shown that the motives and consequences for such behavior are different for women and men (White, Koss, & Kissling, 1991). Women are more likely to be injured, and to feel surprised, scared, angry, and hurt by a partner's aggression than are men (Makepeace, 1986).

The best estimates of sexual assault among college students to date are that 14.4% of college women have experienced unwanted sexual contact; 11.9% have been verbally coerced into sexual intercourse; 12.1% have experienced attempted rape; and 15.4% have been raped (Koss, Gidycz, & Wisniewski, 1987). The estimate of rape found by Koss and her colleagues is 10 to 15 times higher than corresponding FBI estimates. To understand these results, you should realize that the word *rape* or the phrase *sexual assault* was not used to assess whether or not a woman was a rape victim. Instead, behavioral descriptions of the various forms of sexual assault were given, and the women were asked to indicate whether each had happened to them. When asked later in the survey, "Have you ever been raped?" 73% of the women who said they had experienced what meets the legal definition of rape answered "no." Furthermore, half of these women never told anyone about the assault. This survey revealed that most victims knew the perpetrator and the assaults frequently occurred in a dating context. A recent survey found similar rates of reported sexual assault among adolescents, indicating that sexual assault is not just a problem for college students. It is a frequent experience during the high school years as well (White & Humphrey, 1993).

Although research is limited, we know something about dating violence and sexual assault among adolescents who are not white, middle-class, heterosexual college students. Although it is difficult for any young person to admit being victimized by a dating partner, it is especially so for ethnic minorities. The legacy of slavery and distrust of white authority figures have made it difficult for African-American teens to report abusive dating relationships (White, 1991). Women in Asian and Pacific Island communities, too, are reluctant to disclose abuse because of cultural traditions of male dominance and reticence to discuss private relationships in public (Yoshi-hamana, Parekh, & Boyington, 1991). For lesbian teens, the problem is complicated by the fact that, in reporting abuse, they may have to reveal their sexual orientation, something they may not be psychologically ready to do (Levy & Lobel, 1991).

It appears that dating violence and sexual assault among adolescents and college students is so prevalent, in part, because of the *overall structure and meaning of dating in our culture,* which give men greater power. Adolescent dating patterns follow a fairly well-defined script that has not changed much over several decades. A dating script is a set of rules to be followed by girls and boys that affords men greater power relative to women because they are expected to initiate and pay for dates, and because relationships generally are perceived as more important to women than to men (Breines & Gordon, 1983). A component of the dating script is a sexual script that prescribes the man to be the predator and the woman the prey (Weiss & Borges, 1973). Women are assumed to be responsible for how "far things go," and if things "get out of hand," it is their fault.

An in-depth study of college women's peer cultures discovered that young women believe that being attractive, attracting men and having dates and boyfriends are very important (Holland & Eisenhart, 1990). Young women believe they will be judged as more attractive if they have a relationship with an attractive man. The more attractive the man, the more prestige and status a woman gains by dating him. Further, some college women believe that when a woman is more attractive than the man, he must treat her especially well as a means of equalizing power in the relationship, but if the woman is less attractive than the man, he can treat her poorly to compensate for her unattractiveness. The woman, if less attractive than the man, reduces her expectation for good treatment. Her expectations reflect her judgment of her relative attractiveness. Women also use a man's treatment as an index of their attractiveness. When mistreated, women blame themselves rather than the man for their victimization (Holland & Eisenhart, 1990).

Violence in Marriage and Other Committed Relationships

Abusive experiences in committed relationships include not only nonsexual physical violence, but also verbal harassment, insults, intimidation, threats, sexual coercion, sexual assault, rape, forced isolation, lack of control of money, and restrictions on medical visits (Yllo, 1993). Most researchers, however, focus on physical abuse, because it is seen as a more severe threat to safety and life and because it is easier to measure than emotional abuse. Although women report engaging in aggressive behaviors in committed relationships, most researchers acknowledge that these behaviors do not result in the same amount of physical and psychological damage as men's aggression (Straus, 1993).

The greatest threat of violence to women is from their intimate partners; for men, the greatest threat is from other men (Browne, 1993). Women are more likely to be physically or sexually assaulted by an intimate partner than by a stranger. It is estimated that 2 to 3 million women are assaulted by male partners in the United States each year and that at least half of these women are severely assaulted (that is, punched, kicked, choked, beaten, or threatened or injured with a knife or gun) (Straus & Gelles, 1990). As many as 21 to 34% of women will be assaulted by an intimate partner during adulthood (Browne, 1993). Further, it is estimated that 33 to 50% of all battered wives are also victims of partner rape (Randall, 1990). Most researchers agree that these numbers are underestimates and that the actual figures may be much higher. It is likely that many people do not admit to abusive behavior, even when guaranteed that their responses will be anonymous, because of shame, guilt, and the belief that wife abuse is normal (Dutton, 1988).

It isn't unusual for intimate violence to end in homicide. A woman's death can result from a severe beating or from the use of guns, knives, or other weapons. Approximately two-thirds of family violence deaths are women killed by their male partners and over one-half of all murders of women are committed by current or former partners (Browne & Williams, 1989). In contrast, only 6% of male murder victims are killed by wives or girlfriends (Uniform Crime Report, 1985). Murder-suicides are almost always cases where the man kills his partner or estranged partner and then kills himself (Stuart & Campbell, 1989). He also may kill the children or other family members before he kills himself. While men are homicide victims more often than women, if a woman is killed there is a 50% chance that she will be killed by her partner (Browne & Williams, 1989). Although there are instances in which a woman murders a partner who has been abusing her, this happens less frequently than men killing partners they have abused chronically (Browne, 1993).

When women do kill their partners, they often are reacting to abuse rather then initiating it. A recent study found several commonalities among women who kill their partners (Brown, 1987). The women were in situations where they were abused by their partners, and the abuse was increasing in frequency and severity. Along with the increased violence was a rise in the number and seriousness of the women's injuries. It was common for these men to have raped their spouses, to have forced them into other sexual acts, and to have made threats against their lives. The men typically used alcohol excessively each day as well as recreational drugs. Altogether, the desperation of battered women who kill has prompted attorneys to use "the battered woman syndrome" in court cases to describe the woman's psychological state (Walker, 1984).

The issue of gender differences in domestic violence is clouded by data on abuse in lesbian relationships. Until the 1980s, lesbian battery was rarely discussed. The idea of lesbian love as a utopia free of male violence permeated lesbian thought. Supposedly, if two women were together in a relationship, there should be no violence, only peace and harmony (Schilit, Lie, & Montagne, 1990). However, 31% of lesbian women report forced sexual activities in their intimate relationships (Waterman, Dawson, & Bologna, 1989). Even so, a study comparing heterosexual to lesbian women found that both groups of women had been victimized by men (72%) more often than women (28%). In dating relationships, heterosexual women were more likely to have been physically abused by their partner than were lesbian women. However, heterosexual and lesbian couples did not differ on physical abuse in committed relationships or sexual abuse in dating or committed relationships (Brand & Kidd, 1986). In sum, it appears that partner abuse is a problem that occurs with almost the same frequency in heterosexual and lesbian relatinships, although there are differences in dating relationships. Gay male couples report slightly less sexual abuse than lesbian couples, but have more violence associated with abusive acts (Waterman et al., 1989).

UNDERSTANDING GENDERED VIOLENCE

To understand gendered violence, we must first recognize that culturally based socialization practices teach men to be aggressors and women to be victims. As this chapter has described, gendered violence is learned early in life and continues in our different relationships as we age. Although all men are not more powerful than all women, a social analysis focuses on overall patterns found in society. Statistics allow us to examine larger social influences. As this chapter has shown, the statistics reveal that women are the victims of intimate violence more often then men at every stage of development, with the exception of early childhood physical abuse.

Evidence of female abuse of children and spouses and the admission of lesbian violence create disagreement among researchers as to the relationship between gender and violence. Because mothers abuse their children and lesbians abuse their partners, some researchers argue that intimate violence is *not* related to gender and social roles. Other researchers disagree, arguing that patriarchy as a social system carries with it the message that the more powerful are entitled to dominate the less powerful. Because men more often hold higher status positions than women, it follows that men will abuse more than women, and because adults are more powerful than children, children will be victimized more than adults. But not all men are aggressors, and not all women are victims. Similarly, all men are not more powerful than all women.

Inequality in relationships, coupled with cultural values that embrace domination of the weaker by the stronger, creates the potential for violence. Theorists suggest that lesbian battery is motivated by factors common to all Western couples. Both lesbian and heterosexual couples are raised to see families as social units where hierarchical relationships exist. Parents have more power than children, and one partner has more power than the other. The more powerful partner can control money, resources, activities, and decisions. Partner abuse has been associated with issues of power and dependency in both lesbians (Renzetti, 1992) and heterosexual couples (Finkelhor, 1983). Both men and women learn that violence is a method people use to get their way. When individuals use violence and get their way, they are reinforced and thus more likely to use aggression in the future. Research indicates that women are as likely as men to aggress in situations that are congruent with their gender identities, and where they hold relatively more power (Towson & Zanna, 1982). White and Kowalski (1994) conclude that, "to the extent that power corrupts men, it may also corrupt women" (p. 485).

QUESTIONS FOR REFLECTION AND DISCUSSION

1. How might individuals and social systems encourage greater reporting of violence by minority and lesbian and gay individuals?
2. If violence is woven into the broad ideology of Western culture, how can we reduce it?
3. What are the merits of teaching young children about relationship violence? For various ages, what would be some of the ways to approach the topic?
4. Does it appear contradictory to conclude that women are the victims of many forms of intimate violence and yet frequently feel empowered in their day-to-day lives? How can you resolve this contradiction?
5. If a woman experiences several forms of victimization, for example childhood incest, adolescent dating violence, and marital rape, is she to blame? How can you account for her experiences?
6. Should physical abuse be considered "more serious" than verbal or emotional abuse? What kind of evidence would you consider necessary to answer this question?

30

DEATH ON THE HOME FRONT—WARS ABROAD CONTINUE AT HOME
WOMEN IN THE CROSSHAIR

Ann Jones

Wake up, America. The boys are coming home, and they're not the boys who went away.

On New Year's Day, the *New York Times* welcomed the advent of 2009 by reporting that, since returning from Iraq, nine members of the Fort Carson, Colorado, Fourth Brigade Combat team had been charged with homicide. Five of the murders they were responsible for took place in 2008 when, in addition, "charges of domestic violence, rape and sexual assault" at the base rose sharply. Some of the murder victims were chosen at random; four were fellow soldiers—all men. Three were wives or girlfriends.

This shouldn't be a surprise. Men sent to Iraq or Afghanistan for two, three, or four tours of duty return to wives who find them "changed" and children they barely know. Tens of thousands return to inadequate, underfunded veterans' services with appalling physical injuries, crippling post-traumatic stress disorder (PTSD), and suck-it-up sergeants who hold to the belief that no good soldier seeks help. That, by the way, is a mighty convenient belief for the Departments of Defense and Veterans Affairs, which have been notoriously slow to offer much of that help.

Recently Republican Senator John Cornyn from Texas, a state with 15 major military bases, noted that as many as one in five U.S. veterans is expected to suffer from at least one "invisible wound" of war, if not a combination of them, "including depression, post-traumatic stress disorder and mild traumatic brain injury." Left untreated, such wounds can become *very* visible: witness, for example, the recent wave of suicides that have swept through the military, at least 128 in 2008, and 24 in January 2009 alone.

To judge by past wars, a lot of returning veterans will do themselves a lot of damage drinking and drugging. Many will wind up in prison for drug use or criminal offenses that might have been minor if the offenders hadn't been carrying guns they learned to rely on in the service. And a shocking number of those veterans will bring the violence of war home to their wives and children.

That's no accident. The U.S. military is a macho club, proud of its long tradition of misogyny, and not about to give it up. One decorated veteran of the first Gulf War, who credited the army with teaching him to repress his emotions, described his basic training as "long, exhausting marches" and "sound-offs [that] revolved around killing and mutilating the enemy or violent sex with women." (The two themes easily merge.) That veteran was Timothy McVeigh, the unrepentant Oklahoma City bomber, who must have known that blowing up a government office building during business hours was sure to kill a whole lot of women.

Even in the best of times, the incidence of violence against women is much higher in the military than among civilians. After war, it's naturally worse—as with those combat team members at Fort Carson. In 2005, one of them, Pfc. Stephen Sherwood, returned from Iraq and fatally shot his wife, then himself. In September 2008, Pvt. John Needham, who received a medical discharge after a failed suicide attempt, beat his girlfriend to death. In October 2008, Spc. Robert H. Marko raped and murdered Judilianna Lawrence, a developmentally disabled teenager he met online.

These murders of wives and girlfriends—crimes the Bureau of Justice Statistics labels "intimate homicides"—were hardly the first. In fact, the first veterans of George Bush's wars returned to Fort Bragg, North Carolina, from Afghanistan in 2002.

On June 11, 2002, Sgt. First Class Rigoberto Nieves fatally shot his wife Teresa and then himself in their bedroom. On June 29th, Sgt. William Wright strangled his wife Jennifer and buried her body in the woods. On July 9th, Sgt. Ramon Griffin stabbed his estranged wife Marilyn 50 times or more and set her house on fire. On July 19th, Sgt. First Class Brandon Floyd of Delta Force, the antiterrorism unit of the Special Forces, shot his wife Andrea and then killed himself. At least three of the murdered wives had been seeking separation or divorce.

When a *New York Times* reporter asked a master sergeant in the Special Forces to comment on these events, he responded: "S.F.'s [Special Forces members] don't like to talk about emotional stuff. We are Type A people who just blow things like that off..."

The killings at Fort Bragg didn't stop there. In February 2005, Army Special Forces trainee Richard Corcoran shot and wounded his estranged wife Michele and another soldier, then killed himself. He became the tenth fatality in a lengthening list of domestic violence deaths at Fort Bragg.

In February 2008, the *Times* reported finding "more than 150 cases of fatal domestic violence or [fatal] child abuse in the United States involving service members and new veterans" since the Afghan War began in October 2001. And it's still going on.

THE PENTAGON: CONVENIENTLY CLUELESS

In April 2000, after three soldiers stationed at Fort Campbell, Kentucky, murdered their wives and CBS TV's "60 Minutes" broke a story on those deaths, the Pentagon established a task force on domestic violence. After three years of careful work, the task force reported its findings and recommendations to Congress on March 20, 2003, the day the United States invaded Iraq. Members of the House Armed Services Committee kept rushing from the hearing room, where testimony on the report was underway, to see how the brand new war was coming along.

What the task force discovered was that soldiers rarely faced any consequences for beating or raping their wives. (Girlfriends didn't even count.) In fact, soldiers were regularly sheltered on military bases from civilian orders of protection and criminal arrest warrants. The military, in short, did a much better job of protecting servicemen from punishment than protecting their wives from harm.

Years later the military seems as much in denial as ever. It has, for instance, established "anger management" classes, long known to be useless when it comes to men who assault their wives. Batterers already manage their anger very well—and very selectively—to intimidate wives and girlfriends; rarely do they take it out on a senior officer or other figure of authority. It's the punch line to an old joke: the angry man goes home to kick his dog, or more likely, his wife.

Anger may fire the shot, but misogyny determines the target. A sense of male superiority, and the habitual disrespect for women that goes with it, make many men feel entitled to control the lesser lives of women—and dogs. Even Hollywood gets the connection: in Paul Haggis's stark film on the consequences of the Iraq War, *In the Valley of Elah*, a returned vet drowns the family dog in the bathtub—a rehearsal for drowning his wife.

The military does evaluate the mental health of soldiers. Three times it evaluated the mental health of Robert H. Marko (the Fort Carson infantryman who raped and murdered a girl), and each time declared him fit for combat, even though his record noted his belief that, on his twenty-first birthday, he would be transformed into the "Black Raptor," half-man, half-dinosaur.

In February 2008, after the ninth homicide at Fort Carson, the Army launched an inquiry there too. The general in charge said investigators were "looking for a trend, something that happened through [the murderers'] life cycle that might have contributed to this." A former captain and Army prosecutor at Fort Carson asked, "Where is this aggression coming from? . . . Was it something in Iraq?"

WHAT ARE WE FIGHTING FOR?

Our women soldiers are a different story. The Department of Defense still contends that women serve only "in support of" U.S. operations, but in the wars in Iraq and Afghanistan "support" and "combat" often amount to the same thing. Between September 11, 2001, and mid-2008, 193,400 women were deployed "in support of" U.S. combat operations. In Iraq alone, 97 were killed and 585 wounded.

Like their male counterparts, thousands of women soldiers return from Afghanistan and Iraq afflicted with PTSD. Their "invisible wounds," however, are invariably made more complex by the conditions under which they serve. Although they train with other women, they are often deployed only with men. In the field they are routinely harassed and raped by their fellow soldiers and by officers who can destroy their careers if they protest.

On March 17, 2009, the Pentagon reported 2,923 cases of sexual assault in the past year in the U.S. military, including a 25% increase in assaults reported by women serving in Iraq and Afghanistan, assaults committed by men who serve under the same flag. What's more, the Pentagon estimated that perhaps 80% of such rapes go unreported.

And then, when women come home as veterans, they, like their male counterparts, may be involved in domestic homicides. Unlike the men, however, they are usually not the killers, but the victims.

Shortly after Sgt. William Edwards and his wife, Sgt. Erin Edwards, returned to Fort Hood, Texas, in 2004 from separate missions in Iraq, he assaulted her. She moved off base, sent her two children to stay with her mother, brought charges against her husband, got an order of protection, and received assurances from her husband's commanders that they would prevent him from leaving the base without an accompanying officer.

She even arranged for a transfer to a base in New York. However, on July 22, 2004, before she could leave the area, William Edwards skipped his anger management class, left the base by himself, drove to Erin Edwards's house, and after a struggle, shot her in the head, then turned the gun on himself.

The police detective in charge of the investigation told reporters, "I believe that had he been confined to base and had that confinement been monitored, she would not be dead at his hands." Base commanders excused themselves, saying they hadn't known Erin Edwards was "afraid" of her husband. Even if true, since when is that a standard of military discipline? William Edwards had assaulted a fellow soldier. Normally, that would be some kind of crime—unless, of course, the victim was just a wife.

Back in North Carolina, near Fort Bragg and the nearby Marine base at Camp Lejeune, military men murdered four military women in nine months between December 2007 and September 2008. Marine Lance Cpl. Maria Lauterbach, eight months pregnant, went missing from Camp Lejeune in December 2007, not long before she was to testify that a fellow Marine, Cpl. Cesar Laurean, had raped her. In January, investigators found her burned body in a shallow grave in Laurean's backyard. By then, he had fled to Mexico, his native country, and been apprehended there; but Mexico does not extradite citizens subject to capital punishment.

On June 21st, the decomposing body of Spc. Megan Touma, seven months pregnant, was found in a motel room near Fort Bragg. In July, Sgt. Edgar Patino, a married man and the father of Touma's child, was arrested and charged with her murder.

On July 10th, Army 2nd Lt. Holly Wimunc, a nurse, failed to appear for work at Fort Bragg. Neighbors reported that her apartment was burning. Days later, her charred body was found near Camp Lejeune. She had been in the process of divorcing her estranged husband, Marine Cpl. John Wimunc, and had a restraining order against him. He and his friend Lance Cpl. Kyle Ryan Alden were charged with murder, arson, and felony conspiracy.

On September 30th, Army Sgt. Christina Smith was walking with her husband Sgt. Richard Smith in their Fayetteville neighborhood near Fort Bragg when an assailant plunged a knife into her neck. Richard Smith and Pfc. Mathew Kvapil, a hired hit man, were charged with murder and conspiracy.

Striking about these "intimate homicides" is their lack of intimacy. They tend to be planned and carried out with the kind of ruthless calculation that would go into any military plan of attack. Most were designed to eliminate an inconveniently pregnant lover and an unwelcome child, or to inflict the ultimate lesson on a woman about to make good her escape from a man's control. In some of them, in good soldierly fashion, the man planning the killing was able to enlist the help of a buddy. On military websites you can read plenty of comments of comradely support for these homicidal men who so heroically "offed the bitches."

GIVE PEACE A CHANCE

The battered women's movement once had a slogan: World peace begins at home. They thought peace could be learned by example in homes free of violence and then carried into the wider world. It was an idea first suggested in 1869 by the English political philosopher John Stuart Mill. He saw that "the subjection of women," as he called it, engendered in the home the habits of tyranny and violence which afflicted England's political life and corrupted its conduct abroad.

The idea seems almost quaint in competition with the brutal, dehumanizing effectiveness of two or three tours of duty in a pointless war and a little "mild" brain damage.

We had a respite for a while. For nearly a decade, starting in 1993, rates of domestic violence and wife murder went down by a few percentage points. Then in 2002, the vets started coming home.

No society that sends its men abroad to do violence can expect them to come home and be at peace. To let world peace begin at home, you have to stop making war. (Europe has largely done it.) Short of that, you have to take better care of your soldiers and the people they once knew how to love.

Ann Jones is a journalist and the author of a groundbreaking series of books on violence against women, including Next Time She'll Be Dead, *on battering, and* **Women Who Kill,** *a contemporary classic to be reissued this fall by the Feminist Press, with a new introduction from which this post is adapted. She serves as a gender advisor to the UN.*

Copyright 2009 Ann Jones

31

AMERICA AND POLITICAL ISLAM

Mahmood Mamdani

GLOBAL AGENDA 2005

I was in New York City on 9/11. In the weeks that followed, newspapers reported that the Koran had become one of the biggest-selling books in American bookshops. Astonishingly, Americans seemed to think that reading the Koran might give them a clue to the motivation of those who carried out the suicide attacks on the World Trade Center. Recently, I have wondered whether the people of Falluja have taken to reading the Bible to understand the motivation for American bombings. I doubt it.

Why the difference? I suggest we look at the nature of the public debate in America as a key ingredient in shaping public opinion.

The post-9/11 public debate in the US has been inspired by two Ivy League intellectuals—Samuel Huntington at Harvard and Bernard Lewis at Princeton. From Huntington's point of view, the Cold War was a civil war within the west. He says the real war is yet to come. That real war will be a civilizational war, at its core a war with Islam. From this point of view, all Muslims are bad.

Bernard Lewis, in contrast, makes a more nuanced claim. He says that there are good secular Muslims and bad fundamentalist Muslims, and that the west needs to distinguish between them. He identifies a secular point of view with western culture so completely that, for him, a secular Muslim is necessarily a westernized Muslim. A neoconservative guru, Lewis was a major inspiration behind the Iraq War.

Their differences aside, Lewis and Huntington share two assumptions. The first is that the world is divided into two—modern and pre-modern. Modern peoples make their own culture; their culture is a creative act and it changes historically. In contrast, they assume that pre-modern peoples have an unchanging, ahistorical culture, one they carry along with them; they wear their culture as a kind of badge, and sometimes suffer from it like a collective twitch. The second assumption is that you can read people's politics from their culture. I call these two assumptions Culture Talk.

The aftermath of the Iraq War has turned into a crisis for theory. It is increasingly clear that the designation of some Muslims as good and others as bad has little to do with their orientation to Islam, and everything to do with their orientation to America. Simply put, good Muslim is a label for those who are deemed pro-American and bad Muslims are those reckoned anti-American. Culture Talk is not only wrong, it is also self-serving. How convenient it is to see political violence as something wrong with the culture of one party rather than an indication that something has gone wrong in the relationship between two parties.

POLITICAL ISLAM

Contemporary, modern political Islam developed as a response to colonialism. Colonialism posed a double challenge, that of foreign domination and of the need for internal reform to address weaknesses exposed by external aggression.

Early political Islam grappled with such questions in an attempt to modernize and reform Islamic societies. Then came Pakistani thinker Abu ala Mawdudi, who placed political violence at the centre of political action, and Egyptian thinker Sayyed Qutb, who argued that it was necessary to distinguish between friends and enemies, for with friends you use reason and persuasion, but with enemies you use force.

The terrorist tendency in political Islam is not a pre- modern carry-over but a very modern development.

Radical political Islam is not a development of the ulama (legal scholars), not even of mullahs or imams (prayer leaders). It is mainly the work of non- religious political intellectuals. Mawdudi was a journalist and Qutb a literary theorist. It has developed through a set of debates, but these cannot be understood as a linear development inside political Islam. Waged inside and outside political Islam, they are both a critique of reformist political Islam and an engagement with competing political ideologies, particularly Marxism-Leninism.

Let us remember that the period after World War II was one of a decades-long secular romance with political violence. Armed struggle was in vogue in national liberation and revolutionary movements. Many political activists were convinced that a thoroughgoing struggle had to be armed. The development of religious political tendencies that glorify the liberating role of violence is a latter-day phenomenon. Rather than a product of religious fundamentalism, it is best thought of as both religious and secular, a sign of the times.

THE LATE COLD WAR

That said, we are confronted with a singular question: How did Islamist terror, a theoretical tendency that preoccupied a few intellectuals and was of marginal political significance in the 1970s, become part of the political mainstream in only a few decades? To answer it, we need to move away from the internal debates of political Islam to its relations with official America, and back from 9/11 to the period that followed America's defeat in Vietnam, the period I call the late Cold War. My claim is also that this question is best answered from a vantage point inside Africa.

Decolonization reached a momentous point in 1975. The year the Americans were defeated in Vietnam was also the year the Portuguese empire collapsed in Africa. The result was a shift in the centre of gravity of the Cold War from south-east Asia to southern Africa. Who would pick up the pieces of the Portuguese empire in Africa, America or the Soviet Union?

The defining feature of the new phase of the Cold War was the strong anti-war movement within America opposed to direct military intervention overseas. Henry Kissinger, the US secretary of state, designed a strategy in response to the changed context: if America could not intervene overseas directly, it would intervene through others. Thus began the era of proxy war, one that was to mark the period from Vietnam to Iraq.

Angola was the first important American proxy intervention in the post-Vietnam period. Kissinger first looked for mercenaries to counter the independence movement in Angola, and then followed with a nod to apartheid South Africa. The South African intervention was discredited internationally as soon as it became public knowledge and led to a powerful anti- war response in Congress: the Clark Amendment terminated all assistance, overt and covert, to anti- communist forces in Angola.

The administration of Ronald Reagan raised proxy war from a pragmatic response to a grand strategy, called the Reagan Doctrine. Developed in response to two 1979 revolutions—those of the Sandinistas in Nicaragua and the Islamists in Iran—the Reagan Doctrine made two claims. The first was that America had been preparing to fight the wrong war—that against Soviet forces on the plains of Europe—and meanwhile was losing the real war, that against Third World nationalism. Reagan called on America to fight the war that was already on, against yesterday's guerrillas now come to power. Arguing that there could be no middle ground in war, the Reagan administration portrayed nationalist governments newly come to power in southern Africa and central America as Soviet proxies that needed to be nipped in the bud before they turned into real dangers.

The Reagan Doctrine also turned on a second initiative, one that involved a shift from "containment" to "rollback", from peaceful coexistence to a determined, sustained and aggressive bid to reverse defeats in the Third World. To underline the historical legitimacy of this shift, it brought the language of religion into politics. Speaking before the National Association of Evangelicals in 1983, Reagan called on America to defeat "the evil empire".

Evil is a theological notion. As such, it has neither a history nor motivation. The political use of evil is two-fold. First, one cannot coexist with evil, nor can one convert it. Evil must be eliminated. The war against evil is a permanent war, one without a truce. Second, the Manichean battle against evil justifies any alliance. The first such alliance, dubbed "constructive engagement", was between official America and apartheid South Africa.

"Constructive Engagement"

It is through "constructive engagement" that official America provided political cover to apartheid South Africa as it set about developing a strategy for proxy war in the former Portuguese colonies of Mozambique and Angola. As the Reagan administration moved from "peaceful coexistence" to "rollback", so the apartheid government redefined its regional strategy from "détente" to "total onslaught".

The bitter fruit of constructive engagement was Africa's first genuine terrorist movement, called Renamo. Created by the Rhodesian army in the early 1970s and nurtured by the apartheid army after 1980, Renamo consistently targeted civilians in Mozambique to convince them that an independent African government could not possibly assure them law and order. At the same time, when terror unleashed by Renamo became the subject of public discussion, the apartheid regime explained it in cultural terms, as "black on black violence", as an expression of age-old tribal conflict, of the inability of black people to coexist without an outside mediator.

America's responsibility for Renamo was solely political. But without an American political cover, it would have been impossible for apartheid South Africa to organize, arm and finance a terrorist movement in independent Africa for more than a decade—and to do so with impunity.

Constructive engagement was a period of tutorship for official America. America created and wielded the Contras in Nicaragua just as apartheid South Africa did Renamo in south central Africa. Under CIA tutelage, the Contras blew up bridges and health centres, and killed health personnel, judges and heads of cooperative societies. The point of terror was not to win civilian support, but to highlight the inability of the government to ensure law and order. It was to convince the population that the only way to end terror was to hand over power to terrorists. This lesson in the electoral uses of terror was learnt by others, including Charles Taylor in Liberia and the Revolutionary United Front (RUF) in Sierra Leone.

It is worth drawing some lessons from the history of terror after Vietnam. Terror was a strategy America embraced when it had almost lost the Cold War in 1975. Mozambique and Nicaragua were the founding moments of that history. Both Renamo and the Contras, the pioneer terrorist movements, were proxies of South Africa and America. Both were secular in orientation. The development of a religious proxy—terror claiming a religious justification—was characteristic of the closing phase of the Cold War in Afghanistan.

ROLLBACK ON A GLOBAL SCALE: AFGHANISTAN

The Afghan war was the prime example of "rollback". In the history of terror during the last phase of the Cold War, the Afghan war was important for two reasons. First, the Reagan administration ideologized the war as a religious war against the evil empire, rather than styling it a war of national liberation such as that it claimed the Contras were fighting in Nicaragua. In the process, the CIA marginalized every Islamist group that had a nationalist orientation, fearing that these groups might be tempted to negotiate with the Soviet Union, and brought centre-stage the most extreme Islamists in a partnership that would "bleed the Soviet Union white".

Second, the Reagan administration privatized war in the course of recruiting, training and organizing a global network of Islamic fighters against the Soviet Union. The recruitment was done through Islamic charities, and the training through militarized madrasahs. Unlike the historical madrasah, which taught a range of subjects, secular and religious, from theology and jurisprudence to history and medicine, the Afghan madrasah taught a narrow curriculum dedicated to a narrow theology (jihadi Islam) and gave a complementary military training.

The narrow theology recast Islam around a single institution, the jihad; it redefined the jihad as exclusively military and claimed the military jihad to be an offensive war entered into by individual born-again devotees as opposed to defence by an Islamic community under threat. The jihadi madrasahs in Pakistan trained both the Afghan refugee children who were later recruited into the Taliban and the Arab-Afghans who were later networked by the organization called al-Qaeda ("the Base"). If national liberation wars created proto-state apparatuses, the international jihad created a private network of specialists in violence.

America did not create right-wing Islam, a tendency that came into being through intellectual debates, both inside political Islam and with competing secular ideologies, such as Marxism-Leninism. America's responsibility was to turn this ideological tendency into a political organization—by incorporating it into America's Cold War strategy in the closing phase of the Cold War.

Before the Afghan jihad, right-wing political Islam was an ideological tendency with little organization and muscle on the ground. The Afghan jihad gave it numbers, organization, skills, reach, confidence and a coherent objective. America created an infrastructure of terror but heralded it as an infrastructure of liberation.

_____ Mahmood Mamdani is Herbert Lehman Professor of Government, Department of Anthropology and School of International Affairs, Columbia University, New York.

32

THE MANUFACTURE OF ISLAMOPHOBIA: CLASS, IMPERIALISM, AND IDEOLOGY

Chuck O'Connell

Historical background: After the end of world War II in 1945, the United States relied upon Great Britain to police the Middle East and the Persian Gulf region. British bases and alliances were used to keep the area free from foreign encroachment and from any internal rebellions that might topple pro-Western regimes and disrupt the flow of oil. For Britain, however, the cost eventually proved too much and in 1968 it announced that it would, by 1971, abandon its role as guarantor of regional stability. This announcement came at an inopportune moment for the U.S. ruling class because, with a war in Viet Nam (a war that involved invading two countries and bombing four) and with a powerful domestic antiwar movement, the U.S. was not in a position to deploy troops to the Middle East as a replacement for the British. Thus, the Nixon Doctrine was announced in 1969 stating that the U.S. would rely on local powers to provide regional security. Known as the "two pillar" strategy, it involved the Americans arming Saudi Arabia and Iran as the two key U.S. allies. This arrangement lasted until 1979. In that year two major events destroyed the two-pillar strategy and lead to the proclamation of the Carter Doctrine: the Islamic Revolution in Iran transforming Iran from ally to adversary and the Soviet invasion of Afghanistan bringing Soviet power much closer to the Mideast oil fields. Subsequent to these events President Carter announced that, because persian Gulf and Middle East oil was vital to the security of the U.S., its flow to market would be militarily guaranteed by the United States itself. To back up this pledge the U.S.

created a new military command (the Central Command or "CENTCOM") in the 1980s for projecting American power into the Middle East and Central Asia. The first work of CENTCOM was to obtain access rights for military facilities in the Middle East and to them Stockpile ammunition and fuel at these facilities in preparation for future war. By 1990 this was accomplished.

Creating the enemy: Wars, however, require not only logistical preparation; they also require the psychological preparation of the people who will pay for and fight them. Thus, in the 1980s the American mass media through its news reporting and through its entertainment industry (Hollywood) began prepping Americans for combat against Arabs (not all of whom are Muslim) and against Muslims (not all of whom are Arab). In order to wage war Americans had to acquire the politically necessary perspective. This work was done by the mass media through its framing of news events in the Middle East. The interpretative frame has been one that avoids class analysis and the imperial character of modern capitalist economies. American presence in the Middle East is presumed to be necessary and beneficent; any opposition to that presence is therefore wrong. Additionally, the indigenous people are depicted as culturally flawed: they are said to be anti-modern peoples held back from the modern world by their religion: Islam. Not only were television and radio news and opinion shaping talk shows used to advance this view; Hollywood did its part to prepare Americans for war by producing several anti-Arab, anti-Muslim films during the 1980s and 1990s. (For an extensive discussion of Hollywood's anti-Arab bias see Jack Shaheen, *Reel Bad Arabs*).

After the terrorist attacks on September 11, 2001 and the U.S. invasions of Afghanistan (Oct. 7, 2001) and Iraq (March 18, 2003), the ruling class increased the demonization of Muslims. This was done for four reasons:

1. To prepare American soldiers for war in Afghanistan and Iraq by dehumanizing Muslims.
2. To foster indifference to the killing of civilians in Afghanistan and Iraq by building hostility towards Muslims.
3. To intimidate into silence those Muslim-Americans who might be critical of U.S. war policies by creating fear of persecution.
4. To minimize social contacts between Muslims and non-Muslims by creating fear and distrust of Muslims by non-Muslims.

Fear, Inc.—How Islamophobia Appeared: The creation of an ideology of "Islamophobia" was not left to accident. According to an August 2011 report from the Center for American Progress entitled *"Fear, Inc: The Roots of the Islamophobia Network in America"* the emergence of the politics of lslamophobia is the result of the work of "misinformation experts" spreading lies and distortions about Islam through the media and grassroots organizing; this work has been funded by a few "key foundations". Between 2001 and 2009 these foundation gave $42.6 million to certain individuals and their organizations to produce anti-Islamic ideology. The leading anti-Muslim writers, speakers, and "scholars"—men such as Daniel Pipes, David

Horowitz, Steven Emerson, Frank Gaffney, and Robert Spencer—all were sponsored by the following foundations: Donors Capital Fund, Richard Mellon Scaife, Lynde and Harry Bradley Foundation, Newton and Rochelle Becker Foundation, the Russell Berrie Foundation, Anchorage Charitable Fund William Rosenwald Family Fund, and the Fairbrook Foundation.

This foundation funding has paid for the openltion of groups designed to spread fear and distrust of Muslims. These groups and their "experts" identified by the *Fear Inc.* report are:

- The Center for Security Policy (Frank Gaffney)
- Society of Americans for National Existence (David Yerushalmi)
- Middle East Forum (Daniel Pipes)
- Jihad Watch and Stop Islamization of America (Robert Spencer)
- The Investigative Project on Terrorism (Steven Emerson)

The "experts" from these organizations actually have visited State legislatures to advocate legal bans against the "threat" of Islamic Sharia law. Their claims that the majority of mosques in the U.S. have members who are either terrorists or terrorist sympathizers have been repeated in the media. Other political groups such as the Freedom Center of David Horowitz and even U.S. politicians such as Congressman Peter King (R-NY) promote anti-Muslim ideology. The result, according to *Fear, Inc.,* is that an anti-Muslim movement has spread to more than 23 states and "is driving the national and global debates that have real consequences on the public dialogue and on American Muslims". The report cites a Washington Post-ABC opinion poll of September 2010 reporting that the percentage of Americans holding an unfavorable view of Islam had risen from 39% in 2002 to 49% in 2010.

Critique of Fear, Inc: While the report, *Fear, Inc.*, is valuable for describing the process by which anti-Islamic ideology becomes a material force, it frames the intentions and the consequences in politically correct language that avoids issues of class and imperialism. This is done in three ways.

First, the report traces the funding for Islamophobic writings to seven foundations but fails to identify them for what they are: the charitable institutions of a ruling class that has an economic interest in imperialism. These funding organizations are not simply giving money because a few rich guys hate Islam; they give money to get people prepared to kill Muslims in the name of "national security".

Second, the report refers to the men and women promoting Islamophobia as "misinformation experts" when it would be more accurate to describe them as the paid intelligentsia for the ruling class. To call them "misinformation experts" portrays them as either confused men who can't get the information right or as men motivated by religious intolerance (or, as Americans like to say, by "hate"). Taking this point of view makes them appear as dim-witted and irrational. It is more likely, however, that they are entirely rational: they are quite aware that the ruling class will pay good money and give you a bit of public fame if you can ideologically advance the cause of imperialism. The fact that they buy into the intolerance they advocate adds emotional force to their arguments by giving them the appearance of a deep and passionate sincerity.

Third, the report frames the problem of Islamophobia as a problem of religious intolerance that threatens "the fabric and strength of our democracy and our national security" when the real problem of Islamophobia is that it inhibits the development of an anti-imperialist political consciousness within the working class. How likely is it that you would see the people of the Middle East as consisting primarily of workers who have the same class interests as American workers if you've been taught to see them as culturally inferior beings with a retrograde religion? The repeated references to "our democracy", "our national security", and "our Constitution" in the report *Fear, Inc.* are indicative of the nationalism of the writers; this nationalism (or failure to see the class basis of politics) explains their failure to see Islamophobia as nothing more than a pernicious form of religious intolerance when, in fact, it functions as an ideological preparation for war.

33

"FREE TRADE" AND IMMIGRATION: A PRIMER

Raul Fernandez

*Prepared by Raul Fernandez, Ph.D. (Economics) and Professor at
UC Irvine, for the Hemispheric Social Alliance (Alianza Social Continental)
(1/26/08)*

—Beginning in the early 1990s, the great increase in immigration from Mexico, Central America and South America coincides with the imposition of "free trade" policies and agreements –a euphemism for what should be called *investor rights agreements*. The U.S. government, banks and corporations exerted pressure on pliable Latin American governments ruling poor, indebted countries.

—These policies require the elimination of protective tariffs and measures in Latin America while the U.S. continues its protective policies, esp. in agriculture. This so-called "Free trade" has meant no restriction of goods entering into Mexico, now Central America and Peru.

—NAFTA allowed the entry of US agricultural products into Mexico without tariffs or other kinds of barriers. The heavily protected US agro complex could do this while NAFTA required Mexico to dismantle agricultural supports and protection.

—At the time of the passage of NAFTA, some economists predicted that millions of agricultural jobs would be lost in Mexico, as poor farmers could not compete with the heavily subsidized imports dumped there.

—By 2006, Mexico had lost over two million agricultural jobs, including as many as 1.7 million small farmers who were forced off their land and into the migratory stream—all because of cheap corn, milk, chicken, pork, beans, rice, all entering from the United States. Everyday about 600 people leave the Mexican countryside.

—There is little employment in local urban industry because there, too, "free trade" means the import of cheap U.S. manufactured products. The choices are: working in *maquilas* on the border, already saturated and losing employment to even cheaper China, or migrating to the United States.

—Before NAFTA, Mexican wages were 23% of U.S. wages; now they are about 12%.

—Of the millions of undocumented workers currently living in the United States 2/3rds came to the US after the passage of NAFTA in 1994, seeking relief from the disastrous economic conditions in Mexico.

—In 2005, at least 582,000 Mexican *economic refugees* immigrated north to the U.S.; the number was 559,000 in 2006. US responses to the increased migration include: militarization of the border, hunting down undocumented workers as if they were criminals, and the rise of demagoguery a la Lou Dobbs.

—At least 562 immigrants died trying to cross the U.S.-Mexico border in 2007. *The average of the last ten years is one death per day.* Deaths have increased as the militarization of the border has pushed economic refugees to cross over the more deserted and desolate areas.

—Hundreds of thousands of people from other countries that have been enduring these free trade policies have also been displaced, forced to migrate out of their countries. Tens of thousands have left Colombia which "opened" its economy to "free trade" in 1991. In El Salvador hundreds of thousands have migrated, about 1/3 of the entire population, mostly to the United States.

—Many Americans are angry at the presence of about 12 million Mexican, Central American, and South American undocumented migrants in the U.S.; but they have only to blame policies like NAFTA and other US-backed "free trade" policies put into effect in Mexico and other Latin American countries beginning in the early 1990s.

—Other treaties, like CAFTA, the recently approved Free Trade Agreement with Peru, and the proposed Free Trade Agreement with Colombia, will have similar results. In the words of Teamsters President Hoffa: *Subsistence farmers will be forced off their land because cheap U.S. food produced by agribusiness will undercut their prices. The same thing happened with the North American Free Trade Agreement which resulted in millions of poor Mexicans leaving their farms."*

—The goal of the so-called "free trade" agreements is made crystal-clear in a letter sent recently to U.S. Congress Speaker Pelosi from the CEO's of Citibank, Coca-Cola, General Motors, ExxonMobil and others about the proposed Colombian Free Trade Agreement. It says right at the beginning: *"The US-Colombia FTA will: eliminate barriers to U.S. farm products....it will provide new sales opportunities for American farmers and ranchers.* In other words: local agriculture will be destroyed and peasants and rural workers forced to migrate.

—These investor rights agreements and policies are intensifying the economic situation in Latin America, where 200 million people, more than 40% of the population, is living below the poverty line, more than 100 million people are completely impoverished, 40 million children live in the streets, and enormous inequality has been accelerated by these "free trade" policies that benefit multinationals and local groups connected with the import business.

—The beginning of a solution to the "immigration problem" begins with the reversal of the policies of a false "free trade" like NAFTA, CAFTA, and other agreements.

34

ARIZONA'S NEW LAWS: AN ATTEMPT TO SECURE CHEAP LABOR?

Paul Ortiz

"Why are there 40 million poor people in America? When you begin to ask that question, you are raising questions about the economic system, about a broader distribution of wealth. When you ask that question, you begin to question the capitalistic economy. And I'm simply saying that more and more, we've got to begin to ask questions about the whole society. We are called upon to help the discouraged beggars in life's market place. But one day we must come to see that an edifice which produces beggars needs restructuring."
—Dr. Martin Luther King Jr., message
to Southern Christian Leadership Council (1967).

In the debate surrounding Arizona's laws targeting immigrants and ethnic studies, we've heard very little mention of capitalism and its place in American politics. Senate Bill 1070 is an insurance policy for capitalism, a way to ensure that the cheap labor that serves the foundation of the new economy remains cheap forever. House Bill 2281 is part of a package deal. The erasure of ethnic studies courses that show how poor people have changed history—when they have organized—will allow the invention of a historical narrative as one sided as the old myths of the European Conquest. These bills are a gift from a steadily shrinking, white, ruling class to its own posterity and to any white workers and ethnic minorities willing to accept second-class citizenship in order to avoid something far worse. Unless we mobilize to defeat these measures, worse things are on the horizon. Our history proves it.

SB 1070 makes racial profiling the de facto law of the state, but police in Arizona or anywhere else for that matter do not need a law to continue feeding working- class people to the expanding prison industrial complex. (1) We need to listen carefully to Governor Brewer's rationale for this bill. She consulted closely with major business owners before signing the new law. "The bottom line is that when I go about meeting with businesses that come into Arizona," Brewer stated, "they want to know that we have a safe and secure environment into which to move their businesses here....They want to know that their employees are going to have a quality of life that they've had in the places where they're moving from to move here." (2)

ARIZONA, IS THIS AMERICA?

Arizona has a long record of robbing working people in order to provide a "safe and secure environment" for big business. The US conquest of northern Mexico resulted in a dual racial system with similarities to Jim Crow in the southeast. (3) In the copper mining camps of the Grand Canyon State, there were two wage scales in the early 20th century: a "white wage" and a "Mexican wage." In Arizona mines, the top wage for Mexicans was $2.50 per day; $4.00 for "Anglos." (4) Ninety-seven percent of the mine foremen in the copper mine camps were white. Pervasive wage differentials in the southwest gave white workers an incentive to maintain a separate-and-unequal economic system and served as the most visible wedge in the working class. One official exulted, "Mexicans came cheap by the dozen and could be bought for ten cents each." (5) Many Mexican-American miners became union activists in an effort to abolish this system. (6)

Armed vigilantes seized and deported 1,300 striking miners in Bisbee, Arizona, in 1917. Many of the workers were members of the Industrial Workers of the World, who envisioned a world without capitalism. Arizona also gave us the anti-labor crusader Barry Goldwater. Elected to the US Senate in 1953, Goldwater sought to extinguish the New Deal. He was an ardent foe of unions and warred against social welfare programs. After initially supporting civil rights, Goldwater embraced the GOP's "Southern Strategy" of wooing white voters away from the Democratic Party by using coded racial appeals to white masculinity. (7) On the advice of a Republican lawyer by the name of William Rehnquist, Senator Goldwater voted against the passage of the 1964 Civil Rights Act. (8)

During Goldwater's first term, the federal government initiated "Operation Wetback" in Arizona and other southwestern states. Reprising the brutal racial repatriations of the 1930s, Federal agents seized and forcibly deported tens of thousands of Mexican- Americans from the state using what one critic calls a "mass deportation on the Soviet model." (9) Many workers who were repatriated to Mexico were owed back wages by their employers. (10) White leaders have pined for a new Operation Wetback for years. (11) SB 1070 is their new Bill of Rights.

The defeat of the Copper Miners' Strike of 1983–1986 in Arizona was a devastating blow to the labor movement. The victory of the Phelps Dodge Corporation over the miners was made possible by massive state military force as well as infiltration of the unions by the Arizona State Criminal Intelligence Agency. (12) A strong organizing tradition of Mexican-American leadership in mining unionism was wiped out. In the midst of the struggle, a white strikebreaker responded to Mexican-American unionists by asserting: "I'd rather be rich than an ignorant fucking Mexican union-loving son of a bitch." (13) Dozens of union locals were crushed.

Arizona delivered Chief Justice William Rehnquist to the Supreme Court in 1971. Two decades earlier, as a clerk for Justice Robert H. Jackson, Rehnquist defended the Court's 1898 Plessy v. Ferguson decision that validated racial segregation. The young lawyer was also a leader in the Republican Party's "Operation Eagle Eye" in Arizona. According to retired State Senator Manuel Peña, this group deployed what Gregory Palast later called "voter harassment teams" who tried to prevent African-Americans and Chicanos from voting in Phoenix during the 1962 elections. (14) Rehnquist's generation of reactionary Republicans, (to borrow a phrase from A. Phillip Randolph) viewed African- American and Latina/o voting as dangerous and disruptive of white business supremacy.

Among its many anti-labor rulings, the Rehnquist Court ruled in Hoffman Plastic Compounds v. NLRB (2002) that ". . . .a worker who is undocumented could not recover the remedy of back pay under the National Labor Relations Act." How convenient for the bosses! (15) Arizona—and the entire country—is continuously becoming more "safe and secure" for employers and more unsafe for workers who want to get paid for their work, nurture their families and develop their capacities to the fullest.

ACTUALLY EXISTING CAPITALISM

Latina/o workers have been in the forefront of new labor organizing. (16) This has not escaped the attention of employers and the US Immigration and Customs Enforcement (ICE) has carried out so-called "immigration raids" in Iowa, North Carolina and other states targeting workplaces where Latinos were trying to organize unions. (17) These raids are ostensibly carried out to enforce immigration laws. Anyone with common sense knows otherwise. "If anything," David Bacon writes, "ICE seems intent on punishing undocumented workers who earn too much, or who become too visible by demanding higher wages and organizing unions." (18)

Arizona's SB 1070 is capitalism's latest salvo against the American working class. One of my UC-Santa Cruz students, Marisa Verónica Espinosa, wrote a senior thesis in 2005 titled "Capitalism at Work: A Contemporary Look at Mexican Immigration to the United States." In this brilliant essay, Ms. Espinosa showed that the North American Free Trade Agreement (NAFTA) was forcing tens of thousands of Mexican farmers off of the land on terms wildly advantageous to US businesses. She argued that "The capitalist tendency to displace people and force them into migration is not recognized in public policy." (19) Drawing on the work of Jorge Bustamante, Espinosa continued, "Instead, the United States exerts its 'right' as a nation-state to police its borders from 'unwanted' but necessary foreigners. Of course, this occurs because it 'has the function of producing savings for the US economy.'" Espinosa demonstrated that the increasing militarization of the US-Mexico border had the effect of terrorizing many Mexican workers into silence and that ". . . the goal of these operations has been to satisfy the desires of a nativist electorate and big business." Chalk up another victory for capital. (20)

A generation of propagandists claimed that capitalism emancipates the poor as long as the state stays out of the way. Espinosa's thesis proves otherwise. She quotes a 1926 Congressional hearing on immigration that illuminated how capitalism really works:

> Mr. Chairman, here is the problem in a nutshell. Farming is not a profitable industry in this country and in order to make money out of this, you have to have cheap labor . . . [I]n order to allow land owners to make a profit on their farms, they want to get the cheapest labor they can find and if they can get the Mexican labor it enables them to make a profit. That is the way it is along the border and I imagine that is the way it is anywhere else." (21)

Decades later, Jorge Bustamante observes that social conditions for migrant workers in the border states have declined even as NAFTA-fueled agribusiness has thrived. (22)

RACISM

SB 1070 is not only an anti-immigrant bill, it is an anti-labor bill designed to scare a portion of the American working class into accepting their lot. It criminalizes the Latina/o working class the way that Jim Crow criminalized the African-American working class in the South. Segregation, like slavery is a labor system. It is designed to extract wealth from one portion of society in order to distribute it—unequally—to the rest of the nation. (23) Insightful African-American leaders are making this connection. "To my . . . black brothers and sisters that think this is not your fight," Rev. Al Sharpton recently said, "Let me tell you something, after dark, we all look Mexican right now." (24) At the 2010 May Day Immigration Rally in Washington, DC, Rev. Jesse Jackson compared Arizona today with Selma in 1965 and urged a boycott of the state. (25) Congresswoman Barbara Lee (D-California), calls SB 1070 a "national disgrace" and argues that it "It harkens back to the era of Jim Crow or apartheid in South Africa." (26)

Representative Lee is absolutely correct. SB 1070 will help to sustain the Jim Crow style racism that Latino workers face nationally. A survey of recent United States Equal Employment Commission (EEOC) cases demonstrates that sexual and national origin discrimination against Latina/o workers is a pervasive problem. The EEOC recently filed suit against Sizzler Restaurants "for the explicitly targeted harassment of Mexican women by non-Mexican men. Latinas were targeted as 'Mexican bitches only good for sex,' physically and verbally harassed and told 'go back where you come from if you don't like it.'" Latina workers at an Arizona firm were fired after they reported being subjected to discrimination and intrusive body searches. (27)

An analysis of the EEOC cases reveals Latina/o workers are often paid lower wages than their white peers for doing the same work regardless of educational attainment. This confirms contemporary findings of wage discrimination in the scholarly literature on race and wage inequality. (28) A recent survey of labor market studies demonstrates that Latina/o workers "earn lower wages and/or experience higher unemployment than similarly qualified White workers and [they] attribute some portion of the differential (10%–50% of the White- Latino wage gap, equal to about 4%–16% of Hispanic wages) to employment discrimination." (29)

Racial injustice continues to be a major barrier to Latina/o progress. We need immigration reform. However, we also need to launch an all-out offensive against racism. What other than racism explains the slander spread on cable television stations about what Latinos do in the United States? We need more truth tellers. "In case you don't know what immigrants do in this country," Barbara Ehrenreich observes, "the Latinos have a word for it—trabajo. They've been mowing the lawns, cleaning the offices, hammering the nails and picking the tomatoes, not to mention all that dish-washing, diaper-changing, meat-packing and poultry-plucking." (30)

BARRIERS TO UNIONIZATION

Comprehensive immigration reform will not improve the lives of America's working people unless workers regain the right to collective bargaining. Recent reports by Amnesty International and Human Rights Watch show that US workersparticularly Latino workers—who try to organize face severe corporate and state hostility. The obstacles that workers faced in their decade-long quest to organize Smithfield Foods in North Carolina show why few workers are able to form unions in the United States. Employees testified that pro-union employees were harassed and fired while management tried to convince Latino workers that African-Americans were organizing to steal their jobs. One former manager of the firm admitted to Amnesty International that "We were told to fire anyone who advocated for the union." According to the manager, a company lawyer instructed her to deal proactively with a union-inclined employee under her supervision: "Fire the bitch. I'll beat anything she or they throw at me in court." (31)

Local government officials assisted the firm by distributing anti-union propaganda at the workplace. Investigators responded to workers' safety complaints by haranguing them about their union sympathies. The federal government later targeted the firm for a raid on suspected illegal immigrants. Union activist Julio Vargas affirms that Latino and African-American workers believed that the government raided their plant "because people were getting organized." (32) Human Rights Watch concludes "that freedom of association is a right under severe, often buckling pressure when workers in the United States try to exercise it." (33)

HOUSE BILL 2281

In order to maintain an environment that keeps big business safe and secure, Arizona's leaders understand that it is not enough to control contemporary labor markets; they must also control history. HB 2281 is part of a resurgence of white nationalism that wants to make sure that capitalism and the Confederacy are given their proper due in our nation's classrooms. (34) (After all, the antebellum slave owners were possibly the most successful capitalists in history!) If students in Arizona have access to stories of labor and civil rights movements, they would learn critical lessons about how to create social change. They would also learn that many of the contemporary social problems they face are the result of centuries of institutional discrimination. Progressive social history taught by scholars such as Ernesto Galarza, Elizabeth Martinez, Rudy Acuña and others teach us that racism, segregation and anti-immigrant politics feed a very profitable system of exploitation where the few live off of the labors of the many. They also teach us through historical case studies how to end this cycle of victimization. (35)

Sociologist Oliver Cromwell Cox noted, "The capitalist exploitation of colored workers, it should be observed, consigns them to employments and treatment that is humanly degrading. In order to justify this treatment the exploiters must argue that the workers are innately degraded and degenerate, consequently they naturally merit their condition." (36) The target of House Bill 2281 is any courses that " . . . are designed primarily for pupils of a particular ethnic group . . . [or] advocate ethnic solidarity instead of the treatment of pupils as individuals." (37) In other words, students will be taught that they are isolated individuals without recourse to broader networks of solidarity. According to Governor Brewer's spokesperson, "The governor believes . . . public school students should be taught to treat and value each other as individuals and not be taught to resent or hate other races or classes of people." Because many episodes of human rights struggle involved fighting racial and class oppression of one kind or the other, these must not be taught.

HB 2281 means that Arizona students will not learn about the rise of the United Farm Workers nor will they be allowed to study the histories of the Western Federation of Miners or the Mine, Mill and Smelter Workers' Union in Arizona. These organizations taught that unbridled capitalism was not going to solve the problems of the working class. It is fine for scholars to publish articles about these organizations in academic journals, but state educational officials are fighting harder than ever to keep Chicano studies and narratives of resistance out of the high school classroom. The Texas Board of Education is replacing UFW co-founder Dolores Huerta in favor of "conservative hero" Phyllis Schlafly in forthcoming textbooks. (38) House Bill 2281 is designed to ensure that the status quo remains unquestioned. (39)

THE WAY FORWARD

On May 1, 2006—International Workers' Day—Latina/o workers initiated the largest work stoppage in the history of the Americas. Migrant laborers, Nuyoricans, Chicana/os, Afrocubanos, Guatemaltecos and immigrants from every continent on earth united in protest of immigration restriction measures that threatened their families, their livelihoods and their dignity. Hundreds of thousands of Latina/o workers and their allies sought to end the cycle of isolation and alienation from the broader society which has left them vulnerable to exploitation. The protests were marked by a profound sense of urgency.

Latino workers used International Workers' Day to prove that their labor power is an integral part of the New Economy. Indeed, several days in advance of the gigantic protest dubbed as "A Day Without Immigrants," corporations such as Cargill Inc., Tyson Foods and the Seaboard Corporation announced that they would be closing due to a lack of personnel. (40) On the West Coast, entire fast food chains were forced to shut down as truck drivers refused to deliver supplies. The US working class has not exerted this kind of power in decades.

Latina/o marchers expressed a democratic vision of an economy where labor is the source of all wealth instead of being a pitiful captive to capital and paternalistic employers. Nursing home worker Corina Payan, who participated in the Denver march, explained, "I know that without us, they're not going to be able to do anything. They're not going to go out in the field and clean the bathrooms or anything . . . Everywhere you go, Wal- Mart, anything, all you see are Hispanic people filling their carts to the top. . . . We're the ones making them money." (41)

SB1070 is part of a larger effort to crush the nascent Latina/o social movement that has formed the base of the May Day protests. The measure is part of a national trend to steal our rights and to keep us powerless in our workplaces and neighborhoods. HB2281 is designed to enforce a historical amnesia upon younger Americans and to teach them that any problem they may have will be magically solved by the free enterprise system. Never mind organizing for mutual interests. Leave that to the National Association of Manufacturers.

We must support the students, workers and reformers fighting SB1070 and HB 2281. Our future hangs in the balance. If we value a society where human rights are defended, we must act now. Today, the focus is rightly on Arizona. However, we must understand that Arizona is only one part of the problem. Unless we democratize American workplaces, even comprehensive immigration reform will not improve the lives of millions of workers.

Marisa Espinosa's senior thesis serves as a starting point for understanding this crisis, especially her insight that "The capitalist tendency to displace people and force them into migration is not recognized in public policy." Until we grasp what Espinosa is telling us we cannot solve the immigration problem. Workers' rights must be at the foundation of all US trade policies. NAFTA needs a massive overhaul or revocation if it continues to push Mexican farmers to the wall. In the US we need to reconsider the relationship among capitalism, public policy and immigration. For example, Social Security, Workers' Compensation and Unemployment Security implicitly recognize that the free market creates a number of harmful conditions at critical points in human life that must be mitigated by the state. Capitalism also has harmful effects on migrants, but where are the social programs to ameliorate their plight?

Along with assertively stating that "No human being is illegal," we must add the cry "Capitalism needs Perestroika." A system that impoverishes people and imposes harsh public measures to preserve itself, needs to be rethought. (42)

We need to deepen our commitment to grassroots organizing, and we need to listen to the workers who are carrying our rickety economic system on their shoulders. Their voices are missing in the current debate and that is a fatal oversight. As María Elena Durazo, executive secretary-treasurer of the Los Angeles County Federation of Labor, reminds us:

> The most dramatic social changes of the past did not happen because a few politicians and rich people took pity on black people or workers. It did not happen in Congress, or in the White House. It happened in the streets—churches, unions and workplaces. And it needs to happen there again. We must build a movement with thousands of leaders and millions of supporters that can pressure elected and corporations to do the right thing. When we build a movement of the working poor, we will have the power to end poverty. (43)

NOTES

1. Jon Swartz, "Inmates vs. Outsourcing," USA Today, July 6, 2004; Ruth Wilson Gilmore, Golden Gulag: Prisons, Surplus, Crisis and Opposition in Globalizing California (Berkeley: University of California Press, 2006); Robert Perkinson, Texas Tough: The Rise of America's Prison Empire (New York: Metropolitan Books, 2010); Critical Resistance at: http://www.criticalresistance.org/

2. "New Immigration Law Won't Hurt Economy, Arizona Governor Says," CNN.Com, April 26, 2010.

3. I discuss the impact of the Mexican-American War on Latina/o workers in: "¡Si, Se Puede! Revisited: Latino/a Workers in the United States," in Social Work Practice with Latinos, Eds., Richard Furman & Nalini Negi (Chicago: Lyceum Books, 2010), 45–66.

4. Los Mineros. (The American Experience), Dir. Hector Galan. Writer, Paul Espinosa. Perfs. Luis Valdez. PBS. 1992; Katherine Benton-Cohen, "Docile Children and Dangerous Revolutionaries: The Racial Hierarchy of Manliness and the Bisbee Deportation of 1917." Frontiers: A Journal of Women's Studies, (2003, June- September) 24.2–3, 30–50.

5. Carlos M. Larralde and Richard Griswold del Castillo, "Luisa Moreno and the Beginnings of the Mexican-American Civil Rights Movement in San Diego," The Journal of San Diego History, Volume 43, Number 3 (Summer 1997).

6. Zaragosa Vargas, Labor Rights Are Civil Rights: Mexican-American Workers in Twentieth-Century America (Princeton: Princeton University Press, 2005), 220–223.

7. Laura Jane Gifford, "Dixie is no longer in the bag": South Carolina Republicans and the Election of 1960," Journal of Policy History, Vol. 19, No. 2, (2007), 207–233.

8. John W. Dean, The Rehnquist Choice: The Untold Story of the Nixon Appointment That Redefined the Supreme Court (New York: The Free Press, 2001), 129.

9. Pierre Tristam, "'Operation Wetback': Illegal Immigration's Golden-Crisp Myth," Daytona Beach News-Journal, April 5, 2007. For the forced reparations of Mexicans and Mexican-Americans to Mexico in the 1930s, see: Francisco E. Balderrama and Raymond Rodríguez, Decade of Betrayal: Mexican Repatriation in the 1930s (Albuquerque: University of New Mexico Press, 2006)

10. "Owed Back Pay, Guest Workers Comb the Past," The New York Times, November 23, 2008.

11. John Dillin, "How Eisenhower Solved Illegal Border Crossings from Mexico," The Christian Science Monitor, July 6, 2006.

12. Jonathan Rosenblum, "Union Busting: How Arizona's 'CIA' Helped Phelps Dodge Destroy The Unions," The Tucson Weekly, June 29, 1995, http://www.tucsonweekly.com/tw/06-29-95/curr4.htm (Accessed May 22, 2010)

13. Barbara Kingsolver, Holding the Line: Women in the Great Arizona Mine Strike of 1983 (Ithaca: Cornell University Press), 113.

14. "Panel Hears Conflicting Voter Challenge Testimony," Times-News (Hendersonville, NC), August 2, 1986; Gregory Palast, Armed Madhouse, 10th Plume Printing p. 261; Laura Flanders, "A Racist Elephant," Common Dreams.org, December 13, 2000. (Accessed May 22, 2010.); Alan Dershowitz, Telling the Truth About Chief Justice Rehnquist," The Huffington Post, May 20, 2010. http://www.huffington-post.com/alan-dershowitz/telling-the-truth-about-c_b_6844.html (Accessed May 20, 2010); John W. Dean, The Rehnquist Choice (New York: Free Press, 2002).

15. Amy Sugimori, Rebecca Smith, et. al., "Assessing the Impact of the Supreme Court's Decision in Hoffman Plastic Compounds v. NLRB on Immigrant Workers and Recent Developments," National Immigration Law Center, n.d.

16. John Trumpbour and Elaine Bernard, "Unions and Latinos: Mutual Transformation," in Latinos: Remaking America, ed., Marcelo M. Suárez-Orozco and Mariela M. Páez (Berkeley: University of California Press, 2009), 126–145.

17. "Immigration Raid Breaks Up Organizing Drive at Iowa Meatpacking Plant," Labor Notes, August 26, 2008.

18. David Bacon, "Mass Firings, The New Face of Immigration Raids," The Progressive (December 2009/January 2010).

19. Marisa Verónica Espinosa, "Capitalism at Work: A Contemporary Look at Mexican Immigration to the United States," Undergraduate Thesis, UC-Santa Cruz (2005), 33. See Jorge A. Bustamante's important essay, "Mexico—United States Labor Migration Flows, " International Migration Review, Vol. 31, No. 4., Special Issue: Immigrant Adaptation and Native-Born Responses in the Making of Americans (Winter, 1997), 1112–1121.

20. Espinosa, 5. A powerful analysis of the continuing devastation wrought by NAFTA is found in: John Ross, "The Feminization of Mexican Agriculture," Counterpunch.org, May 19, 2010 (Accessed May 21, 2010).

21. Espinosa, 32.

22. Jorge A. Bustamante, "Mexican-United States Labor Migration Flows," 1116.

23. Paul Ortiz, "Before the CIO: Segregation and Black Labor Struggles," Against the Current, (January/February 2009).

24. "Al Sharpton Wears 'Los Suns' Jersey During March to Arizona Capitol Protesting SB 1070," Phoenix New Times Blogs, May 6, 2010 http://blogs.phoenixnewtimes.com/bastard/2010/05/al_sha rpton_wears_los_suns_jer.php (Accessed May 22, 2010)

25. "Immigration Advocates Rally for Change," The New York Times, May 1, 2010.

26. "Dems: Ariz. Law Like Jim Crow, apartheid," Politico, April 28, 2010. http://www.politico.com/news/stories/0410/36503.html (Accessed May 15, 2010).

27. US Equal Employment Opportunity Commission. EEOC Settles Suit Against Arizona Company for $3.5 Million on Behalf of Low-Wage Workers. August 8, 2001; EEOC, Central Casino to Pay $1.5 Million in EEOC Settlement for National Origin Bias. July 18, 2003) EEOC, "EEOC Settles Lawsuit on Behalf of Hispanic Employees," April 12, 2006; EEOC, Statement of William R. Tamayo, February 28, 2007. See also: "Life Under Siege: Life for Low-Income Latinos in the South," Southern Poverty Law Center (April 2009).

28. Daley M. Camoy and Ojeda R. Hinojosa, Latinos in a Changing US Economy: Comparative Perspectives in the Labor Market Since 1939. Inter-University Program for Latino Research, New York: Research Foundation of the City University of New York, 1990; Edwin Melendez, Clara Rodriguez and Janis Barry Figueroa, eds., Hispanics in the Labor Force: Issues and Policies (New York: Plenum Press, 1991).

29. Raul Yzaguirre and Charles Kamasaki, "Comment on The Latino Civil Rights Crisis: A Research Conference," The Civil Rights Project/Proyecto Derechos Civiles, University of California, Los Angeles (2007), Retrieved October 9, 2007 from http://www.civilrightsproject.ucla.edu/research/latino9 7/latino97.php

30. Barbara Ehrenreich, "What America Owes its 'Illegals,'" The Nation. Org. (http://www.thenation.com/doc/20070625/ehrenreich) (Accessed, June 13, 2007).

31. Kristal Brent Zook, "Hog-Tied: Battling It Out (Again) At Smithfield Foods," Amnesty International Magazine (Winter 2003), http://www.amnestyusa.org/Winter_2003/ (Accessed June 4, 2007).

32. David Bacon, "Feds Crack Down on Immigrant Labor Organizers," The American Prospect Online, May 11, 2007, http://www.prospect.org (Accessed June 5, 2007).

33. Human Rights Watch, "Unfair Advantage: Workers' Freedom of Association in the United States under International Human Rights Standards," (New York: Human Rights Watch, 2000), 141–142.

34. "Texas School Board Hears from Critics of Social Studies Changes," The Washington Post, May 21, 2010.

35. Critical work in Chicano and Latino Studies include: Ernesto Galarza, Spiders in the House & Workers in the Field (Notre Dame: University of Notre Dame Press, 1970); Carey McWilliams, Factories in the Field: The Story of Migratory Farm Labor in California (originally published, 1935; Santa Barbara: Peregrine Publishers, Inc., 1971); Rodolfo Acuna, Occupied America: A History of Chicanos (New York : Harper & Row, 1988); Elizabeth Martinez, De Colores Means All of Us: Latina Views for a Multi-Colored Century (South End Press, 1999); Vicki Ruiz, From Out of the Shadows: Mexican Women in Twentieth-Century America (Oxford University Press, 2008); Carlos Muñoz, Youth, Identity, Power: The Chicano Movement (London: Verso, 1989); David Gutiérrez, Walls and Mirrors: Mexican-Americans, Mexican Immigrants and the Politics of Ethnicity (Berkeley: University of California Press, 1995).

36. Oliver C. Cox, Race: A Study in Social Dynamics. New Introduction by Adolph Reed Jr. (Monthly Review Press, 2000), 19.

37. "Arizona Gov. Signs Bill Targeting Ethnic Studies," Yahoo News, May 12, 2010. http://news.yahoo.com/s/ap/20100512/ap_on_re_us/us_arizona_ethnic_studies (Accessed, May 20, 2010)

38. Lauri Lebo, "Texas Textbook Massacre," Religion Dispatches.org, April 27, 2010 (Accessed, May 20, 2010).

39. Bill Bigelow, "Those Awful Texas Social Studies Standards. And What About Yours?" CommonDreams.org May 22, 2010 (Accessed, May 23, 2010); Christine E. Sleeter, "Standardizing Imperialism," Rethinking Schools, Volume 19, (Fall 2004). http://www.rethinkingschools.org/restrict.asp?path=archive/19_01/impe191.shtml (Accessed, May 23, 2010).

40. Immigrants Take to US Streets in Show of Strength," The New York Times, May 2, 2006; "US Latinos expect a momentous May Day," The Star-Ledger (Newark, New Jersey), April 28, 2006.

41. "Prompted By Anger, A Colorado Immigrant Marches for Principle," The Associated Press (Denver), May 2, 2006

42. Mikhail Gorbachev, "Capitalism in Crisis," The Guardian, October 30, 2009.

43. María Elena Durazo, "Living Wage for All: A Plan for a New Living Wage Movement," The Burning Bush: A Publication of the Center for the Working Poor.

http://www.centerforthworkingpoor.org/ (Accessed May 1, 2010). Creative Commons License This work by Truthout is licensed under a Creative Commons Attribution-Noncommercial 3.0 United States License. Support Truthout's work with a $10/month tax-deductible donation today!

Paul Ortiz is an associate professor of history at the University of Florida. He is writing a book titled Our Separate Struggles Are Really One: African American and Latino Histories," that will be published by Beacon Press.

35

THE DUNCAN DOCTRINE:
THE MILITARY-CORPORATE LEGACY
OF THE NEW SECRETARY OF EDUCATION

Andy Kroll

On December 16th, a friendship forged nearly two decades ago on the hardwood of the basketball court culminated in a press conference at the Dodge Renaissance Academy, an elementary school located on the west side of Chicago. In a glowing introduction to the media, President-elect Barack Obama named Arne Duncan, the chief executive officer of the Chicago Public Schools system (CPS), as his nominee for U.S. Secretary of Education. "When it comes to school reform," the President-elect said, "Arne is the most hands-on of hands-on practitioners. For Arne, school reform isn't just a theory in a book—it's the cause of his life. And the results aren't just about test scores or statistics, but about whether our children are developing the skills they need to compete with any worker in the world for any job."

Though the announcement came amidst a deluge of other Obama nominations—he had unveiled key members of his energy and environment teams the day before and would add his picks for the Secretaries of Agriculture and the Interior the next day—Duncan's selection was eagerly anticipated, and garnered mostly favorable reactions in education circles and in the media. He was described as *the* compromise candidate between powerful teachers' unions and the advocates of charter schools and merit pay. He was also regularly hailed as a "reformer," fearless when it came to challenging the educational *status quo* and more than willing to shake up hidebound, moribund public school systems.

Yet a closer investigation of Duncan's record in Chicago casts doubt on that label. As he packs up for Washington, Duncan leaves behind a Windy City legacy that's hardly cause for optimism, emphasizing as it does a business-minded, market-driven model for education. If he is a "reformer," his style of management is distinctly top-down, corporate, and privatizing. It views teachers as expendable, unions as unnecessary, and students as customers.

Disturbing as well is the prominence of Duncan's belief in offering a key role in public education to the military. Chicago's school system is currently the <u>most</u> militarized in the country, boasting five military academies, nearly three dozen smaller Junior Reserve Officer Training Corps programs within existing high schools, and numerous middle school Junior ROTC programs. More troubling yet, the military academies he's started are nearly all located in low-income, minority neighborhoods. This merging of military training and education naturally raises concerns about whether such academies will be not just education centers, but recruitment centers as well.

Rather than handing Duncan a free pass on his way into office, as lawmakers did during Duncan's breezy confirmation hearings last week, a closer examination of the Chicago native's record is in order. Only then can we begin to imagine where public education might be heading under Arne Duncan, and whether his vision represents the kind of "change" that will bring our students meaningfully in line with the rest of the world.

THE MILITARIZATION OF SECONDARY EDUCATION

Today, the flagship projects in CPS's militarization are its five military academies, affiliated with either the Army, Navy, or Marines. All students—or cadets, as they're known—attending one of these schools are required to enroll as well in the academy's Junior ROTC program. That means cadets must wear full military uniforms to school everyday, and undergo daily uniform inspections. As part of the academy's curriculum, they must also take a daily ROTC course focusing on military history, map reading and navigation, drug prevention, and the branches of the Department of Defense.

Cadets can practice marching on an academy's drill team, learn the proper way to fire a weapon on the rifle team, and choose to attend extracurricular spring or summer military training sessions. At the Phoenix Military Academy, cadets are even organized into an academy battalion, modeled on an Army infantry division battalion, in which upper-class cadets fill the leading roles of commander, executive officer, and sergeant major.

In addition, military personnel from the U.S. armed services teach alongside regular teachers in each academy, and also fill administrative roles such as academy "commandants." Three of these military academies were created in part with Department of Defense appropriations—funds secured by Illinois lawmakers—and when the proposed Air Force Academy High School opens this fall, CPS will be the only public school system in the country with Air Force, Army, Navy, and Marine Corps high school academies.

CPS also boasts almost three dozen smaller Junior ROTC programs within existing high schools that students can opt to join, and over 20 voluntary middle school

Junior ROTC programs. All told, between the academies and the voluntary Junior ROTC programs, more than 10,000 students are enrolled in a military education program of some sort in the CPS system. Officials like Duncan and Chicago Mayor Richard M. Daley justify the need for the military academies by claiming they do a superlative job teaching students discipline and providing them with character-building opportunities. "These are positive learning environments," Duncan said in 2007. "I love the sense of leadership. I love the sense of discipline."

Without a doubt, teaching students about discipline and leadership is an important aspect of being an educator. But is the full-scale uniformed culture of the military actually necessary to impart these values? A student who learns to play the cello, who studies how to read music, will learn discipline too, without a military-themed learning environment. In addition, encouraging students to be critical thinkers, to question accepted beliefs and norms, remains key to a teacher's role at any grade level. The military's culture of uniformity and discipline, important as it may be for an army, hardly aligns with these pedagogical values.

Of no less concern are the types of students Chicago's military academies are trying to attract. All of CPS's military academies (except the Rickover Naval Academy) are located in low-income neighborhoods with primarily black and/or Hispanic residents. As a result, student enrollment in the academies consists almost entirely of minorities. Whites, who already represent a mere 9% of the students in the Chicago system, make up only 4% of the students enrolled in the military academies.

There is obviously a correlation between these low-income, minority communities, the military academies being established in them, and the long-term recruitment needs of the U.S. military. The schools essentially function as recruiting tools, despite the expectable military disclaimers. The *Chicago Tribune* typically reported in 1999 that the creation of the system's first military school in the historically black community of Bronzeville grew, in part, out of "a desire for the military to increase the pool of minority candidates for its academies." And before the House Armed Services Committee in 2000, the armed services chiefs of staff testified that 30%–50% of all Junior ROTC cadets later enlist in the military. Organizations opposing the military's growing presence in public schools insist that it's no mistake the number of military academies in Chicago is on the rise at a time when the U.S. military has had difficulty meeting its recruitment targets while fighting two unpopular wars.

It seems clear enough that, when it comes to the militarization of the Chicago school system, whatever Duncan's goals, the results are likely to be only partly "educational."

MERGING THE MARKET AND THE CLASSROOM

While discussing his nomination, President-elect Obama praised the fact that Duncan isn't "beholden to any one ideology." A closer examination of his career in education, however, suggests otherwise. As Chicago's chief executive officer (not to be confused with CPS's chief *education* officer), Duncan ran his district in a most busi-nesslike manner. As he put it in a 2003 profile in *Catalyst Chicago*, an independent magazine that covers education reform, "We're in the business of education." And indeed, managing the country's third-largest school system *does* require sharp busi-ness acumen. But what's evident from Duncan's seven years in charge is his belief that the business of education should, first and foremost, embrace the logic of the free market and privatization.

Duncan's belief in privatizing public education can be most clearly seen in Chicago's Renaissance 2010 plan, the centerpiece of his time in that city. Designed by corporate consulting firm A.T. Kearney and backed by the Commercial Club of Chicago, an organization representing some of the city's largest businesses, Renaissance 2010 has pushed hard for the closing of underperforming schools—to be replaced by multiple new, smaller, "entrepreneurial" schools. Under the plan, many of the new institutions established have been privatized charter or "contract" schools run by independent nonprofit outfits. They, then, turn out to have the option of contracting school management out to for-profit education management organi-zations. In addition, Renaissance 2010 charter schools, not being subject to state laws and district initiatives, can—as many have—eliminate the teachers' union altogether.

Under Duncan's leadership, CPS and Renaissance 2010 schools have adopted a performance-driven style of governance in which well-run schools and their teach-ers and administrators are rewarded, and low-performing schools are penalized. As *Catalyst Chicago* reported, "Star schools and principals have been granted more flex-ibility and autonomy, and often financial freedom and bonus pay." Low-performing schools put on probation, on the other hand, "have little say over how they can spend poverty funding, an area otherwise controlled by elected local school councils [Local school councils] at struggling schools have also lost the right to hire or fire principals—restrictions that have outraged some parent activists."

Students as well as teachers and principals are experiencing firsthand the impact of Duncan's belief in competition and incentive-based learning. This fall, the Chicago Public Schools rolled out a Green for Grade$ program in which the district will pay freshmen at 20 selected high schools for good grades—$50 in cash for an A, $35 for a B, and even $20 for a C. Though students not surprisingly say they support the program—what student wouldn't want to get paid for grades?—critics contend that cash-for-grades incentives, which stir interest in learning for all the wrong reasons, turn being educated into a job.

Duncan's rhetoric offers a good sense of what his business-minded approach and support for bringing free-market ideologies into public education means. At a May 2008 symposium hosted by the Renaissance Schools Fund, the nonprofit financial arm of Renaissance 2010, entitled "Free to Choose, Free to Succeed: The New Market of Public Education," Duncan typically compared his job running a school district to that of a stock portfolio manager. As he explained, "I am not a manager of 600 schools. I'm a portfolio manager of 600 schools and I'm trying to improve the portfolio." He would later add, "We're trying to blur the lines between the public and the private."

A Top-Down Leadership Style

Barack Obama built his campaign on impressive grassroots support and the democratic nature of his candidacy. Judging by his continued outreach to supporters, he seems intent on leading, at least in part, with the same bottom-up style. Duncan's style couldn't be more different.

Under Duncan, the critical voices of parents, community leaders, students, and teachers regularly fell on deaf ears. As described by University of Illinois at Chicago professor and education activist Pauline Lipman in the journal *Educational Policy* in 2007, Renaissance 2010 provoked striking resistance within affected communities and neighborhoods. There were heated community hearings and similarly angry testimony at Board of Education meetings, as well as door-to-door organizing, picketing, and even, at one point, a student walk-out.

"The opposition," Lipman wrote, "brought together unions, teachers, students, school reformers, community leaders and organizations, parents in African American South and West Side communities, and some Latino community activists and teachers." Yet, as she pointed out recently, mounting neighborhood opposition had little effect. "I'm pretty in tune with the grassroots activism in education in Chicago," she said, "and people are uniformly opposed to these policies, and uniformly feel that they have no voice."

During Duncan's tenure, decision-making responsibilities that once belonged to elected officials shifted into the hands of unelected individuals handpicked by the city's corporate or political elite. For instance, elected local school councils, made up mostly of parents and community leaders, are to be scaled back or eliminated altogether as part of Renaissance 2010. Now, many new schools can simply opt out of such councils.

Then there's the Renaissance Schools Fund. It oversees the selection and evaluation of new schools and subsequent investment in them. Made up of unelected business leaders, the CEO of the system, and the Chicago Board of Education president, the Fund takes the money it raises and makes schools compete against each other for limited private funding. It has typically been criticized by community leaders and activists for being an opaque, unaccountable body indifferent to the will of Chicago's citizens.

Making the grade?

Despite his controversial educational policies, Duncan's supporters ultimately contend that, as the CEO of Chicago's schools, he's gotten results where it matters—test scores. An objective, easily quantifiable yet imperfect measure of student learning, test scores have indeed improved in several areas under Duncan (though many attribute this to lowered statewide testing standards and more lenient testing guidelines). Between 2001 and 2008, for instance, the percentage of elementary school students meeting or exceeding standards on the Illinois Standards Achievement Test increased from 39.5% to 65%. The number of CPS students meeting or exceeding the Illinois Learning Standards, another statewide secondary education achievement assessment, also increased from 38% in 2002 to 60% in 2008.

When measured on a national scale, however, Duncan's record looks a lot less impressive. In comparison to other major urban school districts (including Los Angeles, Boston, New York City, and Washington, D.C.) in the National Assessment of Educational Progress, or "The Nation's Report Card," Chicago fourth and eighth graders ranked, with only one exception, in the bottom half of all districts in math, reading, and science in 2003, 2005 and 2007. In addition, from 2004 to 2008, the Chicago Public Schools district failed to make "adequate yearly progress" as mandated by the Bush administration's No Child Left Behind Act.

Even if Duncan's policies do continue to boost test scores in coming years, the question must be asked: At whose expense? In a competition-driven educational system, some schools will, of course, succeed, receiving more funding and so hiring the most talented teachers. At the same time, schools that aren't "performing" will be put on probation, stripped of their autonomy, and possibly closed, only to be reopened as privately-run outfits—or even handed over to the military. The highest achieving students (that is, the best test-takers) will have access to the most up-to-date facilities, advanced equipment, and academic support programs; struggling students will likely be left behind, separate and unequal, stuck in decrepit classrooms and underfunded schools.

Public education is not meant to be a win-lose, us-versus-them system, nor is it meant to be a recruitment system for the military—and yet this, it seems, is at the heart of Duncan's legacy in Chicago, and so a reasonable indication of the kind of "reform" he's likely to bring to the country as education secretary.

Andy Kroll is a writer based in Ann Arbor, Michigan, and a student at the University of Michigan. His writing has appeared at the Nation Online, Alternet, CNN, CBS News, CampusProgress.org, and Wiretap Magazine, among other publications. He welcomes feedback, and can be reached at his website. To listen to a TomDispatch audio interview with Kroll on the new Secretary of Education, click here.

Copyright 2009 Andy Kroll

36

LOOKING FOR SPIES OF A DIFFERENT COLOR
THE CIA REALIZES DIVERSITY IS FOR ITS OWN GOOD IN TODAY'S WORLD

Vernon Loeb

Her family immigrated to the United States when she was a teenager, searching for the kind of opportunity they never had in Latin America. Her parents preached hard work, education, patriotism.

ESPIONAGE

Now she is preparing to put her Latino heritage and her education at a top U.S. university to use in a globe-trotting career—as a spy in countries where, she believes, her language skills and appearance will allow her to operate in ways "a white, blond-haired, blue-eyed American" never could.

"My parents are very proud," she says.

Although CIA officials refused to disclose the woman's name, age or country of birth, they made her available for an interview at the agency's headquarters in Langley, Va., to illustrate the CIA's new push for diversity in its clandestine branch, the Directorate of Operations.

Like other government agencies, the CIA has long viewed affirmative action as a desirable social goal, and its clandestine service has long made use of immigrants capable of blending into foreign locales. But with an increasing focus on terrorists, narcotics traffickers, weapons sellers and other "hard targets" who don't show up at embassy cocktail parties, the agency's need to hire nonwhite spies fluent in many languages has never been greater, top officials say.

"When you're trying to recruit an agent, you're establishing a bond with that person," says David W. Carey, the CIA's executive director, its No. 3 post. "If you're a blond-haired guy from Oklahoma, there are some parts of the world where that's an uphill battle."

In its biggest hiring push in more than a decade, the CIA has run a series of advertisements in newspapers and highbrow magazines, such as the Economist, that depict the Directorate of Operations as a rainbow coalition of good-looking twenty somethings.

The truth, at the moment, is somewhat different. Of the CIA's corps of case officers—believed to number more than 1,000—just 11 percent are minorities and 18 percent are women. And although CIA Director George J. Tenet six months ago appointed an African American, Donald R. Cryer, as his special assistant for diversity programs, the agency's top managers are still predominantly white men.

But CIA officials say that a third of the new operations officers hired in the past year have been women. Although just 11 percent have been minorities as traditionally defined (blacks, Asians or Hispanics), 20 percent of all new operations officers are native speakers of a foreign language and 75 percent have advanced proficiency in foreign languages, many because they have lived abroad. Almost half have advanced degrees.

"We are currently hiring officers in the Directorate of Operations with specialized skills directly applicable to combating terrorism worldwide," such as fluency in Russian, Arabic, Farsi and Chinese, says James L. Pavitt, the agency's deputy director for operations.

"Fluency in these languages, almost by definition, suggests that they may be native born and learned the language at their mother's knee," Pavitt adds. "If you're looking [at diversity] from a purely social perspective, can we do better? You bet. But I'm looking at it now not only from that perspective, but from the business perspective as well: How do I operate in parts of the world where I need a different breed of cat, not somebody who necessarily looks like me or talks like me?"

CIA officials acknowledge that they face some image problems in recruiting minorities, given the agency's past support for coups in Latin America and the Middle East and a belief among some African Americans that CIA operatives helped bring crack cocaine to urban America.

"Are we going to be effective going in and setting up our recruitment booth in Watts? No, clearly not," Carey says.

But the Latino emigre in training to be a CIA spy expresses no such reservations. On the contrary, she says a keen sense of patriotism attracted her to the agency. CIA officials insist that they are able to find many minority candidates who harbor no negative views about the agency.

THE VALUE OF DIVERSITY IN A SPY service that operates in almost every country would seem to be obvious. "You can't have white guys doing operational things in most of the world and expect them to get away with it," says Brian P. Fairchild, a retired operations officer.

Yet Fairchild and a dozen other current and former spies say it is possible to overstate the value of diversity for clandestine operations, since much street-level espionage activity is performed by foreigners.

In CIA parlance, a U.S. citizen working as a professional spy overseas is a "case officer," while a foreigner on the CIA payroll is an "agent." Many agents are not handled directly by a CIA case officer but by a "principal agent" of the same nationality. There are also "access agents," who help CIA officers get closer to their targets, and "support agents," who provide transportation, safe houses and other services.

The need for diversity is also diminished, some former agency officers maintain, by the CIA's frequent use of embassy cover, the practice of having CIA officers work out of U.S. embassies under the guise of State Department employees, which quickly brings them to the attention of foreign intelligence agencies.

One former operations officer scoffs at Tenet's promotion of diversity as an "operational imperative," contending that a skilled case officer of any ethnic background—whether male or female, black, white, Asian or Latino—can operate anywhere in the world, using his or her own skills and those of foreign agents, where necessary.

"Diversity of experience is a necessity," the former officer says. "Ethnic diversity may be a laudable social goal, but it is not by any means an operational imperative."

But most current and former operatives interviewed disagreed, arguing that it is often essential to be able to put, say, an officer of Arabic descent on the ground in Amman or a native speaker of Farsi in Tehran.

Garrett Jones, who served as CIA station chief in Somalia during peacekeeping operations in 1993, cites the example of an African American officer who was able to work undercover for weeks in north Mogadishu, which he says would have been all but impossible for Jones or any of the station's other white officers.

"They've got a new world to operate in," adds Milt Bearden, a former station chief in Khartoum, Islamabad and Bonn. "It's not a bunch of second secretaries chasing second secretaries at embassies in Bern."

Jack Downing, the only person in CIA history to serve as station chief in both Moscow and Beijing, says it was not until the 1970s that the CIA first posted officers in countries from which they, or their parents, had recently emigrated. Until then, the agency feared that such officers would be seriously hampered by the host countries' intense mistrust—and surveillance—of them.

Although such first- and second-generation emigres have indeed faced heavy surveillance, he says, experience has shown that they also have enormous potential once they are able to evade their watchers and function on the streets as natives.

"It's one of our real strengths as a nation, being a nation of nations, to have all these different kinds of people," says Downing, who—like John le Carré's fictional spy master, George Smiley—was brought out of retirement for a few years to rebuild a badly demoralized clandestine service.

"We have a competitive advantage," says Downing, who retired for a second time last year. "Whether it's the Near East or Africa, Latin America or Asia, to have people who have the language and look the part and have that cultural feel, even if it's second generation, is a terrific operational advantage. We have used it on many occasions. We just need more."

ONE FORMER EMPLOYEE SAYS THE CIA now has an officer of Arabic descent who joined the agency in midcareer and has been a "phenomenal" undercover operative in the Middle East. "His Arabic is so native he can do accents," the former employee says. "He's been responsible for some of the agency's best operations."

Similarly, the CIA's best recruiter in one Asian country, a former operative says, is a woman who lived the first 20 or so years of her life there. Men in the country, though unaccustomed to dealing with women as professional equals, "are obviously enthralled with her because she speaks their language and knows their culture," the former operative says.

The young spy in training at CIA headquarters recalls that during a recent vacation at a luxury hotel in Latin America, a tourist saw her in the hallway and asked her for extra towels, assuming she was a chambermaid.

Far from being offended, she says, she was secretly pleased, knowing that her ability to pass for a local may soon be invaluable . . .

37

THE LIMITS OF ANTI-RACISM

Adolph Reed Jr.

Antiracism is a favorite concept on the American left these days. Of course, all good sorts want to be against racism, but what does the word mean exactly?

The contemporary discourse of "antiracism" is focused much more on taxonomy than politics. It emphasizes the name by which we should call some strains of inequality—whether they should be broadly recognized as evidence of "racism"—over specifying the mechanisms that produce them or even the steps that can be taken to combat them. And, no, neither "overcoming racism" nor "rejecting whiteness" qualifies as such a step any more than does waiting for the "revolution" or urging God's heavenly intervention. If organizing a rally against racism seems at present to be a more substantive political act than attending a prayer vigil for world peace, that's only because contemporary antiracist activists understand themselves to be employing the same tactics and pursuing the same ends as their predecessors in the period of high insurgency in the struggle against racial segregation.

This view, however, is mistaken. The postwar activism that reached its crescendo in the South as the "civil rights movement" wasn't a movement against a generic "racism;" it was specifically and explicitly directed toward full citizenship rights for black Americans and against the system of racial segregation that defined a specific regime of explicitly racial subordination in the South. The 1940s March on Washington Movement was also directed against specific targets, like employment discrimination in defense production. Black Power era and post-Black Power era struggles similarly focused on combating specific inequalities and pursuing specific goals like the effective exercise of voting rights and specific programs of redistribution.

CLARITY LOST

Whether or not one considers those goals correct or appropriate, they were clear and strategic in a way that "antiracism" simply is not. Sure, those earlier struggles relied on a discourse of racial justice, but their targets were concrete and strategic. It is only in a period of political demobilization that the historical specificities of those struggles have become smoothed out of sight in a romantic idealism that homogenizes them into timeless abstractions like "the black liberation movement"—an entity that, like Brigadoon, sporadically appears and returns impelled by its own logic.

Ironically, as the basis for a politics, antiracism seems to reflect, several generations downstream, the victory of the postwar psychologists in depoliticizing the critique of racial injustice by shifting its focus from the social structures that generate and reproduce racial inequality to an ultimately individual, and ahistorical, domain of "prejudice" or "intolerance." (No doubt this shift was partly aided by political imperatives associated with the Cold War and domestic anticommunism.) Beryl Satter's recent book on the racialized political economy of "contract buying" in Chicago in the 1950s and 1960s, *Family Properties: Race, Real Estate, and the Exploitation of Black Urban America*, is a good illustration of how these processes worked; Robert Self's book on Oakland since the 1930s, *American Babylon*, is another. Both make abundantly clear the role of the real estate industry in creating and recreating housing segregation and ghettoization.

TASTY BUNNY

All too often, "racism" is the subject of sentences that imply intentional activity or is characterized as an autonomous "force." In this kind of formulation, "racism," a conceptual abstraction, is imagined as a material entity. Abstractions can be useful, but they shouldn't be given independent life.

I can appreciate such formulations as transient political rhetoric; hyperbolic claims made in order to draw attention and galvanize opinion against some particular injustice. But as the basis for social interpretation, and particularly interpretation directed toward strategic political action, they are useless. Their principal function is to feel good and tastily righteous in the mouths of those who propound them. People do things that reproduce patterns of racialized inequality, sometimes with self-consciously bigoted motives, sometimes not. Properly speaking, however, "racism" itself doesn't do anything more than the Easter Bunny does.

Yes, racism exists, as a conceptual condensation of practices and ideas that reproduce, or seek to reproduce, hierarchy along lines defined by race. Apostles of antiracism frequently can't hear this sort of statement, because in their exceedingly simplistic version of the nexus of race and injustice there can be only the Manichean dichotomy of those who admit racism's existence and those who deny it. There can be only Todd Gitlin (the sociologist and former SDS leader who has become, both fairly and as caricature, the symbol of a "class-first" line) and their own heroic, truth-telling selves, and whoever is not the latter must be the former. Thus the logic of straining to assign guilt by association substitutes for argument.

My position is—and I can't count the number of times I've said this bluntly, yet to no avail, in response to those in blissful thrall of the comforting Manicheanism— that of course racism persists, in all the disparate, often unrelated kinds of social relations and "attitudes" that are characteristically lumped together under that rubric, but from the standpoint of trying to figure out how to combat even what most of us would agree is racial inequality and injustice, that acknowledgement and $2.25 will get me a ride on the subway. It doesn't lend itself to any particular action except more taxonomic argument about what counts as racism.

Do What Now?

And here's a practical catch-22. In the logic of antiracism, exposure of the racial element of an instance of wrongdoing will lead to recognition of injustice, which in turn will lead to remedial action—though not much attention seems ever given to how this part is supposed to work. I suspect this is because the exposure part, which feels so righteously yet undemandingly good, is the real focus. But this exposure convinces only those who are already disposed to recognize.

Those who aren't so disposed have multiple layers of obfuscating ideology, mainly forms of victim-blaming, through which to deny that a given disparity stems from racism or for that matter is even unjust. The Simi Valley jury's reaction to the Rodney King tape, which saw King as perp and the cops as victims, is a classic illustration. So is "underclass" discourse. Victimization by subprime mortgage scams can be, and frequently is, dismissed as the fault of irresponsible poor folks aspiring beyond their means. And there is no shortage of black people in the public eye—Bill Cosby and Oprah Winfrey are two prime examples, as is Barack Obama—who embrace and recycle those narratives of poor black Americans' wayward behavior and self-destructive habits.

And how does a simple narrative of "racism" account for the fact that so many black institutions, including churches and some racial advocacy organizations, and many, many black individuals actively promoted those risky mortgages as making the "American Dream of home ownership" possible for "us"? Sure, there are analogies available—black slave traders, slave snitches, "Uncle Toms" and various race traitors—but those analogies are moral judgments, not explanations. And to mention them only opens up another second-order debate about racial authenticity—about who "really" represents the black community. Even Clarence Thomas sees himself as a proud black man representing the race's best interests.

My point is that it's more effective politically to challenge the inequality and injustice directly and bypass the debate over whether it should be called "racism."

I do recognize that, partly because of the terms on which the civil rights movement's victories have been achieved, there is a strong practical imperative for stressing the racially invidious aspects of injustices: they have legal remedies. Race is one of the legal classes protected by anti-discrimination law; poverty, for instance, is not.

But this makes identifying "racism" a technical requirement for pursuing certain grievances, not the basis of an overall political strategy for pursuit of racial justice, or, as I believe is a clearer left formulation, racial equality as an essential component of a program of social justice.

ANTI-MARX

I've been struck by the level of visceral and vitriolic anti-Marxism I've seen from this strain of defenders of antiracism as a politics. It's not clear to me what drives it because it takes the form of snide dismissals than direct arguments. Moreover, the dismissals typically include empty acknowledgment that "of course we should oppose capitalism," whatever that might mean. In any event, the tenor of this anti-Marxism is reminiscent of those right-wing discourses, many of which masqueraded as liberal, in which only invoking the word "Marxism" was sufficient to dismiss an opposing argument or position.

This anti-Marxism has some curious effects. Leading professional antiracist Tim Wise came to the defense of Obama's purged green jobs czar Van Jones by dismissing Jones's "brief stint with a pseudo-Maoist group," and pointing instead to "his more recent break with such groups and philosophies, in favor of a commitment to eco-friendly, sustainable capitalism." In fact, Jones was a core member of a revolutionary organization, STORM, that took itself very seriously, almost comically so.

And are we to applaud his break with radical politics in favor of a style of capitalism that few actual capitalists embrace? This is the substance of Wise's defense.

This sort of thing only deepens my suspicions about antiracism's status within the comfort zone of neoliberalism's discourses of "reform." More to the point, I suspect as well that this vitriol toward radicalism is rooted partly in the conviction that a left politics based on class analysis and one focused on racial injustice are Manichean alternatives.

DEVOLUTIONS

This is also a notion of fairly recent provenance, in part as well another artifact of the terms on which the civil rights victories were consolidated, including the emergence of a fully incorporated black political class in the 1970s and its subsequent evolution. By contrast, examining, for example, the contributions to historian and civil rights activist Rayford Logan's 1944 volume *What the Negro Wants*, one sees quite a different picture. Nearly all the contributors—including nominal conservatives—to this collection of analyses from a broad cross section of black scholars and activists asserted in very concrete terms that the struggle for racial justice and the general struggle for social and industrial democracy were more than inseparable, that the victory of the former largely depended on the success of the latter. This was, at the time, barely even a matter for debate: rather, it was the frame of reference for any black mass politics and protest activity.

As I suggest above, various pressures of the postwar period—including carrots of success and sticks of intimidation and witch-hunting, as well as the articulation of class tensions within the Civil Rights movement itself—drove an evolution away from this perspective and toward reformulation of the movement's goals along lines more consonant with postwar, post-New Deal, Cold War liberalism. Thus what the political scientist Preston Smith calls "racial democracy" came gradually to replace social democracy as a political goal—the redress of grievances that could be construed as specifically racial took precedence over the redistribution of wealth, and an individualized psychology replaced notions of reworking the material sphere. This dynamic intensified with the combination of popular demobilization in black politics and emergence of the post-segregation black political class in the 1970s and 1980s.

We live under a regime now that is capable simultaneously of including black people and Latinos, even celebrating that inclusion as a fulfillment of democracy, while excluding poor people without a whimper of opposition. Of course, those most visible in the excluded class are disproportionately black and Latino, and that fact gives the lie to the celebration. Or does it really? From the standpoint of a neoliberal ideal of equality, in which classification by race, gender, sexual orientation or any other recognized ascriptive status (that is, status based on what one allegedly is rather than what one does) does not impose explicit, intrinsic or necessary limitations on one's participation and aspirations in the society, this celebration of inclusion of blacks, Latinos and others is warranted.

WE'LL BE BACK!

But this notion of democracy is inadequate, since it doesn't begin to address the deep and deepening patterns of inequality and injustice embedded in the ostensibly "neutral" dynamics of American capitalism. What A. Philip Randolph and others— even anticommunists like Roy Wilkins—understood in the 1940s is that what racism meant was that, so long as such dynamics persisted without challenge, black people and other similarly stigmatized populations would be clustered on the bad side of the distribution of costs and benefits. To extrapolate anachronistically to the present, they would have understood that the struggle against racial health disparities, for example, has no real chance of success apart from a struggle to eliminate for-profit health care.

These seem really transparent points to me, but maybe that's just me. I remain curious why the "debate" over antiracism as a politics takes such indirect and evasive forms—like the analogizing and guilt by association, moralistic bombast in lieu of concrete argument—and why it persists in establishing, even often while denying the move, the terms of debate as race vs. class. I'm increasingly convinced that a likely reason is that the race line is itself a class line, one that is entirely consistent with the neoliberal redefinition of equality and democracy. It reflects the social position of those positioned to benefit from the view that the market is a just, effective, or even acceptable system for rewarding talent and virtue and punishing their opposites and that, therefore, removal of "artificial" impediments to its functioning like race and gender will make it even more efficient and just.

From this perspective even the "left" antiracist line that we must fight both economic inequality and racial inequality, which seems always in practice to give priority to "fighting racism" (often theorized as a necessary precondition for doing anything else), looks suspiciously like only another version of the evasive "we'll come back for you" (after we do all the business-friendly stuff) politics that the Democrats have so successfully employed to avoid addressing economic injustice.

Adolph Reed Jr. is a professor of political science at the University of Pennsylvania.

38

CIVIL RELIGION IN AMERICA

Robert N. Bellah

While some have argued that Christianity is the national faith, and others that church and synagogue celebrate only the generalized religion of "the American Way of Life," few have realized that there actually exists alongside of and rather clearly differentiated from the church an elaborate and well-institutionalized civil religion in America. This article argues not only that there is such a thing, but also that this religion—or perhaps better, this religious dimension—has its own seriousness and integrity and requires the same care in understanding that any other religion does.[1]

THE KENNEDY INAUGURAL

Kennedy's inaugural address of 20 January 1961 serves as an example and a clue with which to introduce this complex subject. That address began:

> We observe today not a victory of party but a celebration of freedom—symbolizing an end as well as a beginning—signifying renewal as well as change. For I have sworn before you and Almighty God the same solemn oath our forebears prescribed nearly a century and three quarters ago.
>
> The world is very different now. For man holds in his mortal hands the power to abolish all forms of human life. And yet the same revolutionary beliefs for which our forebears fought are still at issue around the globe—the belief that the rights of man come not from the generosity of the state but from the hand of God.

And it concluded:

> Finally, whether you are citizens of America or of the world, ask of us the same high standards of strength and sacrifice that we shall ask of you. With

a good conscience our only sure reward, with history the final judge of our
deeds, let us go forth to lead the land we love, asking His blessing and His
help, but knowing here on earth God's work must truly be our own.

These are the three places in this brief address in which Kennedy mentioned the
name of God. If we could understand why he mentioned God, the way in which he
did it, and what he meant to say in those three references, we would understand
much about American civil religion. But this is not a simple or obvious task, and
American students of religion would probably differ widely in their interpretation of
these passages.

Let us consider first the placing of the three references. They occur in the two
opening paragraphs and in the closing paragraph, thus providing a sort of frame for
the more concrete remarks that form the middle part of the speech. Looking beyond
this particular speech, we would find that similar references to God are almost
invariably to be found in the pronouncements of American presidents on solemn
occasions, though usually not in the working messages that the president sends to
Congress on various concrete issues. How, then, are we to interpret this placing of
references to God?

It might be argued that the passages quoted reveal the essentially irrelevant role
of religion in the very secular society that is America. The placing of the references
in this speech as well as in public life generally indicates that religion has "only a ceremonial significance"; it gets only a sentimental nod which serves largely to placate
the more unenlightened members of the community, before a discussion of the really
serious business with which religion has nothing whatever to do. A cynical observer
might even say that an American president has to mention God or risk losing votes.
A semblance of piety is merely one of the unwritten qualifications for the office, a bit
more traditional than but not essentially different from the present-day requirement
of a pleasing television personality.

But we know enough about the function of ceremonial and ritual in various societies to make us suspicious of dismissing something as unimportant because it is
"only a ritual." What people say on solemn occasions need not be taken at face value,
but it is often indicative of deep-seated values and commitments that are not made
explicit in the course of everyday life. Following this line of argument, it is worth
considering whether the very special placing of the references to God in Kennedy's
address may not reveal something rather important and serious about religion in
American life.

It might be countered that the very way in which Kennedy made his references
reveals the essentially vestigial place of religion today. He did not refer to any religion in particular. He did not refer to Jesus Christ, or to Moses, or to the Christian
church; certainly he did not refer to the Catholic Church. In fact, his only reference
was to the concept of God, a word which almost all Americans can accept but which
means so many different things to so many different people that it is almost an
empty sign. Is this not just another indication that in America religion is considered

vaguely to be a good thing, but that people care so little about it that it has lost any content whatever? Isn't Eisenhower reported to have said, "Our government makes no sense unless it is founded in a deeply felt religious faith—and I don't care what it is,"[2] and isn't that a complete negation of any real religion?

These questions are worth pursuing because they raise the issue of how civil religion relates to the political society, on the one hand, and to private religious organization, on the other. President Kennedy was a Christian, more specifically a Catholic Christian. Thus, his general references to God do not mean that he lacked a specific religious commitment. But why, then, did he not include some remark to the effect that Christ is the Lord of the world or some indication of respect for the Catholic Church? He did not because these are matters of his own private religious belief and of his relation to his own particular church; they are not matters relevant in any direct way to the conduct of his public office. Others with different religious views and commitments to difference churches or denominations are equally qualified participants in the political process. The principle of separation of church and state guarantees the freedom of religious belief and association, but at the same time clearly segregates the religious sphere, which is considered to be essentially private, from the political one.

Considering the separation of church and state, how is a president justified in using the word *God* at all? The answer is that the separation of church and state has not denied the political realm a religious dimension. Although matters of personal religious belief, worship, and association are considered to be strictly private affairs, there are, at the same time, certain common elements of religious orientation that the great majority of Americans share. These have played a crucial role in the development of American institutions and still provide a religious dimension for the whole fabric of American life, including the political sphere. This public religious dimension is expressed in a set of beliefs, symbols, and rituals that I am calling the American civil religion. The inauguration of a president is an important ceremonial event in this religion. It reaffirms, among other things, the religious legitimization of the highest political authority.

Let us look more closely at what Kennedy actually said. First he said, "I have sworn before you and Almighty God the same solemn oath our forebears prescribed nearly a century and three quarters ago." The oath is the oath of office, including the acceptance of the obligation to uphold the Constitution. He swears it before the people (you) and God. Beyond the Constitution, then, the president's obligation extends not only to the people but to God. In American political theory, sovereignty rests, of course, with the people, but implicitly, and often explicitly, the ultimate sovereignty has been attributed to God. This is the meaning of the motto, "In God we trust," as well as the inclusion of the phrase "under God" in the pledge to the flag. What difference does it make that sovereignty belongs to God? Though the will of the people as expressed in majority vote is carefully institutionalized as the operative source of political authority, it is deprived of an ultimate significance. The will of the people is not itself the criterion of right and wrong. There is a higher criterion in terms of which this will can be judged; it is possible that the people may be wrong. The president's obligation extends to the higher criterion.

When Kennedy says that "the rights of man come not from the generosity of the state but from the hand of God," he is stressing this point again. It does not matter whether the state is the expression of the will of an autocratic monarch or of the "people"; the rights of man are more basic than any political structure and provide a point of revolutionary leverage from which any state structure may be radically altered. That is the basis for his reassertion of the revolutionary significance of America.

But the religious dimension in political life as recognized by Kennedy not only provides a grounding for the rights of man which makes any form of political absolutism illegitimate, it also provides a transcendent goal for the political process. This is implied in his final words that "here on earth God's work must truly be our own." What he means here is, I think, more clearly spelled out in a previous paragraph, the wording of which, incidentally, has a distinctly Biblical ring:

> Now the trumpet summons us again—not as a call to bear arms, though arms we need—not as a call to battle, though embattled we are—but a call to bear the burden of a long twilight struggle, year in and year out, "rejoicing in hope, patient in tribulation"—a struggle against the common enemies of man: tyranny, poverty, disease and war itself.

The whole address can be understood as only the most recent statement of a theme that lies very deep in the American tradition, namely the obligation, both collective and individual, to carry out God's will on earth. This was the motivating spirit of those who founded America, and it has been present in every generation since. Just below the surface throughout Kennedy's inaugural address, it becomes explicit in the closing statement that God's work must be our own. That this very activist and non-contemplative conception of the fundamental religious obligation, which has been historically associated with the Protestant position, should be enunciated so clearly in the first major statement of the first Catholic president seems to underline how deeply established it is in the American outlook. Let us now consider the form and history of the civil religious tradition in which Kennedy was speaking.

THE IDEA OF CIVIL RELIGION

The phrase *civil religion* is, of course, Rousseau's. In Chapter 8, Book 4, of *The Social Contract*, he outlines the simple dogmas of the civil religion: the existence of God, the life to come, the reward of virtue and the punishment of vice, and the exclusion of religious intolerance. All other religious opinions are outside the cognizance of the state and may be freely held by citizens. While the phrase *civil religion* was not used, to the best of my knowledge, by the founding fathers, and I am certainly not arguing for the particular influence of Rousseau, it is clear that similar ideas, as part of the cultural climate of the late eighteenth century, were to be found among the Americans. For example, Franklin writes in his autobiography:

> I never was without some religious principles. I never doubted, for instance, the existence of the Deity; that he made the world and govern'd it by his Providence; that the most acceptable service of God was the doing of good to men; that our souls are immortal; and that all crime will be punished, and virtue rewarded either here or hereafter. These I esteemed the essentials of every religion; and, being to be found in all the religions we had in our country, I respected them all, tho' with different degrees of respect, as I found them more or less mix'd with other articles, which, without any tendency to inspire, promote or confirm morality, serv'd principally to divide us, and make us unfriendly to one another.

It is easy to dispose of this sort of position as essentially utilitarian in relation to religion. In Washington's Farewell Address (though the words may be Hamilton's) the utilitarian aspect is quite explicit:

> Of all the dispositions and habits which lead to political prosperity, Religion and Morality are indispensable supports. In vain would that man claim the tribute to Patriotism, who should labour to subvert these great Pillars of human happiness, these firmest props of the duties of men and citizens. The mere politicians, equally with the pious man ought to respect and cherish them. A volume could not trace all their connections with private and public felicity. Let it simply be asked where is the security for property, for reputation, for life, if the sense of religious obligation *desert* the oaths, which are the instruments of investigation in Courts of Justice? And let us with caution indulge the supposition, that morality can be maintained without religion. Whatever may be conceded to the influence of refined education on minds of peculiar structure, reason and experience both forbid us to expect that National morality can prevail in exclusion of religious principle.

But there is every reason to believe that religion, particularly the idea of God, played a constitutive role in the thought of the early American statesmen.

Kennedy's inaugural pointed to the religious aspect of the Declaration of Independence, and it might be well to look at that document a bit more closely. There are four references to God. The first speaks of the "Laws of Nature and Nature's God" which entitle any people to be independent. The second is the famous statement that all men "are endowed by their Creator with certain inalienable Rights." Here Jefferson is locating the fundamental legitimacy of the new nation in a conception of "higher law" that is itself based on both classical natural law and Biblical religion. The third is an appeal to "the Supreme Judge of the world for the rectitude of our

intentions," and the last indicates "a firm reliance on the protection of divine Providence." In these last two references, a Biblical God of history who stands in judgment
over the world is indicated.

The intimate relation of these religious notions with the self-conception of the
new republic is indicated by the frequency of their appearance in early official documents. For example, we find in Washington's first inaugural address of 30 April
1789:

> It would be peculiarly improper to omit in this first official act my fervent
> supplications to that Almighty Being who rules over the universe, who pre-
> sides in the councils of nations, and whose providential aids can supply
> every defect, that His benediction may consecrate to the liberties and
> happiness of the people of the United States a Government instituted by
> themselves for these essential purposes, and may enable every instrument
> employed in its administration to execute with success the functions allot-
> ted to his charge.
>
> No people can be bound to acknowledge and adore the Invisible Hand
> which conducts the affairs of man more than those of the United States.
> Every step by which we have advanced to the character of an independent
> nation seems to have been distinguished by some token of providential
> agency . . .
>
> The propitious smiles of Heaven can never be expected on a nation that
> disregards the eternal rules of order and right which Heaven itself has
> ordained. . . . The preservation of the sacred fire of liberty and the destiny of
> the republican model of government are justly considered, perhaps, as
> *deeply*, as *finally*, staked on the experiment intrusted to the hands of the
> American people.

Nor did these religious sentiments remain merely the personal expression of the
president. At the request of both Houses of Congress, Washington proclaimed on
October 3 of that same first year as president that November 26 should be "a day of
public thanksgiving and prayer," the first Thanksgiving Day under the Constitution.

The words and acts of the founding fathers, especially the first few presidents,
shaped the form and tone of the civil religion as it has been maintained ever since.
Though much is selectively derived from Christianity, this religion is clearly not itself
Christianity. For one thing, neither Washington nor Adams nor Jefferson mentions
Christ in his inaugural address; nor do any of the subsequent presidents, although
not one of them fails to mention God.[3] The God of the civil religion is not only rather
"unitarian," he is also on the austere side, much more related to order, law, and right
than to salvation and love. Even though he is somewhat deist in cast, he is by no
means simply a watchmaker God. He is actively interested and involved in history,
with a special concern for America. Here the analogy has much less to do with natural law than with ancient Israel; the equation of America with Israel in the idea of

the "American Israel" is not infrequent.[4] What was implicit in the words of Washington already quoted becomes explicit in Jefferson's second inaugural when he said: "I shall need, too the favor of that Being in whose hands we are, who led our fathers, as Israel of old, from their native land and planted them in a country flowing with all the necessaries and comforts of life." Europe is Egypt; America, the promised land. God has led his people to establish a new sort of social order that shall be a light unto all the nations.[5]

This theme, too, has been a continuous one in the civil religion. We have already alluded to it in the case of the Kennedy inaugural. We find it again in President Johnson's inaugural address:

> They came here—the exile and the stranger, brave but frightened—to find a place where a man could be his own man. They made a covenant with this land. Conceived in justice, written in liberty, bound in union, it was meant one day to inspire the hopes of all mankind; and it binds us still. If we keep its terms, we shall flourish.

What we have, then, from the earliest years of the republic is a collection of beliefs, symbols, and rituals with respect to sacred things and institutionalized in a collectivity. This religion—there seems no other word for it—while not antithetical to and indeed sharing much in common with Christianity, was neither sectarian nor in any specific sense Christian. At a time when the society was overwhelmingly Christian, it seems unlikely that this lack of Christian reference was meant to spare the feelings of the tiny non-Christian minority. Rather, the civil religion expressed what those who set the precedents felt was appropriate under the circumstances. It reflected their private as well as public views. Nor was the civil religion simply in the quotation from Franklin above, the civil religion was specific enough when it came to the topic of America. Precisely because of this specificity, the civil religion was saved from empty formalism and served as a genuine vehicle of national religious self-understanding.

But the civil religion was not, in the minds of Franklin, Washington, Jefferson, or other leaders, with the exception of a few radicals like Tom Paine, ever felt to be a substitute for Christianity. There was an implicit but quite clear division of function between the civil religion and Christianity. Under the doctrine of religious liberty, an exceptionally wide sphere of personal piety and voluntary social action was left to the churches. But the churches were neither to control the state nor to be controlled by it. The national magistrate, whatever his private religious views, operates under the rubrics of the civil religion as long as he is in his official capacity, as we have already seen in the case of Kennedy. This accommodation was undoubtedly the product of a particular historical moment and of a cultural background dominated by Protestantism of several varieties and by the Enlightenment, but it has survived despite subsequent changes in the cultural and religious climate.

CIVIL WAR AND CIVIL RELIGION

Until the Civil War, the American civil religion focused above all on the event of the Revolution, which was seen as the final act of the Exodus from the old lands across the waters. The Declaration of Independence and the Constitution were the sacred scriptures and Washington the divinely appointed Moses who led his people out of the hands of tyranny. The Civil War, which Sidney Mead calls "the center of American history,"[6] was the second great event that involved the national self-understanding so deeply as to require expression in the civil religion. In 1835, Tocqueville wrote that the American republic had never really been tried, that victory in the Revolutionary War was more the result of British preoccupation elsewhere and the presence of a powerful ally than of any great military success of the Americans. But in 1861 the time of testing had indeed come. Not only did the Civil War have the tragic intensity of fratricidal strife, but it was one of the bloodiest wars of the nineteenth century; the loss of life was far greater than any previously suffered by Americans.

The Civil War raised the deepest questions of national meaning. The man who not only formulated but in his own person embodied its meaning for Americans was Abraham Lincoln. For him the issue was not in the first instance slavery but "whether that nation, or any nation so conceived, and so dedicated, can long endure." He had said in Independence Hall in Philadelphia on 22 February 1861:

> All the political sentiments I entertain have been drawn, so far as I have been able to draw them, from the sentiments which originated in and were given to the world from this Hall. I have never had a feeling, politically, that did not spring from the sentiments embodied in the Declaration of Independence.[7]

The phrases of Jefferson constantly echo in Lincoln's speeches. His task was, first of all, to save the Union—not for America alone but for the meaning of America to the whole world so unforgettably etched in the last phrase of the Gettysbury Address.

But inevitably the issue of slavery as the deeper cause of the conflict had to be faced. In the second inaugural, Lincoln related slavery and the war in an ultimate perspective:

> If we shall suppose that American slavery is one of those offenses which, in the providence of God, must needs come, but which, having continued through His appointed time, He now wills to remove, and that He gives to both North and South this terrible war as the woe due to those by whom the offense came, shall we discern therein any departure from those divine attributes which the believers in a living God always ascribe to Him? Fondly do we hope, fervently do we pray, that this mighty scourge of war may speedily pass away. Yet, if God wills that it continue until all the wealth piled by the bondsman's two hundred and fifty years of unrequited toil

shall be sunk, and until every drop of blood drawn with the lash shall be paid by another drawn with the sword, as was said three thousand years ago, so still it must be said "the judgements of the Lord are true and righteous altogether."

But he closes on a note if not of redemption then of reconciliation—"With malice toward none, with charity for all. . . ."

With the Civil War, a new theme of death, sacrifice, and rebirth enters the civil religion. It is symbolized in the life and death of Lincoln. Nowhere is it stated more vividly than in the Gettysburg Address, itself part of the Lincolnian "New Testament" among the civil scriptures. Robert Lowell has recently pointed out the "insistent use of birth images" in this speech explicitly devoted to "these honored dead": "brought forth," "conceived," "created," "new birth of freedom." He goes on to say:

> The Gettysburg Address is a symbolic and sacramental act. Its verbal quality is resonance combined with a logical, matter of fact, prosaic brevity. . . . In his words, Lincoln symbolically died, just as the Union soldiers really died—and as he himself was soon really to die. By his words, he gave the field of battle a symbolic significance that it had lacked. For us and our country, he left Jefferson's ideals of freedom and equality joined to the Christian sacrificial act of death and rebirth. I believe this is a meaning that goes beyond sect or religion and beyond peace and war, and is now part of our lives as a challenge, obstacle and hope.[8]

Lowell is certainly right in pointing out the Christian quality of the symbolism here, but he is also right in quickly disavowing any sectarian implication. The earlier symbolism of the civil religion had been Hebraic without being in any specific sense Jewish. The Gettysburg symbolism (". . . those who here gave their lives, that that nation might live") is Christian without having anything to do with the Christian church.

The symbolic equation of Lincoln with Jesus was made relatively early. Herndon, who had been Lincoln's law partner, wrote:

> For fifty years God rolled Abraham Lincoln through his fiery furnace. He did it to try Abraham and to purify him for his purposes. This made Mr. Lincoln humble, tender, forebearing, sympathetic to suffering, kind, sensitive, tolerant; broadening, deepening and widening his whole nature; making him the noblest and loveliest character since Jesus Christ. . . . I believe that Lincoln was God's chosen one.[9]

With the Christian archetype in the background, Lincoln, "our martyred president," was linked to the war dead, those who "gave the last full measure of devotion." The theme of sacrifice was indelibly written into the civil religion.

The new symbolism soon found both physical and ritualistic expression. The great number of the war dead required the establishment of a number of national cemeteries. Of these, the Gettysburg National Cemetery, which Lincoln's famous address served to dedicate, has been overshadowed only by the Arlington National Cemetery, begun somewhat vindictively on the Lee estate across the river from Washington, partly with the end that the Lee family could never reclaim it,[10] it has subsequently become the most hallowed monument of the civil religion. Not only was a section set aside for the Confederate dead, but it has received the dead of each succeeding American war. It is the site of the one important new symbol to come out of World War I, the Tomb of the Unknown Soldier; more recently it has become the site of the tomb of another martyred president and its symbolic eternal flame.

Memorial Day, which grew out of the Civil War, gave ritual expression to the themes we have been discussing. As Lloyd Warner has so brilliantly analyzed it, the Memorial Day observance, especially in the towns and smaller cities in America, is a major event for the whole community involving a rededication to the martyred dead, to the spirit of sacrifice, and to the American vision.[11] Just as Thanksgiving Day, which incidentally was securely institutionalized as an annual national holiday only under the presidency of Lincoln, serves to integrate the family into the civil religion, so Memorial Day has acted to integrate the local community into the national cult. Together with the less overtly religious Fourth of July and the more minor celebrations of Veterans Day and the birthdays of Washington and Lincoln, these two holidays provide an annual ritual calendar for the civil religion. The public-school system serves as a particularly important context for the cultic celebration of the civil rituals.

In reifying and giving a name to something that, though pervasive enough when you look at it, has gone on only semiconsciously, there is risk of severely distorting the data. But the reification and the naming have already begun. The religious critics of "religion in general," or of the "religion of the 'American Way of Life,'" or of "American Shinto" have really been talking about the civil religion. As usual in religious polemic, they take as criteria the best in their own religious tradition and as typical the worst in the tradition of the civil religion. Against these critics, I would argue that the civil religion at its best is a genuine apprehension of universal and transcendent religious reality as seen in or, one could almost say, as revealed through the experience of the American people. Like all religions, it has suffered various deformations and demonic distortions. At its best, it has neither been so general that it has lacked incisive relevance to the American scene nor so particular that it has placed American society above universal human values. I am not at all convinced that the leaders of the churches have consistently represented a higher level of religious insight than the spokesmen of the civil religion. Reinhold Niebuhr has this to say of Lincoln, who never joined a church and who certainly represents civil religion at its best:

> An analysis of the religion of Abraham Lincoln in the context of the traditional religion of his time and place and of its polemical use on the slavery issue, which corrupted religious life in the days before and during the Civil War, must lead to the conclusion that Lincoln's religious convictions were superior in depth and purity to those, not only of the political leaders of his day, but of the religious leaders of the era.[12]

Perhaps the real animus of the religious critics has been not so much against the civil religion in itself but against its pervasive and dominating influence within the sphere of church religion. As S. M. Lipset has recently shown, American religion at least since the early nineteenth century has been predominantly activist, moralistic, and social rather than contemplative, theological, of innerly spiritual.[13] Tocqueville spoke of American church religion as "a political institution which powerfully contributes to the maintenance of a democratic republic among the Americans"[14] by supplying a strong moral consensus amidst continuous political change. Henry Bargy in 1902 spoke of American church religion as "la poésie du civisme."[15]

It is certainly true that the relation between religion and politics in America has been singularly smooth. This is in large part due to the dominant tradition. As Tocqueville wrote:

> The greatest part of British America was peopled by men who, after having shaken off the authority of the Pope, acknowledged no other religious supremacy: they brought with them into the New World a form of Christianity which I cannot better describe than by styling it a democratic and republican religion.[16]

The churches opposed neither the Revolution nor the establishment of democratic institutions. Even when some of them opposed the full institutionalization of religious liberty, they accepted the final outcome with good grace and without nostalgia for an *ancien régime*. The American civil religion was never anticlerical or militantly secular. On the contrary, it borrowed selectively from the religious tradition in such a way that the average American saw no conflict between the two. In this way, the civil religion was able to build up without any bitter struggle with the church powerful symbols of national solidarity and to mobilize deep levels of personal motivation for the attainment of national goals.

Such an achievement is by no means to be taken for granted. It would seem that the problem of a civil religion is quite general in modern societies and that the way it is solved or not solved will have repercussions in many spheres. One need only to think of France to see how differently things can go. The French Revolution was anticlerical to the core and attempted to set upon anti-Christian civil religion. Throughout modern French history, the chasm between traditional Catholic symbols and the symbolism of 1789 has been immense.

American civil religion is still very much alive. [In 1963] we participated in a vivid reenactment of the sacrifice theme in connection with the funeral of our assassinated president. The American Israel theme is clearly behind both Kennedy's New Frontier and Johnson's Great Society. Let me give just one recent illustration of how the civil religion serves to mobilize support for the attainment of national goals. On 15 March 1965 President Johnson went before Congress to ask for a strong voting-rights bill. Early in the speech he said:

> Rarely are we met with the challenge, not to our growth or abundance, or our welfare or our security—but rather to the values and the purposes and the meaning of our beloved nation.
>
> The issue of equal rights for American Negroes is such an issue. And should we defeat every enemy, and should we double our wealth and conquer the stars and still be unequal to this issue, then we will have failed as a people and as a nation.
>
> For with a country as with a person, "What is a man profited, if he shall gain the whole world, and lose his own soul?"

And in conclusion he said:

> Above the pyramid on the great seal of the United States it says in Latin, "God has favored our undertaking."
>
> God will not favor everything that we do. It is rather our duty to divine his will. I cannot help but believe that He truly understands and that He really favors the undertaking that we begin here tonight.[17]

The civil religion has not always been involved in favor of worthy causes. On the domestic scene, an American-Legion type of ideology that fuses God, country, and flag has been used to attack nonconformist and liberal ideas and groups of all kinds. Still, it has been difficult to use the words of Jefferson and Lincoln to support special interests and undermine personal freedom. The defenders of slavery before the Civil War came to reject the thinking of the Declaration of Independence. Some of the most consistent of them turned against not only Jeffersonian democracy but Reformation religion; they dreamed of a South dominated by medieval chivalry and divine-right monarchy.[18] For all the overt religiosity of the radical right today, their relation to the civil religious consensus is tenuous, as when the John Birch Society attacks the central American symbol of Democracy itself.

With respect to America's role in the world, the dangers of distortion are greater and the built-in safeguards of the tradition weaker. The theme of the American Israel was used, almost from the beginning, as a justification for the shameful treatment of the Indians so characteristic of our history. It can be overtly or implicitly linked to the idea of manifest destiny which has been used to legitimate several adventures in imperialism since the early nineteenth century. Never has the danger been greater than today. The issue is not so much one of imperial expansion, of which we are accused, as of the tendency to assimilate all governments or parties in the world which support our immediate policies or call upon our help by invoking the notion of free institutions and democratic values. Those nations that are for the moment "on our side" become "the free world." A repressive and unstable military dictatorship in South Viet-Nam becomes "the free people of South Viet-Nam and their government." It is then part of the role of America as the New Jerusalem and "the last best hope on earth" to defend such governments with treasure and eventually with blood. When our soldiers are actually dying, it becomes possible to consecrate the struggle further by invoking the great theme of sacrifice. For the majority of the American people who are unable to judge whether the people in South Viet-Nam (or wherever) are "free like us," such arguments are convincing. Fortunately President Johnson has been less ready to assert that "God has favored our undertaking" in the case of Viet-Nam than with respect to civil rights. But others are not so hesitant. The civil religion has exercised long-term pressure for the humane solution of our greatest domestic problem, the treatment of the Negro American. It remains to be seen how relevant it can become for our role in the world at large, and whether we can effectually stand for "the revolutionary beliefs for which our forebears fought," in John F. Kennedy's words.

The civil religion is obviously involved in the most pressing moral and political issue of the day. But it is also caught in another kind of crisis, theoretical and theological, of which it is at the moment largely unaware. "God" has clearly been a central symbol in the civil religion from the beginning and remains so today. This symbol is just as central to the civil religion as it is to Judaism or Christianity. In the late eighteenth century this posed no problem; even Tom Paine, contrary to his detractors, was not an atheist. From left to right and regardless of church or sect, all could accept the idea of God. But today, as even *Time* has recognized, the meaning of the world *God* is by no means so clear or so obvious. There is no formal creed in the civil religion. We have had a Catholic president; it is conceivable that we could have a Jewish one. But could we have an agnostic president? Could a man with conscientious scruples about using the word *God* the way Kennedy and Johnson have used it be elected chief magistrate of our country? If the whole God symbolism requires reformulation, there will be obvious consequences for the civil religion, consequences perhaps of liberal alienation and of fundamentalist ossification that have not so far been prominent in this realm. The civil religion has been a point of articulation between the profoundest commitments of the Western religious and philosophical tradition and the common beliefs of ordinary Americans. It is not too soon to consider how the deepening theological crisis may affect the future of this articulation.

THE THIRD TIME OF TRIAL

In conclusion it may be worthwhile to relate the civil religion to the most serious situation that we as Americans now face, what I call the third time of trial. The first time of trial had to do with the question of independence, whether we should or could run our own affairs in our own way. The second time of trial was over the issue of slavery, which in turn was only the most salient aspect of the more general problem of the full institutionalization of democracy within our country. This second problem we are still far from solving though we have some notable successes to our credit. But we have been overtaken by a third great problem which has led to a third great crisis, in the midst of which we stand. This is the problem of responsible action in a revolutionary world, a world seeking to attain many of the things, material and spiritual, that we have already attained. Americans have, from the beginning, been aware of the responsibility and the significance our republican experiment has for the whole world. The first internal political polarization in the new nation had to do with our attitude toward the French Revolution. But we were small and weak then, and "foreign entanglements" seemed to threaten our very survival. During the last century, our relevance for the world was not forgotten, but our role was seen as purely exemplary. Our democratic republic rebuked tyranny by merely existing. Just after World War I we were on the brink of taking a different role in the world, but once again we turned our back.

Since World War II the old pattern has become impossible. Every president since Roosevelt has been groping toward a new pattern of action in the world, one that would be consonant with our power and our responsibilities. For Truman and for the period dominated by John Foster Dulles that pattern was seen to be the great Manichaean confrontation of East and West, the confrontation of democracy and "the false philosophy of Communism" that provided the structure of Truman's inaugural address. But with the last years of Eisenhower and with the successive two presidents, the pattern began to shift. The great problems came to be seen as caused not solely by the evil intent of any one group of men, but as stemming from much more complex and multiple sources. For Kennedy, it was not so much a struggle against particular men as against "the common enemies of man: tyranny, poverty, disease and war itself."

But in the midst of this trend toward a less primitive conception of ourselves and our world, we have somehow, without anyone really intending it, stumbled into a military confrontation where we have come to feel that our honor is at stake. We have in a moment a uncertainty been tempted to rely on our overwhelming physical power rather than on our intelligence, and we have, in part, succumbed to this temptation. Bewildered and unnerved when our terrible power fails to bring immediate success, we are at the edge of a chasm the depth of which no man knows.

I cannot help but think of Robinson Jeffers, whose poetry seems more apt now than when it was written, when he said:

> *Unhappy country, what wings you have! . . .*
> *Weep (it is frequent in human affairs), weep for the terrible magnificence of the means,*
> *The ridiculous incompetence of the reasons, the bloody and shabby*
> *Pathos of the result.*

But as so often before in similar times, we have a man of prophetic stature, without the bitterness or misanthropy of Jeffers, who, as Lincoln before him, calls this nation to its judgment:

> When a nation is very powerful but lacking in self-confidence, it is likely to behave in a manner that is dangerous both to itself and to others.

Gradually but unmistakably, America is succumbing to that arrogance of power which has afflicted, weakened and in some cases destroyed great nations in the past.

If the war goes on and expands, if that fatal process continues to accelerate until America becomes what is not now and never has been, a seeker after unlimited power and empire, then Vietnam will have had a mighty and tragic fallout indeed.

I do not believe that will happen, I am very apprehensive but I still remain hopeful, and even confident, that America, with its humane and democratic traditions, will find the wisdom to match its power.[19]

Without an awareness that our nation stands under higher judgment, the tradition of the civil religion would be dangerous indeed. Fortunately, the prophetic voices have never been lacking. Our present situation brings to mind the Mexican-American war that Lincoln, among so many others, opposed. The spirit of civil disobedience that is alive today in the civil rights movement and the opposition to the Viet-Nam war was already clearly outlined by Henry David Thoreau when he wrote, "If the law is of such a nature that it requires you to be an agent of injustice to another, then I say, break the law." Thoreau's words, "I would remind my countrymen that they are men first, and Americans at a late and convenient hour,"[20] provide an essential standard for any adequate thought and action in our third time of trial. As Americans, we have been well favored in the world, but it is as men that we will be judged.

Out of the first and second times of trial have come, as we have seen, the major symbols of the American civil religion. There seems little doubt that a successful negotiation of this third time of trial—the attainment of some kind of viable and coherent world order—would precipitate a major new set of symbolic forms. So far the flickering flame of the United Nations burns too low to be the focus of a cult, but the emergence of a genuine transnational sovereignty would certainly change this. It would necessitate the incorporation of vital international symbolism into our civil religion, or, perhaps a better way of putting it, it would result in American civil religion becoming simply one part of a new civil religion of the world. It is useless to speculate on the form such a civil religion might take, though it obviously would draw on religious traditions beyond the sphere of Biblical religion alone. Fortunately, since the American civil religion is not the worship of the American nation but an understanding of the American experience in the light of ultimate and universal reality, the reorganization entailed by such a new situation need not disrupt the American civil religion's continuity. A world civil religion could be accepted as a fulfillment and not a denial of American civil religion. Indeed, such an outcome has been the eschatological hope of American civil religion from the beginning. To deny such an outcome would be to deny the meaning of America itself.

Behind the civil religion at every point lie Biblical archetypes: Exodus, Chosen People, Promised Land, New Jerusalem, Sacrificial Death and Rebirth. But it is also genuinely American and genuinely new. It has its own prophets and its own martyrs, its own sacred events and sacred places, its own solemn rituals and symbols. It is concerned that America be a society as perfectly in accord with the will of God as men can make it, and a light to all the nations.

It has often been used and is being used today as a cloak for petty interests and ugly passions. It is in need—as is any living faith—of continual reformation, of being measured by universal standards. But it is not evident that it is incapable of growth and new insight.

It does not make any decision for us. It does not remove us from moral ambiguity, from being, in Lincoln's fine phrase, an "almost chosen people." But it is a heritage of moral and religious experience from which we still have much to learn as we formulate the decisions that lie ahead.

NOTES

1. Why something so obvious should have escaped serious analytical attention is in itself an interesting problem. Part of the reason is probably the controversial nature of the subject. From the earliest years of the nineteenth century, conservative religious and political groups have argued that Christianity is, in fact, the national religion. Some of them have from time to time and as recently as the 1950's proposed constitutional amendments that would explicitly recognize the sovereignty of Christ. In defending the doctrine of separation of church and state, opponents of such groups have denied that the national polity has, intrinsically, anything to do with religion at all. The moderates on this issue have insisted that the American state has taken a permissive and indeed supportive attitude toward religious groups (tax exemption, et cetera), thus favoring religion but still missing the positive institutionalization with which I am concerned. But part of the reason this issue has been left in obscurity is certainly due to the peculiarly Western concept of "religion" as denoting a single type of collectivity of which an individual can be a member of one and only one at a time. The Durkheimian notion that every group has a religious dimension, which would be seen as obvious in southern or eastern Asia, is foreign to us. This obscures the recognition of such dimensions in our society.

2. Quoted in Will Herberg, *Protestant-Catholic-Jew* (New York, 1955), p. 97.

3. God is mentioned or referred to in all inaugural addresses but Washington's second, which is a very brief (two paragraphs) and perfunctory acknowledgment. It is not without interest that the actual word *God* does not appear until Monroe's second inaugural, 5 March 1821. In his first inaugural, Washington refers to God as "that Almighty Being who rules the universe," "Great Author of every public and private good," "Invisible Hand," and "benign Parent of the Human Race." John Adams refers to God as "Providence," "Being who is supreme over all," "Patron of Order," "Foundation of Justice," and "Protector in all ages of the world of virtuous liberty."

Jefferson speaks of "that Infinite Power which rules the destinies of the universe," and "that Being in whose hands we are." Madison speaks of "that Almighty Being whose power regulates the destiny of nations," and "Heaven." Monroe uses "Providence" and "the Almighty" in his first inaugural and finally "Almighty God" in his second. See *Inaugural Addresses of the Presidents of the United States from George Washington 1789 to Harry S Truman 1949*. 82nd Congress, 2d Session, House Document No. 540,1952.

4. For example, Abiel Abbot, pastor of the First Church in Haverhill, Massachusetts, delivered a Thanksgiving sermon in 1799, *Traits of Resemblance in the People of the United States of America to Ancient Israel*, in which he said, "It has been often remarked that the people of the United States come nearer to a parallel with Ancient Israel, than any other nation upon the globe. Hence 'Our American Israel' is a term frequently used; and common consent allows it apt and proper." Cited in Hans Kohn, *The Idea of Nationalism* (New York, 1961), p. 665.

5. That the Mosiac analogy was present in the minds of leaders at the very moment of the birth of the republic is indicated in the designs proposed by Franklin and Jefferson for a seal of the United States of America. Together with Adams, they formed a committee of three delegated by the Continental Congress on July 4, 1776, to draw up the new device. "Franklin proposed as the device Moses lifting up his wand and dividing the Red Sea while Pharaoh was overwhelmed by its waters, with the motto 'Rebellion to tyrants is obedience to God.' Jefferson proposed the children of Israel in the wilderness 'led by a cloud by day and a pillar of fire by night.'" Anson Phelps Stokes, *Church and State in the United States*, Vol. 1 (New York, 1950), pp. 467–468.

6. Sidney Mead, *The Lively Experiment* (New York, 1963), p. 12.

7. Quoted by Arthur Lehman Goodhart in Allan Nevins (ed.), *Lincoln and the Gettysburg Address* (Urbana, Ill., 1961), p. 39.

8. Ibid., "On the Gettysburg Address," pp. 88–89.

9. Quoted in Sherwood Eddy, *The Kingdom of God and the American Dream* (New York, 1941), p. 162.

10. Karl Decker and Angus McSween, *Historic Arlington* (Washington, D.C., 1892), pp. 60–67.

11. How extensive the activity associated with Memorial Day can be is indicated by Warner: "The sacred symbolic behavior of Memorial Day, in which scores of the town's organizations are involved, is ordinarily divided into four periods. During the year separate rituals are held by many of the associations for their dead, and many of these activities are connected with later Memorial Day events. In the second phase, preparations are made during the last three or four weeks for the ceremony itself, and some of the associations perform public rituals. The third phase consists of scores of rituals held in all the cemeteries, churches, and halls of the associations. These rituals consist of speeches and highly ritualized behavior. They last for two days and are climaxed by the fourth and last phase, in which all the separate celebrants gather in the center of the business district on the afternoon of Memorial Day. The separate organizations, with their members in uniform or with fitting insignia,

march through the town, visit the shrines and monuments of the hero dead, and, finally enter the cemetery. Here dozens of ceremonies are held, most of them highly symbolic and formalized." During these various ceremonies Lincoln is continually referred to and the Gettysburg Address recited many times. W. Lloyd Warner, *American Life* (Chicago, 1962), pp. 8–9.

12. Reinold Neibuhr, "The Religion of Abraham Lincoln," in Nevins (ed.), *op. cit.*, p. 72. William J. Wolfe of the Episcopal Theological School in Cambridge, Massachusetts, has written: "Lincoln is one of the greatest theologians of America—not in the technical meaning of producing a system of doctrine, certainly not as the defender of some one denomination, but in the sense of seeing the hand of God intimately in the affairs of nations. Just so the prophets of Israel criticized the events of their day from the perspective of the God who is concerned for history and who reveals His will within it. Lincoln now stands among God's latterday prophets." *The Religion of Abraham Lincoln* (New York, 1963), p. 24.

13. Seymour Martin Lipset, "Religion and American Values," Chapter 4, *The First New Nation* (New York, 1964).

14. Alexis de Tocqueville, *Democracy in America,* Vol. 1 (New York, 1954), p. 310.

15. Henry Bargy, *La Religion dans la Société aux Etats-Unis* (Paris, 1902), p. 31.

16. Tocqueville, *op. cit.*, p. 311. Later he says, "In the United States even the religion of most of the citizens is republican, since it submits the truths of the other world to private judgment, as in politics the care of their temporal interests is abandoned to the good sense of the people. Thus every man is allowed freely to take the road which he thinks will lead him to heaven, just as the law permits every citizen to have the right of choosing his own government" (p. 436).

17. U.S., *Congressional Record*, House, 15 March 1965, pp. 4924, 4926.

18. See Louis Hartz, "The Feudal Dream of the South," Part 4, *The Liberal Tradition in America* (New York, 1955).

19. Speech of Senator J. William Fulbright of 28 April 1968, as reported in the *New York Times*, 29 April 1968.

20. Quoted in Yehoshua Arieli, *Individualism and Nationalism in American Ideology* (Cambridge, Mass., 1964), p. 274.

39

VATICAN KEEPS UP DRUMBEAT AGAINST WAR IN IRAQ

John L. Allen Jr.

Fierce Vatican diplomacy aimed at blocking a war in Iraq continued in late February, with meetings between John Paul II and English Prime Minister Tony Blair, Spanish Prime Minister Jose Maria Aznar, and the speaker of the Iranian parliament Mohammad Reza Khatami, brother of the country's president.

The Vatican also kept up its rhetorical drumbeat, with unusually strong comments suggesting that armed force without United Nations authorization would be illegal, and that the United States may be acting on the basis of its desire to control Iraq's oil resources.

On Feb. 23, John Paul II invited Catholics to a day of fast on Ash Wednesday, March 5, as a way of expressing their desire for peace. *L'Osservatore Romano*, the official Vatican newspaper, featured the pope's words about the possibility of war in its Monday edition, with the word "never" blazed across the front page in enormous type.

"Believers, whatever their religion, should proclaim that we will never be able to be happy opposing each other, and that the future of humanity can never be assured by terrorism and the logic of war," the pope said.

On Feb. 27, the Vatican hosted a briefing session for all its accredited diplomats, more than 300, to explain its view on the fundamental role of the United Nations in resolving the Iraq conflict. One Western diplomat told *NCR* that the move was in response to a high volume of requests from diplomats for the Holy See to explain its strong antiwar line.

The recent flurry of high-profile visits to Pope John Paul II symbolizes the Vatican's attempt to influence all sides in the debate over Iraq, since England and Spain both support the use of force, while Iran is one of the so-called "axis of evil" nations.

In recent weeks, the pope met British Prime Minister Tony Blair, Iraqi Deputy Prime Minister Tariq Aziz, U.N. General-Secretary Kofi Annan and German Foreign Minister Joschka Fischer. He sent Cardinal Roger Etchegaray as a special envoy to Baghdad (NCR, Feb. 21 and 28).

Archbishop Jean-Louis Tauran, the Vatican's foreign minister, warned Feb. 24 at a conference on peace at a Roman hotel that "a war of aggression would be a crime against peace," especially if that war were launched "by one or more states" outside the framework of the United Nations.

"For us, everything must be undertaken and decided in the context of the United Nations," Tauran said.

Meanwhile, the director of Vatican Radio, Jesuit Fr. Pasquale Borgomeo, asserted during a live broadcast Feb. 25 that it is "difficult to explain" American policy in Iraq without respect to the country's oil resources. Iraq has the second-largest oil reserves in the world, estimated at 112 billion barrels.

Despite Blair's recent statement that suggestions of oil interests behind the push in Iraq amount to a "conspiracy theory," Borgomeo said that American antiwar protestors carrying signs reading "no blood for oil" may be on to something. He pointed to reports of November meetings between Iraqi opposition leaders and officials of American oil companies to discuss the postwar development of Iraqi oil fields.

The Bush administration has indicated it would use oil revenue to help finance the rebuilding of Iraq.

Not all Catholic figures were content with the Vatican's full court press against the war.

"I have the impression that by now the Catholics who count are increasingly lined up under the banner of anti-Americanism," said Bishop Alessandro Maggiolini of Como, Italy.

Despite the diplomatic frenzy, senior Vatican officials seem privately pessimistic that war in Iraq can be avoided.

"I hope for it strongly, but I don't have much faith," a senior official told NCR Feb. 25.

"I'm sorry to say this to your countrymen, but my impression is that America wants to get rid of Saddam Hussein at all costs, and even if he does disarm that won't be enough to save himself," the official said.

John L. Allen Jr. is NCR *Rome correspondent. His e-mail address is* **jallen@natcath.org**
National Catholic Reporter, March 7, 2003

40

WE DON'T HAVE TO BE SAINTS

Paul Loeb

> *We can make ourselves whole only by accepting our partiality, by living within our limits, by being human—not by trying to be gods.*
>
> *—Wendell Berry*

I believe many of us feel uneasy about America's fragmentation and relentless self-interest—what Thomas Moore calls "a national persona of hype, ambition, narcissism, and materialism." We would like to find ways to connect with each other and express our compassion, experiencing a sense of purpose impossible to attain through private pursuits alone. When we don't find ways to voice this larger self, our most generous impulses have nowhere to go.

Chief among the obstacles to acting on these impulses is the mistaken belief that anyone who takes a committed public stand, or at least an effective one, has to be a larger-than-life figure—someone with more time, energy, courage, vision, or knowledge than a normal person could ever possess. This belief pervades our society, in part because the media tends not to represent heroism as the work of ordinary human beings, which it almost always is. A few years ago, on Martin Luther King Day, I was interviewed on CNN. So was Rosa Parks, by phone from Los Angeles. "We're very honored to have her," said the host. "Rosa Parks was the woman who wouldn't go to the back of the bus. She wouldn't get up and give her seat in the white section to a white person. That set in motion the year-long bus boycott in Montgomery. It earned Rosa Parks the title of 'mother of the civil rights movement.'"

I was excited to hear Parks's voice and to be part of the same show. Then it occurred to me that the hosts' description—the story's standard rendition—stripped the Montgomery boycott of all its context. Before the day she refused to give up her bus seat, Parks had spent twelve years helping lead the local NAACP chapter, along with the union activist E. D. Nixon from the Brotherhood of Sleeping Car Porters, teachers from the local Negro college, and a variety of ordinary members of Montgomery's African American community. The summer before, Parks had attended a ten-day training session at Tennessee's labor and civil rights organizing school, the Highlander Center, where she'd met an older generation of civil rights activists and discussed the Supreme Court's recent decision in *Brown v. Board of Education* banning "separate but equal" schools. During this period of involvement and education, Parks had become familiar with previous challenges to segregation: Another Montgomery bus boycott, fifty years earlier, successfully eased some restrictions; a bus boycott in Baton Rouge had won limited gains two years before Parks was arrested; and the previous spring, a young Montgomery woman had also refused to move to the back of the bus, causing the NAACP to consider a legal challenge until it turned out that she was unmarried and pregnant, and therefore a poor symbol for a campaign. In short, Parks's decision didn't come out of nowhere. And she didn't single-handedly give birth to the civil rights movement. Rather, she was part of an existing broader effort to create change, at a time when success was far from certain. This in no way diminishes the power and historical importance of her refusal to give up her seat. But it does remind us that this tremendously consequential act might never have taken place without an immense amount of humble and frustrating work that she and others did earlier on.

I often ask students what words they associate with social activists. "Fanatical," they'll say. "Crazy." "Troublemakers." "Angry." "Extremists." Then I'll ask where Martin Luther King, Jr., fits in, and after a pause, they'll characterize him as someone morally superhuman, who stood above or apart from life, a man so rare that nothing he did could be replicated, even on a smaller scale. These judgments, they acknowledge, come not from direct experience but from cultural images. Their high school textbooks, they say, "only mention the conclusions," omitting accounts of how ordinary citizens have repeatedly shaped America. Today, activist stories rarely make the news. Apart from a few pictures, a three-minute feature on a "person of the week," or a brief sound bite here and there, most of us have encountered little that conveys the actual process of social change, with all its passion, frustration, difficult perseverance, and sense of consequence and purpose.

The students' superficial understanding of key events in American history is not unusual. For most of us, the past is a foreign country. The very stories that might remind us of our potential impact and strength are too often forgotten, caricatured, or ignored altogether. Apart from obvious times of armed conflict, or the legends of those few people we've elevated to the status of "hero," most of us know next to nothing of the many battles ordinary men and women have fought to preserve freedom, expand the sphere of democracy, and create a more just society. Of the abolitionist and civil rights movements, we at best recall a few key leaders—and often, as with Rosa Parks, we don't know their actual stories. We know even less about the turn-of-the-century populists who challenged entrenched economic interests and fought for a "cooperative commonwealth." Who these days can describe the union movements that ended eighty-hour workweeks at near-starvation wages? Who knows about the citizen efforts that first pushed through Social Security? How did the women's suffrage movement spread to hundreds of communities, and gather enough strength to prevail?

Many have remarked on America's historical amnesia, but its implications are hard to appreciate without recognizing how much identity dissolves in the absence of memory. In our collective amnesia, we lose the mechanisms through which grass-roots social movements of the past successfully shifted public sentiment and challenged entrenched institutional power. Equally lost are the means by which their participants managed to keep on, sustaining their hope, and eventually prevailing in circumstances at least as difficult as those we face today. As the novelist Milan Kundera writes, "The struggle of man against power is the struggle of memory against forgetting."

Think about the different ways one can frame Rosa Parks' historic action. In the prevailing myth, Parks decides to act almost on a whim, in isolation. She's a virgin to politics, a holy innocent. The lesson seems to be that if any of us suddenly got the urge to do something equally heroic, that would be great. Of course most of us don't, so we wait our entire lives to find the ideal moment.

The real story conveys a far more empowering moral. It suggests that change is the product of deliberate, incremental action, whereby we join together to try to shape a better world. Sometimes our struggles will fail, as did many earlier efforts by Parks, her peers, and her predecessors. Other times they may bear modest fruit. And at times they will trigger a miraculous outpouring of courage and heart—as happened with Parks's arrest and all that followed. We can never know beforehand the consequences of our actions.

"I think it does us all a disservice," says Atlanta activist Sonya Vetra Tinsley, "when people who work for social change are presented as saints—so much more noble than the rest of us. We get a false sense that from the moment they were born they were called to act, never had doubts, were bathed in a circle of light. But I'm much more inspired learning how people succeeded despite their failings and uncertainties. It's a much less intimidating image. It makes me feel like I have a shot at changing things too."

Sonya had previously attended a talk given by one of Martin Luther King, Jr.'s Morehouse professors, in which he mentioned how much King had struggled when he first came to college, getting only a C, for example, in his first philosophy course. "I found that very inspiring, when I heard it," Sonya said, "given all that King achieved."

THE PERFECT STANDARD

Once we enshrine our heroes, it becomes hard for mere mortals to measure up in our eyes. However individuals speak out, we often dismiss their motives, knowledge, and tactics. We fault them for not being in command of every fact and figure, for not being able to answer every question put to them. As Taylor Branch wrote in

Parting the Waters, the first volume of his epic history of the civil rights movement, we're taught to view social activists as people who shout loudly and rudely in a hushed museum, as grandstanders, as "zealots, people who oversimplify the world into good and evil without room for the murky truth, who lack the quality of self-effacement in their enthusiasm for their own views." We can't imagine how an ordinary human being without ordinary flaws might make a critical difference in a worthy social cause.

As a result of such images, many of us have developed what I call the perfect standard: Before we will allow ourselves to take action on an issue, we must be convinced not only that the issue is the world's most important, but that we have perfect understanding of it, perfect moral consistency in our character, and that we will be able to express our views with perfect eloquence.

The perfect standard assumes many forms. At a small Minnesota college, a half-dozen students were sleeping in makeshift cardboard shelters to dramatize the plight of America's homeless. As one participant recalled, "Lots who passed by treated us like a slumber party. They told us we were cute. But when we kept on for a couple days they began to get annoyed. One girl yelled, 'Homeless people don't have blankets. You're being hypocritical.' I was half asleep but I said, 'Yes they do. They have blankets and friends. They just don't have homes.' She looked like she'd be satisfied only if we got soaked in the freezing rain."

In effect, the activists were ridiculed for not being pious enough. Yet even had they demonstrated their commitment by standing in the rain until they became hypothermic, or by launching a hunger strike, odds are the critics still wouldn't have been satisfied. They would have turned their argument around, and accused the activists of being too holy, of taking things to seriously. Whatever the critique, the approach is the same: Identify a perceived flaw, large or small, then use it to dismiss an entire effort.

To hear others invoke the perfect standard is damaging enough. It's worse to subject ourselves to it. As a result, for instance, we often refrain from tackling environmental issues because they're technically complex. We don't address homelessness because we aren't homeless ourselves. Though outraged when moneyed interests corrupt our political system, we believe we lack the authority to insist campaign financing be reformed. Whatever the issue, whatever the approach, we never feel we have enough knowledge or standing. If we do speak out, someone might challenge us, might find an error in our thinking or an inconsistency—what they might call a hypocrisy—in our lives. As the spiritual writer Marianne Williamson says, "We have insidiously convinced ourselves that our wisdom is not wisdom, our common sense is not common sense, and our conscience is not conscience."

If anything, the proliferation of sources of information makes it more likely that we'll use the perfect standard to justify detachment. Now we can spend our lives in solitude trying to garner ever more information from books, magazines, newspapers, the Internet, satellite cable channels, and radio talk shows. Just as America has no notion of economic sufficiency, so the perfect standard leaves us with a permanent insufficiency of knowledge—and a perpetual mistrust of anyone who dares to voice an opinion or offer an objection. As everything that can be known continues to increase, the effort to know everything grows increasingly doomed. Yet we don't dare speak out unless we feel prepared to debate Henry Kissinger on *Nightline*.

IF NOT NOW

According to another version of the perfect standard, we shouldn't begin working for social change until the time is ideal—say, when our kids are grown, when our job is more secure, when we find the most worthy cause, when we retire, or, in Bill Gates–speak, when we "enter philanthropic mode." We wait for when our courage and wisdom will be greatest, the issues clearest, and our supporters and allies most steadfast. Such hesitation is reasonable. We are subject to real pressures and constraints. Yet when in life will we not be subject to pressures, of one kind or another? When will public participation not require a shift from familiar and comfortable habits? What's more, the issues that most need our attention will probably always be complex, forbidding, and difficult to address effectively. As Rachel Naomi Remen reminds us, "Being brave does not mean being unafraid. It often means being afraid and doing it anyway."

If we trust our convictions, we can take stands whether or not we have formal credentials at all. As David Halberstam describes in his wonderful book *The Children*, on the group that led the pivotal Nashville civil rights sit-ins, former Student Nonviolent Coordinating Committee (SNCC) head John Lewis, now a Georgia Congressman, began as the most unsophisticated person imaginable. Lewis was so "country," his friends from the rural South said he made *them* feel like city boys. Stuttering when he talked, preaching to the chickens because he had no other audience (and presiding over chicken births, baptisms, weddings, and funerals), Lewis was the last person one would have expected to change history.

Involvement similarly knows no barriers of age. A young woman named Joby Gelbspan was fourteen when she had a life-changing experience. Her family was on vacation in Ecuador, and a guide was showing them the sights of the rainforest. They came to a series of large, cylindrical holes in the ground, which Joby assumed were made by yet another kind of burrowing animal. But they weren't. They'd been made by an oil company, the guide explained, designed to hold dynamite charges, that would blow up the land and buildings of an uncooperative village that was opposing the company's plan for development—the same village where Joby was staying. The villagers had caught the company employees in the act, and driven them off. But they knew they'd be returning soon with the military.

Joby was shocked. She'd never before realized the destructive power of raw economic greed. Soon after, she encountered some petitioners from the citizen group Infact on a Boston street. They were getting people to support a boycott of General Electric for the corporation's prime role in fostering the arms race. Joby signed, began circulating petitions of her own, and at age sixteen, became the youngest-ever member of Infact's national board. She played a major role in their successful campaign to persuade GE to sell off its weapons division and in mobilizing popular support to hold tobacco companies responsible for the health toll of their actions. Most of the Infact board members, Joby said, "were asking my advice on how to deal with their own kids who were my age. But they also respected and listened to me."

While we wait for the ideal time to arrive, weeks, months, and years pass by. We squander repeated opportunities to involve ourselves in the larger community for causes whose justification may be imperfect and whose outcome is far from certain— in other words, causes that are real. The perfect standard promotes endless deferral.

In part, that's because social justice battles always look safer and more clear-cut in retrospect. In the middle of the Iran-Contra hearings, George Bush came to Seattle to deliver a fund-raising speech; I joined a civil disobedience protest, during which several of us were arrested for sitting down in front of the doors where the guests were due to arrive. One of those taken into custody was the head of a local alternative school who'd worked with Martin Luther King, Jr. in the South. The arraigning judge asked him, as he asked all who came before him, whether he'd had any previous arrests.

"I was arrested in Birmingham," my friend explained. "I was arrested in Selma." And he reeled off a succession of civil rights battles. "No," said the judge, getting testy, because those were the "good" arrests, "I mean recently." "Yes," my friend said with an enormous grin. "I have lots of those, too."

Sometimes we're called to take moral stands not only when the time seems less than ideal but also when we're extremely vulnerable. When Alice Walker was a poor and relatively unknown writer, a major magazine commissioned her to write an autobiographical piece about growing up in the Deep South. Over lunch at a fancy New York restaurant, the magazine editors insisted on changes that Walker felt would make the piece more pleasant and sunny, but also wholly inaccurate. She argued and resisted. Finally, one of the editors said, "Listen to us, Alice. If you want to publish your article, you *have* to make these changes." Walker needed the money and exposure. She was far from being in the perfect situation, where she could begin to call her own shots. But she gathered her manuscript and turned to leave. "Listen to me," she said. "All I *have* to do in life is save my soul."

Contrary to expectation, we're most effective when we realize that there is no perfect time to get involved in social causes, no ideal circumstances for voicing our convictions. What each of us faces instead is a lifelong series of imperfect moments in which we must decide what to stand for. Choices may at times be thrust upon us, as Alice Walker's was on her. More often we'll have to seek them out consciously, in contexts that don't always encourage them and sometimes when we don't feel ready. The wonder is that when we do begin to act, we often gain the knowledge, confidence, and strength that we need to continue.